Jewish Experiences across the Americas

JEWISH EXPERIENCES ACROSS THE AMERICAS

Local Histories through Global Lenses

EDITED BY
Katalin Franciska Rac and
Lenny A. Ureña Valerio

University of Florida Press
Gainesville

Publication of this work made possible by a Sustaining the Humanities through the American Rescue Plan grant from the National Endowment for the Humanities.

Copyright 2022 by Katalin Franciska Rac and Lenny A. Ureña Valerio
All rights reserved
Published in the United States of America

First cloth printing, 2022
First paperback printing, 2023

28 27 26 25 24 23   6 5 4 3 2 1

Library of Congress Cataloging-in-Publication Data
Names: Rac, Katalin Franciska, editor. | Ureña Valerio, Lenny A., 1977– editor.
Title: Jewish experiences across the Americas : local histories through global lenses / edited by Katalin Franciska Rac and Lenny A. Ureña Valerio.
Description: Gainesville : University of Florida Press, [2022] | Includes bibliographical references and index.
Identifiers: LCCN 2021027317 (print) | LCCN 2021027318 (ebook) | ISBN 9781683402565 (hardback) | ISBN 9781683403074 (pdf) | ISBN 9781683403845 (pbk.)
Subjects: LCSH: Jews—United States—History. | Judaism—United States—History. | United States—Civilization—Jewish influences. | BISAC: SOCIAL SCIENCE / Jewish Studies | HISTORY / Latin America / General
Classification: LCC E184.35 .J45 2022 (print) | LCC E184.35 (ebook) | DDC 296.0973—dc23
LC record available at https://lccn.loc.gov/2021027317
LC ebook record available at https://lccn.loc.gov/2021027318

University of Florida Press
2046 NE Waldo Road
Suite 2100
Gainesville, FL 32609
http://upress.ufl.edu

Contents

List of Illustrations vii

Note on Transliteration ix

Acknowledgments xi

Introduction 1
   Katalin Franciska Rac and Lenny A. Ureña Valerio

Part I. Imperial Intersections

1. Muslims and Jewish Converts in the Early Modern Hispanic World 37
   Tamar Herzog

Insert Carta ejecutoria de hidalguía for the Ortega y Vilches family (Granada, 1725) 53
   Neil Weijer

2. The Struggle for Jewish Naturalization from Jamaica to London, 1748–1753 56
   Dana Rabin

Part II. Network Empires

3. Gifts from the Center: Gifting and Religious Authority in Colonial Curaçao 83
   Hilit Surowitz-Israel

4. Jews and New Christians in the Iberian Empires in a Global Context, 1492–1800 108
   José C. Moya

Part III. Perceptions of Migrants and Migration

5. Navigating Citizenship: Consular Practices and the Brazilian Jewish Community in Nineteenth-Century Morocco 149

    Lucas de Mattos Moura Fernandes

6. A *Yanqui's* Gaze: Maurice Schwartz's South American Travelogues from 1930 176

    Zachary M. Baker

7. Going Where? The Trope of Migration in Yiddish Movies from the Year 1939 201

    Elisa Kriza

8. Deforestation and Jewish Settlement in Fazenda Quatro Irmãos: A History of the Jewish Colonization Association's Activities in Rio Grande do Sul, Brazil 232

    Isabel Rosa Gritti

Part IV. Global Struggles and Community Organizing

9. Antifascist Jewish Women in Argentina and Uruguay: Inclusion and Identities, 1941–1945 249

    Sandra McGee Deutsch

10. Out of the "Ghetto" and into the World: Argentine Sephardi Youth, 1940s–1950s 277

    Adriana M. Brodsky

11. Defying Traditional *Shtadlanut*: Jewish Self-Defense in Argentina 302

    Raanan Rein

List of Contributors 325

Index 329

Illustrations

Figures

1.1. Ordenanzas Reales para la Casa de la Contratacion de Sevilla, y para otras cosas de las Indias, y de la navegacion y contratacion de ellas. Cover 41

1.2. Ordenanzas Reales para la Casa de la Contratacion de Sevilla, y para otras cosas de las Indias, y de la navegacion y contratacion de ellas. Fol. 30r 41

Insert 1. Genealogy tree from Carta ejecutoria de hidalguía for the Ortega y Vilches family 54

Insert 2. Two pages from Carta ejecutoria de hidalguía for the Ortega y Vilches family 55

6.1. Photograph of Maurice Schwartz's family 177

7.1. Fishke and Hodl encroached by death and darkness during their wedding 208

7.2. A beard and a tallit do not define a good Jew 209

7.3. The Ukrainian wedding dress is a symbol of Chave's apostasy 212

7.4. Tevye and his family seem rooted in the Ukrainian countryside 214

7.5. A proper Sabbath table 219

7.6. Hymie's gang illustrates a view of non-Jews as leading a life of vice 221

8.1. Map of Quatro Irmãos 237

Table

1. Translation of Hebrew words that appeared in *Hanoar Hasefaradí*, March–April 1949 295

Note on Transliteration

This volume adopts Brill's simple transliteration system. In the case of Yiddish words, it complies with YIVO rules. In chapters 10 and 11, the reader will encounter Hebrew terminology transliterated according to Spanish orthography. Here, as in the case of Arabic terms in chapter 5, the transliteration follows convention. In each chapter, the authors provide an English definition for the Arabic, Hebrew, Latin, Portuguese, Spanish, and Yiddish words and expressions.

Acknowledgments

This book is the result of many interconnected conversations, exchanges of ideas, and collaborative work between old and newly acquainted colleagues, mentors and mentees, teachers and students about and centered around the study of Jewish experiences in the Americas. We editors first met while working at the University of Florida's Isser and Rae Price Library of Judaica and Center for Latin America Studies, respectively. Supported by a National Endowment for the Humanities Challenge Grant, the Price Library had been collecting and preserving records of Jewish communities in Latin America, the Caribbean, and Florida. This endeavor was extended into a collaboration between our units, the Latin American and Caribbean Collections, and the former Alexander Grass Chair in Jewish Studies to promote scholarly research on Jewish history and culture in the Americas. The former Alexander Grass Chair and a Title VI grant from the US Department of Education awarded to the Center provided additional financial support for this project. The University of Florida Center for Latin American Studies' 68th Annual Conference in 2019, "Jews and the Americas," was a major part of our collaborative work. At this conference, over twenty scholars from across the Americas, Germany, and Israel addressed a cornucopia of themes and took us on the high roads and hidden paths of historical, literary, anthropological, political, psychological, and philosophical inquiry that again and again met at surprising and thought-inducing intersections. We would like to use the space these pages provide us to thank the participants of the conference for including us in their fascinating conversations and thus taking us on an amazing intellectual journey that ultimately led to the project of editing this volume.

Working on this volume, we aimed to capture a divergence of themes and organize histories belonging to different periods and geographical areas in a way that the points of conjuncture they create would themselves construct continuities and highlight historical change. We found that by simultaneously exploring the local specificities and global connections of the Americas' Jewish histories, we can achieve the narrative aspirations of our project. We contacted some of the participants of the 2019 conference and approached scholars with whom we had not yet worked together and whose contributions enhanced the perspectives and topics addressed in the volume. We are manifoldly indebted to the authors featured in this volume. In addition to the generosity that they extended to us in the form of invigorating scholarship, they demonstrated unconditional intellectual openness and engaged with our vision by also offering invaluable insights and comments to our introduction to the volume.

We are thankful to Nina Caputo, Mitchell Hart, Rebecca Jefferson, and Paul Losch, together with whom we organized the 2019 conference. They supported our intellectual ambitions by offering feedback on our editorial efforts at different stages of this project. Nina Caputo's careful reading of our drafts and Mitchell Hart's insightful suggestions were central to the evolution of our work. We are also grateful to Monica Grin and Jeffrey Lesser for their assistance in navigating the bountiful waters of Brazilian scholarship on Jewish history.

Publishing this volume could not have been possible without the academic and financial help of the University of Florida's Isser and Rae Price Library of Judaica and the Center for Latin American Studies or the assistance of our colleagues in these units. We also thank the University of Florida Press, particularly Stephanye Hunter and Marthe Walters, for supporting us throughout the process of turning the project into the book it is today. Finally, our special thanks go to the reviewers whose insightful comments helped strengthen the narrative presented in the following pages.

Introduction

KATALIN FRANCISKA RAC AND LENNY A. UREÑA VALERIO

What tied Jews to their local communities, the broader societies in the Americas, and the world beyond the continent? How did Jews' local and global connections shape their lived experiences between the sixteenth and twentieth centuries?[1] The chapters in this volume offer a broad range of answers to these questions as they explore episodes in the centuries-long history of Jews in the Americas. They elucidate the diversity of Jewish experiences and identifications in the continent by stressing the significance of the institutions and sense of belonging that Jews developed in their local communities and countries of domicile. Additionally, the chapters of the volume direct attention to global cultural, economic, and political interconnections underlying the historical transformation of Jewish experiences in the Americas. Together, the contributions confirm that, throughout the centuries, local and global influences simultaneously shaped Jewish lives across the hemisphere while also transforming the continent, and, as a result, weaving together the histories of the Americas and the Americas' Jewish inhabitants.[2]

Beyond the volume's immediate interest in Jewish histories in the Western Hemisphere, the parallel attention paid to the local and the global is conducive to the study of the Americas' multicultural societies. The volume contends that the focus on the Jewish minority can be instructive of the examination of the history of other minorities. Furthermore, it stresses that Jewish communities in the Americas have been living alongside other Jewish and non-Jewish groups—ethnic and religious minorities—whose histories and roots further nuance our understanding of the Americas' global interdependencies and the ways in which their polities faced the challenges of social and cultural heterogeneity. Without claiming that an exhaustive hemispheric panorama unfolds throughout the pages of this volume, we aim to emphasize the relevance of Jewish history to the deeper exploration of the Americas' multicultural pasts and to contribute to the global history of the Americas.

Approaching the Study of Jewish Experiences in the Americas

We relied on a number of premises when compiling this volume. In contrast to the conventional, fragmented research on the Americas, the volume treats Latin America, the Caribbean, and North America as one geographically continuous entity, while also taking into consideration regional specificities. Accordingly, the epithet "American" is descriptive of the entirety of the Western Hemisphere.[3] As noted, conscious of geographical and cultural hiatuses, the volume as a whole scouts the continent's Anglo-Saxon, Hispanic, and Lusophone regions across political borders and the north–south divide. The contributors to this book investigate how local conditions impacted the processes of Jewish integration and exclusion, Jewish engagement with local institutions, the advancement of Jewish political and economic interests locally and regionally, and the cultivation of Jewish cultural and religious values. In our analysis, local conditions include the agency with which Jews in the Americas shaped their communities, surroundings, and relationships with their non-Jewish neighbors and the political regimes in which they participated or to which they were subjected. The study of local institutions that promoted acculturation and participation in national organizations among Jewish constituencies or those that devised and executed policies of exclusion are of special relevance to our inquiries. The essays in this volume tangibly depict that, by strengthening emotional, economic, and political ties to their localities and as they gained citizenship across the Americas during the modern period, Jews actively influenced their respective countries and societies, while either resisting or succumbing to discrimination through a broadening range of practices.

The emphasis on local settings and conditions enables us to explore the heterogeneous landscape of Jewishness in the Americas. The different origins of Jewish immigrants, their linguistic practices, and ties to Ashkenazic, Sephardic, and Mizrahi cultures or Italian or Romaniote rites, just to name a few examples, played an important role in how Jews self-identified in the Americas. Moreover, Jews defined themselves as individuals and community members in more than one way, depending on different religious, legal, political, professional, and cultural contexts. They have been in a constant dialogue with their non-Jewish surroundings, negotiating their understanding of what it meant to be Jewish and the significance of Jewish difference. The political and institutional divisions within Jewish communities in the Americas played important roles in situating Jews in their broader communities as well. Yet, the quest for civic and political rights often eclipsed the primacy of their Jewish identity. The volume emphasizes the complexity of each historical context in which Jewishness was rearticulated and reinterpreted by Jews and non-Jews alike.

The special attention this volume pays to the cultural and political heterogeneity of the Americas' Jewries further advances our goal to promote the study of the Americas' multicultural character.[4] This book is in direct conversation with recent scholarship on both North and South American Jewish histories, which situates Jews among the many groups that conform to the religious and ethnic diversity of the continent and advance the study of Jewish identities in dialogue with other ethnic and religious groups.[5] Several contributions in the volume address scholarship on migration, diaspora, and transnational connections in which scholars recognize the major sources of the multicultural nature of the Americas' societies.[6] As José C. Moya, the author of one of the essays in this book argued elsewhere, the "transcontinental migration" of the aboriginal population of the Western Hemisphere and, after 1492, the arrival of "sixty million Europeans, eleven million Africans, and five million Asians" defined the continent's cultural diversity that is unlike any other ethnically diverse region of the globe.[7] The inquiry into the social, economic, and political impact of ethnic and religious diasporas and transnational cultural and professional connections of the continent's Jewish and other ethnic and religious communities contributes to our understanding of the Americas as a culturally diverse continent in the past and the present alike.[8] Equally important are racial constructs, though less unique to the understanding of how the societies of the Americas interpret cultural differences. Interlaced with the study of ethnicity, religion, gender, and class, they further complicate our understanding of the lived experience of Jews and their neighbors in the multicultural setting of the continent throughout the centuries.[9] That, in this volume, racial constructs receive relatively little attention highlights the uneven challenges and diverse roles racial ideas presented to or played in the histories of the Americas' societies and minorities. Nevertheless, readers will note that over time, notions of lineage, ideas of belonging, and observations of appearance merged into complex systems of social and cultural distinctions, giving birth to a broad range of categories and definitions of difference. The volume's stress on multiple diversities manifesting themselves on the cultural, political, social, and economic planes and as products of various transnational phenomena reinforces the correlations between the local and the global and supports our global framework of analysis.

Our understanding of the global is rooted in the two monumental events of 1492—the expulsion of Spanish Jewry and the beginning of the European discovery of the Americas—and their far-reaching effects viewed as one historical continuum. Separated only by days, the temporal proximity of these two events accentuates that, according to the original Spanish design, the histories of Jews (as well as other groups) and the Americas would not conjoin.[10] The spirit of the Edict of Expulsion dictated that Jews were not to be allowed to set foot in any Spanish domain.[11] Yet, the very act of the expulsion opened up multiple passages for Jews to engage with the "new" continent. Right from the early days of Spanish colonial rule, Jewish relations to the Americas rested on the contradictory fact that, even in their absence, the legacy of Jewish presence in Spain could still be perceived in the institutional and legal frameworks that Spaniards developed vis-à-vis multiple others in Europe and then carried overseas. Forced to either convert to Catholicism or be exiled, many Iberian Jews and their Jewish and Christian descendants found refuge in and became beneficiaries or even agents of overseas expansion—not only of Spain and Portugal, but also of other empires that competed for colonial influence and resources in the Americas. This volume explores the global forces emerging as repercussions of the two, almost simultaneous events of 1492 that inaugurated European overseas imperialism binding the American continent to the rest of the world and the expansion of the Jewish Diaspora to the Western Hemisphere.[12]

Early modern empires in the Americas present the first avenues of globalization.[13] The theoretical creativity evolving in the scholarship on imperial frameworks lends us tools to further conceptualize continuities and discontinuities in the history of the Americas and the Jewish Diaspora at the global level. Hence, we also examine the nexuses that replaced toppled imperial structures.[14] We are interested in exploring both their horizontal and vertical dimensions; that is, both their geographical extension and the ways in which they manifest themselves in different layers of social formation and cultural production. In the horizontal sense, these global connections entail multiple asymmetrical power relations unfolding across, between, and beyond imperial and non-imperial actors. We look at the vertical axis of global relationships when probing intra-imperial material, ideological, and artistic exchanges that also contributed to, in Tony Ballantyne's terminology, web-like interdependencies and nexuses between the colonizer and the colonized, the imperial center and periphery, as well as different colonies and territories.[15]

Organizing the volume into four parts stresses the theoretical connections we draw between global structures erected by empires and communal networks and diasporas, paths of migration, and ideological movements emerging in the geographical space once dominated by colonial powers. Accordingly, our definition of "global" fluctuates between the early modern European sense of continuous expansion and the material, social, political, and ideological connections that bridge societies in Europe, the Middle East, and the Americas.[16] The arrangement of the four parts in chronological order also illuminates the causal relationships connecting these four global structures. We are interested in tracing these four channels of globalization affecting the continent or Jewish communities only, as they unfolded on political, social, or cultural planes, creating parallel and interlaced, quasi-imperial and global nexuses for the Americas and the Americas' Jewries. We note that these occasionally reinforced each other or produced divergent effects. The contributions to the volume elucidate how imperial centers and peripheries shifted across the hemisphere and how the connections between them transformed into ties linking cultural and ideological trendsetters and followers. They also demonstrate how Jewish communities effectively influenced the economic, political, cultural, and religious aspects of the lives of Jewish communities in other regions. The Sephardic, Ashkenazic, and other Jewish diasporas, or the Jewish Diaspora as a whole, established structures similar to those of formal empires, and through global commerce, migration, and international ideological movements developed overlapping layers of connections that we explore on the following pages. Furthermore, the essays in the volume examine how local conditions could affect the engagement with global ideological and political movements and how the transcontinental movement of people, objects, ideas, and ideologies interfered with local dynamics. These studies document that an awareness of global dynamics within the Jewish Diaspora and beyond, in conjunction with diverse articulations of Jewish identity, effectively shaped local contexts. In addition to recording intensifying and diversifying courses of Jewish integration at the local level, the essays draw a long historical arc between the experiences of Jewish subjects in different empires and Jewish members in international Jewish and non-Jewish ideological movements. In doing so, the chapters of the volume reconstruct the transformations of Jewish agency and its roles in shaping global dynamics.

The Global and the Local

The first part of the book, "Imperial Intersections," contributes to the scholarship on empires, legal conceptualization of religious differences, competing political influences, and belonging in the early modern Atlantic world. While Tamar Herzog analyzes metropolitan developments, Dana Rabin highlights the triangular power dynamics and legislative interactions between the British metropole, the colonies, and Jewish subjects. Both authors stress a relational and comparative examination of the status and experiences of Jews in Europe and the Americas in light of differences in regulating the collective and individual rights of imperial subjects and changing colonial realities.

In her essay, Herzog elucidates that the categories of legal status based on descent and religion that the Spanish authorities established and specified in the *limpieza de sangre* (purity of blood) decrees also reflect assumptions about religious conviction in a society, which, beginning from the eighth century, witnessed multiple and multidirectional, both enforced and voluntary, conversion waves. The statutes are considered by many scholars as early promulgations of state-mandated, religiously coded racial ideology that defined the status of Jewish converts to Catholicism in Spain and, consequently, in the Americas.[17] Until the seventeenth century, Muslims were subjected to similar legislation. Herzog inquires about the reason for the consequent divergence in attitudes toward granting Jews and Muslims who became Christians the right to reside and access economic opportunities, taking into account the historical role of the emotional ties and sense of belonging that Jews and Muslims respectively developed toward Spain. The essay also notes that the legal categories and social practices that aimed to exclude former Jews and Muslims had deeply impressed the identity discourse of the Catholic majority since the early modern period.

To illustrate how, aside from the exclusion of minority groups, the preoccupation with descent remained salient in the stratification of Spanish society and the effective articulation of individual identity in the centuries to come, we include Neil Weijer's description of an eighteenth-century record of a Spanish family's noble ancestry—the *Carta ejecutoria de hidalguía for the Ortega y Vilches family*—following Herzog's essay. Scholars of the medieval and early modern periods are familiar with this genre. Thanks to the relative abundance of surviving samples, such as the source included here, the importance and practice of recording lineage in early modern Spain comes to full light.[18]

Rabin likewise uses legal records to highlight that similarly to Spain, in the course of the eighteenth century, the British Empire had defined the status of Jews both in Britain and the American colonies in the context of its governance over a multicultural population. Identifying Jews as nonwhite and religious others was a pretext to the continued denial of their political rights. Focusing on the reception and implementation of the Plantation Act of 1740 and the Jewish Naturalization Act, aka "Jew Bill," from 1753 in Jamaica and in London that granted citizenship to Jewish subjects, Rabin sheds light on the ways in which colonial and metropolitan elites interpreted, acted on, and protested it. Furthermore, she reconstructs how Jewish individuals wished to exercise their citizenship and negotiated their political rights. In addition to the law, the conceptualization of skin color, religious identity, and economic interests also shaped Jewish struggles for the right to vote and hold office in the colonies and the metropole, and influenced the articulation of belonging and inclusion in the British nation and empire. Thus, instead of examining exclusion in the imperial context as a top-down process, Rabin suggests that the power relations between the metropole, the colonies, and Jewish subjects proved to be central to the negotiations over Jewish citizenship and rights in the empire. Together, the two essays by Rabin and Herzog offer a broad overview of the early modern transformation of racial discrimination, in which religion remained salient, while skin color took prominence over lineage. Moreover, not unlike the case in Spain, the debates over the definition of the political and cultural outsider, which targeted Jews who formed one of the smaller minority groups of the British Empire, thoroughly impacted the evolution of Christian British identity as well.

The two essays in the second part "Network Empires," turn to the history of the Western Sephardic Diaspora and their global nexuses. In continuation of Herzog's comparative analysis of Spain's legal approach to New Christians (i.e., converts and their immediate descendants), the two essays examine how Sephardic Jewish identification transformed and diversified in the transatlantic Iberian world and beyond. Hilit Surowitz-Israel's essay introduces the Dutch maritime empire as another major player in the European colonial expansion in the Atlantic region that crucially shaped Jewish experiences in the Caribbean. Many of the expelled Jewish families as well as *conversos* who moved from Spain to Portugal consequently found refuge in Amsterdam, where religious tolerance provided higher security and stability. They also took advantage of the commercial opportunities the Dutch imperial expansion had to offer.[19] As Judith Laikin Elkin, the prominent historian of Latin American Jewries notes, "From Amsterdam, Curaçao, and other Dutch-protected areas, Sephardic merchants fanned out to other Caribbean islands and contiguous areas of the mainland."[20] Surowitz-Israel's study focuses on the Jewish community in Curaçao in the eighteenth century, whose members drew their family trees back to Iberian conversos and considered themselves part of the transatlantic Portuguese Jewish Diaspora. Using a broad lens to observe the transformations of the Iberian Jewish Diaspora, José C. Moya's essay explores the fluidities and multiple threads of continuity and discontinuity between Jewish, converso or New Christian, and Crypto-Jewish identities on the one hand, and between Sephardic and Portuguese Jewish identifications on the other, by mapping intertwining routes of migration and commerce. While Surowitz-Israel highlights quasi-imperial relations between centers and peripheries in the Western Sephardic Diaspora, Moya presents early modern Sephardic and New Christian nexuses as inseparable from the development of global mercantile capitalism driven by Portuguese and Spanish imperial ambitions.

To explain Curaçao's connections to other Jewish communities in the Caribbean and beyond, Surowitz-Israel reconstructs the mechanisms through which, in the eighteenth century, the island superseded Amsterdam as a new quasi-imperial center in the region. In doing so, she revisits the status of Curaçao as the "mother community of all the Caribbean Islands" in the Atlantic Portuguese Diaspora.[21] By gifting religious objects, issuing charitable donations, and offering financial support, Curaçao asserted its religious authority over other congregations in the Americas and across imperial borders. Additionally, Surowitz-Israel's work elucidates correlations between the study of material culture, religiosity, and power relations in the Caribbean Jewish Diaspora. The example of Portuguese Jews offers lessons about how religious identity was regulated in the dawn of the modern era outside formal imperial frameworks. By documenting Curaçao's emergence as a Jewish religious hegemonic power in the Caribbean, like Rabin's essay, Surowitz-Israel's study pinpoints the versatility of center-periphery relations. Accordingly, it contributes to the historiographical conceptualization of the south-north axes of exchange in the early modern histories of the Americas. It equally fosters the exploration of the relational nature of the identities that Jews in the Americas embraced.

Moya's work closes the discussion of early modern empires and the ways in which Jewish cross-communal ties and networks both mirrored and defied imperial frameworks and commercial ambitions before the nineteenth century. It traces the voluntary and forced migration patterns of Iberian Jewry from before 1492 between the Spanish and Portuguese kingdoms, to the Atlantic colonies of Spain and the Portuguese territory of Brazil, as well as to the Mediterranean and the Middle East. As a result, Moya places the migration of Iberian Jewry to the Americas into the larger context of the Iberian maritime expansion, and situates the Western Sephardic Diaspora in the larger context of the dispersion of Iberian Jewry. In doing so, he underscores the effect of global migration on the evolution of the hardly detectable gradients of Sephardic identities both before and after 1492 and as they transcended religious and cultural divides. In his conclusion, he notes that concomitant with the decline of the Western Sephardic Diaspora's global commercial activities, the growth of Europe's Ashkenazic population and westward migration to the Americas—not independent from the intensifying waves of global migration, the ripples of which engulfed Sephardic communities on the eastern Mediterranean as well—transformed the Jewish Diaspora in the nineteenth century.[22] Migration trends and Jewish population patterns transformed globally during the 1800s also in reaction to the rise of the independent republics in Latin America that long preceded the crumbling of centuries-old imperial polities in Central, Eastern, and Southern Europe, while European imperialism in Africa and Asia peaked, the Dominion of Canada became established, and the United States expanded its borders and entered global politics.

For Jews on both sides of the Atlantic—as Hasia Diner has emphasized— "Migration represented one of the most characteristic aspects of Jewish life in the century between 1820 through the 1920s."[23] By the early interwar period, close to three million Jewish newcomers from the European continent, the Mediterranean, and North Africa along with masses of non-Jews arrived in the United States alone, and close to four hundred thousand reached Latin America.[24] From 1840 to 1942, the total number of Jewish migrants worldwide reached 3.9 million. The overwhelming majority, about 3.6 million people, came from mostly Yiddish-speaking communities in Eastern Europe.[25] They migrated due to the combined impact of the allure of the Americas' promise and worsening socioeconomic conditions at home. Emigration from the Russian, Austro-Hungarian, German, and the Ottoman empires was not independent of local authorities' heightening efforts to suppress what they deemed political dissidence and to maintain these multiethnic and multireligious empires' territorial integrity. Modern political and social movements, among them Zionism, nonetheless continued to rise in the successor nation states as well and affected everyday life and legal status alike. Equally important was the role of Jewish philanthropists and their colonial agents in attracting Jewish immigrants to the Americas, Palestine, and other regions. At the end of the eighteenth century, the Habsburg Emperor Joseph II's Edicts of Tolerance had pressed Jews to become "productive" by engaging with agriculture, crafts, and industry. Pursuing similar objectives, yet also driven by philantropic considerations, less than a century later, Jewish financiers and entrepreneurs aimed to assist Jews to move to newly established agricultural colonies. As a result, former imperial frameworks that created commonalities between Jewish experiences in Central, Eastern, and Southern Europe, mutatis mutandis, endured in different forms of migration and occupational patterns. In their new homelands, Jews engaged with new professions such as farming while also continuing long-practiced ones, chiefly peddling.

The Jewish Colonialization Association (JCA), established in 1891 by Baron Maurice Hirsch (1831–1896), promised new, repression-free, and prosperous lives for Jews, and played an unparalleled role in the establishment of Jewish agricultural settlements in Argentina, Brazil, and Uruguay, as well as Canada and parts of the United States. The fact that Jewish colonial settlements became new homes only for a minority of Jewish immigrants from Europe while the majority gravitated toward urban and industrial centers does not diminish these settlements' or the Jewish agricultural movement's historical importance. Isabel Rosa Gritti's essay in this volume also stresses that the JCA's activities aligned with government interests to attract a European labor force and earn revenues from the extraction of natural resources and the introduction of agriculture on previously "unused" land—often the home of indigenous populations. Therefore, the history of the Jewish and non-Jewish colonization companies and their negotiations with different national and imperial governments elucidates additional interconnections between the migration of Jews and other groups, as well as the relationship between global migration and agendas of colonization in the late nineteenth and early twentieth centuries.

It is against the backdrop formed by these linkages that the essays in the third part of the volume—"Perceptions of Migrants and Migration"—study images of migrants and migration and describe views of and discourses about the Jewish migrant and Jewish migration as social and economic phenomena. By focusing on Brazil's imperial ambitions in Africa, US immigrant Jewish artists' descriptions of Latin America and Jewish life in Eastern Europe, and, as noted above, the correlation between governmental policies of settlement, economic activities, and immigrant labor, these contributions explore connections between imperial structures and migration from late nineteenth century. Registering such connections, the essays record the diminishing of the Jewish migrant's agency to a point where, from the migration narrative, his or her figure almost completely disappears.

The first essay in this part, by Lucas de Mattos Moura Fernandes, chooses a unique angle to explore a relative late period in the migration to the Amazon region animated by the booming rubber industry—a rather understudied chapter of the late nineteenth-century history of Jewish migration to the Americas. He follows Moroccan Jewish immigrants who became naturalized Brazilian citizens moving not to a different region in the Americas but back to North Africa—a region of competing European colonial and imperial presence.[26] Fernandes points out that the Empire of Brazil (1822–1889) participated in the European competition for influence in Africa, which largely defined the first consul, the trained orientalist José Daniel Colaço's (1831–1907) attitude toward the local population, and his eagerness to extend protections to Brazilian citizens living in Morocco. By looking at Colaço's and consequently appointed consuls' correspondences in addition to the records of Brazil's consular services in various Moroccan cities, Fernandes examines perceptions that the representatives of the Brazilian government held of the Jewish expats on the one hand, and those Moroccan Jewish individuals—who presented themselves as Brazilian citizens for unveiled practical ends—on the other. Fernandes's work closely corresponds with Jeffrey Lesser's examination of the Moroccan Jewish immigration to Brazil and the mobility that naturalization in Brazil afforded to these immigrants.[27] Tracing the lives of the returnees to Morocco, Fernandes demonstrates how they deployed their former Brazilian citizenship to ensure not only protection against the perceived abuses of fellow Moroccans and local authorities, but also success in their commercial dealings.

Resembling Rabin's reconstruction of Jewish experiences in Britain's Caribbean colonies in the early modern period, Fernandes's study, thus, reminds us of the importance of citizenship in creating and enhancing opportunities of mobility for the Jewish minority in both the geographical and social sense. In addition, the case of the Jewish Brazilian expats in modern Morocco signals that, despite their small number, the Jewish minority could also invigorate imperial ambitions in the modern period. When viewed through the prism of Brazilian political and economic interests, the Jewish minority's visibility sharpened. Moreover, the history of the Brazilian Jews in Morocco highlights that next to the main tides of migration, smaller streams diverted, and even reversed, the flow of movement, and thus, simultaneously contributed to the extension and contraction of the North African Jewish Diaspora in the west. Their stories weave together, thus establishing reciprocity between the transnational histories of Brazilian and Moroccan Jewries.

The next two chapters turn to the history of emigration from Eastern Europe and the concomitant geographical and cultural extension of the Ashkenazic world to the west. As the term "Yiddishland" referenced by Zachary M. Baker indicates, the Yiddish language became a global vernacular and literary language due to the intensifying East European Jewish emigration in the last third of the nineteenth century. Yiddish connected not only the northern and southern parts of the Americas, but was equally instrumental in establishing, maintaining, and—after the Holocaust—replacing the ties between various centers of Yiddish culture and arts, literature, theater, and film globally.[28] Its influence extended even further. As Rebecca Kobrin found in studying the global dispersal of the Bialystok Jewish community, the geographical reconfiguration of Yiddish and Yiddish-speaking communities inspired some Jewish authors in the Americas to liken their cultural and economic ties to former compatriots who migrated to other destinations to an invisible, "imagined" empire.[29] Indeed, the worldwide expansion of Yiddish theater was compared to the British Empire, (while it could have equally been likened to the Habsburgs' global empire in the early modern period) where "the sun never set."[30] The two essays by Baker and Elisa Kriza direct the reader's attention to views and representations of Jewish migration by taking the analysis to the 1930s' Yiddish cultural sphere of the Americas, created by Yiddish-speaking American artists, often themselves immigrants to the United States. The iconic figure of New York's Yiddish Art Theater, actor-director Maurice Schwartz connects the two contributions. Baker examines Schwartz's travelogues written during his travels in South America and published in the Yiddish press in the United States beginning from 1930. One of the three Yiddish films produced in the United States and premiered in 1939 that Kriza studies was written and directed by Schwartz. These two essays by Baker and Kriza highlight the ways in which this migration shaped Jewish identities and artistic expression in the Americas especially when emigration was less and less achievable for European Jews trying to flee worsening conditions in their respective homelands. The two essays underscore the significant role that cultural production and the arts play in articulating and mediating national, ethnic, and religious identities in an increasingly globalized world.

Schwartz's travelogues offer an insight into how a North American Jewish celebrity viewed, often with disparaging eyes, Latin America. According to Baker's analysis, Schwartz's impressions of Argentina, Brazil, and Uruguay were devoid of a colonial agenda, yet arguably reproduced a colonial gaze. Contrary to the power relations suggested by Surowitz-Israel on Curaçao's quasi-imperial networks, the discussion of Schwartz's travels demonstrates that by the early twentieth century, the north had established itself as a cultural hegemon in the hemisphere. His pivotal role in the North American Yiddish theater, even after its heyday, could lend an air of superiority to Schwartz when traveling south. His travelogues discussing Jewish life in South America and Eastern Europe clearly reflected a New York- or US-centric worldview according to which North America was a cultural and artistic trendsetter for the international Yiddish theater world—with Second Avenue as its "Hollywood"—and South America figured in it as periphery.[31] In addition to the sites he visited, Schwartz, himself an immigrant to the United States at the beginning of the century, discussed migration to the Americas, especially to South America, as a process that could enrich both immigrants and South American countries. He supported the idea of Argentina and the Southern Cone in general as a land of opportunities for Yiddish-speaking immigrants. In this regard, the actor and director followed the footsteps of European authors who, in the nineteenth century, used travelogues to advance migration and the foundation of settler colonies and ethnic enclaves in Latin America while spreading both enticing and negative images about the region.[32]

However, Schwartz's tone about immigration changed when it came to directing motion pictures. His film, *Tevye the Milkman,* an adaptation of the renowned Yiddish author Sholem Aleichem's short stories, for example, weighed Jewish futures in Eastern Europe and options of migration. Kriza elucidates that on the eve of World War II, Jewish immigrant filmmakers in the United States—Schwartz among them—discussed Jewish emigration from Eastern Europe as a reflection of and resolve to ease cultural and existential anxieties. Migration both embodied and responded to spiritual and physical danger threatening Jewish communities in Eastern Europe and the United States. Accordingly, these movies juxtaposed ideal and corrupt ways of Jewish life, sincere and enlightened religiosity opposing superstition-riddled ignorance and the abandonment of Judaism altogether. While some of the filmmakers suggested that life in Eastern Europe should be relegated to the past, others mused that immigration to the Land of Israel and to the Americas would lead to new lives of polar opposites. (Tevye considers the Americas as a non-option.) These movies drew a global map of East European Jewry in both the geographical and spiritual sense, and also reinterpreted cultural continuities in the Yiddish-speaking world of North America and Eastern Europe at a point when the Yiddish film industry was about to be robbed of its Eastern European audiences. Through their examination of the associative links between migration and threat, like journalists and literati, Jewish filmmakers in the United States produced critical and complex narratives on Jewish migration and spirituality, void of pro-immigration arguments that Schwartz as a travelogue writer promoted during his visit to Latin America. Kriza's essay highlights the importance of film studies in studying Yiddish culture around the globe.

The closing essay in this third part returns the narrative to Brazil, to the history of the Eastern European immigrants in the agricultural colony Fazenda Quatro Irmãos founded by the JCA in the southern part of the country. Instead of emphasizing temporality and lack of success in attracting large masses and offering lasting existences to Jewish families (as during the 1930s Maurice Schwartz had noted as well), Isabel Rosa Gritti's study reconstructs the JCA's economic activities and its contractual exchanges with the local government and focuses on the economic interests behind the support for Jewish colonial settlements. With the JCA-run timber industry in Quatro Irmãos at the forefront of her examination, the image of the immigrant is relegated to the background, where it almost completely vanishes. It is her emphasis on the promise of profitable deforestation that accentuates the lack of perception of the Jewish migrant from the part of the JCA. Gritti's inquiry reaches even deeper, as she demonstrates that beginning in the mid-1800s, that is, prior to the arrival of the JCA, the expansion of agricultural activities led to the destruction of the area's natural pine forests that had served as dwelling areas and food resources for the subsequently displaced indigenous population. Thus, she transforms the history of East European Jewish immigrants in the south of Brazil into a narrative about the commodification of land causing subsequent ecological and humanitarian crises, neatly fitting the longer history of colonial exploitation in the Americas in general, and in Brazil in particular, heralded by the arrival of the Spaniards and the Portuguese at the turn of the sixteenth century.[33]

The inquiry into the East European Jewish colonization movement and the efforts of the JCA in southern Brazil also introduces the fourth part of this volume: "Global Struggles and Community Organizing." This part primarily focuses on the postwar history of Argentine Jewry. Not only were Argentine Jewish colonists among the founders of Jewish colonies in the south of Brazil, but, as we later note, beginning from the late nineteenth century, the global reach of the intertwined history of Jewish migration, the agricultural settlements, and their ideational foundations geographically overlap with the extent of Jewish involvement in international ideological movements.

The histories told in the fourth part of the volume examine different ideological movements through which Jewish communities and individuals established international connections and aimed to alter their position in Argentina and Uruguay between the 1940s and 1960s. Moreover, the three essays in this part focus on the activism of marginalized groups within the Jewish community—women and youth—as a means to either join or fight against worldwide ideological movements, both outside and as part of Jewish politics. As such, these contributions study Jewish activism along two axes: within and beyond Jewish organizations, and as it affected Jewish organization members' local and global involvements. They highlight that the local and global interests together likewise informed Jewish engagements with international ideologies not rooted in Jewish religious or political thought.[34] Through their local memberships, Jewish activists could see themselves as part of an international community that, in turn, strengthened their identification in the region.

Sandra McGee Deutsch's chapter introduces the reader to the world of Jewish women of different linguistic, cultural, educational, and socioeconomic backgrounds in Argentina and Uruguay. Many of them, as recent immigrants from Eastern and Central Europe, had affiliated with leftist ideologies in their former homelands. Jewish women activists together with their new compatriots—Jews and non-Jews, women and men equally—contributed to the antifascist struggle during World War II by both sending aid packages to the Soviet Union and participating in organizations that promoted democratic and pluralistic values domestically. Deutsch's essay offers important lessons about the correlations between Jewish integration, citizenship, and womanhood in the two countries also through continuing engagement with Raanan Rein's work on the Argentine identification of Jews in Argentina and Adriana M. Brodsky's research on Sephardic women in the same country, whose lived experience in the first half of the twentieth century was markedly different from that of Ashkenazic women.[35] This essay continues the previous research Deutsch conducted on women's struggle against fascist political forces at home and on the international front prior to the outbreak of World War II in sharply contrasting political circumstances and against the backdrop of different Jewish institutional structures in Argentina and Uruguay. Here, the comparative approach opens a window to the global connections of Argentine and Uruguayan democratic movements and the ways in which Jewish participation in the international antifascist struggle effectively advanced Jewish integration in both countries.

From national and international antifascist politics, Brodsky shifts attention to transnational Zionist politics in which the Sephardic community participated throughout the 1940s and early 1950s. She sheds light on the history of Zionism in Argentina, exploring the ways in which the State of Israel affected Jewish Argentines' Zionist activism after 1948. Studying this history from the perspective of young Sephardic Zionists, especially women, she records the differences between their and Ashkenazic women's public and private lives, and how the Ashkenazic-Sephardic divide spiraled into the two groups' attitudes toward the Zionist cause and commitments to the Jewish state. The differences became especially apparent in the ways Ashkenazic Jews in Argentina internalized the political divisions within the Zionist movement, while Sephardic Jews, at least initially, remained mostly non-partisan. Yet, like Deutsch's interpretation of women's involvement in the antifascist struggles, Brodsky's study suggests that Zionist activism advanced women's local integration and galvanized their civic engagement.

Moreover, Brodsky draws a collective portrait of the Sephardic Zionist youngsters with great sensitivity, inquiring about how they balanced their activities between multiple goals, such as the support for Israel and initiation of change in the leadership of Argentine Sephardic Zionist institutions. In so doing, she reconstructs a scenario similar to the one that Surowitz-Israel presents about Curaçao: in both cases, on the road to power, the challengers of the status quo internalized techniques of influence and organization practiced by the challenged. The young activists in the Sephardic Zionist movement redefined their Zionist, Jewish, and Argentine identifications by initiating change in Zionist organizations, extending their connection to the Uruguayan community, and participating in activities in Argentina and Israel that were either organized or supported by Israeli Zionist institutions.

Rein's concluding work connects to both Brodsky's through his focus on youth, and to Deutsch's when he depicts Jewish self-defense youth groups' fights against antisemitism in the periods before and following Israel's Six-Day War in 1967. Rein reconstructs the history of these groups within the overlapping contexts of the Argentine society's deterioration into the Dirty War, the state-level connections between Argentina and Israel, Latin America's complex involvement in the growing tension between Israel and the Arab countries and the Palestinian movement, as well as the global youth movements. He elucidates the connections and parallels in the emergence, self-organization, training practice, and the culture of these groups with the early radical Zionist groups in Mandatory Palestine and contemporary Argentine militant cells on the right and the left equally. Rein's analysis of the global and the local forces molding the Jewish self-defense youth movement in Argentina resonates with the scholarship on youth movements throughout the Americas and across the political spectrum.[36] Young people were at the epicenter of cultural and political struggles in the 1960s, and their militancy led them to the streets to protest what they perceived as oppression emanating from global economic inequalities and, particularly in Latin American countries, repression and state-sponsored physical violence.[37]

The radicalization of young Jews followed just a short generation after the initiation of the activities of the young Sephardic women and men in Brodsky's study. In the Argentina of the 1960s, Jewish youngsters broke with earlier community politics and chose distinctly different tactics. The youth that decided to put on an armed fight against the Argentine agents of the increasingly aggressive antisemitic movement rebelled against the earlier generation of community leaders who favored peaceful compromise with anti-Jewish and antisemitic authorities. However, unlike the women whose lives both Deutsch and Brodsky examine, many of the former self-defense group members ended up emigrating to Israel. In other words, the fight against antisemitism and fascism on the one hand and support for Zionism on the other produced results of geometrical opposites: forces that connected Argentine and Uruguayan Jewry to the world and deepened Jewish integration in the Southern Cone strengthened, while emigration to Israel from the 1950s also intensified.

Together with the rest of the essays in the volume, these three studies demonstrate that, shaped by global and local influences, power relations, the culture of belonging, and individual agency both deepened Jewish communities' integration and exacerbated processes of exclusion throughout the Americas. The authors instruct us that one cannot understand the significance of either imperial power or the international ideological and political movements in shaping Jewish life in the Americas without considering Jewish organizational structures that governed the religious and political activities of individuals and communities alike. The opposite is equally relevant to the interpretations provided by the volume's contributors: the ways in which Jewish organizational structures and the institutionalization of religious practice and political life evolved since the early modern period shaped Jewish attitudes toward imperialism, hegemonic power, and modern Jewish politics. Neither the forces guiding migration—cross-Atlantic and cross-continental—nor Jewish perceptions of migration can be adequately assessed without taking into account the cultural and ideological values attached to migration, migration's place in Jewish historical consciousness, or the Jewish organizational and international political backdrop against which immigration and emigration had taken place.

Other Readings of This Book

The long-view historical arc of this book complements the geographical dimension of the concept of globality with a chronological one. In other words, the book articulates our interest in the transformation of not only global structures, but also the central institutions and values of Jewish lives in the Americas and the continent itself through extended periods by bringing into conversation essays focusing on different eras in the five-century-long history of Jews in the Americas. The essays elaborate on a broad range of topics that shed light on the contours of localized Jewish life and its global entanglements, including gender relations, generational connections, national identification and belonging, politics, law, charity, philanthropy, suffrage, and violence. The contributions combine legal, social, and cultural historical inquiries using sources coming from correspondences, legal treatises, travelogues, diplomatic and consular documentation, and oral history that accentuate thematic continuities and discontinuities. For example, the chapters by Herzog, Surowitz-Israel, Moya, and Brodsky emphasize Jewish emotional connections to Spain that the expulsion left uninterrupted. As a result, identification with the Iberian past remained salient in the Americas and beyond.[38] The center-periphery binary constitutes a central narrative thread in the first part of the volume. The binary is picked up in the discussions of Baker and Kriza on the deterritorialization of East European Jewish identities and the concomitant rise of Yiddish cultural centers, as well as in Brodsky's examination of how young Sephardic activists gained control of community organizing. Research on empires, migration, or the impact of Zionism and the State of Israel, in addition, elucidates the relational aspect of Jewish self-understanding in the Americas.

The geographical and the chronological reach of the volume underlines that the Americas, much like Palestine or other destinations of emigrants from Europe, the Mediterranean region, and the Middle East, brought different Jewish communities into close physical proximity. Across the Americas, Jewish communal life—whether religious or cultural in character—has been conducted not in one but in several languages. At least during the lifetime of the first generation of migrants, the "language of the land" coexisted with the language of religious practice, communal organization, and the one spoken at home. It was the purpose of this volume's contributors and editors to record and demonstrate the idioms of the different cultures and lived experiences of Jews in the Americas throughout the volume and thus sample Jewish linguistic practices in the Americas. The essays illustrate how, for example, modern Hebrew was used in Zionist circles in Argentina and how certain Hebrew words, integrated into the local vocabularies and infused with Spanish orthography, were endowed with specific meaning.[39] Less prominent, organizational structures reflected the members' multiple ideological allegiances. Whether linguistic, political, economic, or religious, Jewish difference presented itself within the majority society and the Jewish community at the same time, posing challenges to both first and second generations as well as their descendants living in the Americas.

Furthermore, the volume conceptualizes global connections as avenues through which the study of the history of Jewish communities in the Americas can fruitfully inform the study of the history of Jews in other geographical regions. For instance, the comparative analysis of Hispanicity and status of Jews and Muslims in early modern Spain offers parallels with how Jews and Muslims among other non-Christian groups fared in medieval kingdoms and early modern and modern multiethnic empires.[40] Tangentially related is the growing comparative scholarship on the presence of Jewish and Arab (both Christian and Muslim) communities in Latin American countries that takes the perspective of ethnic studies and also emphasizes the Arab identity of Jewish migrants from Arabic-speaking countries in Latin America.[41] The history of those Moroccan Jews who returned to their homelands as Brazilian citizens may serve as a geographical and ideational conduit between these histories. Their twofold self-representation as both locals and foreigners in Morocco sheds light on the opportunities and limitations global imperial competition presented for not only local elites, but also minorities in the late nineteenth and early twentieth centuries.

East European Jewish immigrant experiences in nineteenth- and twentieth-century urban and rural Americas are equally shaped by the migrants' strong cultural, religious, and ideological ties to other destinations of Jewish immigration—Germany, Western Europe, or Palestine and as far as Australia and South Africa. The history of Jewish colonial settlements, closely connected to the history of Jewish agricultural movement, serves as an important example. Israel Bartal emphasizes that, beginning from the earliest years of the nineteenth century, resettlement of Jews in the recently occupied and annexed southern regions of the Russian Empire continued in the emigration to Palestine and the Americas as well as the Russian Empire's Central Asian areas during the latter part of the century. It also enfolded in the evolution of the ideology of Jewish agriculturalism.[42] The rarely addressed ecological aspects of their settlements' history further diversifies the intertwining histories of Jewish migration and engagement with agriculture. Gritti's presentation of the history of Jewish colonial settlement in southern Brazil as part of an ecologically negligent enterprise diverges from narratives of Jewish agricultural projects in neighboring Argentina, North America, and especially Palestine and Israel—not to mention those early nineteenth-century settlements in Ukraine, Romania, and Bessarabia. As a report of Israeli Foreign Minister Moshe Sharett's visit to Brazil in 1953 noted, while the Israeli kibbutzim were praised for making the desert flourish, Jewish colonies in Brazil had an opposite impact on the natural environment.[43] Depicting immigration to Brazil, Jewish and non-Jewish alike, as a potential contributor to environmental disasters and subsequent emigration, Gritti's study addresses the broader inquiry into the correlation between man-made ecological and natural climate crises and migration in the modern era.

Finally, Jewish women's political activism in the Southern Cone, as studied here by Deutsch and Brodsky, ties into the longer history of the transformation of gender relations in Jewish families and communities. It likewise raises questions relevant to the study of Jewish women's participation in both the feminist and the social democratic movements in, for example, Central Europe.[44] The focus on their political agency counterbalances the attention scholarship pays to white slavery as an important aspect of Jewish women's immigration to Latin America.

By widening and narrowing the analytical lens, the essays in this volume capture localized histories of Jews and their neighbors in the Americas also from hemispheric and global vantage points. The various interpretations and readings of Jewish experiences emerge from an ongoing conversation across academic cultures that, in itself, is transnational.[45] We hope that the dialogue presented on these pages will continue to build additional bridges between Jewish histories of the American continent and beyond. Hopefully, these bridges will also facilitate dialogues about the historical experiences of the Americas' multicultural societies.

Notes

1. The exploration of the interactions and interconnections between the local and global is a familiar subject for world historians and shapes the historiography on Jewries in the Americas. For example, Hasia Diner's introduction to *Voices of Lombard Street* by the Jewish Museum of Maryland emphasizes the simultaneously local and transnational character of the modern Jewish experience. Diner argues that "Wherever they made their homes, Jews recognize themselves as belonging to a transnational people to whom they maintained connections and bore responsibilities. Yet, their local settings shaped them." Hasia Diner, "The Local and the Global: Lombard Street and the Modern Jewish Diaspora," in *Voices of Lombard Street: A Century of Change in East Baltimore*, eds. Deborah R. Weiner, Anita Kassof, and Avi Y. Decter (Baltimore: Jewish Museum of Baltimore, 2007), 10. Casting a broad picture of Jewish immigrants' perspectives across Latin America in the modern period, Judith Laikin Elkin presents a similar argument. Elkin demonstrates that the balancing of local circumstances, such as religious toleration and economic opportunities, and global forces, for example "massive immigration of heterogeneous peoples," is a key factor in Latin American Jewish experiences. Judith Laikin Elkin, *The Jews of Latin America*, rev. ed. (Ann Arbor: Michigan Publishing, University of Michigan, 2011), 49–50.

2. We suggest that the parallel global influences on the Western hemisphere and the Jewish communities living there and the impact of local conditions produced points of convergence between the histories of the Americas and Jews in the Americas. For a different approach to the interlaced histories of Jews and the Americas, see Paolo Bernardini's "A Milder Colonization: Jewish Expansion to the New World, and the New World in the Jewish Consciousness of the Early Modern Era," in *The Jews and the Expansion of*

Europe to the West, 1450–1800, vol. 2, eds. Paolo Bernardini and Norman Fiering (New York: Berghahn Books, 2001), 1.

3. At the time of its foundation, as well as in its recent biannual scholarly meetings, the American Jewish Historical Society advances a similar, geographically inclusive approach to the study of Jewish life in the Americas. The Schusterman Center for Jewish Studies at University of Texas at Austin also promotes a similar scholarly agenda. For a comparison between Jewish experiences in the US and Latin America, see chapter 9 "Jews North and South," in Elkin, *The Jews of Latin America*, 215–29.

4. See Jeffrey Lesser, *Immigration, Ethnicity, and National Identity in Brazil, 1880 to the Present* (Cambridge: Cambridge University Press, 2013); Raanan Rein, Stefan H. Rinke, and Nadia Zysman, eds., *New Ethnic Studies in Latin America* (Boston: Brill, 2017); Leonard Dinnerstein and David M. Reimers, *Ethnic Americans: A History of Immigration* (New York: Columbia University Press, 2009). More recently, a rising interest in food studies has also advanced the study of the Americas' ethnic diversity.

5. See Jeffrey Lesser and Raanan Rein, eds., *Rethinking Jewish Latin Americans* (Albuquerque: University of New Mexico Press, 2008); Wieke Vinke, *Creole Jews: Negotiating Community in Colonial Suriname* (Leiden: KITLV Press, 2010); Elkin, *The Jews of Latin America*, vii–ix; Susannah Heschel, David Biale, and Michael Galchinsky, eds., *Insider/Outsider: American Jews and Multiculturalism* (Berkeley: University of California Press, 1998). The promotion of comparative ethnic studies can also be seen in recent works on Asian Latin Americans. For example, see Edward R. Slack Jr., "The Chinos in New Spain: A Corrective Lens for a Distorted Image," *Journal of World History* 20, no. 1 (March 2009): 35–65; and Chisu Teresa Ko, "Between Foreigners and Heroes: Asian Argentines in a Multicultural Nation," in *Rethinking Race in Modern Argentina*, eds. Paulina Alberto and Eduardo Elena (Cambridge: Cambridge University Press, 2016), 268–88.

6. For a thorough theoretical discussion of the two concepts' usage in the study of Latin American Jewry, see Margalit Bejarano et al., eds., *Jews and Jewish Identities in Latin America: Historical, Cultural, and Literary Perspectives* (Boston: Academic Studies Press, 2017), especially the essays in part 1: "Globalization, Transnationalism, and Latin American Judaism and Jewishness," 1–100. Additionally, scholars studying North American Jewish history have emphasized that the transnational perspective reinvigorate the historiography on North American Jewry. Recently, in the periodical *American Jewish History* Miriam Rürup noted that "American Jewish studies will always have to take into account both the origin of American Jews and their lasting networks that are shared within families and passed on to future generations. Therefore, Jewish Studies, and the approach to Jewish history, always needs to be transnational." Miriam Rürup, "Transnational Perspectives on Jewish and American-Jewish Studies," *American Jewish History* 101, no. 4 (October 2017): 556.

7. José C. Moya, introduction to *The Oxford Handbook of Latin American History* (Oxford: Oxford University Press, 2011), 4.

8. The interest in considering the parallels of Jewish and other diasporas in the Americas can be gauged by Jay P. Dolan's review of Lawrence J. McCaffrey's *Irish Diaspora*

in America, published in 1976. Dolan opens with a quote from the bestseller author of *Exodus*, Leon Uris, who had just published the novel *Trinity*, saying, "In the Irish I found somebody more fouled up than the Jews." Jay P. Dolan, review of *The Irish Diaspora*, by Lawrence J. McCaffrey, *Reviews in American History* 5, no. 2 (June 1977): 174. For a comparative overview of Asian communities in Latin America, see Evelyn Hu-DeHart and Kathleen López, "Asian Diasporas in Latin America and the Caribbean History: An Historical Overview," *Afro-Hispanic Review* 27, no.1: "Afro-Asia" (Spring 2008): 9–21. The impressive number of diaspora studies programs and courses offered by universities worldwide is also an indication of interest in comparative diaspora studies. Finally, for a thorough treatment of the two concepts both in connection to the study of Jewish communities and the comparative study of ethnic and religious dispersal, see Eliezer Ben-Rafael and Yitzhak Sternberg with Judit Bokser Liwerant and Yosef Gorny, eds., *Transnationalism Diasporas and the Advent of a New (Dis)order* (Leiden: Brill, 2009).

9. For example, Aviva Ben-Ur's examination of the relations between Suriname's Sephardic and Ashkenazic congregants and former slaves who were manumitted and converted to Judaism, thus becoming congregants, demonstrates that the community's internal hierarchies mirrored colonial power relations without the overt employment or direct internalization of racial theory. This type of differentiation between community members, however, from the late eighteenth century has been gradually removed from the community's bylaws. Aviva Ben-Ur, *Jewish Autonomy in a Slave Society: Suriname in the Atlantic World, 1651–1825* (Philadelphia: University of Pennsylvania Press, 2020). Studying the late nineteenth-century US, Eric Goldstein points out that until the 1870s, Jews refrained from employing racial terminology to define their own collective identity. They did so not only because of fear of negative stereotyping, but because it was alien to the vocabulary of Judaism: "But by the 1870s, when concern for their group identity began to accompany the desire for Americanization, Jews discovered that 'race,' a term widely accepted in the non-Jewish world, would allow them to express their desire to maintain a distinct identity without the unwanted political connotations." Eric L. Goldstein, *The Price of Whiteness: Jews, Race, and American Identity* (Princeton: Princeton University Press, 2006), 17. In Mitchell Hart's edition, and with his illuminating foreword, the book *Jews and Race: Writings on Identity and Difference, 1880–1940* (Waltham: Brandeis University Press, 2016) opens a broad horizon of the multitude of opinions and arguments made in the United States, Europe, and Mandatory Palestine both for and against identifying the Jewish collective as a race. About the fluidity of racial identity in current Latin America, see Edward Telles and Tianna Paschel, "Who is Black, White, or Mixed Race? How Skin Color, Status, and Nation Shape Racial Classification in Latin America," *American Journal of Sociology* 120, no. 3 (November 2014): 864–907. This article is related to the research project PERLA, available from perla.princeton.edu, which explores correlations between skin color, ethnicity, and racial identification in current Brazil, Colombia, Mexico, and Peru. A detailed summary of the findings is included in Edward Telles, *Pigmentocracies: Ethnicity, Race, and Color in Latin America* (Chapel Hill: University of North Carolina Press, 2014). Finally, for the impact of racial thinking on Jewish integration in Argentina, see Sandra McGee Deutsch, "Insecure Whiteness:

Jews between Civilization and Barbarism 1880–1940s," in Paulino Alberto and Eduardo Elena, eds., *Rethinking Race in Modern Argentina* (Cambridge: Cambridge University Press, 2016), 25–52.

10. According to the dictates of the Alhambra Decree promulgating the expulsion of the Jews from Spain dated March 31, 1492, Jews were to leave Spain no later than the end of July of the same year. Columbus set sail on August 3, that is, three days later. As José C. Moya notes in his essay included in this volume, records suggest that Columbus's departure was postponed to after the Jewish fasting day on the ninth day of the month of Av, Tish'a B'av, that usually falls at the beginning of August. About Columbus's observation of the coincidence of the two events and its historical significance see also Jane S. Gerber, "An Enigma of 1492," introduction to *The Jews of Spain: A History of the Sephardic Experience* (New York: Free Press, 1992), ix–x.

11. For more details, see Tamar Herzog's essay, "Muslims and Jewish Converts in the Early Modern Hispanic World," in this volume.

12. For the interest in the role of global nexuses shaping Latin American and Jewish histories see for example, Jeffrey Lesser and Matthew C. Gutmann, eds., *Global Latin America: Into the Twenty-First Century* (Oakland: University of California Press, 2016). The editors introduce their volume by arguing that "Latin Americans have always been intertwined in wholly uneven global relationships that have encompassed every aspect of their lives" (Lesser and Gutmann, 4). Sarah Abrevaya Stein's study on Lithuanian Jewish emigrants to South Africa engaging with the global ostrich plume trade, or Hasia Diner's work on Jewish peddlers that focuses on North America both call attention to how Jews in different regions engaged with globally pursued commercial activities. See Sarah Abrevaya Stein, *Plumes: Ostrich Feathers, Jews, and a Lost World of Global Commerce* (New Haven: Yale University Press, 2008); Hasia Diner, *Roads Taken: The Great Jewish Migrations to the New World and the Peddlers Who Forged the Way* (New Haven: Yale University Press, 2015).

13. Our ideas about the correlation between empires and globalization correspond with Antony Gerald Hopkins's broadly accepted arguments of how empires serve as agents of globalization. He notes that in addition to empires, "diasporas, mercantile networks, and universal systems of belief, such as Islam" can be considered promoters of global frameworks. See Antony Gerald Hopkins, *American Empire: A Global History* (Princeton: Princeton University Press, 2018), 27.

14. Kristin L. Hoganson and Jay Sexton, eds., *Crossing Empires: Taking US History into Transimperial Terrain* (Durham: Duke University Press, 2020), 11.

15. Tony Ballantyne, *Webs of Empire: Locating New Zealand's Colonial Past* (Vancouver, Toronto: University of British Columbia Press, 2012), 16. We thank Dana Rabin for calling our attention to Ballantyne's approach.

16. Frederick Cooper, *Colonialism in Question: Theory, Knowledge, History.* (Berkeley: University of California Press, 2005), 10.

17. Spain's engagement with the concept of blood purity and regulation of social and political exclusion and inclusion have intrigued historians for decades. For discussions of how the blood purity laws introducing genealogy as a corrective to religious identity contributed to practices of exclusion and the evolution of racial notions, on the one

hand, and how historians evaluated their role in European racial thinking and Spanish and Portuguese colonial rule, on the other, see the insightful review by Rachel L. Burk, "Purity and Impurity of Blood in Early Modern Iberia," in *The Routledge Companion to Iberian Studies*, eds. Javier Muñoz-Basols, Laura Lonsdale, and Manuel Delgado (New York: Routledge, 2017), 173–83. For a selection of in-depth studies on ideologies of exclusion and inclusion in Spain, see Max S. Hering Torres, María Elena Martínez, and David Nirenberg, eds., *Race and Blood in the Iberian World* (Berlin: Lit, 2012) that includes Herzog's essay "Beyond Race: Exclusion in Early Modern Spain and Spanish America," 151–67, highlighting the legal and social categories, other than "race," along which different groups—Indians, Africans, and Gypsies—were excluded. For the distinction between religiously coded and color-coded racism, see Margaret R. Gree, Walter D. Mignolo, and Maureen Quilligan, eds., introduction to *Rereading the Black Legend: The Discourses of Religious and Racial Difference in the Renaissance Empires* (London and Chicago: Chicago University Press, 2007), 2, 10–11.

18. We would like to thank Neil Weijer for suggesting this book both as an object and example of the genre known also outside of Spain. For more information on the *carta ejecutoria* genre, see Mauricio Drelichman, "Sons of Something: Taxes, Lawsuits, and Local Political Control in Sixteenth-Century Castile," *Journal of Economic History* 67, no. 3 (2007): 608–42.

19. For a review of the Sephardic migration to the Dutch Republic and how the Dutch expansion served as a backdrop to Jewish commercial activities in the Atlantic see Jonathan Israel, "Sephardic Immigration into the Dutch Republic, 1595–1672," *Studia Rosenthaliana* 23 (Fall 1989): 45–53.

20. Elkin, *The Jews of Latin America*, 17.

21. Isaac Samuel Emmanuel and Suzanne Emmanuel, *History of the Jews of the Netherlands Antilles I* (Cincinnati: American Jewish Archives, 1970), chap. VIII, 151–80, 174; Jonathan I. Israel, "The Jews of Dutch America," in *The Jews and the Expansion of Europe to the West, 1450–1800*, 336.

22. Devi Mays has demonstrated the "hypermobility" of Sephardic migrants from the eastern Mediterranean to the Americas and Western Europe in the late nineteenth and the early twentieth centuries in her *Forging Ties, Forging Passports: Migration and the Modern Sephardi Diaspora* (Stanford, CA: Stanford University Press, 2020.)

23. Hasia Diner, *The Jews of the United States: 1654 to 2000* (Berkeley: University of California Press, 2004), 74.

24. About immigration to Latin America also in relation to the US and Canada, see Elkin, *The Jews of Latin America*, 52. She relies on the statistics included in Jacob Lestchinsky's "Jewish Migrations, 1840–1956," in *The Jews: Their History, Culture, and Religion*, vol. 2, ed. Louis Finkelstein (New York: Harper & Bros., 1960), 1536–96. Like other scholars, Elkin sees the numbers provided by Lestchinsky as reliable also in light of recent research, such as Jeffrey Lesser's on the Jewish population in Brazil. See her unnumbered footnote on page 53.

25. Jacob Lestchinsky, *The Jewish Migration for the Past Hundred Years* (New York: YIVO, 1944), 6.

26. Ariel Segal, *Jews of the Amazon: Self-Exile in Earthly Paradise* (Philadelphia: Jewish Publication Society, 1999), 48.

27. Jeffrey Lesser, *Immigration, Ethnicity, and National Identity in Brazil* (Cambridge: Cambridge University Press, 2013), 120.

28. Through the example of Jewish emigrants from the Polish town Bialystok to the US (about 50,000), Argentina (20,000), and Australia (5,000) Rebecca Kobrin outlines global nexuses, both material and spiritual, emerging from the turn-of-the-century East European Jewish emigration. See Rebecca Kobrin, *Jewish Bialystok and Its Diaspora* (Bloomington: Indiana University Press, 2010), 7. Kobrin's research on the Bialystoker Diaspora points to questions about center and periphery in the transnational Yiddish-speaking community and belonging to different cultural spheres outside of Eastern Europe. These nexuses destabilize the religious understanding of a Jewish world in which Zion figures as center and the diaspora is the collective for peripheries.

29. Rebecca Kobrin, "Rewriting the Diaspora: Images of Eastern Europe in the Bialystok Landsmanshaft Press, 1921–45," *Jewish Social Studies* 12, no. 3 (Spring–Summer 2006): 13–17.

30. Debra Caplan, "Nomadic Chutzpah: The Vilna Troupe's Transnational Yiddish Theatre Paradigm, 1915–1935," *Theatre Survey* 55, no. 3 (September 2014): 303.

31. We thank Zachary Baker for the insight. In an email, he explained that the Vilna Troupe and the State Jewish Theatre in Moscow were equally important centers of Yiddish theatre. After World War I and through the 1930s, Second Avenue became the locus of Yiddish popular culture and Schwartz's Yiddish Art Theatre represented its highbrow ambitions.

32. The best examples here are the early nineteenth-century travelogues about Latin America by Alexandre von Humboldt and Aimée Bonpland. Humboldt's descriptions generated North Europeans' fascination with and interest in the former Spanish and Portuguese colonies to the point that he was often hailed as a second Columbus, as someone who rediscovered the lands through his scientific observations. Numerous European travelers followed his example in exploring the region and promoting it as a destination for European migrants. For works analyzing travel literature in Latin America and its connection to migration and colonial agendas, see Mary Louise Pratt, *Imperial Eyes: Travel and Transculturation* (London: Routledge, 1992); Gabi Kathöfer, "Devouring Culture: Cannibalism, National Identity, and Nineteenth-Century German Emigration to Brazil," in *KulturConfusão—On German-Brazilian Interculturalities*, eds. Anke Finger, Gabi Kathöfer, and Christopher Larkosh (Berlin: DeGruyter, 2015), 71–94; and Lenny A. Ureña Valerio, "Creating the Polish Nation Abroad," in *Colonial Fantasies, Imperial Realities: Race Science and the Making of Polishness on the Fringes of the German Empire, 1840–1920*, (Athens: Ohio University Press, 2019), 148–71. For an interesting discussion of the legacy of Humboldt in Jewish emigrants' photographic representations of Bolivia, see Leo Spitzer, *Hotel Bolivia: The Culture and Memory in a Refuge from Nazism* (New York: Hill and Wang, 1998). About the European colonial gaze's imprint on Yiddish travel writing in the twentieth century see Mariusz Kałczewiak, "Meeting the Gaucho and Searching for Indians: The Trajectories of Exoticization," in *Polacos in Argentina: Polish*

Jews, Interwar Migration, and the Emergence of Transatlantic Jewish Culture (Tuscaloosa: University of Alabama Press, 2020), 88–108.

33. Arnold Wiznitzer noted that in the first decade of the Portuguese colonization of Brazil, a group of New Christian investors "pioneered the Brazilian timber industry" and export. Arnold Wiznitzer, *Jews in Colonial Brazil* (New York: Columbia University Press, 1960), 8. See also, Moya's essay in chapter 4 of this volume, "Jews and New Christians in the Iberian Empires in a Global Context, 1492–1800," 121.

34. For example, the Bund—the General Union of Jewish Workers in Lithuania, Poland, and Russia—and the Zionist Organization, were both secular Jewish institutions of worldwide outreach. For a comparison of the two movements, see Derek Jonathan Penslar, "1897: The Year of Jewish Revolutions?" *Jewish Quarterly Review* 108, no. 4, (Fall 2018): 520–25.

35. Deutsch's work is in close dialogue with what Katherine M. Marino calls "Popular Front Pan-American Feminism" and describes as "an internationalist feminism that combined social democratic labor concerns with international equal rights demands in the context of an antifascist, inter-American solidarity." Rooted in global dynamics, it was a movement that responded to tangible local needs across the whole hemisphere, where women's rights varied greatly from country to country, ranging from having voting rights to no political rights at all. See, Katherine M. Marino, *Feminism for the Americas: The Making of an International Human Rights Movement* (Chapel Hill: University of North Carolina Press, 2019), 122. Specifically, see chapter 5 "The Birth of Popular Front Pan-American Feminism," 120–44.

36. The Cold War period provided a fertile ground for the mobilization of youths and spread of training sites for young revolutionaries engaged in urban and rural armed groups. Anticommunists and communists (in their different varieties: pro-Cuba, pro-Soviet, or pro-Maoist alignments) competed to enroll members to their cause. The Tupamaros in Uruguay, Black Panthers and Young Lords in the US, communist-led self-defense groups in Colombia's rural area, to name a few, are examples of left-wing activist movements that resorted to violence to challenge what they saw as repressive governments. They responded to local politics while also establishing international connections. US-sponsored trainings and resources provided to police and military forces throughout Latin America were crucial to suppressing many of these movements. For further information see Lyndsay Churchill, *Becoming the Tupamaros: Solidarity and Transnational Revolutionaries in Uruguay and the United States* (Nashville: Vanderbilt University Press, 2014); Johana Fernández, *The Young Lords: A Radical History* (Chapel Hill: University of North Carolina Press, 2019); and, for an interesting discussion of rural guerrillas in Latin America, Richard J. Evans, *Eric Hobsbawm: A Life in History* (Oxford: Oxford University Press, 2019).

37. For example, the *Halconazo* or Corpus Christi massacre against students on June 10, 1971, was carried out by the paramilitary group named Halcones. In Alfonso Cuarón's film *Roma* (2018), the character of Fermín, obsessed with martial arts, can be understood as a member of the Halcones. See Isabel Torrealba, "The Surprising Piece of Mexican (and American) History at the Center of *Roma*," *Slate Magazine*, November 21, 2018,

accessed May 9, 2020, https://slate.com/culture/2018/11/roma-corpus-christi-student-massacre-el-halconazo.html.

38. The autobiography of the Argentine Jewish textile merchant and Zionist leader Nissim Teubal entitled *El inmigrante: de Alepo a Buenos Aires* illustrates the enduring Iberian identification and Zionist politics of Sephardic Jews in the twentieth century. Born in Aleppo, Syria, in 1893, Teubal traced the origins of his family back to Medieval Iberia. The way his family celebrated the Jewish holidays of Hanukkah and Purim confirmed the likelihood that his family was of Iberian origins. He arrived in Argentina and joined his brothers and their business ventures, a rather common path that many immigrants followed throughout the twentieth century. Active in the Jewish community, Teubal was invested in the modernization of religious studies for young boys and in popularizing the Zionist movement. In his autobiography he listed the organizations in which he participated and held prominent positions, such as the Jewish organization B'nai Brit, the Zionist Macabi Sports Club, as well as the non-Jewish Rotary Club de Vincente López. For further details, see Nissim Teubal, *El inmigrante: de Alepo a Buenos Aires* (Buenos Aires: n.p., 1953), 13–14, 173. We would like to thank Adriana Brodsky who helped us learn about Nissim Teubal.

39. Indirectly, they also elaborate the role of language in Jewish community organizing nationally and across political borders. In contrast to the Jewish Labor movement in New York where, in the historian Tony Michels's view, the use of Yiddish in exchanges with Jewish activists in Russia did not play a role in demonstrating or confirming the activists' Jewish identity, the use of Hebrew described in the essays by Brodsky and Rein was instrumental in tying Jewishness to identification with the State of Israel. For details see Tony Michels, "Toward a History of American Jews and the Russian Revolutionary Movement," in *A Century of Transnationalism: Immigrants and Their Homeland Connections*, eds. Nancy L. Green and Roger Waldinger (Urbana: University of Illinois Press, 2017), 185–208.

40. For two chronologically distinct examples, which also underscore the differences between state-level and municipal regulatory practices, see Nora Berend, *At the Gate of Christendom: Jews, Muslims and 'Pagans' in Medieval Hungary, c. 1000–c. 1300* (Cambridge: Cambridge University Press, 2010) and Emily Greble, *Sarajevo, 1941–1945: Muslims, Christians, and Jews in Hitler's Europe* (Ithaca: Cornell University Press, 2011). See also Ethan B. Katz et al., eds., *Colonialism and the Jews* (Bloomington: Indiana University Press, 2017). Highlighting the many crossroads between the histories of Jews and modern European colonialism, this edited volume also includes chapters about Jews and Muslims in modern France and its North African colonies in the nineteenth and twentieth centuries.

41. See, for example, Ignacio Klich and Jeffrey Lesser, eds., *Arab and Jewish Immigrants in Latin America: Images and Realities* (London and Portland: Frank Cass, 1998); Raanan Rein, ed., *Árabes y judíos en Iberoamérica: similitudes, diferencias y tensiones*, Colección Ánfora (Seville: Fundación Tres Culturas del Mediterráneo, 2008).

42. Israel Bartal, "Farming the Land on Three Continents: Bilu, Am Oylom, and Yefe-Nahar," *Jewish History* 21, no. 3/4 (2007): 255.

43. Meir Chazan, "The Creation of the Relations between Israel and Brazil from a

Pioneering Perspective: Between Diplomacy and Kibbutz," in *Jews and Jewish Identities in Latin America*, eds. Bejarano et al., 208.

44. Harriet Pass Freidenreich, *Female, Jewish, and Educated: The Lives of Central European University Women* (Bloomington: Indiana University Press, 2002), especially chap. 6. Judith Szapor et al., eds., *Jewish Intellectual Women in Central Europe, 1860–2000: Twelve Biographical Essays* (Lewiston: Edwin Mellen Press, 2012).

45. The transnational dialogue presented in the volume coincides with Eli Lederhendler's call to transform also (North) American Jewish studies into a transnational study field. Eli Lederhendler, "Modern Historians and Jewish Transnational Perspectives," *American Jewish History* 101, no. 4 (October 2017): 561.

Bibliography

Alberto, Paulina, and Eduardo Elena, eds. *Rethinking Race in Modern Argentina*. Cambridge: Cambridge University Press, 2016.

Avni, Haim. "Antisemitism in Argentina: The Dimension of Danger." In *Approaches to Antisemitism: Context and Curriculum*, edited by Michael Brown, 57–77. New York: American Jewish Committee, 1994.

Ballantyne, Tony. *Webs of Empire: Locating New Zealand's Colonial Past*. Vancouver, Toronto: University of British Columbia Press, 2012.

Bartal, Israel. "Farming the Land on Three Continents: Bilu, Am Oylom, and Yefe-Nahar." *Jewish History* 21, no. 3/4 (2007): 249–61.

Bejarano, Margalit, Yaron Harel, Marta Francisca Topel, and Margalit Yosifn, eds. *Jews and Jewish Identities in Latin America: Historical, Cultural, and Literary Perspectives*. Boston: Academic Studies Press, 2017.

Ben-Rafael, Eliezer, and Yitzak Stemerg, with Judit Bokser Liwerant and Yosef Gorny, eds. *Transnationalism Diasporas and the Advent of a New (Dis)order*. Leiden: Brill, 2009.

Ben-Ur, Aviva. *Jewish Autonomy in a Slave Society: Suriname in the Atlantic World, 1651–1825*. Philadelphia: University of Pennsylvania Press, 2020.

Berend, Nora. *At the Gate of Christendom: Jews, Muslims and 'Pagans' in Medieval Hungary, c. 1000–c. 1300*. Cambridge: Cambridge University Press, 2010.

Bernardini, Paolo. "A Milder Colonization: Jewish Expansion to the New World, and the New World in the Jewish Consciousness of the Early Modern Era." In *The Jews and the Expansion of Europe to the West, 1450–1800*. Vol. 2, edited by Paolo Bernardini and Norman Fiering, 1–23. New York: Berghahn Books, 2001.

Burk, Rachel L. "Purity and Impurity of Blood in Early Modern Iberia." In *The Routledge Companion to Iberian Studies*, edited by Javier Muñoz-Basols, Laura Lonsdale, and Manuel Delgado, 173–83. New York: Routledge, 2017.

Caplan, Debra. "Nomadic Chutzpah: The Vilna Troupe's Transnational Yiddish Theatre Paradigm, 1915–1935." *Theatre Survey* 55, no. 3 (September 2014): 296–317.

Churchill, Lyndsay. *Becoming the Tupamaros: Solidarity and Transnational Revolutionaries in Uruguay and the United States*. Nashville: Vanderbilt University Press, 2014.

Cooper, Frederick. *Colonialism in Question: Theory, Knowledge, History*. Berkeley: University of California Press, 2005.

Deutsch, Sandra McGee. "Anti-Semitism and the Chilean Movimiento Nacional Socialista, 1932–1941." In *The Jewish Diaspora in Latin America: New Studies on History and Literature*, edited by David Sheinin and Lois Baer Barr, 161–81. New York: Gerland, 1996.

———."Insecure Whiteness: Jews between Civilization and Barbarism 1880–1940s." In *Rethinking Race in Modern Argentina*, edited by Paulina Alberto and Eduardo Elena, 25–52. Cambridge: Cambridge University Press, 2016.

Diner, Hasia. *The Jews of the United States: 1654 to 2000.* Berkeley: University of California Press, 2004.

———. "The Local and the Global: Lombard Street and the Modern Jewish Diaspora." In *Voices of Lombard Street: A Century of Change in East Baltimore*, edited by Deborah R. Weiner, Anita Kassof, and Avi Y. Decter, 8–21. Baltimore: Jewish Museum of Baltimore, 2007.

———. *Roads Taken: The Great Jewish Migrations to the New World and the Peddlers Who Forged the Way.* New Haven: Yale University Press, 2015.

Dinnerstein, Leonard, and David M. Reimers. *Ethnic Americans: A History of Immigration.* New York: Columbia University Press, 2009.

Drelichman, Mauricio. "Sons of Something: Taxes, Lawsuits, and Local Political Control in Sixteenth-Century Castile." *Journal of Economic History* 67, no. 3 (2007): 608–42.

Dolan, Jay P. Review of *The Irish Diaspora*, by Lawrence J. McCaffrey. *Reviews in American History* 5, no. 2 (June 1977): 174–79.

Elkin, Judith Laikin. *The Jews of Latin America.* Rev. ed. Ann Arbor: Michigan Publishing, University of Michigan, 2011.

Emmanuel, Isaac Samuel, and Suzanne Emmanuel. *History of the Jews of the Netherlands Antilles I.* Cincinnati: American Jewish Archives, 1970.

Evans, Richard J. *Eric Hobsbawm: A Life in History.* Oxford: Oxford University Press, 2019.

Fernández, Johana. *The Young Lords: A Radical History.* Chapel Hill: University of North Carolina Press, 2019.

Freidenreich Pass, Harriet. *Female, Jewish, and Educated: The Lives of Central European University Women.* Bloomington: Indiana University Press, 2002.

Gerber, Jane S. "An Enigma of 1492." Introduction to *The Jews of Spain: A History of the Sephardic Experience.* New York: Free Press, 1992.

Goldstein, Eric L. *The Price of Whiteness: Jews, Race, and American Identity.* Princeton: Princeton University Press, 2006.

Graetz, Heinrich. *History of the Jews.* Vol. 4. Philadelphia: Jewish Publication Society of America, 1956.

Greble, Emily. *Sarajevo, 1941–1945: Muslims, Christians, and Jews in Hitler's Europe.* Ithaca: Cornell University Press, 2011.

Gree, Margaret R., Walter D. Mignolo, and Maureen Quilligan, eds. Introduction to *Rereading the Black Legend: The Discourses of Religious and Racial Difference in the Renaissance Empires*, 1–24. London and Chicago: Chicago University Press, 2007.

Hart, Mitchell, ed. *Jews and Race: Writings on Identity and Difference, 1880–1940.* Waltham: Brandeis University Press, 2016.

Herzog, Tamar. "Beyond Race: Exclusion in Early Modern Spain and Spanish America." In *Race and Blood in the Iberian World*, edited by Max S. Hering Torres, María Elena Martínez, and David Nirenberg, 151–67. Berlin: Lit, 2012.

Heschel, Susannah, David Biale, and Michael Galchinsky, eds. *Insider/Outsider: American Jews and Multiculturalism*. Berkeley: University of California Press, 1998.

Hoganson, Kristin L., and Jay Sexton, eds., *Crossing Empires: Taking US History into Transimperial Terrain*. Durham: Duke University Press, 2020.

Hopkins, Antony Gerald. *American Empire: A Global History*. Princeton: Princeton University Press, 2018.

Hu-DeHart, Evelyn, and Kathleen López. "Asian Diasporas in Latin America and the Caribbean History: An Historical Overview." *Afro-Hispanic Review* 27, no. 1: "Afro-Asia" (Spring 2008): 9–21.

Israel, Jonathan. "Sephardic Immigration into the Dutch Republic, 1595–1672." *Studia Rosenthaliana* 23 (Fall 1989): 45–53.

Kałczewiak, Mariusz. "Meeting the Gaucho and Searching for Indians: The Trajectories of Exoticization." In *Polacos in Argentina: Polish Jews, Interwar Migration, and the Emergence of Transatlantic Jewish Culture*, 88–108. Tuscaloosa: University of Alabama Press, 2020.

Kathöfer, Gabi. "Devouring Culture: Cannibalism, National Identity, and Nineteenth-Century German Emigration to Brazil." In *KulturConfusão—On German-Brazilian Interculturalities*, edited by Anke Finger, Gabi Kathöfer, and Christopher Larkosh, 71–94. Berlin: DeGruyter, 2015.

Katz, Ethan, Lisa Moses Leff, and Maud Mandel. *Colonialism and the Jews*. Bloomington: Indiana University Press, 2017.

Klich, Ignacio, and Jeffrey Lesser, eds. *Arab and Jewish Immigrants in Latin America: Images and Realities*. London and Portland: Frank Cass, 1998.

Ko, Chisu Teresa. "Between Foreigners and Heroes: Asian Argentines in a Multicultural Nation." In *Rethinking Race in Modern Argentina*, edited by Paulina Alberto and Eduardo Elena, 268–88. Cambridge: Cambridge University Press, 2016.

Kobrin, Rebecca. *Jewish Bialystok and its Diaspora*. Bloomington: Indiana University Press, 2010.

———. "Rewriting the Diaspora: Images of Eastern Europe in the Bialystok Landsmanshaft Press, 1921–45." *Jewish Social Studies* 12, no. 3 (Spring-Summer 2006): 1–38.

Leal Villamizar, Lina María. *Colombia frente al antisemitismo y la inmigración de judíos polacos y alemanes, 1933–1948*. Bogotá: Academia Colombiana de Historia, 2015.

Lederhendler, Eli. "Modern Historians and Jewish Transnational Perspectives." *American Jewish History* 101, no. 4 (October 2017): 557–61.

Lesser, Jeffrey. *Immigration, Ethnicity, and National Identity in Brazil, 1880 to the Present*. Cambridge: Cambridge University Press, 2013.

Lesser, Jeffrey, and Michael C. Gutmann, eds. *Global Latin America: Into the Twenty-First Century*. Oakland: University of California Press, 2016.

Lesser, Jeffrey, and Raanan Rein, eds. *Rethinking Jewish Latin Americans*. Albuquerque: University of New Mexico Press, 2008.

Lestchinsky, Jacob. *The Jewish Migration for the Past Hundred Years*. New York: YIVO, 1944.

———. "Jewish Migrations, 1840–1956." In *The Jews: Their History, Culture, and Religion*. Vol. 2, edited by Louis Finkelstein, 1536–96. New York: Harper & Bros., 1960.

Marino, Katherine M. *Feminism for the Americas: The Making of an International Human Rights Movement*. Chapel Hill: University of North Carolina Press, 2019.

Mays, Devi. *Forging Ties, Forging Passports: Migration and the Modern Sephardi Diaspora*. Stanford, CA: Stanford University Press, 2020.

Michels, Tony. "Toward a History of American Jews and the Russian Revolutionary Movement." In *A Century of Transnationalism: Immigrants and Their Homeland Connections*, edited by Nancy L. Green and Roger Waldinger, 185–208. Urbana: University of Illinois Press, 2017.

Moya, José C. Introduction to *The Oxford Handbook of Latin American History*, edited by José C. Moya, 1–24. Oxford: Oxford University Press, 2011.

Newton, Ronald C. "German Nazism and the Origins of Argentine Anti-Semitism." In *The Jewish Diaspora in Latin America: New Studies on History and Literature*, edited by David Sheinin and Lois Baer Barr, 199–217. New York: Gerland, 1996.

Penslar, Derek Jonathan. "1897: The Year of Jewish Revolutions?" *Jewish Quarterly Review* 108, no. 4, (Fall 2018): 520–25.

Perlmann, Joel. *Ethnic Differences: Schooling and Social Structure Among the Irish, Italians, Jews, and Blacks in an American City*. Cambridge: Cambridge University Press, 1989.

Pratt, Mary Louise. *Imperial Eyes: Travel and Transculturation*. London: Routledge, 1992.

Rein, Raanan. "The Eichmann Kidnapping: Its Effects on Argentine-Israeli Relations and Local Jewish Relations." *Jewish Social Studies New Series* 7, no. 3 (Spring–Summer 2001): 101–30.

———, ed. *Árabes y judíos en Iberoamérica: similitudes, diferencias y tensiones*. Colección Ánfora. Seville: Fundación Tres Culturas del Mediterráneo, 2008.

Rein, Raanan, Stefan H. Rinke, and Nadia Zysman, eds. *New Ethnic Studies in Latin America*. Boston: Brill, 2017.

Rürup, Miriam. "Transnational Perspectives on Jewish and American-Jewish Studies." *American Jewish History* 101, no. 4 (October 2017): 553–56.

Segal, Ariel. *Jews of the Amazon: Self-Exile in Earthly Paradise*. Philadelphia: Jewish Publication Society, 1999.

Slack, Edward R., Jr. "The Chinos in New Spain: A Corrective Lens for a Distorted Image." *Journal of World History* 20, no. 1 (March 2009): 35–65.

Spitzer, Leo. *Hotel Bolivia: The Culture and Memory in a Refuge from Nazism*. New York: Hill and Wang, 1998.

Stein, Sarah Abrevaya. *Plumes: Ostrich Feathers, Jews, and a Lost World of Global Commerce*. New Haven: Yale University Press, 2008.

Stites Mor, Jessica. "The Question of Palestine in the Argentine Political Imaginary: Anti-Imperialist Thought from Cold War to Neoliberal Order." *Journal of Iberian and Latin American Research* 20, no. 2 (2014): 183–97.

Szapor, Judith, Andrea Pető, Maura Hametz, and Marina Calloni, eds. *Jewish Intellectual Women in Central Europe, 1860–2000: Twelve Biographical Essays*. Lewiston: Edwin Mellen Press, 2012.

Telles, Edward. *Pigmentocracies: Ethnicity, Race, and Color in Latin America*. Chapel Hill: University of North Carolina Press, 2014.
Telles, Edward, and Tianna Paschel. "Who is Black, White, or Mixed Race? How Skin Color, Status, and Nation Shape Racial Classification in Latin America." *American Journal of Sociology* 120, no. 3 (November 2014): 864–907.
Teubal, Nissim. *El inmigrante: de Alepo a Buenos Aires*. Buenos Aires: n.p., 1953.
Torrealba, Isabel. "The Surprising Piece of Mexican (and American) History at the Center of *Roma*." *Slate Magazine*, November 21, 2018. https://slate.com/culture/2018/11/roma-corpus-christi-student-massacre-el-halconazo.html.
Ureña Valerio, Lenny A. "Creating the Polish Nation Abroad." In *Colonial Fantasies, Imperial Realities: Race Science and the Making of Polishness on the Fringes of the German Empire, 1840–1920*, 148–71. Athens: Ohio University Press, 2019.
Vinke, Wieke. *Creole Jews: Negotiating Community in Colonial Suriname*. Leiden: KITLV Press, 2010.
Wiznitzer, Arnold. *Jews in Colonial Brazil*. New York: Columbia University Press, 1960.

I

IMPERIAL INTERSECTIONS

1

Muslims and Jewish Converts in the Early Modern Hispanic World

TAMAR HERZOG

Between 1609 and 1614, some 300,000 individuals of Muslim descent were ordered to leave the Iberian Peninsula.[1] Historians who have studied these measures remarked that they were issued against persons who were at least nominally Christian. They explained that, from as early as 1500, Muslims living on Spanish soil were encouraged or even forced to convert, first by mass conversions and then by decrees that in 1502 and 1526 gave them the choice between conversion and exile. Consequently, in the early seventeenth century, when these individuals were ordered into exile, all of them were, by definition, Christians.

The question of why Christians of Muslim descent were expelled from Spain has generated a huge bibliography. Historians have argued that, although most Muslims chose conversion over exile, in the aftermaths of this decision they hardly modified their ways of being. Separate and distinct from all other Spaniards, they remained in the same communities and obeyed the same authorities. Also persisting were intellectual and commercial ties with Muslim authorities and individuals across the seas.[2] Many observers—both past observers and present-day historians—thus concluded that converts of Muslim origin had their bodies in Iberia but their souls in Dar-al-Islam, that is, in lands where Islam dominated.

According to this narrative, this continuity despite conversion was initially tolerated. However, gradually, the Christian authorities began censoring this persistence, among other things, because they considered it an indication of either insincere or incomplete conversion. Thereafter, these authorities began banning certain customs which they identified as Muslim, while devising projects targeting the redistribution of *converso*

Muslims across Spain with the aim of ensuring both the breakup of existing communities as well as the insertion of individuals and families into new, Christian-dominated, enclaves. Eventually, the Spanish kings decreed their expulsion in the early seventeenth century, having concluded that most former Muslims were permanent and dangerous religious and cultural renegades.

The decision favoring expulsion was accompanied by constant debate as to whether certain individuals could or should be spared—children, for example, or persons who had already lived in Christian communities, who had severed ties will all other former Muslims, were married to Christians, or who had manifested in other ways their sincere Christian belief. In the end, however, in most cases the sincerity of conversion was deemed mostly irrelevant, and all former Muslims were ordered into exile regardless of how they behaved.

The social sector formed by former Muslims was not the only one treated this way. As is well known, attempts to convert Jews were also frequent in late medieval Spain where, on many occasions, Jews were baptized in ceremonies of mass conversion. The coexistence, side-by-side, of Jews and Christians ended in 1492 when the royal authorities gave Jews an option similar to the one they would give former Muslims a few decades later, namely, either to convert or to go into exile. Those who converted were both integrated and rejected simultaneously. As would happen with conversos of Muslim origin some hundred years later, contemporaries constantly questioned whether the conversion of the Jews who preferred to remain in Spain was sincere and whether it was complete. The suspicion that conversion might have been disingenuous or incomplete allowed rebels in Toledo as early as 1449 to pass a *sentencia decreto* (decision), which excluded all converts of Jewish descent from occupying public offices and ecclesiastical benefices in the jurisdiction. Exclusion soon expanded to many other institutions and geographies. In 1482, the Colegio Mayor de San Bartolomé of the University of Salamanca barred converts from membership, and, in the following years, so did many other colleges as well as several religious and military orders and a number of dioceses.[3] Eventually, exclusion by reference to descent (the so-called *limpieza de sangre* [purity of blood] decrees) would also be applied to converts from Islam, who would be equally barred from many privileges reserved for those now identified as "Old Christians."

If conversos of both Jewish and Muslim descent had lived through a somewhat parallel experience in the fifteenth and sixteenth centuries, by the early seventeenth century this was no longer true. While Christians who descended from Jews, even if they were on occasion persecuted or discriminated against, could thereafter remain in Spain and, indeed, were considered Spaniards, those who descended from Muslims were ordered into exile regardless of their religious belief. The question historians have asked ever since is why. Why allow conversos of Jewish origins to remain yet expel those of Muslim descent?

This question was meaningful on both sides of the ocean. Theoretically, conversos belonging to both groups were barred from migrating to the New World. According to decrees dated 1501, repeated in 1518 and 1530, and later integrated into the most important compilation of royal decisions—the *Recopilación de Indias*, dated 1681, "no one newly converted" to Catholicism of Muslim or Jewish descent nor their sons, could migrate to the Americas without obtaining a special license.[4] To ensure obedience, the authorities began requiring all candidates for immigration to present, before they boarded the ships, a judicial information certifying, among other things, that they were not of these prohibited types.[5] Although not always supplied, or not always trustworthy, these briefs were to be elaborated at the hometown of candidates and were to document who they and what their origins were.

Though similar orders were given regarding New Christians of both Jewish and Muslim descent in the New World it was mainly the potential presence of those originating in Jews that caused most preoccupation. Historians still debate how many had crossed the Atlantic, but they tend to agree that anxieties regarding who they were and whether their conversion was truthful exploded during the union of the crowns of Castile and Portugal (1580–1640) because, in contemporary appreciation, being Portuguese and having Jewish descent were one and the same thing. According to these perceptions, all Portuguese were New Christians and most New Christians were Portuguese.

The propensity to assume that practically all Portuguese were new converts of Jewish descent and most new converts of Jewish descent were Portuguese was linked to the belief that many Spanish Jews had fled to Portugal in the late medieval period, thus considerably augmenting the size and importance of the Portuguese Jewish community. According to popular views, the forced conversion of the Portuguese Jews in 1497 had been less successful than that of Spanish Jews, paradoxically because Portuguese Jews were not given the option of exile but instead were all forced to convert. The absence of inquisitorial persecution in Portugal until 1536 (when the first inquisitorial court was established) further enhanced these conclusions, which now pointed both to the prevalence of former Jews in Portugal as well as to the likelihood—because of the lack of persecution—of widespread persistence of Jewish beliefs.[6] The fact that many Portuguese who emigrated to the Americas during the union between Spain and Portugal were merchants only intensified this association between the Portuguese and converts of Jewish origin because, according to contemporary convictions, Jews and former Jews now turned Christians were mostly merchants and merchants were mostly Jews.

The conclusion that the Portuguese and conversos of Jewish origin formed part of the very same community was so immediate and so strong in Spanish America that most interlocutors never questioned it. It resulted in a constant suspicion against all Portuguese, suspicion that greatly intensified in periods of heightened political tensions between both crowns. These political tensions resulted usually in the persecution of the Portuguese in Spanish America, now accused not only of political infidelity but also of secretly practicing their Judaism. Particularly famous in this regard were the campaigns unleashed by the Inquisition against such individuals in major Spanish American centers and port towns such as Mexico City, Lima, or Cartagena de Indias in the 1630s and 1640s, coinciding with the uprising and then independence of Portugal.[7]

Though the presence of individuals in Spanish America who should not have crossed the Atlantic preoccupied the authorities, most efforts were invested not in expelling the new converts of Jewish descent but in questioning their faith and their political allegiance. It was almost as if Jewish descent was commonly known (or assumed), at least in many cases, the only question being whether it indicated (or not) some political, social, or religious danger. Yet, while former Jews had to demonstrate their loyalty, most individuals accused of being of Muslim descent (equally banned from the jurisdiction) in Spanish America instead tended to deny their origin.[8] Rather than insisting on their correct religious belief as most Christians of Jewish descent (or suspected of having Jewish descent) did, when it was suspected that they were new converts, most conversos of Muslim descent typically replied that they were not.

If this was indeed true, that is, if in both Spain and Spanish America, converts of Jewish descent had to mainly prove the sincerity of their conversion while those of Muslim descent had to renounce their origins or else be forced to leave, how can we account for these differences?

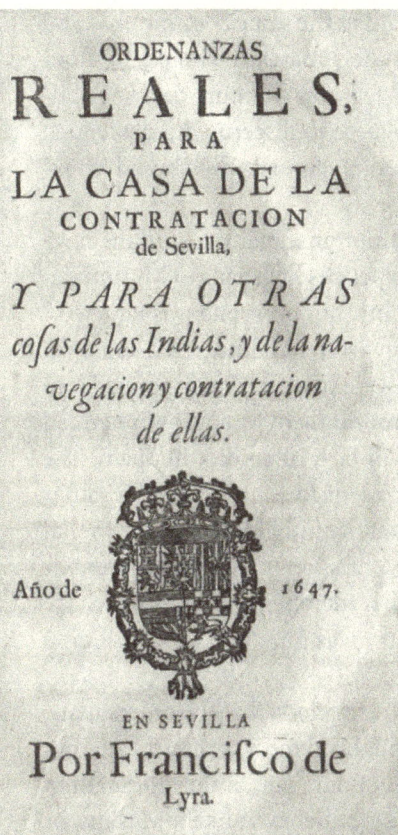

Figures 1.1 and 1.2. Francisco de Lyra, *Ordenanzas reales para la Casa de la Contratacion de Sevilla, y para otras cosas de las Indias, y de la navegacion y contratacion de ellas* (1647). Cover and fol. 30r listing the groups prohibited from travelling to the Americas. Courtesy of the Harold and Mary Jean Hanson Rare Book Collection, Special and Area Studies Collections, George A. Smathers Libraries, University of Florida.

Can You Tell a Convert When You See One?

The early seventeenth-century decrees that ordered the expulsion of all converts of Muslim descent did not define who these individuals were or how they could be distinguished from all other Spaniards. Most historians explain that, in the aftermaths of their religious transformation, these Christians could still be easily recognizable because they continued to exhibit cultural traits that distinguished them from all other Christians, such as their use of Arabic or the wearing of a particular dress, their following social practices that let many of them remain in the same communities and restrict most of their activities, as well as their marriage choices to other members of the group. These identifying features—culture and sociability—helped the authorities and society-at-large to discern who descended of Muslims and thus, in the early seventeenth century, who should be expelled from the Iberian Peninsula.

Yet, despite these common sense assumptions, many historians have also affirmed that, although the order to expel all Christians of Muslim descent barely allowed for exceptions, in reality, not everyone was targeted.[9] If, initially, those who could prove that they were well integrated could remain in Iberia, eventually, only those who were so utterly incorporated into the local fabric that both they and those around them forgot (or pretended to forget) their origin could remain and, in fact, often did, in Spain. The ambition to apprehend and identify all those of Muslim descent, in other words, was circumscribed by the need to classify individuals, a process that guaranteed that only those known as New Christians of Muslim descent or behaving as such would be targeted. All other members of the group whose behavior was normative and whose ancestry was forgotten (or considered irrelevant) were necessarily left alone.

These developments led some scholars to conclude that the orders mandating expulsion were, paradoxically, the final and most successful attempt to assimilate Spaniards of Muslim descent. Simply put, in the aftermath of the decrees no one who looked like a Muslim, behaved like a Muslim, or with a known Muslim past was allowed to be present in Spain. The decrees, therefore, might have not eliminated all those of Muslim origin, but they did succeed in erasing the memory, and often the visibility, of their existence. These decrees instituted an imaginary watershed enabling Spaniards to reimagine both who they were and what Spain had been. This watershed sustained a historical fiction according to which, in the post-expulsion period, de jure, even if not de facto, Spaniards of Muslim descent simply ceased to exist. They were to become an impossible oxymoron.

Detecting traces of silent assimilation—that is, the presence of those individuals who could remain in Spain despite their origin because they no longer were considered former Muslims or their origin was no longer deemed relevant—is of course much harder to accomplish than finding indications of open resistance or persecution. Yet, clues for the prevalence of assimilation are not wanting in the historical record. Already a century before the expulsion, for example, the number of conversos of Muslim descent mentioned in archival sources gradually diminished, as if either they had materially vanished or, more probably, the memory of their presence was slowly fading away.[10] The ability to avoid detection was sometimes related to mobility, as many former Muslims who originated in Granada were dispersed across the Peninsula, becoming a highly volatile population, which was hard to control and often distinguish.[11] But memory was also failing in other Iberian territories, most particularly in Castile, where integration was apparently exceptionally successful. It was precisely at this conjuncture that some actors, preoccupied with oblivion, sought to institute and ensure recollection. As the actual number of subjects categorized as former Muslims was diminishing, their once-upon-a-time existence, these individuals argued, had to be remembered. The instrument these actors selected to perform this task were the (in)famous limpieza de sangre decrees. Instituting new distinctions between those whose blood was allegedly pure because they were Old Christians and those whose blood was contaminated because they were not was therefore paradoxically a means to remember what was otherwise no longer clear or visual.

Ironically, we now know that many of the converts who were stigmatized in the sixteenth and seventeenth centuries by their Muslim descent were in fact of Jewish or Christian origin. Many among them were offspring of Peninsular families who were either forced or enticed to convert to Islam after the territory was conquered by Muslims in the eighth and ninth centuries. Others descended of captives, who were equally pressed to convert. Many of these former Jews and Christians adopted Arabic as their language and even pretended to be of Arab descent in order to ensure their survival and improve their living conditions under Muslim control. Yet, despite their attempts to pass as Old Muslims, their status as converts and New Muslims was sufficiently well known to propel the last Muslim ruler of Granada, Boabdil, to request to allow them to maintain their new Muslim faith and their adhesion to Islam even after the Christian takeover and the treaty of capitulation he signed with the Catholic Kings in 1491.[12]

If accusations of newness depended on memory, claims for antiquity were based on oblivion. Discussions regarding old and new adopted as historically true the phantasmagoric convention that all communities, whether Christian or Muslim, had some members whose ancestors had always belonged to the polity and others whose ancestors did not.[13] Affirmations of authenticity and fantasies of purity necessarily depended on such fictions, as well as on the presence or absence of information, or the willingness or reluctance to ask difficult questions. But just as important was what was remembered and what was forgotten as those claiming the need for discrimination remembered certain things but not others. They remembered, for example, that some Spaniards descended of Jews and Muslims, but they forgot that many Muslims were of Jewish or Christian descent. They also did not ask who the other Spaniards descended from.[14]

While some interlocutors insisted on forgetting who they were but on remembering who others had been, others adopted the contrary policy. In early modern Spain there were also individuals who were willing to refute claims for exclusivity and fantasies of purity by invoking memory. Privileges, these individuals argued, could not be granted on the basis of antiquity in Spain because "no one can prove that he is a descendant of the companions of Tuval, who because of the confusion of the languages [tower of Babel] came to live in Spain, Spain having been so flooded with innumerable nations that even the most genealogical person cannot boast an origin previous to the Goths, who came to Spain after many other nations did."[15] Indeed, until now, they insisted, no one had imagined or thought to form a genealogical tree that would declare his degree of antiquity in Spain in order to prove that he was fully a Spaniard.[16] In a melting pot like Spain at any rate, it would be utterly impossible to distinguish an original from a non-original member, Romans from Goths, Spaniards from foreigners.[17]

Comparing Different Types of New Christians

Returning to the question of conversos of Jewish descent and why they could remain in Spain (even if on occasions they were persecuted) while conversos of Muslim descent could not, the typical answer the literature gives is that, while converso Jews did their best to draw as little attention to themselves as possible, those of Muslim descent refused to follow this road. Instead, they were obstinate in stressing their differences and in marking the boundaries that separated them from all other Spaniards.[18]

Regardless of the question of whether this interpretation is accurate (and many now consider it is not), most historians nevertheless agree that, paradoxically, in the long run, what most distinguished conversos of Jewish descent was not their supposed allegiance to Judaism or their doubtful Christian beliefs, but their enduring attachment to the Iberian Peninsula. Whether they were practicing Jews, orthodox Christians, or go-betweens, even proto-atheists, Spaniards of Jewish origins ended up forming a diaspora that—although spread throughout Europe, Africa, Asia, and the Americas—coalesced around a common identity that was not religious but instead was grounded on their common Iberian past. While they continued to associate with one another despite religious differences, the members of this diaspora retained their attachment to their Hispanic traditions. They spoke Spanish, sang Spanish songs, and followed Spanish customs. They also identified themselves as Spaniards.

The memory of having belonged to Spain and of having been Spanish was constantly reenacted by the circulation of members who had returned to the Iberian Peninsula and had left it once again.[19] Some, moved by economic opportunities, family ties, their affinity to the Iberian culture, or the inability to acculturate to Jewish society outside Spain, ended up resettling permanently in Iberia. Although their numbers are difficult to establish, hundreds might have followed this road. Contacts between conversos of Jewish origins and Spain were also reenacted by the refusal to admit Jews of non-Iberian origin as members of Sephardic communities, or the general prohibition of marrying outside the group.[20] In other words, while some (perhaps many) converts of Jewish origin hesitated regarding their religious identity, most were adamantly Spanish.

Recent scholarship confirms that, initially, Spaniards of Muslim descent adopted attitudes similar to those of Spaniards of Jewish descent. There are indications, for example, that, after their expulsion, some converts of Muslim descent returned to the Iberian Peninsula, while others were identified as either Christians or as Iberians in the territories where they found refuge, territories where they attempted to maintain some degree of separation or the host community imposed separation on them.[21] Many former Spaniards of Muslim descent also engaged in endogamous practices while others vindicated their Spanish past. Nonetheless, converts of Muslim origins did not form a dense international community as did the Spaniards of Jewish origin, and most did not maintain a memory of difference beyond the first few generations.[22] That is, regardless of their initial reaction, these Christians of Muslim descent eventually ended up integrating back into Muslim culture as well as (often) Islam.

Fascination with the endurance of recollection, the persistence of loyalty to Spain (or the memory of Spain), and the existence of a Sephardic world that was Hispanic rather than necessarily Jewish, was perhaps already captured by early modern Spaniards, who allowed former Jews to remain in the Iberian Peninsula, but it certainly intrigued not only historians, not only Jews, but also contemporary Spanish legislators. Timidly during the government of Primo de Rivera in the early twentieth century and more clearly with the return of democracy to Spain in the 1980s, these legislators (and the Portuguese legislators following them) gave special privileges to the descendants of Iberian Jews (but not Iberian Muslims). Distinguishing yet again between the treatment of former Spaniards of Jewish descent and former Spaniards of Muslim origin, these legislators established that those descending from Spanish Jews, regardless of the question of whether they were Jewish or Christian, should be allowed readmission to Spain in the form of an accelerated process of naturalization.

Notes

1. Antonio Domínguez Ortiz, "Los moriscos granadinos antes de su definitiva expulsión," *Miscelánea de Estudios Árabes y Hebraicos* 12–13 (1963): 113–28; Enrique Soria Mesa, *Los últimos moriscos. Pervivencias de la población de origen islámico en el reino de Granada (siglos XVII–XVIII)* (Valencia: Universidad de Valencia, 2014); Trevor J. Dadson, *Los moriscos de Villarubia de los Ojos (siglos XV–XVIII). Historia de una minoría asimilada, expulsada y reintegrada* (Madrid: Iberoamericana-Vervuert, 2007); Rafael M. Pérez García and Manuel Fernández Chaves, "La política civil y religiosa sobre el matrimonio y la endogamia de los moriscos en la España del siglo XVI," *Dimensioni e problemi della ricerca storica* 2 (2012): 61–103; Manuel Lomas Cortés, *El proceso de expulsión de los moriscos de España (1609–1614)* (Valencia: Universidad de Valencia, 2011); Rafael Benítez Sánchez-Blanco, *Tríptico de la expulsión de los moriscos. El triunfo de la razón de estado* (Montpellier: Presses Universitaires de la Méditerranée, 2012); Carlos Garriga, "Enemigos domésticos. La expulsión católica de los moriscos (1609–1614)," *Quaderni Fiorentini* 38, no. 1 (2009): 225–87.

2. Kathryn Miller, *Guardians of Islam: Religious Authority and Muslim Communities of Late Medieval Spain* (New York: Columbia University Press, 2008).

3. Albert A. Sicroff, *Los estatutos de limpieza de sangre: controversias entre los siglos XV y XVII*, trans. Mauro Armiño (Madrid: Taurus, 1985). Also see David Nirenberg, "Mass Conversion and Genealogical Mentalities: Jews and Christians in Fifteenth-Century Spain," *Past and Present* 174 (2002): 3–41 and Mercedes García-Arenal, "Creating Conversos: Genealogy and Identity as Historiographical Problems (after a recent book by Ángel Alcalá)," *Bulletin for Spanish and Portuguese Historical Studies* 38, no. 1 (2013): 1–19, 2.

4. "Ninguno nuevamente convertido a nuestra santa fe católica de moro o judío ni sus hijos, puedan pasar a las indias sin expresa licencia nuestra." *Recopilación de Indias*, Law 15, title 26, Book 9. Following are prohibitions for the passage of those who were found guilty by the Inquisition or were heretic (dated 1518 and, again, 1530 and 1539), those who were slaves, independently of the question of whether they were white, black, mulatto or North African (dated 1530), Africans who had already spent at least two years in Spain or Portugal (1526, 1532), slaves that had been raised by Muslims (1526, 1532, and 1550), Gypsies (1570), or Mulattos (1543). Available from https://www.boe.es/biblioteca_juridica/publicacion.php?id=PUB-LH-1998-62&tipo=L&modo=2 (accessed March 4, 2020). See vol. 3, p. 312.

5. Francisco Lyra, *Ordenanzas reales para la Casa de la Contratacion de Sevilla* (Seville, 1647), fol. 30R, citing a decree dated April 5, 1552. The first *ordenanzas* (ordinances) of the Casa, dated 1503, only dealt with control over merchandise not people. However, by 1510 the ordinances referred to people whose passage to the Americas was prohibited. The first regulation of such passage was apparently contained in the instructions given to Nicolás de Ovando after he was named governor of the Americas in 1501. These included a prohibition that Moors, Jews, conversos, or those sentenced by the Inquisition would immigrate to the Americas. Nevertheless, it is possible that the implementation of these instructions was not required until 1508 when the *procuradores* (representatives) of La Española requested to prohibit the passage of those people because of the danger they might pose to the conversion of the Indians. The king agreed but limited the prohibition to descendants of Moors and Jews to the second generation and only the first generation in the case of those sentenced by the Inquisition. On these issues see Francisco Fernández López, "La Casa de la Contratación de Indias: una oficina de expedición documental," (Ph.D diss., Universidad de Sevilla, 2015), 192–95. Fernández López published this dissertation as *La Casa de la Contratación: una oficina de expedición documental para el Gobierno de las Indias (1503–1717)* (Séville: Editorial Universidad de Sevilla, 2018). Also see Esteban Mira Caballos, "Los prohibidos en la emigración a América (1492–1550)," *Estudios de Historia Económica y Social de América* no. 12 (1995): 37–54; Yolanda Quesada Morillas, "La expulsión de los judíos andaluces a finales del siglo XV y su prohibición de pase a Indias," in *Actas del I Congreso Internacional sobre Migraciones en Andalucía*, eds. Francisco Javier García Castaño and Nina Kressova (Granada: Instituto de Migraciones, 2011), 2103. The first prohibition, included in Archivo General de Indias, Indiferente, 418, lib. 1, fol. 41v, capítulo 23 reads: "Ytem, por quanto nos, con mucho cuydado, hemos de procurar la conversión de los yndios a nuestra santa fee católica e si allá fuesen personas sospechosas en la fee a la dicha conversión podrían dar algun impedimento, no consyntiréis ni daréys lugar que allá vayan moros nin judíos nin herejes nin reconçiliados nin personas nuevamente convertidas a nuestra fee, salvo si fueren esclavos negros o otros esclavos que ayan naçido en poder de christianos nuestros súbditos e naturales." Yet, conversos of Jewish origin were still able to cross the Atlantic if they received special licenses. This practice came to a halt in 1552 when new procedures were put in place to check the *limpieza de sangre* of those who wanted to immigrate and were thereafter reproduced in the *Recopilación de Indias*.

6. The Spanish Inquisition was instituted in 1478. Some of these issues are discussed in David L. Graizbord, *Souls in Dispute: Converso Identities in Iberia and the Jewish Diaspora, 1580–1700* (Philadelphia: University of Pennsylvania Press, 2004), 20–21, 44, 48–49, and 50–53.

7. Harry E. Cross, "Commerce and Orthodoxy: A Spanish Response to Portuguese Commercial Penetration in the Viceroyalty of Peru, 1580–1640," *The Americas* 35, no. 2 (1978): 151–67; Stanley M. Hordes, "The Inquisition as Economic and Political Agent: The Campaign of the Mexican Holy Office against the Crypto-Jews in the Mid-Seventeenth Century," *The Americas* 39, no. 1 (1982): 23–38; and Alonso W. Quiroz, "The Expropriation of Portuguese New Christians in Spanish America, 1635–1649," *Ibero-Amerikanisches Archiv*, n.s., 11, no. 4 (1985): 407–65.

8. Karoline P. Cook. *Forbidden Passages. Muslims and Moriscos in Colonial Spanish America* (Philadelphia: University of Pennsylvania Press, 2016).

9. James B. Tueller, "Los moriscos que se quedaron o que regresaron," in *Los moriscos: expulsión y diáspora. Una perspectiva internacional,* eds. Mercedes García Arenal and Gerard Albert Wiegers (Valencia: Universidad de Valencia, 2013), 191–209. Also see François Martinez, "La permanence morisque en Espagne après 1609 (discours et réalités)," (Ph.D. diss., Université Paul Valéry, 1997).

10. William Childers, "Disappearing Morisco," in *Cross-Cultural History and the Domestication of Otherness,* eds. Michael J. Rozbicki and George O. Ndege (New York: Palgrave, 2012), 51–56; see also Sara N. Cavanaugh, *The Morisco Problem and the Politics of Belonging in Sixteenth-Century Valladolid* (Toronto: University of Toronto, 2016); M. F. Gómez Vozmediano, *Mudéjares y moriscos en el Campo de Calatrava* (Ciudad Real: Diputación Provincial, 2000); Esteban Mira Caballos, "Unos se quedaron y otros volvieron: moriscos en la Extremadura del siglo XVII," in *XXXIX Coloquios Históricos de Extremadura* (Trujillo: Asociación Cultural Coloquios Históricos de Extremadura, 2011), 459–88; Santiago Otero Mondéjar, "'Que siendo yo cristiano viejo la justicia procedió contra mí . . .' La instrumentalización de la imagen del morisco," *Historia y Genealogía* 1 (2011): 113–31. Francisco Márquez Villanueva, *El problema morisco (desde otras laderas)* (Madrid: Podhufi, 1991) insists on the importance of integration.

11. Francisco J. Moreno Díaz del Campo, "Los padrones moriscos de la gobernación calatrava de Almodóvar a finales del siglo XVI," *Cuadernos de Historia Moderna* 44, no. 1 (2019): 60.

12. Isabelle Poutrin, *Convertir les musulmans. Espagne, 1491–1609* (Paris: Presses Universitaires de France, 2012), 42–45 and 57–58. The situation in Valencia was not radically different: see pages 77–78. Also see Felipe Maíllo Salgado, *De la desaparición de al-Andalus* (Madrid: Abada Editores, 2004), 23–24, 35, and 38.

13. Ernest Renan, *Qu'est-ce qu'une nation?* (Paris: Calmann Lévy, 1882), 7–8. Renan continued affirming that, as a result, history was a dangerous pursuit for any national project because it illuminated the violence that had been at the origin of all political formations.

14. The "expiration" of memory could be encouraged by "appropriate" behavior, such as marrying an Old Christian. In this case, it was sometimes possible to receive the status of Old Christian even when one was new, or alternatively, giving this status to the mixed offspring. See Max Deardorff, "The Ties that Bind: Intermarriage between Moriscos and Old Christians in Early Modern Spain, 1526–1614," *Journal of Family History* 42, no. 3 (2017): 255.

15. Consulta of November 9, 1742, in Biblioteca del Palacio Real (Madrid), II 2755, no. 24, 153v–160v, 157v. The original reads: "nadie podrá probar ser descendiente de los compañeros de Tuval que de resulta de la confusión de las lenguas vinieron a poblar a España, habiendo sido ésta tan inundada de innumerables naciones que por gran timbre el más lingudo suele alegar su origen de la nación goda (mucho posterior a otras que dominaron la España) . . . hasta ahora, nadie ha imaginado ni pensado en formar un árbol genealógico declarando qué grados de antigüedad en el origen se necesita para comerciar en Indias."

16. Consulta of November 9, 1742, in Biblioteca del Palacio Real (Madrid), II 2755, no. 24, 153v–160v, 157v.

17. Opinion of the representative of royal interests (*fiscal*) of the council of state, as reproduced and adopted in the Consulta of February 26, 1774, in Archivo Histórico Nacional (Madrid), Estado 5042, fols. 75–80. The original reads: "dos naciones enemigas, en virtud de dichas leyes, se convirtieron en una, guerrera y poderosa... acudían personas de toda la cristiandad según crónicas antiguas." Present-day research partially affirms this image, insisting, for example, on the role of foreigners in both the *reconquista* and the resettlement of Castile.

18. Antonio Domínguez Ortiz and Bernard Vincent, *Historia de los Moriscos. Vida y tragedia de una minoría* (Madrid: Revista de Occidente, 1978), 9, and Rafael Benítez Sánchez-Blanco, "Control político y explotación económica de los moriscos: régimen señorial y protección," *Chronica Nova* 20 (1992): 19.

19. Graizbord, *Souls in Dispute*.

20. Thomas Glick, "On Converso and Marrano Ethnicity," in *Crisis and Creativity in the Sephardic World*, ed. Benjamin R. Gampel (New York: Columbia University Press, 1997), 59–76; Miriam Bodian, "Men of the Nation: The Shaping of Converso Identity in Early Modern Europe," *Past and Present* 143 (1994): 49–76, and *Hebrews of the Portuguese Nation: Conversos and Community in Early Modern Amsterdam* (Bloomington: Indiana University Press, 1997); and Yoseph Kaplan, "Exclusión y autoidentidad," in *Judíos nuevos en Amsterdam: estudios sobre la historia social e intellectual del judaísmo sefardí en el siglo XVII* (Barcelona: Editorial Gedisa, 1996), 56–77.

21. Miguel de Espalza and Abdel-Hakim Slama-Gafsi, *El español hablado en Túnez por los moriscos o andalusíes y sus descendientes (siglos XVII–XVIII)* (Valencia: Universidad de Valencia, 2010).

22. Natalia Muchnik, "Ibériques en exil: marranes et morisques aux prises avec le référent-origine," in *Les musulmans dans l'histoire de l'Europe*, vol. 2, *Passages et contacts en Méditerranée*, ed. Jocelyne Dakhlia and Wolfgang Kaiser (Paris: Albin Michel, 2013), 165–89, and "Judeoconversos y moriscos frente a la diáspora," in *Los moriscos: expulsión y diáspora. Una perspectiva internacional*, eds. Mercedes García Arenal and Gerard Albert Wiegers (Valencia: Universidad de Valencia, 2013), 415–40.

Bibliography

Primary Sources

Archives

Archivo General de Indias (Seville)
Archivo Histórico Nacional (Madrid)
Biblioteca del Palacio Real (Madrid)

Printed Sources

Lyra, Francisco. *Ordenanzas reales para la Casa de la Contratacion de Sevilla*. Seville: Francisco Lyra, 1647.
Recopilación de Indias. Book 9, Title 26, Law 15. Accessible online at https://www.boe.es/biblioteca_juridica/publicacion.php?id=PUB-LH-1998-62&tipo=L&modo=2.
Renan, Ernest. *Qu'est-ce qu'une nation?* Paris: Calmann Lévy, 1882.

Secondary Sources

Benítez Sánchez-Blanco, Rafael. "Control político y explotación económica de los moriscos: régimen señorial y protección." *Chronica Nova*, 20 (1992): 9–26.
——. *Tríptico de la expulsión de los moriscos. El triunfo de la razón de estado*. Montpellier: Presses Universitaires de la Méditerranée, 2012.
Bodian, Miriam. *Hebrews of the Portuguese Nation: Conversos and Community in Early Modern Amsterdam*. Bloomington: Indiana University Press, 1997.
——. "Men of the Nation: The Shaping of Converso Identity in Early Modern Europe," *Past and Present* 143 (1994): 49–76.
Cavanaugh, Sara N. *The Morisco Problem and the Politics of Belonging in Sixteenth-Century Valladolid*. Toronto: University of Toronto, 2016.
Childers, William. "Disappearing Morisco." In *Cross-Cultural History and the Domestication of Otherness*, edited by Michael J. Rozbicki and George O. Ndege, 51–64. New York: Palgrave, 2012.
Cook, Karoline P. *Forbidden Passages. Muslims and Moriscos in Colonial Spanish America*. Philadelphia: University of Pennsylvania Press, 2016.
Cross, Harry E. "Commerce and Orthodoxy: A Spanish Response to Portuguese Commercial Penetration in the Viceroyalty of Peru, 1580–1640." *The Americas* 35, no. 2 (1978): 151–67.
Dadson, Trevor J. *Los moriscos de Villarubia de los Ojos (siglos XV–XVIII). Historia de una minoría asimilada, expulsada y reintegrada*. Madrid: Iberoamericana Vervuert, 2007.
Deardorff, Max. "The Ties that Bind: Intermarriage between Moriscos and Old Christians in Early Modern Spain, 1526–1614." *Journal of Family History* 42, no. 3 (2017): 250–70.
De Espalza, Miguel, and Abdel-Hakim Slama-Gafsi. *El español hablado en Túnez por los moriscos o andalusíes y sus descendientes (siglos XVII–XVIII)*. Valencia: Universidad de Valencia, 2010.
Domínguez Ortiz, Antonio. "Los moriscos granadinos antes de su definitiva expulsión." *Miscelánea de Estudios Árabes y Hebraicos* 12–13 (1963–1964): 113–28.
Domínguez Ortiz, Antonio, and Bernard Vincent. *Historia de los moriscos. Vida y tragedia de una minoría*. Madrid: Revista de Occidente, 1978.
Fernández López, Francisco. "La Casa de la Contratación de Indias: una oficina de expedición documental." Ph.D. diss., Universidad de Sevilla, 2015.
García-Arenal, Mercedes. "Creating Conversos: Genealogy and Identity as Historiographical Problems (after a recent book by Ángel Alcalá)." *Bulletin for Spanish and Portuguese Historical Studies* 38, no. 1 (2013): 1–19.

Garriga, Carlos. "Enemigos domésticos. La expulsión católica de los moriscos (1609–1614)." *Quaderni Fiorentini* 38, no. 1 (2009): 225–87.

Glick, Thomas. "On Converso and Marrano Ethnicity." In *Crisis and Creativity in the Sephardic World*, edited by Benjamin R. Gampel, 59–76. New York: Columbia University Press, 1997.

Graizbord, David L. *Souls in Dispute: Converso Identities in Iberia and the Jewish Diaspora, 1580–1700*. Philadelphia: University of Pennsylvania Press, 2004.

Hordes, Stanley M. "The Inquisition as Economic and Political Agent: The Campaign of the Mexican Holy Office against the Crypto-Jews in the Mid-Seventeenth Century." *The Americas* 39, no. 1 (1982): 23–38.

Kaplan, Yoseph. *Judíos nuevos en Amsterdam: estudios sobre la historia social e intelectual del judaísmo sefardí en el siglo XVII*. Barcelona: Editorial Gedisa, 1996.

Lomas Cortés, Manuel. *El proceso de expulsión de los moriscos de España (1609–1614)*. Valencia: Universidad de Valencia, 2011.

Maíllo Salgado, Felipe. *De la desaparición de al-Andalus*. Madrid: Abada Editores, 2004.

Márquez Villanueva, Francisco. *El problema morisco (desde otras laderas)*. Madrid: Podhufi, 1991.

Martinez, François. "La permanence morisque en Espagne après 1609 (discours et réalités)." Ph.D. diss., Université Paul Valéry, 1997.

Miller, Kathryn. *Guardians of Islam: Religious Authority and Muslim Communities of Late Medieval Spain*. New York: Columbia University Press, 2008.

Mira Caballos, Esteban. "Los prohibidos en la emigración a América (1492–1550)." *Estudios de Historia Económica y Social de América*, no. 12 (1995): 37–54.

———. "Unos se quedaron y otros volvieron: moriscos en la Extremadura del siglo XVII." In *XXXIX Coloquios Históricos de Extremadura*. Trujillo: Asociación Cultural Coloquios Históricos de Extremadura, 2011.

Mondéjar, Santiago Otero. "'Que siendo yo cristiano viejo la justicia procedió contra mí . . . ' La instrumentalización de la imagen del morisco." *Historia y Genealogía* 1 (2011): 113–31.

Moreno Díaz del Campo, Francisco J. "Los padrones moriscos de la gobernación calatrava de Almodóvar a finales del siglo XVI." *Cuadernos de Historia Moderna* 44, no. 1 (2019): 37–62.

Muchnik, Natalia. "Ibériques en exil: marranes et morisques aux prises avec le référent-origine." In *Les musulmans dans l'histoire de l'Europe*. Vol. 2, *Passages et contacts en Méditerranée*, edited by Jocelyne Dakhlia and Wolfgang Kaiser, 165–89. Paris: Albin Michel, 2013.

———. "Judeoconversos y moriscos frente a la diáspora." In *Los moriscos: expulsión y diáspora. Una perspectiva internacional*, edited by Mercedes García Arenal and Gerard Albert Wiegers, 415–40. Valencia: Universidad de Valencia, 2013.

Nirenberg, David. "Mass Conversion and Genealogical Mentalities: Jews and Christians in Fifteenth-Century Spain." *Past and Present* 174 (2002): 3–41.

Pérez García, Rafael M., and Manuel Fernández Chaves. "La política civil y religiosa sobre el matrimonio y la endogamia de los moriscos en la España del siglo XVI." *Dimensioni e problemi della ricerca storica* 2 (2012): 61–103.

Poutrin, Isabelle. *Convertir les musulmans. Espagne, 1491-1609*. Paris: Presses Universitaires de France, 2012.
Quesada Morillas, Yolanda. "La expulsión de los judíos andaluces a finales del siglo XV y su prohibición de pase a Indias." In *Actas del I Congreso Internacional sobre Migraciones en Andalucía*, edited by Francisco Javier García Castaño and Nina Kressova, 2099-2106. Granada: Instituto de Migraciones, 2011.
Quiroz, Alonso W. "The Expropriation of Portuguese New Christians in Spanish America, 1635-1649." *Ibero-Amerikanisches Archiv*, n.s., 11, no. 4 (1985): 407-65.
Sicroff, Albert A. *Los estatutos de limpieza de sangre: controversias entre los siglos XV y XVII*. Translated by Mauro Armiño. Madrid: Taurus, 1985.
Soria Mesa, Enrique. *Los últimos moriscos. Pervivencias de la población de origen islámico en el reino de Granada (siglos XVII-XVIII)*. Valencia: Universidad de Valencia, 2014.
Tueller, James B. "Los moriscos que se quedaron o que regresaron." In *Los moriscos: expulsión y diáspora. Una perspectiva internacional*, edited by Mercedes García Arenal and Gerard Albert Wiegers, 191-209. Valencia: Universidad de Valencia, 2013.
Vozmediano, M. F. Gómez. *Mudéjares y moriscos en el Campo de Calatrava*. Ciudad Real: Diputación Provincial, 2000.

Insert

Carta ejecutoria de hidalguía for the Ortega y Vilches family
(Granada, 1725)

NEIL WEIJER

Though its articulations changed with time and location, ancestry proved a remarkably durable way of demarcating identity, social privilege, and even time in the Iberian world. This eighteenth-century manuscript recognizes the *hidalguía*, or noble status, of members of the Ortega y Vilches family of Aziarcollar, near Seville. Known as a *carta ejecutoria*, the text commemorates two decades of litigation during which the Ortegas produced documents and witnesses to attest to their hidalguía being recognized in their city for at least two generations. The origins of such *cartas* and the legal proceedings that produced them trace back to the late Middle Ages. *Hidalgos* were exempt from taxation, imprisonment for debt and from certain types of corporal punishment, and could hold royal benefices. The sixteenth and eighteenth centuries, in particular, witnessed dramatic increases in litigation as families either contested or sought to formally establish hidalguía in the chancery courts of Granada and Valladolid. Cartas like these were produced until the nineteenth century, often by teams of scribes and artists working in close proximity to the courts and in commercial centers such as Seville.

Genealogies also served the dual purpose of asserting a family's bloodline to be free from any religious commingling; assertions of *limpieza de sangre* followed a similar legal procedure. The accompanying genealogical diagram, drawing on the distinctive iconography of the tree of Jesse, traces the lineage of the Ortega family back eight generations, rather than the required two. The two leaves preceding the genealogy display a family coat of arms as well as portraits of the petitioners kneeling before a pietà,

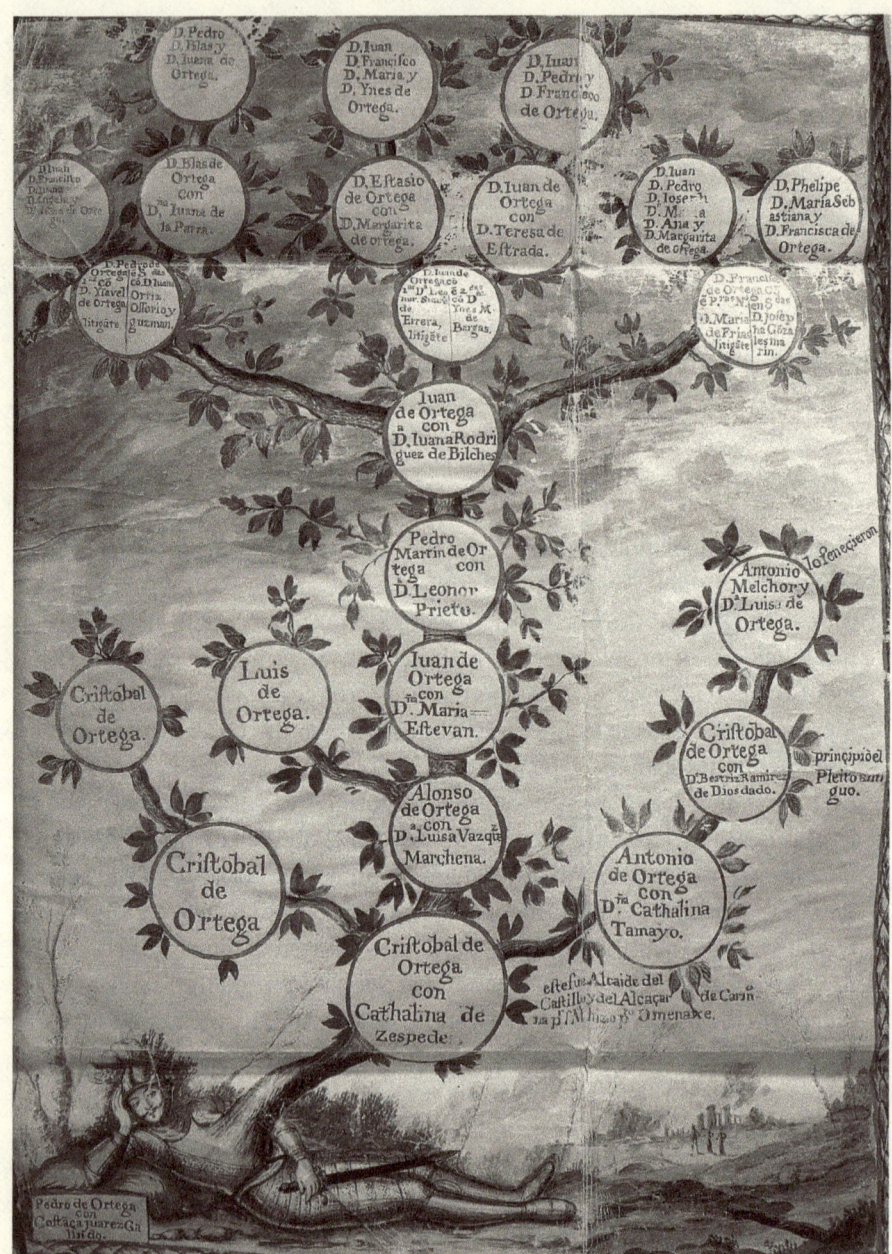

Insert Figure 1. Genealogical tree from *Carta ejecutoria de hidalguía* for the Ortega y Vilches family (1725). Courtesy of the Harold and Mary Jean Hanson Rare Book Collection, Special and Area Studies Collections, George A. Smathers Libraries, University of Florida.

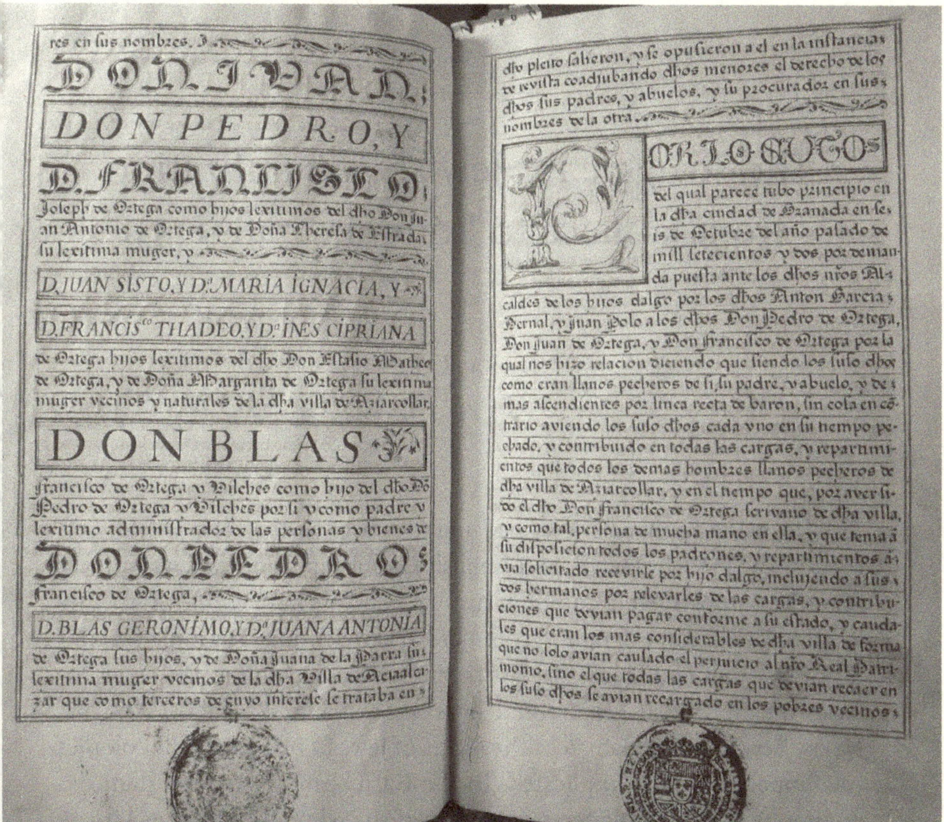

res en ſus nombres.
DON JUAN;
DON PEDRO, Y
D. FRANCISCO;
Joseph de Ortega como hijos lexitimos del dho Don Juan Antonio de Ortega, y de Doña Theresa de Estrada, ſu lexitima muger, y
D. JUAN SISTO, Y Dª. MARIA IGNACIA, Y
D. FRANCISCO THADEO, Y Dª. INES CIPRIANA
de Ortega hijos lexitimos del dho Don Eſtasio Matheo de Ortega, y de Doña Margarita de Ortega ſu lexitima muger vecinos y naturales de la dha villa de Arjarcollar,
DON BLAS
Francisco de Ortega y Vilches como hijo del dho Don Pedro de Ortega y Vilches por ſi y como padre y lexitimo administrador de las perſonas y bienes de
DON PEDRO;
Francisco de Ortega,
D. BLAS GERONIMO, Y Dª. JUANA ANTONIA
de Ortega ſus hijos, y de Doña Juana de la Parra ſu lexitima muger vecinos de la dha Villa de Alcaudete que como terceros de cuyo interese ſe trataba en

dho pleito ſalieron, y ſe opuſieron a el en la instancias de revista coadjubando dhos menores el derecho de los dhos ſus padres, y abuelos, y ſu procurador en ſus nombres de la otra.
... ORIGINALES
del qual parece tubo principio en la dha ciudad de Granada en ſeis de Octubre del año paſado de mill ſetecientos y dos por demanda pueſta ante los dhos nros Alcaldes de los hijos dalgo por los dhos Anton Garcia Bernal, y Juan Polo a los dhos Don Pedro de Ortega, Don Juan de Ortega, y Don Francisco de Ortega por la qual nos hizo relacion diciendo que ſiendo los ſuſo dhos como eran llanos pecheros de ſi, ſu padre, y abuelo, y demas aſcendientes por linea recta de baron, ſin coſa en contrario aviendo los ſuſo dhos cada uno en ſu tiempo pechado, y contribuido en todas las cargas, y repartimientos que todos los demas hombres llanos pecheros de dha villa de Arjarcollar, y en el tiempo que, por aver ſido el dho Don Francisco de Ortega ſcrivano de dha villa, y como tal, perſona de mucha mano en ella, y que tenia á ſu diſpoſicion todos los padrones, y repartimientos avia ſolicitado recevirle por hijo dalgo, incluyendo a ſus dos hermanos por relevarles de las cargas, y contribuciones que devian pagar conforme a ſu eſtado, y caudales que eran los mas conſiderables de dha villa de forma que no ſolo avian cauſado el perjuicio al nro Real Patrimonio, ſino el que todas las cargas que devian recaer en los ſuſo dhos ſe avian recargado en los pobres vecinos

Insert Figure 2. Opening (fols. 6r–7v) from *Carta ejecutoria de hidalguía for the Ortega y Vilches family* (1725) showing the names of the petitioners. Each folio bears the notarized stamp of Philip V of Spain. Courtesy of the Harold and Mary Jean Hanson Rare Book Collection, Special and Area Studies Collections, George A. Smathers Libraries, University of Florida.

a program of illustration common to the beginnings of these documents, and one that preserved the connections between social and confessional identity.

The additional leaves of notarized paper inserted at the back of the book record the presentation of the carta ejecutoria at different locations in the years following its creation. Although the litigants in this suit all appeared to have remained in the exurbs of Seville, documents such as these—based on documented or imagined genealogical connections to the past—were the basis for interaction with society in the Spanish Empire on both sides of the Atlantic in the early modern world.

2

The Struggle for Jewish Naturalization from Jamaica to London, 1748–1753

Dana Rabin

By 1550 many Sephardic Jews had found refuge in the New World. Settling in the French, Dutch, and English Caribbean colonies Jews in these imperial outposts had a common history. Scholars have identified themes of intra-Caribbean migration, commercial activity, and interimperial connection within and across the Northern European empires.[1] My work focuses on the British Empire and Jews in Suriname, Barbados, Antigua, Nevis, Bermuda, and Jamaica. The status of Jews in Britain and its colonies was important and complicated. In the Caribbean it was important demographically: Jews made up 5 percent of the white (i.e., of non-African origin) population in 1680, rising to 9.5 percent in 1720, and 7.5 percent of the white population in 1740. For comparison, consider that in Barbados, Jews were 1.5 percent of whites in 1680, a figure that rose to 3 percent in 1750.[2] I use the word white to describe the Jewish population to signal the examination of whiteness as a process and its connection to the story of naturalization and Jewish suffrage that is the focus of this chapter.

Commercially, the presence of Jews was important in both the colonies and the metropole. England's Jews had been expelled by Edward I in 1290. There is evidence of a continued Jewish presence in England throughout the centuries when they were officially banned.[3] They began to return more openly to England in the middle of the seventeenth century. The financial revolution combined with Britain's imperial expansion made London the center of foreign trade, luxury goods, the insurance industry, public borrowing, and investment. By the first decades of the eighteenth century, London's Jews were involved in every aspect of the city's financial and commercial activity. They held stock in the Bank of England, traded in the money market, and advised the government on its financial policies. Jews provisioned soldiers and supplied the government with loans; they imported bullion, worked as stockbrokers and stock jobbers, and traded in global commodities. Their commercial networks made Jews international trade agents across the British Empire. They invested in colonial enterprises, including the Royal African Company and the South Sea Company.[4]

The record of Jewish investment in colonial enterprises is quite dramatic. Between 1691 and 1712, 58 Jewish names show up among the investors in the Royal African Company while in the same time period, thirty-four Jewish shareholders invested in the South Sea Company. Jewish merchants actively promoted trade in India, the Caribbean, North America, and South America. They were particularly prominent in the diamond trade from India to Europe and active in the coral trade, importing this luxury good to London from the Mediterranean and reexporting it to India.[5]

While Jews in Britain were active in overseas trade importing and reexporting commodities and exporting British goods, Jewish colonial communities complemented the commercial and financial work of their coreligionists in the metropole.[6] The Jewish community in Madras, for example, exported diamonds to London throughout the eighteenth century.[7] In the Caribbean, taxes on the lively sale of commodities by Jewish merchants and shopkeepers filled the coffers of Britain's Exchequer.[8] The cultivation of sugar and the expansion of slavery reshaped the Atlantic economy and the needs of the colonies. In addition to owning slaves and managing plantations, Jews became involved in many of the financial and commercial endeavors that supported the new cash crop economy: shipping and credit, wholesaling dried goods and manufactures, and marine insurance.[9] In certain key imperial sites, this tiny minority was ubiquitous.

Nowhere is the status of Jews more complicated than in the legal realm. English law defined an array of statuses for those living in England or its colonial holdings. The legal commentator, William Blackstone, attempted to summarize the complicated legal categories in his four-volume *Commentaries on the Laws of England* first published in 1765. Blackstone claims that "The first and most obvious division of the people is into aliens and natural-born subjects. Natural-born subjects are such as are born within the dominions of the Crown of England, that is within the ligeance, or as it is generally called, the allegiance of the king; and aliens such as are born out of it."[10] Such born subjects were termed liege subjects: native or natural-born subjects who owed allegiance to the Crown by birth. Of course, status as a liege subject did not carry with it legal equality. Between subject and alien there were levels or gradations of persons with different rights and privileges or disabilities on a continuum between subject and alien.

London was known as "the foreigners' mecca" of "diverse immigrants."[11] The alien status of those who migrated to London or to England's colonies denied them the legal right to own land or other real property, to own or hold a share in a British sailing vessel, or to engage in the lucrative colonial trade. Those who did engage in foreign trade despite these restrictions were required to pay alien duties including custom rates and special port fees. These "diverse immigrants" could purchase letters of patent of denization in order to be made "free denizens." Denization allowed them to engage in colonial trade, but it did not exempt them from paying alien duties. A denizen could purchase and own land but not inherit. Children of denizens born in England were subjects by birth, but they could inherit only if they were born after their father's denization.[12]

The wealthiest immigrants to England, particularly prominent merchants, sought naturalization. Naturalization was the legal means of adopting aliens and incorporating them. It could only be granted by a private Act of Parliament. It conferred a higher status and more extensive privileges than denization because it was permanent and retroactive. Blackstone summarized the difference between these statuses, proclaiming that denization "put a man in a kind of middle state, between an alien and a natural-born subject" while naturalization put him in "exactly the same state as if he had been born in the king's liegeance."[13]

Jews who immigrated to Britain bought letters of patent which allowed them to engage in the profits of colonial trade. But those Jews who could afford the expense of naturalization were blocked from it because it required an Anglican oath as well as proof of receiving the sacrament.[14] As Jews returned to Britain and its Empire, there were more Jews born in England as liege subjects. They lived with the legal limits imposed on other non-Anglicans including Catholics and Dissenters, also known as non-Conformists. Because of the oaths involved and the sacramental requirement, Jews and other non-Anglicans could not serve on juries, hold municipal office, be called to the bar, obtain a naval commission, take a degree in the two universities, vote, or be elected to Parliament.[15]

English people disagreed about how to integrate the religious, racial, and cultural diversity of Britain and its colonies into a legal frame. While some objected to and resisted cultural mixing, others envisioned a global empire directed, inspired, and led by a cosmopolitan metropole. In my book *Britain and its Internal Others, 1750–1800: Under Rule of Law* (2017),

I argue that neither at home nor abroad did access to law emerge neatly or coherently from abstract principles of English justice. Despite Blackstone's artificially simplified statement that implied they were age-old products of legal thought and principle, English legal status was a product of imperial contact. The relationship between colony and metropole, outsiders and insiders, foreigners and "good subjects" operated within boundaries defined opportunistically, depending on the circumstances. Imperial relationships would be continuously and repeatedly negotiated with the tension and arbitrariness of the line drawn and constantly redrawn between those considered English, British, or imperial. In the imperial setting, both metropolitan and colonial, the law promoted and responded to British expansion—creating empire and eventually, by the end of the eighteenth century, defining a new category of difference in whiteness that assigned and reassigned the promise of equality before the law.[16]

Whiteness emerged as both important and complicated. The discourse of equality in the eighteenth century often resulted in hierarchies of race that revolved around definitions of whiteness. The noun "whiteness" was used in the eighteenth century to refer to "the state or condition of being white conceived in terms of racial or cultural identity."[17] The intersection of discourses of class, gender, sexuality, ethnicity, and religion produced definitions of whiteness and signaled the extent to which people were thought to be eligible for the rights and privileges of belonging. The legal category of whiteness was produced through at least three different collisions: between those considered insiders and those considered strangers, by the clash of metropole and colony, and by the clash between those I call "cosmopolitans" and those who resisted cosmopolitanism, even as they embraced empire, both situated in the metropole. Over the course of the second half of the eighteenth century, the legal category of whiteness emerged with male Anglicans of English heritage and middling status as its normative, "core," subjects.[18] Created through imperial contact and reinforced by legal process, this new category contradicted the ideology of universal equality before the law often used to justify imperial expansion.[19]

This chapter examines two related statutes passed in the mid-eighteenth century and the controversies that ensued. The first is the Plantation Act of 1740, which, among other provisions, allowed Jews in the colonies to be naturalized without an Anglican oath.[20] The second is the Jewish Naturalization Act, known as the "Jew Bill," passed in 1753. Both faced intense resistance. After an overview and analysis of each statute, I will suggest the significance of treating these two incidents in the same frame and what that might tell us about law, empire, religion, and whiteness as a process in the eighteenth century.

The Plantation Act of 1740

Menasseh ben Israel's publication of *Hope of Israel* in 1650 entreated Oliver Cromwell to lift the ban on Jews and allow them to settle in England. Five years later, in December 1655, ben Israel obtained an audience with Cromwell, known as the Whitehall Conference. The stakes were higher in 1655 because the Dutch had recently lost Pernambuco, displacing the Dutch Jews who had been there, and Jewish families were looking for new homes. Although Menasseh did not succeed in convincing Cromwell to readmit Jews officially to England and its colonies or to issue an edict of return, the expulsion order from 1290 was no longer enforced. Jews were allowed in England, Jamaica, and Barbados and they could practice Judaism privately. Their legal status was that of aliens. When Charles II was restored to the throne in 1660, he faced pressure to reinstate the expulsion order. He did not do so. With the Windsor Proclamation issued on December 14, 1661, and brought to Jamaica in August 1662 by Governor Thomas, Lord Windsor, Charles incentivized Europeans from non-English nationalities to settle in Jamaica, promising that their children born there would be "free denizens" and have "the same privileges to all intents and purposes of our free borne subjects."[21] The first Jew received denizen status in Barbados in 1661 and in England in 1675. Although there were already Jews in Jamaica, they began to arrive in greater numbers in the 1670s.

Despite some triumphalist accounts of the status of Jews in the colonies that argue for the expansion of their rights at the periphery before, or in anticipation of, Jewish emancipation in Great Britain in the mid-nineteenth century, Jews in the colonies faced unequal treatment.[22] Starting in 1686 and lasting into the eighteenth century, the Jews of Jamaica were assessed a tax for them specifically to fund the defense of the island with the justification that they were exempt from the other duties and responsibilities of citizens. The Jewish community in Jamaica actively resisted this tax on them as "a people apart," a medieval tradition that trapped them in an ascribed status. What that history—reconstructed most recently by Stanley Mirvis[23]—exemplifies is that the Jews in Jamaica were legally literate and willing, active agents on behalf of their community. Metropolitan authorities (the Board of Trade and the king) intervened on their behalf. Although their work was unsuccessful, their repeated attempts to use the legal instruments at their disposal reveal their conceptions of themselves as subjects entitled to and actively claiming rights they believed they were owed. In the exchanges with London, we see the imperial authorities attempting to change colonial policy as well as colonial resistance from white English Protestants in the Jamaican Assembly.

The issue of suffrage was another site of confrontation. When the name of David Nuñes appeared on a list of those who voted in a local election of three representatives from the town of Port Royal in August 1702, a brief discussion of Jews, voting, and representation appeared in the *Journals of the Assembly of Jamaica*.[24] In 1711 the Assembly passed the "Act for Regulating Fees" which specified "That no Jew, Mulatto, Indian or Negro, shall be capable to officiate or be employed to write in or for any of the above offices upon any pretence whatsoever."[25] In other words, Jews, people of color, and indigenous people were barred from voting or holding office. An official who failed to enforce this prohibition was subject to a fine of £100.[26] The racial and religious othering in this Act excluded both non-Christians and people of color from the group acknowledged as rights-bearing subjects.

The right to naturalization and expanding the rights of subjects came up again in 1740.[27] To revive trade spearheaded by Jewish merchants constrained by the Navigation Acts, the British Parliament passed the Plantation Act, "An Act for Naturalizing such foreign Protestants and others therein mentioned, as are settled or shall settle in any of His Majesty's Colonies in America."[28] Citing the argument that "the increase of people is a means of advancing the wealth and strength of any nation or country" and hoping that "many foreigners and strangers from the lenity of our government, the purity of our religion, the benefit of our laws, the advantages of our trade, and the security of our Property" might be convinced to settle in "his majesty's colonies in America," the Plantation Act allowed colonial subjects to apply for naturalization when they had resided in any American colony for at least seven years.[29] All applicants took an oath testifying to their profession of Christianity before a justice in an open court. In addition to the oath, two witnesses signed a certificate supporting the applicant's claim to have taken communion in a Protestant congregation. The key provision of the Act was the exemption of Jews and Quakers from the requirement of both the oath and the certificate of communion.

What was Parliament doing? After all, questions of local political and commercial privileges were already the subject of legislation passed by local assemblies in many American colonies as in the Jamaican case just mentioned. The Plantation Act bypassed these law-making bodies and imposed new law from the center. Unlike the patchwork of laws made by colonial assemblies or governors that applied only locally and sometimes, as in the case of slave laws, contradicted or were disavowed by some metropolitan authorities, this 1740 Act overrode local authorities. In addition to the profits at stake, Parliament was most certainly moved to action by the lengthy correspondence with Jamaica's Jews over the higher levels of taxation at which they were assessed. The repeated resistance of Jamaica's Assembly may have prompted Parliament's legislative intervention.[30] Sheldon and Judith Godfrey ascribe the motive for the Plantation Act to the British government's awareness of the profits generated in the free port of St. Eustatius, a Dutch colony, since 1730 when Jews had been allowed to trade there without impediment. The Plantation Act was designed to replicate those conditions in Jamaica in order to ensure similar profits.[31]

The Plantation Act attempted to standardize the process of naturalization for all white colonists across the American British colonies no matter what their religion. While some scholars have interpreted the Act as an invitation to Jews to come and settle in the colonies, I argue that it recognized and accommodated their existing presence, opportunistically redrawing the line between belonging and exclusion to serve imperial interests, with little apparent concern for religious purity. For the imperial government in London, the Act would facilitate trade conducted by Jews, Quakers, and other non-Anglican merchants living in the Caribbean and in other colonial spaces and also fill the treasury with the income from the taxes generated by that trade.

Abraham Sanches Tries to Vote

In an attempt to realize all of the rights promised by the Plantation Act, Abraham Sanches submitted a petition to the Jamaica Assembly (dated October 4, 1750) explaining that he had been turned away when he tried to vote for William George, a candidate in the parish of St. John. This was no secret; voting was a public act for all to see. Sanches had been naturalized on May 25, 1742, and had a "considerable freehold" in the parish. Maintaining his right to vote as a naturalized subject, Sanches stated simply that "he humbly apprehends that he is entitled to all the rights and privileges of the rest of his majesty's liege subjects" and asked Jamaica's House of Assembly to "enquire into the truth of the allegations of his petition, and grant him such relief, as this honorable house should seem meet."[32] The house resolved to form a committee of the whole and consider the petition and its parties or their lawyers a week later. The Assembly ordered that Sanches's petition was to be circulated and published and that the attorney general appear at their discussion "in support of the custom of not admitting the Jews to give their votes at elections."[33]

In response to the Sanches petition, three different groups of "Christians, freeholders, and other inhabitants" from Kingston, the parish of St. Andrews, and the parish of St. Catherine, each presented petitions at the Assembly's meeting on October 12, 1750. They objected to the Assembly's granting Sanches a vote based on several interlocking arguments. Jews could not be liege subjects, they claimed. First and foremost, they pointed out that "the said Sanches is a Jew" and "could not give a vote to return a representative to sit in any Christian assembly, unless he first became a Christian." The petitions went on to explain that Jews "are a transient people," that they had been so since "they renounced their right of government to the governor Pontius Pilate, in favour of the Roman emperors," and that their religion, culture, laws, and rituals have prevented them from having "a share in the legislature of any country upon earth."[34]

In the Kingston petition these age-old antisemitic claims turned to contemporary conceptions of color and religion. The petition declared that "though a mulatto of the fourth descent may vote at elections, yet the Jews (many of whom are mulattoes of that degree), are, by our wise legislature, [by the "Act for Regulating Fees" passed in 1711] absolutely excluded from that privilege." A mulatto of fourth descent would be considered legally white if he or she were a free person of mixed ancestry, four degrees removed from his or her ancestor of color. As the petitioners explained, "the said mulattoes shall enjoy all the privileges and immunities of his majesty's white subjects of this island, provided that they are brought up in the Christian religion." Jews, the petition points out, are barred from holding "offices of record" and "in that regard [Jews are] on the foot of [i.e., below] mulattoes and negroes."[35]

Brooke Newman and Daniel Livesay (among others) have recently shown that in the first half of the eighteenth century British and Jamaican officials allowed for the legal whitening of mixed-race elites.[36] This was a right demanded by white slave owners who wished to legitimate their children with slave women. Officials agreed in the hopes of broadening the small white population and growing an indigenous elite to provide leadership in the colony.[37] Although their religion excluded Jews from the whitest category, so too did their Spanish and Portuguese ancestry. The prejudice against Spain was rampant; its racialized quality is evident in a pro-slavery commentary on the James Somerset case that appeared in June 1772. The writer clearly sided with the planters who wished to move their slaves around imperial sites and even bring them to England, but he advocated a heavy tax on such movement to discourage the practice and "to preserve the beauty and fair complexion of our people, which otherwise is in a probable way of becoming Morisco, like the Spaniards and Portuguese."[38]

Referring to the historical relationship of Jewish populations to the monarch and their personal tie to him, known in Europe as *servi camerae regis*, or serfs of the royal chamber, the petition describes the legal status of Jews in England from the time of William the Conqueror until their expulsion by Edward I in 1290 "as absolutely the slaves and property of the king, as the African negro slaves are of their masters the planters in this island."[39] A second reference to this personal tie to the monarch cautions that "the Jews, in all countries, look on themselves as under the power of the chief magistrates, rather than under the laws and government." The petitioners insisted that Jews as a religious group formed a "foreign nation" and that their difference extended to law and governance, adding that "they are at this instant governed by laws and magistrates of their own, and pay no voluntary obedience to our laws."[40] In other words, they are described as existing beyond or outside the bounds of law and law-making—slaves, or at best absolutely subject to a sovereign, but not free, liege subjects—in other words, permanent aliens.

For the island's white Christian petitioners, the stakes were very high: they argued that "if the Jews are admitted into the legislature of this island, either by holding offices of power, or voting at elections of a representative to serve in this assembly, [the petitioners] must inevitably be ruined in those things they hold most dear and sacred; their religion, liberty, lives, and property." The petitioners from St. Catherine's worried that voting would be only the first step and that it would inevitably lead to Jews as members of juries, justices, judges, and vestrymen. They pointed out that Britain did not allow Jews "judicial or legislative authority." If the Jews were granted the vote, the petitioners predicted that they themselves "would be reduced to the most abject slavish state, of being obliged to sit like insignificant cyphers, and see themselves out-voted by the Jews."[41] This evidence points to a contrast in the scholarly modes of explanation. While Jewish historians see age-old antisemitic tropes, imperial and legal historians see Jamaica's context and this personal tie to the king or governor as reflecting the antagonistic relationship between the king and the Jamaican Assembly. Cultural historians see Jamaica's racial hierarchies. For these petitioners, the emancipation of the Jews, who they described as having the status of slaves, would enslave the white Christian petitioners. There were only two possibilities here—Jews as slaves of the king or white Christian petitioners slaves of the Jews. As anyone who works on this period knows, these references to slavery are everywhere and especially awful when made by white slave owners.

The petitioners pivoted back to an argument about the racial balance in Jamaica and warned that expanding the franchise to include the Jews would "defeat the measures the legislature hath taken, or shall take, to people this island with whites" because it would "prevent white Christians to come settle in this island but also prove the destruction of those already settled in it." This was not an incidental inclusion or a hypothetical suggestion. The session at which these petitions were presented and debated had already heard a bill to extend or reissue an "Act for introducing White People into this island and Providing them with land that they may become settlers" that had expired in 1749. The petition elaborated on this last warning that "even Christianity itself may be brought into contempt, and Christian people forced from this island, to seek shelter elsewhere."[42] The argument was that granting Jews the vote would imperil whiteness, Christianity, and Jamaica's place in the Empire.

Four days later, on October 16, Daniel Almeyda "and several others of the Jewish nation" submitted a petition to the Assembly. The main point of their petition was not suffrage, but damage control. Countering what they referred to as the "many harsh reflections on the whole body of the Jews" contained in the Christian petitions which they "humbly hope will appear groundless and the effect of blind prejudice," they expressed their surprise at "such indecent reproaches from their fellow subjects." They reiterated their "unalterable attachment" and "dutiful obedience" to the "free and protestant government, admired for its charity in religious matters, for its lenity, and the justice and equality of its laws." Citing "laws of the island, and . . . some acts of parliament of our mother country, in particular the act of parliament passed in 1740," they reminded the Assembly that "they have a right to all the privileges and advantages of the rest of his majesty's natural born subjects," including the "right to vote at elections, if they should see fit." Saying that "they are well entitled" to vote and that they had been lobbied for their votes in the past, they asserted that "being satisfied with the tranquility they enjoy under the government" and not wishing to "inflame the jealousy and incur the displeasure of their fellow subjects" they had not pursued this right. They presented Sanches as a solitary actor whose attempt to vote "was without the knowledge, privity, or participation of the petitioners" and clarified that their petition "did not flow from a forwardness to vote at elections, but to assert the darling privilege" they "had a right to in common with all the rest of his majesty's subjects that have freeholds."[43] In other words, they concluded that civil rights could wait lest they imperil those commercial rights they already had. Again, whiteness is a process: the petition reflects a consensus that the Jewish community had enough to maintain their livelihoods, Jewish practice, and community. Fearing that insisting on more rights would lead to scrutiny and the possible contraction of the rights they had already secured, they signaled a commitment to halting any quest to achieve full civil rights.

The following day, October 17, the Assembly resolved that "the people called Jews ... have no right by law to give their votes, at elections for choosing representatives to sit in the assembly." Implying that Jews remained in their age-old relationship with the monarch, the Assembly ruled that the Jews had no right to "exercise any part of the legislative or judicial authority of this island, or to have any share in the administration of the government thereof" and that their participation, if allowed, would have "the most dangerous consequence to the religion and constitution of this island." The Assembly ordered the "committee of correspondency ... to write to the agent for this island in Great Britain." They charged their agent, John Sharpe, whose appointment they had renewed the previous year, "to make all the opposition in his power, to any application that may be made to his majesty, or to the British Parliament, by the people called Jews" should they demand to participate in the legislative or judicial authority or the administration of the island.[44]

With regard to economic policy, privileges based on religion were deemed outmoded by metropolitan elites acting to ensure British profits and imperial trade networks. These metropolitan policies engendered resistance from colonial populations unwilling to accept the cosmopolitan values and imperial realities thrust on them from the metropole. They also inspired resistance at home. Lest we take metropolitan discourse for truth and imagine London as the liberal, capacious, and inclusive opposite of Jamaica, we need look no farther than the controversy over the "Jew Bill of 1753," three years after Abraham Sanches tried to vote in Jamaica.

The Jew Bill of 1753

On April 3, 1753, George Montagu Dunk, the second earl of Halifax, introduced the Jewish Naturalization Act in the House of Lords. The bill allowed "persons professing the Jewish Religion," born outside of England, to "be naturalized by Parliament, without receiving the Sacrament of the Lord's Supper."[45] Naturalization would require the passage of a private Act of Parliament, something within the reach of only a few of the wealthiest of England's eight thousand Jews.[46] The Jew Bill, as it came to be known, promised no remedy for those limits on the civil rights of Jews born in England who shared the restrictions of all non-Anglicans.[47]

On April 16, 1753, the bill passed London's House of Lords and made it through the House of Commons on May 22 of the same year. Although it met with little initial dispute inside or outside of Parliament, the Act elicited a tremendous popular furor immediately after its passage: pamphlets and prints, sermons, petitions, and newspaper coverage argued over the significance of the Act throughout the summer and fall of 1753. Jewish peddlers were insulted and harassed in the streets and the murder of Jonas Levi in November of 1753 may have resulted from the passions sparked by the bill's passage.[48] In that month, immediately after Parliament reconvened, the Act was repealed.[49]

The storm over the bill rehearsed disquiets about Britain and its integrity as a nation illustrating contemporary apprehensions about the deep religious and political divisions within the polity and the fissured nature of Christian Britain. In the context of the imperial expansion of the eighteenth century these worries signaled disagreement or at least a heated debate about the place and treatment of those considered strangers, foreigners, or Britain's "internal others." While the controversy surrounding the Jew Bill has been studied in the context of Anglo-Jewish history, when placed beside the Act of 1740 and its consequences in Jamaica, this incident can also highlight the relationship between colony and metropole and the competition between law, religion, and race in definitions of difference.

Like the more muted record of Sanches and his attempt to enact his naturalization in Jamaica in 1750, the Jew Bill offers a way to understand the British and their images of themselves as white Christians.[50] The discussion of religion that surrounded the bill points again to the disjuncture between the imagined legal subject: Anglican, English, white, and male and the reality of eighteenth-century imperial Britain. The image titled *The Consequence of Naturalizing Foreigners* published in 1730 and republished in 1753 with the title *The Dreadful Consequences of Naturalizing Jews* illustrates a threatening flood of immigrants, from all parts of the world, each actively seeking to join the ranks of English subjects while Britannia holds out a cornucopia. Beneath the earlier image appeared a lengthy poem with a stanza about each of the groups represented. The poet referred to "this motley Troop," who included a "Palatine," a "Spaniard," a "Blackamoor," a "Dutchman," an "Italian," and a "Musselman."[51]

The initiative for the Jew Bill of 1753 was one of many naturalization bills discussed in Britain's Parliaments since the 1690s. The advocates of naturalization known as "populationists" believed that the strength of any nation depended on a steady growth of its population and its access to new markets. Most of the naturalization bills failed, and the two that passed were later repealed. Despite these setbacks, the Spanish and Portuguese Jewish community in London decided to agitate for similar legislation on their behalf with support from the government and the Church of England.[52]

The London-born merchant Joseph Salvador (1716–1786) became the Act's unofficial spokesman. Like many of the Jews in England, he too had colonial American connections. He advocated for Jewish naturalization for a very personal reason: his brother, Jacob, died in 1749 leaving two sons. Joseph worried that if his nephews died, their land would be forfeit to the Crown because the land's owner, Jacob Salvador, Joseph's brother, was foreign-born. It was Joseph who petitioned the Duke of Newcastle on January 14, 1753, for a Jewish Naturalization Act. Salvador's life and writings provide a window into what Jews wanted and how they saw themselves fitting into Britain's national and imperial scene. They established and maintained global connections, but they also aspired to the highest honors bestowed by metropolitan society.

In his pamphlets promoting the passage of the bill, written under the apt pseudonym of Philo-Patria, Salvador made a direct appeal to law, protesting that withholding naturalization from Jews "is destroying Men's Rights, on a false supposition; all Subjects have Rights according to the Law of the Land; they [the Jews] have been many Times acknowledged Subjects, by the Legislature: How then can it be doubted they are Subjects, and that they have the Rights of a Subject."[53] The quid pro quo is clear: having proven their economic utility, Jews were due their well-earned reward—the civil and political rights of Englishmen.[54]

Opponents of the bill argued that Jewish naturalization threatened the British nation in religious, legal, and economic terms. It would, they contended, undermine Christianity, destabilize the English Constitution, and increase poverty. Furthermore, the Jew Bill imperiled the very ownership of land as Jewish merchants would increase their market share at the expense of British merchants and then buy up landed estates.[55] The propaganda images and articles expressed fears that the naturalization of Jews would inaugurate a vast Jewish conspiracy to circumcise British men and to rob them of their masculinity and virility.[56]

Like the fears expressed in the Jamaican petitions, the pamphlets and prints depicted the stereotypical, uncontested, and what were considered innate, elements of British culture: law, liberty, and Protestantism, as contingent, contested, and at risk from Jews portrayed as lawless rebels and scheming interlopers. In a rebuttal to these suspicions about the loyalty of the Jews, proponents of the Jewish Naturalization Act contended that the Jews had "distinguished themselves" in loyal service to the government during the Jacobite rebellion of 1745 by joining the city militia and loaning the government money and restoring confidence in its financial institutions.[57]

By maintaining the essential difference of Jews from Catholics, Dissenters, and all other foreign elements, and by staking his claim on their exceptional loyalty, Salvador presented a counterargument to those who contended that the admission of the Jews into the body politic would necessitate the inclusion of all other groups defined either as non-English or non-Christian.[58] Scholars have noted that the controversy over the Jew Bill fueled a conversation over national identity ongoing in Britain throughout the eighteenth century. P. J. Marshall has called Britain at this time "a nation defined by empire," and the discussions of Jewish naturalization in the midcentury reveal an emergent national identity, distinct from an imperial identity, formulated as a process of repeatedly delineating lines of inclusion and exclusion.[59]

How do we explain this insistence on a national identity defined by a single faith and practice? England had been confessionally divided since the sixteenth century, and the idea that foreigners posed a threat and were a source of danger was not new in 1753. However, in the mid-eighteenth century, the resonances of otherness were quite different from earlier connotations. Given Britain's imperial project and its aspirations abroad, the idea of the foreigner and of foreignness carried a more ambiguous message. The task of empire necessitated some change in these perceptions of those defined as other and necessitated some flexibility in that opportunistically shifting line. Britain's financial, commercial, and imperial endeavors depended on the networks—both colonial and metropolitan—established and maintained by Jews. But many resisted redrawing the line of inclusion. There were those who wished to repeal the Plantation Act 1740 at the same time, during the debates about the Jewish Naturalization Act and the discussions of its repeal. The question came to a vote on December 4, 1753. It failed 208 to 88.

Conclusion

The history of the legal events recounted here illustrates several trends and themes at the intersections of Jewish, imperial, and cultural history. Whiteness emerges as a process—not unidirectional, never final. The axis of race and religion in Jamaica became religion and ethnicity in London. Parliament overreached in both Jamaica and London when it attempted to impose cosmopolitan values and legal structures that would reinvent categories of difference.

Through both legislative Acts, metropolitan practice attempted to supplant and incorporate older, traditional kinds of difference through law. As Nasser Hussein put it so well in his *Jurisprudence of Emergency*, metropolitan legislators wished to use the law "to hierarchicize, bureaucratize, mediate and channel power"[60] such that, once integrated into the sinews of the legal system, "entire populations [would be] rendered comprehensible—and thus manageable."[61] Although legal and governing authorities sought this neat and rational outcome, the reality reveals a much messier, less linear story of integration, resistance, and exclusion. These metropolitan policies engendered resistance from white colonial populations unwilling to accept the cosmopolitan values and imperial realities thrust on them from the metropole. That process unfolded from London across the Atlantic Ocean to its Caribbean colonies and back.

Defining whiteness as both a cultural concept and a legal category was essential to the process of defining difference, setting the limits of equality, and, ultimately, creating empire. And Jews were the limit, the measure that authorities used to define whiteness and English identity within a British Empire. Whiteness emerged as a legal category in the context of a thriving transatlantic slave trade in which freedom and whiteness were equated, not just in Virginia but at home in London, among Africans, South Asians, East Asians, Irish, and Jews.[62] Bermuda's 1674 Act reissued in 1730 "for Extirpating all Free Negroes, Indians and Mulattoes" attempted to eliminate any confusion should the lines of color and freedom blur by simply expelling all free people of color within six months of their emancipation.[63] The color line existed already in the middle of the eighteenth century, and Jews were just inside of it. Othering of Jews had a racial quality about it in London as defined around the Eucharist, the body marked and unmarked by circumcision, and the oath of loyalty.

Clearly, communication between colony and metropole was not unidirectional. Jews in both London and Jamaica believed in the ideology of the rule of law and their claim to the rights of "free born Englishmen." In Jamaica they met resistance from white Christians who predicted that granting Jews the franchise would unleash chaos as "every election will be obstinately contested at the several polls, and, by their means controverted."[64] They feared that allowing Jews all the privileges of whiteness would impugn and dilute white status and cause whites to lose their grip on power. In London, the fear was a loss of Christian men's hold on land ownership and its measure as a very real hold on power.

The two incidents allow us to see how Jamaica's organization as a racial hierarchy based on white supremacy plays on and reorganizes London's emphasis on law, liberty, and Protestantism. The degrees of whiteness defined by Jamaican law made Jewish suffrage more threatening. In London, the different Protestant sects held the same threat. In each case, allowing for the Jewish exception threatened to open a floodgate of undesirable others: free Black and mixed-race people (who were not "whitened" as "mulattoes of the 4th descent")[65] in the colonies, Dissenters and Catholics in the metropole. The toggle between metropole and colony brings into view the co-constituted nature of empire and colony and throws into relief instances of the center pressing on the periphery, the periphery's resistance, and the periphery's impact on the center. The case of Abraham Sanches is a counter example for me. My work in *Under Rule of Law* identified cases where outsiders in London claimed the rights of Englishmen and used the courts to fight for their rights. Jamaica's Jews, as articulated by Daniel Almayda and the other petitioners, retreated from that rights-claiming position taken by Abraham Sanches to protect the limited rights they already had. Perhaps that is one reason that the next known attempt by a Jew to vote in Jamaica was Levy Hyman's in 1820, 70 years later.

Notes

1. Barry L. Stiefel, "Experimenting with Acceptance, Caribbean-Style: Jews as Aliens in the Anglophone Torrid Zone," in *The Torrid Zone: Caribbean Colonization and Cultural Interaction in the Long Seventeenth-Century*, ed. L. H. Roper (Columbia: University of South Carolina Press, 2018), 163–70.

2. Stephen Fortune, *Merchants and Jews: The Struggle for British West Indian Commerce, 1650–1750* (Gainesville: University of Florida Press, 1984), 47–49. For an overview, see Natalie Zacek, "The Freest Country: Jews of the British Atlantic, ca. 1600–1800," in *The Atlantic World*, eds. D'Maris Coffman, Adrian Leonard, and William O'Reilly (London: Routledge, 2015), 364–75.

3. Kathy Lavezzo, *The Accommodated Jew: English Antisemitism from Bede to Milton* (Ithaca: Cornell University Press, 2016).

4. Harold Pollins, *Economic History of the Jews in England* (London and Rutherford: Fairleigh Dickinson University Press, 1982).

5. Gedalia Yogev, *Anglo-Dutch Jews and Eighteenth-Century Trade* (Leicester: Leicester University Press, 1978); Pollins, *Economic History of the Jews*, 48–53; and Alan Singer, "Aliens and Citizens: Jewish and Protestant Naturalization in the Making of the Modern British Nation," (Ph.D. diss., University of Missouri, 1999), chap. 2, 66–73.

6. Yogev, *Anglo-Dutch Jews*; Pollins, *Economic History of the Jews*, 48–53; and Singer, "Aliens and Citizens," chap. 2, 66–73.

7. Fortune, *Merchants and Jews*, 47–49.

8. Ibid.; Singer, "Aliens and Citizens," chap. 2, 72. In North America most Jews were shopkeepers, and the few who engaged in shipping restricted their trade to the West Indies.

9. Pollins, *Economic History*, 50–53.

10. William Blackstone, *Commentaries on the Laws of England*, 4 vols. (Chicago: University of Chicago Press, 1979), vol. 1, 235.

11. Daniel Statt, *Foreigners and Englishmen: The Controversy over Immigration and Population, 1660–1760* (Newark: University of Delaware Press, 1995), 31.

12. James Kettner, *The Development of American Citizenship, 1608–1870* (Chapel Hill: University of North Carolina Press, 1978), 30–32.

13. Blackstone, *Commentaries*, vol. 1, 235.

14. Todd Endelman, *The Jews of Georgian England, 1714–1830* (Ann Arbor: University of Michigan Press, 1999), 25. 7 Jac. I, c.2., passed in 1609 allowing naturalization by private act of Parliament, attempted to enforce uniformity among non-Anglican sects. H.S.Q. Henriques, *The Jews and the English Law* (London: J. Jacobs, 1908), 238.

15. Edinburgh and other Scottish universities abolished the oaths in the eighteenth century and Jews sought degrees there.

16. Dana Rabin, *Britain and its Internal Others, 1750–1800: Under Rule of Law* (Manchester: University of Manchester Press, 2017).

17. *Oxford English Dictionary Online*, s.v. "whiteness (n.)," accessed October 15, 2021, https://urldefense.proofpoint.com/v2/url?u=https-3A__www-2Doed-2Dcom.proxy2 .library.illinois.edu_view_Entry_228626-3FredirectedFrom-3Dwhiteness&d=Dw IFAg&c=sJ6xIWYx-zLMB3EPkvcnVg&r=VQjBkfrMBDA_1uED6zqRtwszm314WIQY PEoxQGfDFS0&m=9oLPLDVx4u-WWio-QLBwKSq8DhihrI-9CpnHtrWseio&s=zN DwZcPgJdOvjClqYyktqWKrc-QPwq6mOAkkFGFcUMQ&e=. From now on cited as OED.

18. Rabin, *Under Rule of Law*, introduction.

19. For the treatment of non-white defendants in court, see Peter King, "Ethnicity,

Prejudice, and Justice: The Treatment of the Irish at the Old Bailey, 1750–1825," *Journal of British Studies* 52 (2013): 390–14; and King, *Ethnicity, Crime and Justice 1700–1830* (Oxford, Oxford University Press), forthcoming.

20. Holly Snyder has written extensively about Jamaica's Jews and the claims they made to rights in the eighteenth century. For more see, *A Sense of Place: Jews, Identity and Social Status in Colonial British America, 1654–1831* (Ph.D. diss., Brandeis University, 2000), especially chap. 3; and Holly Snyder, "Rules, Rights and Redemption: The Negotiation of Jewish Status in British Atlantic Port Towns, 1740–1831," *Jewish History* 20, no. 2 (2006): 147–70.

21. Windsor Proclamation, 1661.

22. Samuel J. Hurwitz and Edith Hurwitz, "The New World Sets an Example for the Old: The Jews of Jamaica and Political Rights 1661–1831," *American Jewish Historical Quarterly* 55 (1965): 37–56.

23. Stanley Mirvis, "Between Assembly and Crown: The Debate over Jewish Taxation in Jamaica, 1692–1740," *Journal of Early American History* 6, no. 2–3 (2016): 196–219. Four percent of the population paid 10 percent of the taxes.

24. *Journals of the Assembly of Jamaica*, vol. 1, 253.

25. *Acts of Assembly, Passed in the Island of Jamaica, From 1681 to 1754, Inclusive*, vol. 1 (London: Printed for Curtis Brett and Company, St. Jago de la Vega, Jamaica, 1756), 94–104.

26. "An Act for Regulating Fees," act 56, section 273, in *Acts of Assembly, Passed in the Island of Jamaica, From 1681 to 1754, Inclusive*, vol. 1 (London: Printed for Curtis Brett and Company, St. Jago de la Vega, Jamaica, 1756), 103.

27. The Navigation Acts of 1673, the Plantation Duty Act, 1696 and 1773, the Molasses Act, closed the loopholes of the previous Navigation Acts and increased taxes.

28. 13 Geo II, c. 7. Sheldon J. and Judith C. Godfrey, *Search Out the Land: The Jews and the Growth of Equality in the British Colonies* (Montreal: McGill-Queen's University, 1995), 52–61. The text of the act is in John Raithby and Thomas Edlyne, eds., *Statutes at Large, of England and of Great Britain: From Magna Carta to the Union of the Kingdoms of Great Britain and Ireland*, vol. 9 (London: G. Eyre and A. Strahan, 1811), 672–75.

29. Many Jews became naturalized under this act, most of them residents of Jamaica. J. H. Hollander, "The Naturalization of Jews in the American Colonies under the Act of 1740," *Publications of the American Jewish Historical Society* 5 (1897): 103–17. Thomas Perry, *Public Opinion, Propaganda, and Politics in Eighteenth-Century England: A Study of the Jew Bill of 1753* (Cambridge: Harvard University Press, 1962), 15.

30. On the Jewish complaints about special taxes assessed in Jamaica, see Holly Snyder, *A Sense of Place*, 100–108. While Parliament in Westminster generally had legislative supremacy, the precise relationship with other elected assemblies was regularly debated. Most legal commentaries agreed that parliamentary statutes only applied in the colonies if they specifically stated that they did so. If a statute addressed the colonies (such as the Plantation Act or later the Slavery Abolition Act), it automatically became law. If not, then it held no force there. For more on the constitutional relationship between colony and metropole, see Jack Greene, *The Constitutional Origins of the American Revolution* (Cambridge: Cambridge University Press, 2011) and Mary Sarah Bilder, *The Transatlantic*

Constitution: Colonial Legal Culture and the Empire (Cambridge: Harvard University Press, 2004).

31. Godfrey, *Search Out the Land*, 52–61.

32. *Journals of the Assembly of Jamaica*, vol. 4, 238.

33. Ibid., 239.

34. Ibid., 247.

35. Ibid., 247. One degree = mulatto; two degrees = quadroon; three degrees = mustee; four degrees = mustafina (white by law, or one-sixteenth black).

36. Daniel Livesay, *Children of Uncertain Fortune: Mixed-Race Jamaicans in Britain and the Atlantic Family, 1733–1833* (Chapel Hill: University of North Carolina Press, 2018) and Brooke Newman, *A Dark Inheritance: Blood, Race, and Sex in Colonial Jamaica* (New Haven: Yale University Press, 2018).

37. Newman and Livesay demonstrate that Tacky's Revolt in 1760 reversed this trend. Although slave resistance was a constant in Jamaican society, Tacky's Revolt was one of the largest revolts in the eighteenth-century Caribbean, spreading across the island and including up to 30,000 slaves. Although the government eventually suppressed the rebellion brutally, it took over a year to do so and cost the lives of hundreds of slaves in addition to whites and free people of color. Tacky's Revolt slowed, constrained, and reversed the ability to whiten people of mixed race and undoubtedly muted efforts on the part of the Jewish community to exercise the rights they claimed as "his majesty's natural born subjects."

38. "Some Observations upon the Slavery of Negroes," *Scots Magazine* 34 (1772): 301. Similar sentiments are expressed in Samuel Estwick, *Considerations on the Negroe Cause Commonly So Called Addressed to the Right Honourable Lord Mansfield* (London: J. Dodsley, 1772).

39. *Journals of the Assembly of Jamaica*, vol. 4, 247. The term *servi camerae regis* means "servants of the royal chamber." Cecil Roth, *A History of the Jews in England* (Oxford: Clarendon Press, 1941), 96.

40. *Journals of the Assembly of Jamaica*, vol. 4, 247. For more on the relationship between monarchs and their Jewish populations, see David B. Ruderman: *Early Modern Jewry: A New Cultural History* (Princeton: Princeton University Press, 2011). For more on the medieval period, see Albert M. Hyamson, *A History of Jews in England* (London: Chatto & Windus, 1908). The petitioners went on to say "that the Jews (standing in need of many indulgencies not allowable in the law) wait on the chief magistrates on their arrival, in order to make them some considerable present; so that admitting the Jews to vote at elections would, in so dependent a state, throw such a weight into the scale of power in the hands of a chief magistrate, by carrying a majority at elections, as all the interest and weight of the Christians would never be able to counter-balance." St. Andrews also says that the Jews would always side with the chief magistrate and "they would carry such a majority in their favour, as would totally destroy the well-adjusted balance in our happy constitution."

41. *Journals of the Assembly of Jamaica*, vol. 4, 248.

42. Ibid., 247–48.

43. Ibid., 250–51.

44. Ibid., 251.

45. 26 Geo. II, c.26, "The Act to permit Persons professing the Jewish Religion to be Naturalized by Parliament; and for other Purposes therein mentioned." John Raithby and Thomas Edlyne, eds., *Statutes at Large*, vol. 11, 219.

46. The bill itself mentions as its objects the "many Persons of considerable Substance, professing the Jewish Religion."

47. My analysis of the pamphlets and prints that surrounded the Jew Bill builds on the work of Todd Endelman on the role of the Jews as "foils for the forging of English and British identities." Endelman argued that "the agitation sparked by passage of the Jew Bill in 1753 functioned as a lightning rod for the articulation of nationalist sentiments at the time." Endelman, *The Jews of Britain, 1656 to 2000* (Berkeley: University of California Press, 2002), 6. In his 1999 dissertation Alan Singer examined the importance of this incident as a catalyst for the formation of a British identity. Singer, "Aliens and Citizens," and Singer, "Great Britain or Judea Nova? National Identity, Property, and the Jewish Naturalization Controversy of 1753," in *British Romanticism and the Jews: History, Culture, Literature*, ed. Sheila A. Spector (New York: Palgrave Macmillan, 2008), 19–36.

48. Todd Endelman, *The Jews of Georgian England, 1714–1830* (Ann Arbor: University of Michigan Press, 1999), 114. The details of the Act, its passage and repeal are detailed in Thomas Perry, *Public Opinion, Propaganda, and Politics in Eighteenth-Century England: A Study of the Jew Bill of 1753* (Cambridge: Harvard University Press, 1962) and David Katz, *The Jews in the History of England, 1485–1850* (Oxford: Clarendon, 1994), chap. 6.

49. The Act of Repeal, 27 Geo. II, c.1, passed in the House of Lords on November 22 and the House of Commons on November 28. John Raithby and Thomas Edlyne, eds., *Statutes at Large*, 11, 254.

50. All gentile discussions of Jews do this cultural work; however, each is differentiated by its geographical location and historical circumstance. Each discussion varies as any specific discourse about Jews is based on actual knowledge of and contact with Jews balanced with a Christian projection of Jews and Jewishness based on a small number of experiences and encounters with Jews and a heavy reliance on stories and stereotypes.

51. *The Consequence of Naturalizing Foreigners*. F. G. Stephens and Dorothy George, *Catalogue of Prints and Drawings in the British Museum*, 11 vols. (London: Trustees British Museum, 1870–1954), vol. 3, part 2, #3124, 813–814. The stanza about Jews reads as follows:

The Phiz that next attends my view/ Is Aaron, my good Friend, the Jew, A Rogue he is, a perfect Bite/And cheating is his sole Delight; Yet Jesus must live, and why not here,/Where's Wealth enough, and much to spare?/We buy their Baubles and their Toys,/And pay full dearly for their Lies;/Yet as good Christians we forgive,/ For Men must by their Calling live.

According to the OED the word "phiz" is a shortened version of the word "physiognomy," a face or facial expression, countenance. *The Dreadful Consequences of Naturalizing Jews*, AR 820, Jewish Museum of London, was published in 1753 without the poem.

52. Louis Hyman, *The Jews of Ireland from Earliest Times to the Year 1910* (Shannon:

Irish University Press, 1972), chap. 8; Katz, *Jews in the History of England*, 243; and Robert Liberles, "The Jews and their Bill: Jewish Motivation in the Controversy of 1753," *Jewish History* 2, no. 2 (1987): 29–36.

53. Philo-Patriae [J. Salvador], *Further Considerations on the Act to Permit Persons Professing the Jewish Religion, to be Naturalized by Parliament. In a Second Letter from a Merchant in Town to His Friend in the Country. In this Part, the Utility of the Jews in Trade, Their Situation in Other Nations; and the Expediency of Continuing Them on the Present Footing, Are Fully Considered and Proved* (London: R. Baldwin, 1753), 65–66. The first pamphlet was called *Considerations on the Bill to Permit Persons Professing the Jewish Religion to Be Naturalized by Parliament*.

54. Other advocates of the Jew Bill made religious, philosophical, and economic arguments. Most frequently the proponents of Jewish naturalization emphasized its promise for commercial prosperity. For more on Tucker, see Walter Ernest Clark, *Josiah Tucker, Economist: A Study in the History of Economics* (New York: Columbia University Press, 1903).

55. For an overview of the pamphlets produced during the Jew Bill controversy, see Albert M. Hyamson, "The Jew Bill of 1753," *Transactions of the Jewish Historical Society of England* 6 (1912): 156–88. An excellent analysis of newspaper coverage against the bill is found in G.A. Cranfield, "The *London Evening Post* and the Jew Bill of 1753," *Historical Journal* 8 (1965): 16–30.

56. Dana Rabin, "Seeing Jews and Gypsies in 1753," *Cultural and Social History* 7 (2010): 35–58 and Frank Felsenstein, *Anti-Semitic Stereotypes: A Paradigm of Otherness in English Popular Culture, 1660–1830* (Baltimore: Johns Hopkins University Press, 1995), chap. 8. Nadia Valman sets out nineteenth-century English perceptions of Jewish masculinity in "Muscular Jews: Young England, Gender, and Jewishness in Disraeli's 'Political Trilogy,'" *Jewish History* 10 (1996): 57–88.

57. Philo-Patriae [J. Salvador], *Further Considerations*, 41–42.

58. *A Looking-Glass for the Jews: Or, the Credulous Unbelievers* (London: B. Dickinson, 1753), iv.

59. P. J. Marshall, "A Nation Defined by Empire, 1755–1766," in *Uniting the Kingdom: The Making of British History*, eds. Alexander Grand and Keith Stringer (London: Routledge, 1995), 208–22.

60. Nassar Hussain, *The Jurisprudence of Emergency: Colonialism and the Rule of Law* (Ann Arbor: University of Michigan Press, 2003), 32.

61. Jane Carey, Leigh Boucher, and Katherine Ellinghaus, "Reorienting Whiteness: A New Agenda for the Field," in *Re-Orienting Whiteness*, eds. Jane Carey, Leigh Boucher, and Katherine Ellinghaus (New York: Palgrave Macmillan, 2009), 8.

62. The American colonies have been the focus of much historical research on racial formation. For more, see Ariela J. Gross, *What Blood Won't Tell: A History of Race on Trial in America* (Cambridge: Harvard University Press, 2008), chap. 1 and the works cited there.

63. Michael Craton, James Walvin, and David Wright, eds., *Slavery, Abolition and Emancipation: Black Slaves and the British Empire* (New York: Longman, 1976), 180.

64. *Journals of the Assembly of Jamaica*, vol. 4, 247.
65. *Journals of the Assembly of Jamaica*, vol. 4, 247.

Bibliography

Primary Sources

Archives

Jewish Museum of London

Periodicals

Journals of the Assembly of Jamaica (Vols. 1, 3, and 4)

Printed Sources

Acts of Assembly, Passed in the Island of Jamaica, From 1681 to 1754, Inclusive. 2 vols. London: Printed for Curtis Brett and Company, St. Jago de la Vega, Jamaica, 1756.
Estwick, Samuel. *Considerations of the Negroe Cause.* London: J. Dodsley, 1772.
Long, Edward. *Candid Reflections Upon the Judgment Lately Awarded by the Court of King's Bench in Westmister Hall on What is Commonly Called the Negroe Cause.* London: T. Lowndes, 1772.
A Looking-Glass for the Jews: Or, the Credulous Unbelievers. London: B. Dickinson, 1753.
Philo-Patriae [J. Salvador]. *Further Considerations on the Act to Permit Persons Professing the Jewish Religion, to be Naturalized by Parliament. In a Second Letter from a Merchant in Town to His Friend in the Country. In this Part, the Utility of the Jews in Trade, Their Situation in Other Nations; and the Expediency of Continuing Them on the Present Footing, Are Fully Considered and Proved.* London: R. Baldwin, 1753.
Raithby, John, and Thomas Edlyne, eds. *Statutes at Large, of England and of Great Britain: From Magna Carta to the Union of the Kingdoms of Great Britain and Ireland.* 20 Vols. London: G. Eyre and A. Strahan, 1811.
"Some Observations upon the Slavery of Negroes." *Scots Magazine* 34 (1772): 299–301.

Secondary Sources

Bilder, Mary Sarah. *The Transatlantic Constitution: Colonial Legal Culture and the Empire.* Cambridge, MA: Harvard University Press, 2004.
Blackstone, William. *Commentaries on the Laws of England.* Vol. 1. Chicago: University of Chicago Press, 1979.
Carey, Jane, Leigh Boucher, and Katherine Ellinghaus. "Reorienting Whiteness: A New Agenda for the Field." In *Re-Orienting Whiteness*, edited by Jane Carey, Leigh Boucher, Katherine Ellinghaus, 1–14. New York: Palgrave Macmillan, 2009.
Clark, Walter Ernest. *Josiah Tucker, Economist; A Study in the History of Economics.* New York: Columbia University Press, 1903.

Cranfield, G. A. "The *London Evening Post* and the Jew Bill of 1753." *Historical Journal* 8 (1965): 16–30.
Craton, Michael, James Walvin, and David Wright, eds. *Slavery, Abolition and Emancipation: Black Slaves and the British Empire*. New York: Longman, 1976.
Endelman, Todd M. *The Jews of Britain, 1656 to 2000*. Berkeley: University of California Press, 2002.
———. *The Jews of Georgian England, 1714–1830*. Ann Arbor: University of Michigan Press, 1999.
Felsenstein, Frank. *Anti-Semitic Stereotypes: A Paradigm of Otherness in English Popular Culture, 1660–1830*. Baltimore: Johns Hopkins University Press, 1995.
Fortune, Stephen. *Merchants and Jews: The Struggle for British West Indian Commerce, 1650–1750*. Gainesville: University of Florida Press, 1984.
Godfrey, Sheldon J., and Judith C. Godfrey. *Search Out the Land: The Jews and the Growth of Equality in the British Colonies*. Montreal: McGill-Queen's University Press, 1995.
Greene, Jack. *The Constitutional Origins of the American Revolution*. Cambridge: Cambridge University Press, 2011.
Gross, Ariela J. *What Blood Won't Tell: A History of Race on Trial in America*. Cambridge: Harvard University Press, 2008.
Henriques, H.S.Q. *The Jews and the English Law*. London: J. Jacobs, 1908.
Hollander, J. H. "The Naturalization of Jews in the American Colonies under the Act of 1740." *Publications of the American Jewish Historical Society* 5 (1897): 103–117.
Hurwitz, Samuel J., and Edith Hurwitz. "The New World Sets an Example for the Old: The Jews of Jamaica and Political Rights 1661–1831." *American Jewish Historical Quarterly* 55 (1965): 37–56.
Hussain, Nassar. *The Jurisprudence of Emergency: Colonialism and the Rule of Law*. Ann Arbor: University of Michigan Press, 2003.
Hyamson, Albert M. *A History of Jews in England*. London: Chatto & Windus, 1908.
———. "The Jew Bill of 1753." *Transactions of the Jewish Historical Society of England* 6 (1912): 156–88.
Hyman, Louis. *The Jews of Ireland from Earliest Times to the Year 1910*. Shannon: Irish University Press, 1972.
Katz, David. *The Jews in the History of England, 1485–1850*. Oxford: Clarendon, 1994.
Kettner, James. *The Development of American Citizenship, 1608–1870*. Chapel Hill: University of North Carolina Press, 1978.
King, Peter. *Ethnicity, Crime and Justice 1700–1830*. Oxford: Oxford University Press, forthcoming.
———. "Ethnicity, Prejudice, and Justice: The Treatment of the Irish at the Old Bailey, 1750–1825." *Journal of British Studies* 52 (2013): 390–414.
Lavezzo, Kathy. *The Accommodated Jew: English Antisemitism from Bede to Milton*. Ithaca: Cornell University Press, 2016.
Liberles, Robert. "The Jews and Their Bill: Jewish Motivation in the Controversy of 1753." *Jewish History* 2 (1987): 29–36.
Livesay, Daniel. *Children of Uncertain Fortune: Mixed-Race Jamaicans in Britain and the Atlantic Family, 1733–1833*. Chapel Hill: University of North Carolina Press, 2018.

Marshall, P. J. "A Nation Defined by Empire, 1755–1766." In *Uniting the Kingdom: The Making of British History,* edited by Alexander Grand and Keith Stringer, 208–22. London: Routledge, 1995.

Mirvis, Stanley. "Between Assembly and Crown: The Debate over Jewish Taxation in Jamaica, 1692–1740." *Journal of Early American History* 6 (2016): 196–219.

Newman, Brooke. *A Dark Inheritance: Blood, Race, and Sex in Colonial Jamaica.* New Haven: Yale University Press, 2018.

Perry, Thomas. *Public Opinion, Propaganda, and Politics in Eighteenth-Century England: A Study of the Jew Bill of 1753.* Cambridge: Harvard University Press, 1962.

Pollins, Harold. *Economic History of the Jews in England.* London and Rutherford: Fairleigh Dickinson University Press, 1982.

Rabin, Dana. *Britain and its Internal Others, 1750–1800: Under Rule of Law.* Manchester: University of Manchester Press, 2017.

———. "Seeing Jews and Gypsies in 1753." *Cultural and Social History* 7 (2010): 35–58.

Roth, Cecil. *A History of the Jews in England.* Oxford: Clarendon Press, 1941.

Ruderman, David B. *Early Modern Jewry: A New Cultural History.* Princeton: Princeton University Press, 2011.

Singer, Alan. "Aliens and Citizens: Jewish and Protestant Naturalization in the Making of the Modern British Nation." Ph.D. diss., University of Missouri, 1999.

———. "Great Britain or Judea Nova? National Identity, Property, and the Jewish Naturalization Controversy of 1753." In *British Romanticism and the Jews: History, Culture, Literature,* edited by Sheila A. Spector, 19–36. New York: Palgrave Macmillan, 2008.

Snyder, Holly. "Rules, Rights and Redemption: The Negotiation of Jewish Status in British Atlantic Port Towns, 1740–1831." *Jewish History* 20, no. 2 (2006): 147–70.

———. *A Sense of Place: Jews, Identity and Social Status in Colonial British America, 1654–1831.* Ph.D. diss., Brandeis University, 2000.

Statt, Daniel. *Foreigners and Englishmen: The Controversy over Immigration and Population, 1660–1760.* Newark: University of Delaware Press, 1995.

Stiefel, Barry L. "Experimenting with Acceptance, Caribbean-Style: Jews as Aliens in the Anglophone Torrid Zone." In *The Torrid Zone: Caribbean Colonization and Cultural Interaction in the Long Seventeenth-Century,* edited by L. H. Roper, 162–75. Columbia: University of South Carolina Press, 2018.

Valman, Nadia. "Muscular Jews: Young England, Gender, and Jewishness in Disraeli's 'Political Trilogy.'" *Jewish History* 10 (1996): 57–88.

Yogev, Gedalia. *Anglo-Dutch Jews and Eighteenth-Century Trade.* Leicester: Leicester University Press, 1978.

Zacek, Natalie. "The Freest Country: Jews of the British Atlantic, ca. 1600–1800." In *The Atlantic World,* edited by D'Maris Coffman, Adrian Leonard, and William O'Reilly, 364–75. London: Routledge, 2015.

II

NETWORK EMPIRES

3

Gifts from the Center
Gifting and Religious Authority in Colonial Curaçao

HILIT SUROWITZ-ISRAEL

Without their material expressions, religions float in the theological ether, and spiritualities enter the void, lifeless and deracinated.[1]

In 1760, a Curaçaoan Jew, Abraham Mendes de Castro, ordered a Bible from Joseph, Iacob, & Abraham de Salomon Proops (aka Proops Hermanos) publishers in Amsterdam. Frustrated by the lack of Spanish and Hebrew Bibles for Jewish students in Curaçao,[2] de Castro proposed printing a two-column Bible, where the Hebrew and Spanish text would appear side-by-side. Though Hebrew and Yiddish Bibles were relatively common in the sixteenth century, and Spanish and Ladino Bibles had been printed since the Ferrara Bible of 1553,[3] this was the first Hebrew/Spanish Bible. Interestingly, then, the first Hebrew book commissioned by and for an American was contracted from Curaçao, a colonial Dutch trade entrepôt in the Leeward Antilles, established in 1634, with a small Jewish community. The book's introduction pays homage to the Jewish leadership in Amsterdam's Talmud Torah asserting the colony's dependence on the Dutch mother-congregation. The Bible's production signals a significant turn in the relationship between the Dutch and Curaçaoan Jewish communities. One aspect of this shift is economic. The island community had become wealthy enough that it did not need to petition Talmud Torah for aid, and some of its members could commission expensive volumes that required innovative typesetting and a high level of aesthetic detail. But the bilingual Bible also reflected a deeper religious transformation. It was, after all, initiated by a member of Curaçao's Sephardic[4] congregation—Mikvé Israel—for the specific religious and pedagogic needs of the congregation, suggesting Curaçao was no longer dependent upon Amsterdam's Portuguese Jewish religious authorities for direction in such matters. Moreover, de Castro, in addition to gifting a copy to Curaçao's Mikvé Israel, printed the Bible with the explicit instructions that all profit made from the sale of the Bible be gifted to the impoverished Jewish community of Hebron.[5] One of the arguments presented in this essay is that Curaçao claimed independence from its former mother-congregation, eventually replacing it as the mother-congregation of the Americas, influencing the development of Jewish communal life in the Americas.[6] Further, this rich event alongside de Castro's wishes serve as introductory anecdotes most of which highlight the importance of gifting and materiality in the Portuguese Jewish[7] early modern Atlantic.

Building the Americas' Jewish Communities

By the eighteenth century, Curaçao was the most important economic and religious hub for Portuguese Jews in the Americas. Curaçao's commercial status rapidly rose as more colonists settled the area that was ideal for sea trade. By the 1660s, Curaçao was a major hub of international trade, trading with Spanish, French, and English holdings throughout the Americas,[8] with Jews as central actors. In the early 1700s, the population of Curaçao boomed, and the island soon gained the status of a free port. The economic success of Jews in Curaçao is well known and traditionally understood as immaterial to Mikvé Israel's subservience to the mother-congregation in Amsterdam. The communal and religious life of Curaçao has been largely overlooked on the grounds that the Caribbean's subservience to Amsterdam renders its religious life of little independent interest. Curaçao's contribution in much scholarship lies in its roguish and stereotypically Caribbean addition of sailors and privateers to the stock of Jewish characters. The island community and its members are not to be taken seriously as religious actors in the Atlantic, or as a significant community in terms of theological production.

However, through a process that was somewhat mimetic of Amsterdam's relationship with its satellite communities and a process that also nods to the creolization of this American religious community, Curaçao's Mikvé Israel rose to a position of economic success, had a powerful and centralized Portuguese Jewish community, and assumed a position of religious authority among burgeoning American Jewish communities, which it enacted, partially through gifting.

There is little doubt that Curaçao's *ma'amad*,[9] the authoritarian congregational board, was a hegemonic and powerful force that governed both the private and public lives of the island's Jews. Modeled on the Portuguese Jewish communal systems of Amsterdam, the Curaçao Ma'amad was most concerned with maintaining its own authority, and the homogenization of religious practice on the island. As Curaçao's Jewish community became increasingly established both in terms of its population (at its peak, Portuguese Jews composed anywhere from a third to half of the island's free population), the ma'amad, in many ways following the earlier model of Amsterdam, sought to extend its power beyond its island borders. Just as Amsterdam transferred religious objects, personnel, and money to form new Portuguese Jewish communities, Curaçao's Mikvé Israel likewise used this same method to affirm its centrality and to assert its power. An excellent prism through which to explore this process is the transfer of gifts—primarily taking the form of money and Jewish ritual objects.

Curaçao began to replace Amsterdam as an Americas center by aiding new and less fortunate Portuguese Jewish communities in the Americas to acquire ritual objects and build religious spaces. This had previously been Amsterdam's role, and in fact Amsterdam did this for Curaçao as well. Just as Amsterdam's Talmud Torah sent two shipments of assorted religious ceremonial objects to Barbados in 1657 and a Torah scroll with an expensive black and red silk mantle to St. Eustatius in 1738, by the beginning of the eighteenth century, Mikvé Israel had sent ritual objects and funds to these communities as well.[10] The communities on both islands were deeply tied to Curaçao through commerce and family—much as Curaçao had been to Amsterdam. Under the command of the West India Company, the free port of St. Eustatius became a hub for both legal and illicit colonial trade. Portuguese Jews, many with ties to Curaçao, moved to the island in droves looking to expand their trade networks. This connection made St. Eustatius a frequent recipient of aid from Curaçao. And, as many of the St. Eustatius Jews had ties to Curaçao, they sent Salomon de Leon to Curaçao (among many other emissaries) to raise money for them. In response to de Leon, and others, there were *nedabot*, free-will (or voluntary) offerings, for the community, and money was sent to aid.[11] Later disputes between the Ashkenazim and Sephardim in St. Eustatius led the Sephardim to seek economic relief from Curaçao's Mikvé Israel in 1761.[12] Free-will offerings were made, and additional money was contributed from the community chest.[13] In 1772, a hurricane destroyed the island's synagogue, causing Mikvé Israel to once again contribute to its rebuilding. In addition to direct financial assistance in 1750, 1752, and 1770, St. Eustatius sent Torah scrolls to Curaçao for repair.[14]

Curaçao's financial aid extended beyond the Caribbean as the island played an integral role in establishing the earliest communities in North America as well. New York's Shearith Israel, the oldest congregation in the United States of America, was founded around 1654, when a group of Sephardic Jews arrived from Recife, Brazil, following its secession by the Dutch to the Portuguese. In 1729, after years of meeting in rented quarters, the congregation began construction of its first building, which would be known as the Mill Street Synagogue. At this time, Rabbi Jeshurun in Curaçao received a letter from Shearith Israel's *parnasim* (administering body of the synagogue), requesting that "the members of your holy Kahal [Jewish congregation] . . . may contribute all they can to the building of a holy synagogue," so that the congregation would not have to continue congregating "in a Synagogue rented from a Goy."[15] Ḥakham Jeshurun[16] organized a fundraising drive in 1729, despite the fact that Mikvé Israel had raised funds for their own building only a year earlier. This resulted in the largest donation of any outside congregation.[17] And a later 1730 receipt enumerates the funds New York's Shearith Israel congregation received from Mikvé Israel.[18] The successful fundraising effort on behalf of Shearith Israel reflects both the general practice of aiding other congregations in the Americas, and the ties between Curaçao and the New York synagogue. The *ḥazan*[19] of Shearith Israel during this period was Mosseh Lopez da Fonseca, son of Curaçao's Ḥakham Lopez. Lopez da Fonseca had served the New York congregation since the 1720s, and was not the first Curaçaoan to do so. Saul Pardo, son of Ḥakham Josiau Pardo, was the first known ḥazan of Shearith Israel. He led the congregation beginning in 1685 and was responsible for all aspects of ritual life including circumcision and ritual slaughtering.[20]

In the early 1760s, the Newport, Rhode Island, community appealed to various congregations to construct their synagogue; among those congregations was Bevis Marks in London. Though considered the mother-congregation to the British Caribbean, Bevis Marks was unable to procure funds. Moseh de Jacob Franco, of Bevis Marks, wrote to the Newport congregation: "We praise you very much, but at the present time it would not be convenient for us, nor are we able to comply with your request. May

God be the one who assists all and of those whose grace we would desire that He give to you as He is able and may He prosper you in your pious plans."²¹ Ironically, the London congregation sent the Newport congregation two ornamental charity boxes. The funds for the synagogue, however, were drawn primarily from American congregations such as Curaçao and New York. Following the construction of the synagogue, in 1764, in a plea for financial help to help pay the mortgage and interest, the Newport congregation appealed to the regional powerhouse, Curaçao's Mikvé Israel, once again. Curaçao again complied, as they would also in 1768. In the early 1780s, Philadelphia's Mikvé Israel found itself in need of a larger synagogue. During the American Revolutionary War, the congregation had absorbed many new community members who had arrived from places such as Savannah, New York, and Charleston. Among them was Shearith Israel's ḥazan Gershom Mendes Seixas, who would become ḥazan in Philadelphia as well. Seixas initially came to Philadelphia from New York with his congregants as he did not wish to operate the synagogue in "British-occupied New York." Joining Philadelphia's small extant community, he implemented the Spanish-Portuguese rite and was instrumental in the community's growth and development. One major undertaking was the construction of a new building to house the congregation. In 1782, under his tutelage, Philadelphia's Mikvé Israel "appealed to the Jews of the West Indies for financial help on the occasion of the erection of the first Synagogue building in that city."²² Curaçao assisted by sending money. Mikvé Israel showed its generosity with contributions to communities throughout the Americas, which continued throughout the nineteenth and into the twentieth century with monies being sent to Charleston (1816), New York (1816, 1898), Caracas (1844), Rio Hacha (1850), St. Thomas (1867), Venezuela (1875), Jamaica (1882), Suriname (1887, 1928), and Panama (1913), among others.²³

Of course, charitable donations in and of themselves do not signify religious patronage. However, in these cases, the transaction was not merely financial, but rather an opportunity for Curaçao to exert religious influence on its sister congregations. The relationship between the receiving community and Curaçao is generally recognized through prayer or gifts. For example, New York's Shearith Israel congregation recites special prayers twice a year for the health and success of Mikvé Israel.²⁴ The 1729 Mikvé Israel gift to New York's Shearith Israel was made on the condition that the "ritual and *minhag* (custom)²⁵ of the synagogue should [always] remain Sephardic."²⁶

The accompanying letter from Ḥakham Jeshurun further stipulates, "in accordance with the donors' wishes" that the Ashkenazic members should not "have any More Votes nor Authority than they have had hitherto and for the performance of Which you are to get them to Signe an agreement of the Same by all of them,"[27] thereby ensuring that the rapidly growing number of Ashkenazim do not have more votes or representation than the Sephardic members. To make certain that they would fulfill both of these conditions, Ḥakham Jeshurun instructed them to send him a copy of the communal minutes in this respect. The first condition—that of the retention of the Sephardic rite—was not only a typical demand by Curaçao but was a replica of an earlier Amsterdam condition. The second condition is more unusual as it bespeaks intimate knowledge of the demographics of the New York community and the concomitant fear that the necessary inclusion of non-Sephardic Jews into communal life may risk the future of Sephardic traditions in the Americas. It was not enough to demand that the Sephardic custom be retained—Sephardic empowerment was important as well. This is not an isolated case, as Mikvé Israel's leadership also demanded of Newport's Jeshuat Israel (recognized as the Touro Synagogue after 1820) that it maintain the Sephardic rite.[28] Further, the congregation was to recognize the patronage of the island community each year on Yom Kippur.

A further indication of Curaçao's rise to the position of a regional mother-congregation is the aid it offered to a group of poor Jews of the Portuguese Nation. A society founded in 1715 ostensibly to aid transients with the help of the community chest helped the group settle in Tucacas, Venezuela.[29] In gratitude for the assistance extended to them, the Tucacas Jews sent a thank you letter on September 2, 1720, with 340 pesos for the purchase of a Scroll of the Law with its ornaments for the use of the Curaçao synagogue.[30] This society also exemplifies the multidirectional exchange and the social complexity involved in Portuguese Jewish settlement in the Americas. It is likely that the emigrants either received aid, or were part of a larger group of Portuguese Jews from Europe who were sent to settle in Curaçao. The Curaçao community, facing some of the same fears and limited resources for dealing with the poor as Amsterdam was, aided the group of emigrants so that they could continue to Tucacas. Once in Tucacas, they would expand existing trade networks without being a burden on the Curaçao community. In exchange for Curaçaoan aid, the new Venezuelan community presented the Dutch Antillean community with money for the purchase of ritual objects; thus, money moved from the smaller community to the more established one.

Likewise, Mikvé Israel's rising prominence and strong leadership allowed its religious authorities (*ḥakhamim*), and religious leadership, to exert influence on other Americas congregations. This was especially true under the leadership of Ḥakham Mendes de Sola who tried to regulate the kosher meat trade among Curaçao, Jamaica, and New York. In 1753, de Sola even went so far as to raise his concerns about the level of observance of kosher slaughtering and tagging in New York's Shearith Israel community. In his 1753 letter to the leadership of that congregation, he addresses the status of kosher meat shipped to the island from New York. De Sola informs the recipients that he has "made an announcement that the meats which come from your place without a certificate of the hazan and without your prescribed brand, shall be considered prohibited." He continued to explain that he decided to do this because, from what he has "been able to ascertain from some Jews from your place who have sold said meat . . . your Hazan neither sees the meat nor knows whether it has been properly or improperly killed, and . . . your Somer [supervisor], in order to have it passed, or for his own profit, pretends that said Hazan has duly signed the certificates."[31] De Sola then proceeds to instruct the recipients about the supervision of kosher slaughtering and even asserts that "at different times pieces of pork have also been found in some casks of mackerel coming from your place."[32] The Curaçaoan rabbi assumed responsibility for addressing the proper implementation of Jewish dietary laws. His letter is written with a tone of religious authority, and with disdain for the perceived laxity found in New York. De Sola's tone and the subject of the exchange points clearly to the transition of Curaçao to an authoritative religious center in the Americas, serving Portuguese Jewish communities in much of the same manner as Amsterdam had. The letter does not raise questions or seek to gain greater understanding of the northern community. Rather, it scolds, from a position of religious authority, the Shearith Israel community for not abiding by Jewish law and communal regulations for certifying kosher meat.

Throughout the course of the eighteenth century, Curaçao's Mikvé Israel began to replace Amsterdam's Talmud Torah in a number of areas: the transfer of money and ritual objects to newer and languishing communities, a sense of authority as demonstrated through the regulation of kosher meat and ritual supervision, and finally, demands for patronage from Americas congregations. That the European mother-congregation could not fund the American community and that funds came from Curaçao and New York signal a shift in status, wealth, and power to the Americas. Had it not been for the American communities, perhaps, the Newport congregation would not have been able to establish itself. The parallels between Mikvé Israel and Talmud Torah continue, as the American congregation sought to participate and influence the global Portuguese Jewish community as well, much as its predecessor had.

Global Reach

Curaçao emerged, just as Amsterdam had done earlier, as a recognized global center of Sephardic life and prosperity. Curaçao's Jews donated to funds globally and were routinely visited by emissaries of Jewish communities from around the world. The first recorded gift given to a community outside of the Americas was in 1744, when Mikvé Israel gave over one thousand pesos to Ḥakham Yahacob Saul from Smyrna (Izmir), who had come to the island to raise money for his ailing community. The Curaçao community also paid his passage to Holland.[33] Five years later, Mikvé Israel gave a more modest 350 pesos to the congregation in Saida, Morocco, that had—following the successful example of Smyrna—sent an emissary (Ribbi Ishac Colly) to Curaçao for this purpose. When Salonica was devastated by a powerful earthquake in 1759, Mikvé Israel sent monies to aid in the rebuilding process. This was followed by a second donation to Smyrna (1774) and initial gifts to the Jewish communities of Maraha (Maraghe), Persia (1792), and Essaouira (formerly Mogador), Morocco (1838).[34]

Donations also came from standing charities that helped both the local and global Jewish communities. Most of the charities or fraternities met for regular study sessions with the ḥakham and were thus called either *hermandades* or *yeshivas*—formal groups that provided Jewish instruction. The seventeenth and eighteenth centuries saw the creation of over a dozen such organizations. Many of these yeshivas looked beyond the island community and reinforced the building of a transatlantic community. According to Jacob Marcus, "Curaçaoan Jews emulating their fathers in Amsterdam and Recife, also did their part in maintaining the Holy Land cities of Jerusalem, Safed, Hebron and later Tiberias. They contributed regularly every year, probably since 1671 if not earlier."[35] These funds from the congregation, the yeshivas, and from individuals helped establish new Sephardic communities in the Holy Land as well as assist already existing communities. Some yeshivas set, as a primary goal, raising money for those in Palestine, such as the Honen Dalim society, which raised money for Hebron. However, even those yeshivas that had other purposes still made regular contributions to Palestine. The Abi Yetomin ve Dayan Almanoth society, founded in 1733, that focused on caring for orphans and widows, sent money to Hebron on a regular basis; the Neve Sedek society contributed twenty-five pesos annually to Hebron and Tiberias, along with many other such contributors.

Two such brotherhoods present both in Europe and the Americas, Tierra Santa and Tierra Captiva, were responsible for raising money for Sephardic communities in Palestine and for paying the ransom to release captive Jews globally. Amsterdam's Portuguese Jewish community was also connected with non-Iberian Jewish communities globally and regularly sent money to support them in order to "help to the utmost of our ability that holy city, our Land."[36] The island community carried on this tradition, as demonstrated by a section from the Order of Study and Prayer in the Talmudic academy in Hebron, which shows that its students offered daily exaltation to the communities that gave those in Hebron financial aid.[37]

> Your mercies have aided us up to this point and your grace has not departed from us, and you have provided us with sustenance by the hand of your sons and companions . . . [T]hey are the mighty men whose luminosity and [glow] are eternal and spread throughout the world, who sustain the world and raise up the flag to Torah. These are none other than our brothers and redeemers, the elevated lords, men of grace and mercy, who are in the glorious city Amsterdam and Hague and Hamburg and London and America, and in all the cities and provinces of Italy, and in all the cities and provinces of Romagna, and in all the cities and provinces of France—men whose generosity of spirit moved them to pour gold from their pockets, each man giving a free-will offering annually in the aid of the Lord through these mighty men, to sustain the hands of the students of Torah, and to establish four walls of Jewish Law in Qiryat Arba, that is, Hebron.[38]

Individuals also made contributions, with these contributions intended for various occasions—"the birth of a son was a special occasion for rejoicing and donating to the Holy Land"[39]—and as part of wills. For example:

> Jacob Andrade's mother did that in 1721 and so did Abraham Mendes de Castro in 1762. De Castro's will specified that, after the payment of

certain local bequests, half of the remainder of the estate was to go to Jerusalem and the other half to Hebron. The Holy Land bequest was not to be under 2,000 pesos. He directed each of those communities to buy a house in his name. These were never to be sold or mortgaged, and all the rents earned were to be distributed among the poor.[40]

It is striking that the commitment to Jewish communities globally went beyond the institutional level, with private wills serving as a platform that reinforced these connections. Even de Castro's Bible was printed with the specific instruction that the proceeds of its sales were to be divided between the Jewish communities of Jerusalem and Hebron.

Gifting, Exchange, and Power

One could spend dozens of pages enumerating the exchange of gifts on both the communal and individual levels. Already mentioned are the gifts circulating from Curaçao to other communities, but this process took place, with a similar spirit, on the island as well. A prime example is Curaçao's main synagogue, the Snoa,[41] which attributes many of its foundational elements and ritual objects to gifts from community members. The construction of the synagogue, which lasted from 1730 to 1732, was an expensive undertaking that the island community was constantly raising money to fund (they had outgrown their five previous synagogue structures). With the move to erect a new and larger building, which would seat 400 men and 200 women, there was an announcement on March 31, 1730 (13 Nissan), for a *nedaba* (free-will offering)[42] for the said construction. Also, "to sell the four [corner] stones ... any of the *Yehidim* [community members] that purchase them will also receive a *Misheberakh*[43] each year and even after their death."[44] Two days later, the four cornerstones were sold to Mordy [Mordechay] Alvares Correa for 410 pesos, Samuel de Casseres for 315 pesos, Yacob Henriques Morao for 325 pesos, and Manuel Levy for 355 pesos. Soon, more money was necessary and the parnasim "sold the four stones of the four [interior] columns" to Daniel Aboab Cardozo for 155 pesos, Ribica da Daniel Aboab Cardoze for 142 pesos, Abraham Aboab Cardoze for 140 pesos, and Lea de Abraham Aboab Cardoze for 156 pesos.[45] And, just as the brass chandeliers had been donated to the "Old Synagogue" of 1703 by Abraham de Chaves in 1706 and by the brothers Abraham, Isaac, and Jacob de Benjamin Henriquez in 1709, two additional chandeliers to light the large space were ordered from Amsterdam. Isaac and Esther de Marchena purchased one.⁴⁶ The donors of the cornerstones, pillars, and brass chandeliers received a *misheberakh* (an annual prayer for wellbeing) and memorial prayer after death in return for their generous donation.

The gifts traversing the Atlantic and given domestically are all representative of the manner in which money and material culture are indicative of power dynamics and religious identity. Long gone were the days when Émile Durkheim could write "What is a gift . . . but an exchange without reciprocal obligations?"⁴⁷ The twentieth century gave rise to a broad scale interrogation of "the theoretical distinction between commodities, money, and objects of social exchange."⁴⁸ In order to better understand the Portuguese Jews of the early modern Atlantic, here Curaçao specifically, it is necessary to frame these gifts and the act of gifting as a type of dialogue. These gifts are complete with intentionality and powerful meaning. Nonetheless, somehow, the gifts and the act of gifting within this Jewish diasporic context have generally been understood as either a natural extension of diaspora consciousness, or a sort of self-evident aid that Jewish communities provide to one another. In fact, one element of diaspora consciousness assumes gifts and remittances. This, then, allows them to evade the same scrutiny as other gifts and to elude theoretical analysis. Moreover, the gifts have largely been assumed to be devoid of meaning, power, and even symbolism.⁴⁹

In his seminal work, *The Gift* (1925), Marcel Mauss argues that gifts are never free, that they are "juridical, religious, economic, have important aesthetic and emotional aspects and 'are clearly structural' in that they underpin the cohesiveness and interdependence observed between and across individual institutions."⁵⁰ Subsequent to Mauss' work, inquiry into the practice of gifting proliferated primarily among sociologists and anthropologists. Their work pointed to the complicated and powerful realm of gifts. By moving this work into a framework of the field of religion, a further analysis of these gifts can shed light on questions of belief and practice. David Morgan, drawing on the work of Webb Keane, observes that "Religions may not always demand beliefs, but they will always involve material forms."⁵¹ Rather than trying to evaluate the belief of the Portuguese Jews of the early modern Caribbean, an assessment of the constant engagement with the materiality of religion through the act of gifting reveals robust and vibrant Jewish communal religious life.

Alongside the theoretical work on gifts, there has been an examination of the materiality of religion. In many ways, people like David Morgan argue that through an analysis of the "stuff" of religion—ritual objects, spaces, et cetera—we have another avenue for understanding one of the categories most associated with, but most difficult to interrogate in, religious studies—belief. He explains that "[m]ateriality is a compelling register in which to examine belief because feeling, acting, interacting, and sensation embody human relations to the powers whose invocation structures social life. Most believers live their religion in the grit and strain of a felt-life that embodies their relation to the divine as well as to one another."[52] Further, materiality provides the opportunity to focus on the relationship between Atlantic world Portuguese Jewish communities and the dynamics of power that are associated with gifting.

For the first category—belief—in some ways, materiality alleviates some of the empirical nature of the study of religion, especially in regard to Portuguese Jews, and *conversos*. A question that often emerges in regard to this community, but one which is more fully thrust upon the Caribbean communities due to sociocultural and historical biases, is what did the Caribbean Portuguese Jews *really* believe? Were the Portuguese Jews of the Caribbean theologically engaged? Were the communities religiously productive, or were they passive recipients and somewhat reticent participants in European institutional religious life?

The religiosity of Sephardic Jews in the early Americas has generally been overlooked and/or challenged. The Sephardim are seen as a merchant community with little in the way of religious production. Often, their religious institutions are presented as mimetic expressions of Amsterdam's rich and vibrant Jewish communal life. There is no doubt that the fledging American Portuguese Jewish communities utilized Amsterdam's organization as a template, and this has been noted extensively. This approach recognizes Mikvé Israel as a religious community, but understands it as wholly subservient to the mother-congregation in Amsterdam. While many scholars have written on the centrality and power of the Amsterdam Ma'amad and some have focused on London and on other continental ma'amadot, the Curaçao Ma'amad, along with its Caribbean and Latin American brethren, have remained largely overlooked on the grounds that the Caribbean's subservience to Amsterdam (and later, in the British Atlantic, London) renders its religious life of little independent interest. According to Yosef Kaplan,

> From the very beginning, the Jews of Curaçao considered themselves as a branch of the Portuguese community of Amsterdam. The

regulations of the "Mikvé Israel" community were laid down in accordance with the "style of the holy congregation of Talmud Torah of Amsterdam, which may God increase and which we ought to follow." They considered the Amsterdam community as a model to be emulated, and the supreme authority in every aspect of the organization and leadership of their own community.[53]

Yosef Hayyim Yerushalmi echoes this sentiment when he characterizes Curaçaoan Jewry as "a fascinating microcosm of the great Amsterdam community which gave birth to it and to which it remained intimately linked."[54] And while Yerushalmi avers that the community "also betrayed important features of its own,"[55] these are not religious or communal in nature:

[W]hen I first saw the tombstone reproductions in Dr. Emmanuel's *Precious Stones of Curaçao*, I was struck above all by those which displayed maritime motifs, some showing a ship tossed on stormy seas. In 1638 the Venetian rabbi, Simone Luzzatto wrote that Jews are seldom shipowners, except for a few in Amsterdam, Rotterdam and Hamburg. He could not yet know that in Curaçao Jews would not only own some two hundred vessels, but that there would be Jewish captains and sailors, and even Jewish privateers.[56]

More pointedly, Mordechai Arbell recognizes that Curaçao was "often called the 'mother' of the Jewish communities of the Americas in the seventeenth and eighteenth centuries. Its religious administration and its rabbinical academy influenced all the communities in the area." However, he then pivots, while introducing Samuel Mendes de Sola, an eighteenth-century Curaçao ḥakham, to explain that "one can see the growing difference between the Hahams, who wanted to introduce customs acquired in Amsterdam, influenced by the proximity to the German communities, and the Caribbean Jews, who had become accustomed to the lax tropical atmosphere in their everyday life and who had no desire to change the familiar traditional ways inherited from their forefathers in Spain and Portugal."[57] He continues by explaining that "These pious Hahams [from Europe] had to adapt themselves to the special conditions of the Caribbean." Moreover, he continues that the "lack of suitable Hahams forced the Curaçao community to use leaders from their own midst . . . as substitute Hahams." And, that the "Caribbean communities had to rely on the services of itinerant emissaries from the Holy Land or from the Mediterranean ports for guidance, instruction, and maintenance of Jewish ideals."[58] This reveals the biases in the scholarship of the early modern Caribbean's Jewish communities, and points to a larger issue in the field of religious studies, which is the often narrow window within which religion is defined, and the skepticism with which Caribbean religions are often approached.

Much of the literature on Portuguese Jews utilizes a traditional, and dated, Euro-western framework in which "western" religion is shaped by the idea that religiosity can be solely understood by interrogating "what someone believes, which consists of a discrete, subjective experience of assent to propositions concerning the origin of the cosmos, the nature of humanity, the existence of deities, or the purpose of life."[59] David Morgan suggests opening up the discourse of religion to include

> their embodied forms of practice such as prayer, liturgy, and pilgrimage, their sensations of sound in corporate worship, their visual articulations of sacred writ, their creation of spaces that sculpt sound and shape living architectures of human bodies—all these [which] vastly exceed the narrow idea of religion as the profession of creeds or catechetical formulae singularly understood to represent an inner state of volition.[60]

By pushing scholars of religion to consider the categories of belief and its manifestations, he broadens the discussion so that the material culture of religious communities can be considered as an articulation or performance of faith or religiosity. Morgan suggests that "[r]ather than marginalizing belief, we need a more capacious account of it, one that looks to the embodied, material features of lived religion."[61] In fact, if we heed Morgan's advice, then Jewish life in the Caribbean is as theologically oriented and as concerned with religious identity as its European contemporaries. Thus, the Curaçaoan Portuguese Jewish community's lived religious practice, which encompasses belief, practice, and performance, among other acts can be better understood as various aspects of the articulation of religious identity and community. With my focus on gifting and on material culture, Curaçao's Portuguese Jewish community's religious life reveals the active participation in religious community, and a desire to replicate religious institutions to consolidate religious practice and power.

Second, in terms of the idea that these gifts served as a means of establishing power, the work of a number of theorists reveals the complex nature of gifts circulating in the Portuguese Jewish Atlantic world. On the one hand, the gifting of the various ritual objects falls very clearly within the realm of Marcel Mauss's theory of gifts. For him, gifts not only satisfy material needs (here, think of a new Jewish community that needs a Torah scroll) but also strengthen social bonds. The gift, for Mauss, had to appear "disinterested and free, though in fact it was part of a three-fold obligation: to give, to receive, and to repay."[62] Mauss asks: "What power resides in an object that causes its recipient to pay it back?" Differently from Durkheim, Mauss argues that no gift is free. Rather, that the gift becomes a spiritual artifact that is irreversibly tied to the giver. The gift is "never completely separated from the men who exchange them."[63] This then, created a social bond between the gift giver and the recipient. The social bond is important, and the recipient of the initial gift then has a gift-debt, which then obligates them to reciprocate. This returned gift is also tied to the giver, and further strengthens the bond between those who exchanged the gifts. If we consider this in the framework of nedabot, which represent the gifts circulating in the early modern Portuguese Jewish Atlantic world, and other gifts of ritual objects given by Portuguese Jews in honor of various life-cycle events to the various communities and congregations, then Mauss's theory of the gift, and the powers that gifts embody, illuminates the dynamics of these transactions.

For example, when Newport's Jeshuat Israel petitioned Curaçao's Mikvé Israel for money to erect their synagogue, and Mikvé Israel obliged and required an annual public recognition of this event, they are performing Mauss's theory of gifting and reciprocity. The gift—though solicited—from Mikvé Israel to Jeshuat Israel created a closer bond between the two communities, or, materialized the kinship bonds that already existed. What follows is Jeshuat Israel's indebtedness to Mikvé Israel, which is repaid annually with a public prayer for health and well-being that performs the power dynamic between the new mother-congregation and the burgeoning satellite communities. Additionally, Mauss argues that in some cultures (like the Polynesian societies that he utilizes as examples) these gifts can also have spiritual implications, especially if they are not returned. Mauss explains that not fulfilling the obligation may have detrimental spiritual implications and would certainly have significant impact on societal bonds. In this example, the gift-debt is paid with religious capital. For Curaçao's Mikvé Israel, repayment was in the form of homage, centralization of power, and recognition of patronage.

This argument is further supported by later theories such as those put forth by Helmuth Berking and Pierre Bourdieu. Berking, who builds upon C. A. Gregories's ideas of commodities and gifts, focuses on the relational significance of gifting: "if brothers make gifts, then gifts make brothers."[64] Bourdieu, in terms of gift exchange, argues, "there has to be a collectivity maintained and approved self-deception without which symbolic exchange, a fake circulation of fake use, could not operate."[65] Meaning, that the gift has to conceal its self-interest "within an envelope that 'mystifies' its efficacy for the participants in the exchange. This is not to deny the importance of the transaction: properly conducted with the affirmation of approved and accepted symbols . . . it can possess great affective power."[66]

Thus, if we look more closely at these gifts and the context within which they are given, three possibilities are brought to the fore: first, that Curaçao utilized the act of gifting in a deliberate manner as a form of exerting religious control and establishing itself as the mother-congregation of the Americas. Second, that these gifts are a means to more deeply understand the religious identity and the religious networks that existed throughout the Portuguese Jewish Atlantic—in essence they are performances of religious identity and practice. And, third, if we consider these gifts within various theoretical frameworks, recognizing that the meaning of the gift and materiality is both dynamic and changes in various societies and periods—that is, the value in further theorizing these gifts and not viewing them simply as natural extensions of Jewish brotherhood or Portuguese Jewish Diaspora consciousness—then the process of giving, the affective relationship between the actors, and the nature of the material—separated both from the category of a normal commodity and from regular exchange—helps determine the nature of the gifted object, its donation, and its value in terms of its social contract, and of issues of power and identity.

Conclusion

Over the course of the eighteenth century, Curaçao's Mikvé Israel community established itself as a mother-congregation to the Americas. Though recognizing the importance of Amsterdam as a religious center, Mikvé Israel established itself as a center of religious authority and production that would influence early American Jewish communities. The utilization of gifts to establish power and relationships was just one such manifestation of this process. By focusing on gifts and the circulation of the gifts, as well as the stipulations with which they are given, the religious outlook and commitment of the community are expressed through materiality. Here, for this community, gifting both reflected and projected understandings of the boundaries of community and the intersection of belief and practice.

Through the act of gifting, Curaçao's Mikvé Israel was performing its centrality to Jewish life in the Americas. The gifts simultaneously reflect a position of wealth, the performance of religious authority, and the participation in the continued growth of the Western Sephardic Diaspora. Mikvé Israel's act of gifting is, of course, complicated. On the one hand it established relationships built on shared Portuguese Jewish history, theology and destiny. The gifts marked the boundary of community—which congregations and communities were worthy of gifts and who Mikvé Israel felt a responsibility for. The gifts articulated the diaspora consciousness of the Portuguese Jews and the renewed commitment to sustaining their community. Perhaps this is why these gifts have largely remained undertheorized. On the other hand, these gifts are more complicated as they signal a shift in power, the establishment of an Americas mother-congregation, and the complex system of indebtedness and obligation that was implemented.

Further illuminating matters is what David Morgan cleverly calls "the matter of belief." As mentioned, scholarship on the Portuguese Jews of the Caribbean has often pointed to the lack of textual production and the dearth of rabbinic scholars and texts locally produced in the early Americas as evidence that somehow these communities were different, that these communities are largely mercantile in nature, and need not be considered in the same manner as their European counterparts. Scholarship on early modern Caribbean communal bylaws focused on their punitive nature and similarity to the regulations in European Sephardic communities. Close inspection of Caribbean synagogues fixated on the similarities of their structures to those of Talmud Torah in Amsterdam or the incorporation of features necessary for Caribbean religious life—not the creativity and religious dynamism that resulted in their production. While these examples might largely point to similarities not difference, the assumptions were such that the Caribbean communities naturally replicated what members knew in Europe, but that it was a matter of replicating infrastructure, not the foundation for a religious community that could function unaided by, for example, answering religious queries, creating ritual, and training its own scholars. Nonetheless, over the course of the eighteenth and nineteenth centuries, Curaçao commenced these aspects of religious life as well.

However, once we view the act of gifting as a means to interrogate belief and "the religious," Curaçao's Mikvé Israel, early on, becomes a site of religious authority, production, and creativity. Understanding religion "as an embodied epistemology, the sensuous and material routines that produce an integrated (and culturally particular) sense of self, community, and cosmos,"[67] makes clearer the belief, religiosity, and ethos of Curaçao's Mikvé Israel. Mikvé Israel was establishing itself as a mother-congregation in the Americas and a center of religious authority for the Portuguese Nation in the region.

Finally, it can be concluded that the multidirectional relationships of early modern Portuguese Jewish communities have been mapped and discussed for decades utilizing the migration of people, the flow of goods, and the mapping of families. A focus on, and theorization of, the materiality of religion have been absent from this larger cartography of Sephardic Jewish life in the Atlantic world. By examining the circulation of gifts and the conditions under which gifts are given, dynamics of power, as well as the performance of identity and belief are revealed. Religious material both constructs and reveals world beliefs. As Curaçao's Mikvé Israel engaged in gifting both ritual objects and money—understood through a theological obligation or necessity—it was simultaneously enacting its status in the Americas, performing its identity, and ritualizing relationships with other colonial Jewish communities.

Notes

1. Elisabeth Arweck and William Keenan, *Materializing Religion: Expression, Performance and Ritual* (Aldershot, England: Ashgate Publishing, 2006), 1.

2. See his comments in the introduction to *Biblia en dos Colunas Hebrayco y Espanol* (Amsterdam: Joseph, Jacob, and Abraham, sons of Salomon Proops, 1762). Housed in the John Carter Brown Library, Providence, Rhode Island.

3. The Ferrara Bible is a 1553 publication of the Ladino version of the Bible utilized by Spanish Jews. Unlike other Bibles, the text is printed in Latin characters rather than Hebrew characters.

4. Sephardim (Sephardic Jews) trace their ancestry to Spain and Portugal. Ashkenazim (Ashkenazic Jews) trace their ancestry to northern France, Germany, and Eastern Europe. There are some Jews who do not fit into this bifurcated distinction, such as Yemenite Jews and Ethiopian Jews. This essay focuses on a subgroup of Sephardic Jews, the Portuguese Jews of the western Sephardic diaspora, descendants of Jews who lived as *conversos* in Iberia and its diaspora, which occurred following the forced expulsion of Jews from Spain in 1492 and Portugal in 1497. A converso typically refers to an individual of Jewish ancestry who converted, or whose ancestors converted, to Catholicism in Iberia during the fourteenth or fifteenth centuries.

5. Hebron, considered the second holiest site for Jews, is the site of the Cave of Patriarchs/Cave of Makhpelah, where, according to the Book of Genesis, Judaism's three patriarchs and three of their wives are buried (see Gen. 23:1–20, Gen. 35:29, Gen. 49:28–33, Gen. 50: 4–5, and Gen. 50:12–13). Additionally, the Inquisition led some notable Sephardic Jewish kabbalists to settle in Hebron in the sixteenth century. The Jewish com-

munity of Hebron may have only numbered 20–30 families during the period. Under early Ottoman rule, the Jewish community of Hebron was especially impoverished due to ongoing debts to Ottoman religious and governmental figures. Jacob Barnai writes that debts to Ottoman leadership quadrupled in the early eighteenth century, and nearly decimated the city's Jewish community. Barnai, *The Jews in Palestine in the Eighteenth Century: Under the Patronage of the Istanbul Committee of Officials for Palestine*, trans. Naomi Goldblum (Tuscaloosa: University of Alabama Press, 1992). Jewish emissaries from Hebron were regularly sent to solicit funds for communal survival. Why Mendes de Castro chose the Jews of Hebron as his beneficiary could have been due to his knowledge of the plight of the Jews of the city, the holy status that the city held, or his knowledge of the city as a site of Sephardic kabbalist production.

6. The first synagogues throughout the Americas were Sephardic, and the congregations that were established and aided by Curaçao's Mikvé Israel were primarily part of the western Sephardic diaspora.

7. "Portuguese Jews," "Spanish and Portuguese Jews," or "Jews of the Portuguese Nation" also known as *A Nação*, refers to this group of Western Sephardim. These terms were used by both insiders and outsiders to the community, and highlight not only the Iberian heritage and ancestry of the community, but the ongoing usage of Portuguese (rather than Spanish) as their communal language—this is especially evident in congregational records.

8. Jonathan I. Israel, *Diasporas within a Diaspora: Jews, Crypto-Jews, and the World of Maritime Empires (1540–1740)* (Boston: Brill, 2002); William Klooster, "The Jews in Suriname and Curaçao," in *The Jews and the Expansion of Europe to the West, 1450 to 1800*, eds. Paolo Bernardini and Norman Fiering (New York: Berghahn, 2001), 350–68.

9. The *ma'amad* (plural: *ma'amadot*) is the Sephardic congregational board. During the period, the ma'amad was known for its authoritarian rule, and was often punitive when disobeyed. The ma'amad wrote the communal *ascamot*, the laws and regulations of the congregation that touched upon all aspects of communal life, ritual, and practice, and even many aspects of community members' domestic and economic lives.

10. Though the precise amount is not recorded, the gift of Curaçao's Mikvé Israel "must have been especially rewarding." See I. S. Emmanuel and S. A. Emmanuel, *History of the Jews of the Netherlands Antilles* (Cincinnati: American Jewish Archives, 1970), 166.

11. *Memorias Curiel 1716–1739*, Mongui Maduro Library Archives, Curaçao; Senior, Jacob de David, *Memorias Senior 1713–1763*, Mongui Maduro Library Archives, Curaçao, 18 Tebet 5498, according to the Gregorian date, circa January 10, 1738.

12. The Americas, during the early modern period, was home to both Sephardic and Ashkenazic congregations. On the whole, into the nineteenth century, Sephardic congregations tended to be wealthier and more established, especially in the Caribbean Basin. Though there was significant interaction, mercantile and otherwise, between these two Jewish communities, there were also disputes. For many reasons, some of which have to do with religious identity and religious custom, Sephardic Jewish communities in the Americas often had ascamot, which limited congregational membership to Portuguese Jews. Other bylaws sought to retain Portuguese Jewish ritual and tradition. The tension between the Sephardic and Ashkenazic communities can especially be seen in the

ascamot that attempted to regulate Jewish marriage as permissible only between Portuguese Jews. For more, see Laura Leibman, Michael Hoberman, and Hilit Surowitz-Israel, *Jews in the Americas, 1776-1826* (London: Taylor & Francis, 2017).

13. *Memorias Senior 1713-1763*, Menahem [Av] 13 5521, according to the Gregorian date, circa August 13, 1761 (see n. 11, p. 101, herein). The entry lists the month as Menahem, which is more generally known as Av, but is sometimes referred to as Menachem Av.

14. Emmanuel and Emmanuel, *History of the Jews of the Netherlands Antilles*, 520.

15. Joel Israel, Abraham Isaacs, and Jonas N. Phillips, "Items Relating to Congregation Shearith Israel, New York," *Publications of the American Jewish Historical Society*, no. 27 (1920): 2-3.

16. Within the western Sephardic context, the *ḥakham*, literally, a wise person, typically refers to the religious leader of the congregation who has a Talmudic education. This position of religious authority is comparable to a rabbi. Ḥakham Jeshurun arrived in Curaçao from Amsterdam in 1717 to lead the island congregation.

17. Emmanuel and Emmanuel, *History of the Jews of the Netherlands Antilles*, 131.

18. October 13, 1729: By 264 pieces of 8/8 recd by the hands of Moses Gomez and Benja Pacheco sent by the Chacham of Curacoa wch was gethrd by him of sundry Jews of Curacao in a larger sum hereafter CR. Given the sd 264 pieces of 8/8 weighing 229 ounces & 3/8h sold to Thomas Day at 8/9 p. oz"

- Feb. 23, 1730: By 43 oz. & 1/8 of markt Silver recd by hands of Mos. Gomez & Benja Pacheco sent by the Chacham of Curacoa wch was gethrd by him of sundry Jews of Curacoa in a larger sum hereafter CR. Given the sd 264 pieces of 8/8 weighing 229 ounces & 3/8h sold to Thomas Day at 8/9 p. oz"
- Feb. 23, 1730: By 43 oz. & 1/8 of markt Silver recd by hands of Mos. Gomez & Benja Pacheco sent by the Chacham of Curacoa Getherd by him of the Congregation at Curacoa at 8/7 ½ p. oz
- 7 Apr, 1730: By Cash recd in advance on 43 ¼ oz Silver wch I Cr. this Sina the 23d Feby last at 1d ½ p. oz
- 16 June 1730: By 24 heavy ps 8/8 weighing 20¾ oz. and 19 oz. in small Money recd by Capt Mathlin fro Curacoa Consignd to myself from the Chacham Israel Jeshurun wch was getherd by y Sd Chacham of the Kahal of Curacoa & sent for the use & building of the Sinagogue at 8/9 p/ oz. (The Jacques Judah Lyons Collection, AJHS, Box 1 [oversized 14], folder 63)

The receipt of above funds is confirmed in a receipt written in both Portuguese and English in the hand of Jacob Franks, treasurer of New York's Shearith Israel, who "Receivd on ye [the] 7th of October last past by hand of Messrs Moses Gomez & Rodrigo Pacheco two hundred twenty Nine Ounces, and three Eaightes of Silver as Also Likewise Receivd of said Gentlemen on the 24th feby forty three Ounces, and one Eight of Silver which two sums together are applyd for and toward the building of a Sinagogue in this place of which Signed tow recepts of this date, New York the 9 of Nisan 5490 [March 27, 1730]." ("Receipt of Jacob Franks for silver from Curaçao towards building synagogue in New York." Jacques Judah Lyons Collection, AJHS, box 1 [oversized 14], folder 63.)

19. In western Sephardic congregations, the ḥazan was generally the leader of the congregation. The ḥazan tended to have less training than a ḥakham.

20. Curaçao serving as the origin for both the first and, then, a later ḥakham is also significant because we can see that Curaçao must have had a religious influence on the mainland community.

21. Jacob Rader Marcus, *The Jew in the American World: A Source Book* (Detroit: Wayne State University Press, 1996), 282.

22. Isidor Paiewonsky, *Jewish Historical Development in the Virgin Islands, 1665–1959* (Saint Thomas, VI: s.n., 1959).

23. For the full list see Emmanuel and Emmanuel, *History of the Jews of the Netherlands Antilles*, 165–71.

24. Ibid., 131.

25. *Minhag* (plural: *minhagim*) refers to the custom or tradition of the congregation. The minhagim of Sephardic and Ashkenazic communities sometimes differed. As Ashkenazic Jews began to outnumber Sephardic Jews in America, some Sephardic leaders feared that the customs and traditions of the synagogue would change to reflect the practices of the Ashkenazic "newcomers."

26. David de Sola Pool and Tamar de Sola Pool, *Old Faith in a New World: Portraits of Shearith Israel 1654–1954* (New York: Columbia University Press, 1955), 21 (see also pages 26 and 40).

27. Joel Israel, Abraham Isaacs, and Jonas N. Phillips, "Items Relating to Congregation Shearith Israel, New York," *Publications of the American Jewish Historical Society*, no. 27 (1920): 3–4; Emmanuel and Emmanuel, *History of the Jews of the Netherlands Antilles*, 131.

28. Emmanuel and Emmanuel, *History of the Jews of the Netherlands Antilles*, 166–169.

29. There was a Portuguese Jewish practice from Amsterdam of relocating poor Jews to other cities or the new American colonies. This group was called *despechados*. One of the largest groups of despechados, numbering 73 individuals, was relocated to Curaçao. The despechados were most commonly sent to Suriname and Curaçao. For more see Wieke Vink, *Creole Jews: Negotiating Community in Colonial Suriname* (Leiden: Kitlv Press, 2010).

30. *Memorias Senior 1713–1763* and *Memorias Curiel 1716–1739* (see n. 11, p. 101 herein for archive location); Mordechai Arbell, *The Jewish Nation of the Caribbean: the Spanish-Portuguese Jewish Settlements in the Caribbean and the Guianas* (Jerusalem: Gefen, 2002), 163.

31. "Letter from the Parnassim of Curaçao to K.K.S.I. (Portuguese, translation from *Publications of the American Jewish Historical Society*)," 1753, Jacques Judah Lyons Collection, box 2, folder 106, American Jewish Historical Society.

32. Ibid.

33. *Memorias Senior 1713–1763*, Mongui Maduro Library Archives, Curaçao, 26 Kislev 5504, according to the Gregorian date, circa December 12, 1743.

34. The full list of Mikvé Israel's donations is in Emmanuel and Emmanuel, *History of the Jews of the Netherlands Antilles*, 155–65.

35. Marcus, *The Jew in the American World: A Source Book*, 154.

36. For more on the amount of support that Amsterdam's Jewish community sent

to the Holy Land see I. S. Emmanuel, "The Assistance of the Sephardic Communities of Amsterdam and Curaçao to the Holy Land and Safed," *Sefer Safed,* vol. 1 [Hebrew] (Jerusalem: n.p., 1962): 399-424.

37. The Amsterdam and Curaçao communities continued to correspond with and support Hebron through 1872. Evidence for the continuing relationship between Hebron and these communities is seen in the January 1872 letter entitled Kol Sheva'at, National Library of Israel, Jerusalem, Israel. [Hebrew].

38. Order of Study and Prayer in Yeshivah of Hebron (HaYeshiva V'Seder HaLimud . . .), Amsterdam, 1770, National Library of Israel, Jerusalem, Israel. [Hebrew]. In addition to such prayers, there are also reciprocal shipments to the island community. The Amsterdam community wrote, "We have received two cases of sand from the Holy Land that were sent to us from Safed, through Messrs Da Costa and Lameira of Smirna (Izmir), one for our synagogue and the other for Curaçao which we are forwarding." Gerard Nahon, "Les Relations . . .," in *Dutch Jewish History: Proceedings of the Symposium on the History of the Jews in the Netherlands, November 28-December 3, 1982, Tel-Aviv and Jerusalem,* vol. 1 of 2 vols., ed. Joseph Michman, 59-78 (Tel-Aviv: Tel-Aviv University, 1984). In Nahon, see n. 66 citing Copiador de Cartas, PA 334, 93 fol. 319, housed in Gemeente Archief Amsterdam (Amsterdam Municipal Archives), as cited in Arbell, *The Jewish Nation of the Caribbean.*

39. Marcus, *The Jew in the American World: A Source Book,* 154.

40. Ibid.

41. Curaçao's Mikvé Israel synagogue is known as the Snoa, an abbreviated form of *esnoga,* the old Portuguese and Ladino word for synagogue.

42. *Nedaba* is a biblical sacrifice that is not linked to any religious obligation or commandment, but rather offered willingly.

43. A *misheberakh* is a blessing recited for the well-being of a community member.

44. *Memorias Curiel 1716-1739,* Mongui Maduro Library Archives, Curaçao, 13 & 15 Nissan 5490, according to the Gregorian date, circa March 31 and April 2, 1730.

45. *Memorias Curiel 1716-1739,* Mongui Maduro Library Archives, Curaçao, Tebet 7 5490, according to the Gregorian date, circa December 27, 1729.

46. The donor of the fourth chandelier is unknown; Congregation Mikvé Israel-Emanuel (Willemstad, Curaçao). *Our "Snoa," 5492-5742* (Curaçao, Netherlands Antilles: Congregation Mikvé Israel-Emanuel, 1982), 40-41.

47. Émile Durkheim and George Simpson, *Émile Durkheim on the Division of Labor in Society; Being a Translation of His De La Division Du Travail Social, with an Estimate of His Work by George Simpson* (Glencoe, IL: Free Press, 1949), 124.

48. Maurice Godelier, *Perspectives in Marxist Anthropology* (Cambridge: Cambridge University Press, 1977), 129.

49. Though there is much disagreement about the parameters of diaspora, many rely on an ethos of remittances or gifting between the diasporic community and those in the homeland. I would argue that due to emotion and sense of obligation to those often times in far less fortunate conditions, there has been little interrogation into these gifts or remittances—in a sense, the capital becomes easily conflated and understood through emotional capital, which is then presented as self-evident.

50. Christian Free, "Reflections on Marcel Mauss and the (gift as a) 'total social fact,'" *Academia* (website), accessed March 7, 2020, https://www.academia.edu/38018011/Reflections_on_Marcel_Mauss_and_the_gift_as_a_total_social_fact,_2.

51. David Morgan, introduction to *Religion and Material Culture: The Matter of Belief* (Abingdon and New York: Routledge, 2010), 8.

52. Ibid.

53. Yosef Kaplan, "The Curaçao and Amsterdam Jewish Communities in the 17th and 18th Centuries," *American Jewish History* 72, no. 2 (December 1982): 198.

54. Yosef Hayim Yerushalmi, "Between Amsterdam and New Amsterdam: The Place of Curaçao and the Caribbean in Early Modern Jewish History," *American Jewish History* 72, no. 2 (1982): 191.

55. Ibid.

56. Ibid. It is worth noting that the title of this article highlights the marginalization of the Caribbean in Jewish studies. The title reflects the teleology embedded in the field as the title glosses over the "new Amsterdam" of the Americas (Curaçao) and creates a link between Amsterdam and New York (called New Amsterdam until 1664).

57. Mordechai Arbell, "Early Relations between the Jewish Communities in the Caribbean and the Guianas and Those of the Near East 17th to 19th Centuries," accessed November 5, 2021, https://www.rodriguezuribe.co/histories/Mordechai%20Arbell.pdf.

58. Ibid.

59. Morgan, *Introduction to Religion and Material Culture*, 1.

60. Ibid., 2–3.

61. Ibid., 7.

62. Felicity Heal, *The Power of Gifts*, (Oxford: Oxford University Press, 2014), 6.

63. Marcel Mauss, *The Gift: The Form and Reason for Exchange in Archaic Societies* (London: Routledge, 1990), 31.

64. Helmuth Berking, *A Sociology of Giving*, trans. Patrick Camiller (London: Sage, 1999), 39.

65. Pierre Bourdieu, *Outline of a Theory of Practice*, trans. Richard Nice (Cambridge: Cambridge University Press, 1977), 6.

66. Heal, *The Power of Gifts*, 6.

67. Morgan, *Introduction to Religion and Material Culture*, 8.

Bibliography

Primary Sources

Archives

American Jewish Historical Society (AJHS, New York)
John Carter Brown Library (Providence, Rhode Island)
Mongui Maduro Library Archives (Curaçao)
The National Library of Israel (Jerusalem)

Secondary Sources

Arbell, Mordechai. "Early Relations between the Jewish Communities in the Caribbean and the Guianas and Those of the Near East 17th to 19th Centuries." Accessed November 5, 2021. https://www.rodriguezuribe.co/histories/Mordechai%20Arbell.pdf.
———. *The Jewish Nation of the Caribbean: The Spanish-Portuguese Jewish Settlements in the Caribbean and the Guianas*. Jerusalem: Gefen, 2002.
Arweck, Elisabeth, and William Keenan. *Materializing Religion: Expression, Performance and Ritual*. Aldershot, England: Ashgate Publishing, 2006.
Barnai, Jacob. *The Jews in Palestine in the Eighteenth Century: Under the Patronage of the Istanbul Committee of Officials for Palestine*. Translated by Naomi Goldblum. Tuscaloosa: University of Alabama Press, 1992.
Berking, Helmuth. *A Sociology of Giving*. Translated by Patrick Camiller. London: Sage, 1999.
Bourdieu, Pierre. *Outline of a Theory of Practice*. Translated by Richard Nice. Cambridge: Cambridge University Press, 1977.
De Sola Pool, David, and Tamar de Sola Pool. *Old Faith in a New World: Portraits of Shearith Israel 1654–1954*. New York: Columbia University Press, 1955.
Durkheim, Émile, and George Simpson. *Émile Durkheim on the Division of Labor in Society; Being a Translation of His De la Division du Travail Social, with an Estimate of His Work by George Simpson*. Glencoe, IL: Free Press, 1949.
Emmanuel, Isaac Samuel. "The Assistance of the Sephardic Communities of Amsterdam and Curaçao to the Holy Land and Safed." *Sefer Safed*. Vol. 1 [Hebrew]. Jerusalem: N.p., 1962.
Emmanuel, Isaac Samuel, and Suzanne Amazalak Emmanuel. *History of the Jews of the Netherlands Antilles*. Cincinnati: American Jewish Archives, 1970.
Free, Christian. "Reflections on Marcel Mauss and the (gift as a) 'total social fact.'" *Academia* (website). https://www.academia.edu/38018011/Reflections_on_Marcel_Mauss_and_the_gift_as_a_to al_social_fact.
Godelier, Maurice. *Perspectives in Marxist Anthropology*. Cambridge: Cambridge University Press, 1977.
Heal, Felicity. *The Power of Gifts*. Oxford: Oxford University Press, 2014.
Israel, Joel, Abraham Isaacs, and Jonas N. Phillips. "Items Relating to Congregation Shearith Israel, New York." *Publications of the American Jewish Historical Society* no. 27 (1920): 1–125.
Israel, Jonathan I. *Diasporas within a Diaspora: Jews, Crypto-Jews, and the World of Maritime Empires (1540–1740)*. Boston: Brill, 2002.
Kaplan, Yosef. "The Curaçao and Amsterdam Jewish Communities in the 17th and 18th Centuries." *American Jewish History* 72, no. 2 (December 1982): 193–211.
Klooster, William. "The Jews in Suriname and Curaçao." In *The Jews and the Expansion of Europe to the West, 1450 to 1800*, edited by Paolo Bernardini and Norman Fiering, 350–68. New York: Berghahn, 2001.
Leibman, Laura, Michael Hoberman, and Hilit Surowitz-Israel. *Jews in the Americas, 1776–1826*. London: Taylor & Francis, 2017.

Marcus, Jacob Rader. *The Jew in the American World: A Source Book*. Detroit: Wayne State University Press, 1996.
Mauss, Marcel. *The Gift: The Form and Reason for Exchange in Archaic Societies*. London: Routledge, 1990.
Morgan, David, ed. *Religion and Material Culture: The Matter of Belief*. Abingdon and New York: Routledge, 2010.
Nahon, Gerard. "Les Relations entre Amsterdam et Constantinople au XVIIIe siècle d'après le 'Copiador de Cartas' de la Nation Juive Portugaise d'Amsterdam." In *Dutch Jewish History: Proceedings of the Symposium on the History of the Jews in the Netherlands, November 28–December 3, 1982, Tel-Aviv and Jerusale*. Vol. 1 of 2 vols. Edited by Joseph Michman, 59–78 Tel-Aviv: Tel-Aviv University, 1984. (In Nahon, see n. 66 citing Copiador de Cartas, PA 334, 93 fol. 319, housed in Gemeente Archief Amsterdam [Amsterdam Municipal Archives], as cited in Arbell, *The Jewish Nation of the Caribbean*).
Our "Snoa," 5492–5742. Curaçao, Netherlands Antilles: Congregation Mikvé Israel-Emanuel, 1982.
Paiewonsky, Isidor. *Jewish Historical Development in the Virgin Islands, 1665–1959*. Saint Thomas, VI: N.p., 1959.
Vink, Wieke. *Creole Jews: Negotiating Community in Colonial Suriname*. Leiden: Kitlv Press, 2010.
Yerushalmi, Yosef Hayim. "Between Amsterdam and New Amsterdam: The Place of Curaçao and the Carribean in Early Modern Jewish History." *American Jewish History* 72, no. 2 (December 1982): 172–92.

4

Jews and New Christians in the Iberian Empires in a Global Context, 1492–1800

José C. Moya

When the *Nina*, the *Pinta*, and the *Santa Maria* sailed from Palos on the morning of August 3, 1492, so did, according to tradition, the last vessels carrying expelled Jews out of Spain, a country that had had a larger Jewish population than all the others in medieval Europe combined.[1] A related account asserts that the three caravels were set to sail a day earlier, that Columbus postponed the departure so it would not coincide with Tish'a B'Av, a somber and inauspicious day in the Jewish calendar, and that this is part of the evidence for the Admiral of the Ocean Sea's Jewish origins. The coincidence of the dates is plausible. The Edict of Expulsion had decreed July 31 as the last day that unconverted Jews could remain in Spain, but later extended the deadline by nine days. The assertion about Columbus's Jewishness rests on weaker foundations. Most professional historians dismiss it as they do similar claims about Columbus's Catalan, Portuguese, Galician, Corsican, Sardinian, Greek, Polish, Norwegian, and Scottish origins.[2] None would dispute, however, the Jewish presence not only in the ships crossing the Mediterranean but also in the three that would cross the Atlantic. The year 1492 marked, then, the last medieval expulsion of Jews in Western Europe and the first Jewish presence in the New World.

This essay explores the presence in the early modern Iberian world of Jews and New Christians, that is, Jews forcefully converted *en masse* in Portugal in 1497, most of them of Spanish-birth or origin.[3] The first of the essay's six sections centers on the move from Spain to the Americas in the century following 1492, estimating the size of the outflow and the persistence of Judaism in the colonies. The second section discusses the larger migration from Spain to Portugal during the fifteenth century, showing how the exodus's size and selectivity transformed the host country's Jewry by making it much larger, more urban and bourgeois, more religious, and particularly conscious of its Hispanicity. These traits can enhance our understanding of the New Christians overseas. We cannot comprehend the immigrant experience—in this case and in general—by studying it only after the migrants land at their destinations, as if the immigrants were tabula rasa and their previous history irrelevant. With this understanding at the forefront, the third segment examines the ethnogenesis of New Christians. Rather than falling into the binary of whether they were treated as a race or not, it analyzes how the concept *and practice* of "purity of blood" resembled and differed from what are commonly considered the first racial systems: the hypodescent-based racial taxonomies that would emerge in the Americas in the following centuries.

The fourth section of the essay returns the focus to the exodus from Iberia—in this case the more global migrations of Portuguese New Christians to Lusitanian colonies in Africa, India, Brazil, and eventually to Spanish America during the union of the Iberian Crowns (1580–1640). It examines the formation of a mercantile diaspora that connected the destinations not only to the homeland but also to each other. For example, most of the first New Christians in Brazil came not from Portugal but from São Tomé, Cape Verde, Angola, and other Portuguese colonies in Africa, which underlines the value of a diasporic approach. It also explores the role of the New Christian diaspora in the Atlantic economy, in sugar and slave trading, and the degree to which New Christians revived Judaism in Spanish America. The fifth section compares the Jewish experience in the early modern Iberian world to that of contemporary Jews elsewhere in terms of visibility, religious practices, class and cultural homogeneity, global spread, and imperial connections. The sixth, and final, section examines how economic and political trends during the late 1700s and the nineteenth century dwindled what may have been the most geographically widespread and economically prominent ethnic mercantile diaspora in global history.

From Spain to the Indies

Recently baptized *conversos* formed part of the crew of the first transatlantic voyage. These included the comptroller of the fleet (Rodrigo Sanchez), the second mate (Alfonso de la Calle), the apothecary (Maestro Bernal, who had been reconciled two years earlier for Judaizing), and Columbus's interpreter (Luis de Torres).[4] The latter, according to lore, uttered the first words in a non-Amerindian language heard in the New World (one would assume after Old Norse in Newfoundland) when he addressed the Lucayan people of the Bahamas in Hebrew, then Aramaic, and finally Arabic, all to no avail.[5] Given the large number of Jews involved in maritime activities and in the towns of origins of the crew, they must have accounted also for a good proportion of the lesser known eighty-seven sailors and explorers that embarked on the first crossing of the Atlantic. The confiscation of the property of expelled Jews provided much of the royal funding for Columbus's second voyage. The Americas, in turn, would provide an unexpected shelter for conversos and Crypto-Jews despite official, but often contradictory and ineffective, bans and restrictions. They participated in the conquest of the Caribbean, but their exodus picked up, as it did with Spaniards in general, after the conquest of the Aztec and Inca Empires and the start of the longest lasting silver boom in history. There they engaged mainly in trading, mining, and crafts such as tailoring and shoemaking.

The number of Spanish conversos that crossed the Atlantic during the sixteenth century is impossible to ascertain, but several factors indicate that it must have been considerable. One was the ease with which they circumvented restrictions. As in most times and places, the cunning of migrants tended to trump the rigidity of bureaucracies. Schemes abounded. Migrants would falsify papers, bribe officials, or purchase fake permits easily available on the streets of Seville for a modest price. Those who could not afford it relied on other ploys well known to contemporary authorities, who nonetheless admitted their inability to curb them. They would enlist as sailors or soldiers and vanish into the vast expanses of the Indies, or find American-bound travelers in Seville willing to hire them as servants.[6]

Indirect evidence also points to a large exodus. In his study of the Inquisition in New Castile, Jean-Pierre Dedieu showed that the number of convictions pronounced for Jewish practices fell from 87 percent of the total in the years 1483–1530 to 11 percent in 1531–1620, and that the average age of the accused rose considerably.[7] He interpreted the trend as evidence of assimilation, stating that by 1540 Judaism in Castile had become residual. This is valid but so is the assumption that emigration reduced the number of conversos and, as in most migratory flows, particularly among the younger ones. The Americas offered two clear attractions: a less restrictive cultural/religious milieu, and more economic opportunities.

The Spanish Indies became El Dorado in the Old World's imaginary and "rich as Peru" became a common phrase in Western European languages. While every other European Empire had to inveigle or force their subjects to move to the colonies, Spain's challenge was how to prevent them from leaving; yet 450,000 left between 1492 and 1600 in the first massive long-distance migration in the history of humanity.[8] The 300,000 or so conversos in Castile in around the year 1500 accounted for 7 percent of the kingdom's denizens.[9] If they migrated at the same rate as their Old Christian neighbors, then 31,500 would have crossed the Atlantic during the sixteenth century. Bigotry and discrimination acted as an extra push factor for conversos, while their relative concentration in cities, trade, and maritime activities made it easier for them to migrate, so the actual number may easily double that estimate. This at least may have been the case for some occupations. In his gargantuan *The Jews and Medicine* (1944), Harry Friedenwald maintained that medicine in Spain had been so associated with Jews that after 1492 just entering the profession exposed one to suspicions of Crypto-Judaism, leading large numbers of converso physicians to leave for the Americas.[10]

Regarding the preservation of Judaism in the Americas, Seymour Liebman asserted that conversos practiced Judaism openly in the Viceroyalty of New Spain up to the 1560s, and that they were accepted as Jews by coreligionists in places where Judaism was legal such as Curaçao, Jamaica, and Italy. The claim seems valid. The Inquisition first appeared in the Spanish colonies in 1570, almost a century later than in Spain (1478). It had only two offices (in Mexico City and Lima), with a third added in Cartagena in 1610, and before the inflow of Portuguese New Christians following the union of the Iberian Crowns in 1580, inquisitorial activity had targeted mainly indigenous "idolatry" and Protestant "heresy." By the end of the sixteenth century, one could find conversos and evidence of Judaism throughout Spanish America from New Mexico to Chile.[11]

From Spain to Portugal

Iberian Jews' participation in Europe's overseas expansion, however, preceded 1492 by almost a century. Indeed, late fourteenth-century accounts about trading opportunities in sub-Saharan Africa told by Jewish merchants operating in Muslim-controlled, overland commercial routes, provided much of the original impetus for Portugal's Atlantic explorations.[12] Around the same time, that country's Jewish population was swelling with refugees from the 1391 pogroms in Spain and from the aftermath of restrictions that culminated with the 1412 Ayllon laws in Castile and similar ones promulgated in Aragon in 1414.[13] A year later, a Portuguese fleet of 200 ships and 50,000 men conquered Ceuta, beginning a process of overseas expansion that would go on for over a century. Many of the Spanish exiles would eagerly join their Portuguese brethren in faith in this process, participating in the settlement of Ceuta and of the unoccupied archipelagos of Madeira (1420), Azores (1433), and Cape Verde (1462). They also settled in Safi, Azamor, Agadir, Mogador (present-day Essaouira), and other colonial outposts on the North African Atlantic coast, where they received communal recognition and legal assurances from the Portuguese monarchs.[14] In fact, their overrepresentation was so marked that historian António de Almeida Mendes described the Portuguese-led first colonization of the Atlantic as "the work of Jews, renegades, and young men who abandoned their villages to seek a better life."[15]

The 1492 expulsions in Spain further augmented the Jewish population in Portugal and affected its sociocultural composition. Over four-fifths of the refugees who left Spain in 1492 headed for Portugal.[16] The proportion was even higher for neighboring Castile, which contained about 85 percent of Spain's Jews at the time. The inflow swelled Portugal's Jewry to over 100,000, or one-tenth of the total population of the country.[17] Jews in Portugal had been less persecuted and were wealthier than in the rest of the Iberian Peninsula, or for that matter than in the rest of Europe.[18] The 1492 exodus, however, accentuated the wealth part. Exiles in general boast higher socioeconomic background than those left behind because leaving requires a certain level of resources and/or connections. In this case, however, King João II of Portugal increased the selectivity by allowing refugees to settle in his domain permanently only if they could pay 100 crusados per person, excepting only "children at the breast."[19] Another form of selectivity related to religiosity. Norman Roth showed in his classic work on conversion and expulsion that the "overwhelming majority" of Jews in Spain had converted to Catholicism during the late fourteenth and fifteenth centuries.[20] Those moving to Portugal both after the 1391 pogroms and in 1492, were thus representative *not* of Spanish Jewry in general but of its most religious members, those who had refused to convert in spite of plenty of sticks and carrots proffered over the span of a century.

This should inform any analysis of the consequences of the expulsion order and mass baptism of the Jewish population in Portugal five years later. Recent historians have rightly contested the entrenched assumption that Jews in Spain converted to Catholicism only by force, and that therefore most conversos were Crypto-Jews, depicting the supposition as essentialist and ahistorical. Obviously, millions of people worldwide have converted to other religions freely and often in the face of retaliation, and continue to do so. The Portuguese 1497 conversion, however, differed from previous ones in Spain in four critical aspects. First, it took place all at once rather than over centuries. Second, although the original decree resembled the Spanish one of 1492 in that it ordered the expulsion of all Jews who had not converted within three months, in practice, expulsion was not a choice. The Portuguese Crown forbade the departure of children, required that adults could leave only in royal ships, provided few of these, and finally prohibited exits altogether in 1499. This meant that tens of thousands who would have preferred to leave rather than convert, as in Spain, ended up being christened. The policy thus turned Jews into Christians by fiat. Third, Judaism was more deeply entrenched in Portugal than in Spain, where mass conversions had been going on for more than a century.[21] Moreover, the fact that Spaniards who had left everything behind just to continue being Jewish likely constituted the majority of Jews in Portugal increased overall commitment to Judaism even more. Finally, the rigidity of the mass christening came along with a particularly relaxed implementation. King Manuel I set a period of twenty years, and later extended it, in which no one could inquire into the orthodoxy of the religious practices of the *cristãos-novos* (New Christians).

All of this guaranteed that the vast majority of New Christians in Portugal would continue to be Jewish in everything but name, and apparently in not particularly cryptic ways. Rabbis became "masters" (mestre), ethno-religious endogamy continued at the same levels as before, and even Castilian repentant conversos continued moving to Portugal after 1497 because they kept hearing from family and friends that Jews there could live as Jews.[22]

Making Race? The Ethnogenesis of Cristãos-Novos

The sixteenth century, however, witnessed a slow but steady process of ethnogenesis that turned the cristãos-novos into an ethnoracial group. Because merchants are more likely to generate documents than the general population, this process is more visible—and more studied—among mercantile classes. Before 1492, merchant houses in Portugal, as elsewhere in medieval Europe, were patently identifiable by ethno-religious markers: Portuguese Christian or Jewish, Castilian Jewish, Genoese, Flemish, German, et cetera. The foreign identifiers continued but the mass arrival of Castilian Sephardim and the legal erasure of Jews in both Spain and Portugal began to erode the intra-Iberian distinctions. Certain prospects, then, opened to New Christians that had been denied to them as Jews. As had happened before in Castile and Aragon—where conversos came to occupy half of all the important offices at Court by 1480—New Christians took advantage of these new opportunities.[23] The Catholic Church officially rejected the very category of New Christian because it undermined the notion of conversion in a proselytizing religion. When antisemitic riots broke out in Lisbon in 1506, King Manuel I harshly put then down and executed the leaders. Intermarriage between New and Old Christian merchants increased to such a degree that by the end of the sixteenth century, the majority of New Christian merchants were of mixed religious ancestry. Yet, instead of being absorbed and thus disappearing, they became increasingly more dominant. By the 1540s, New Christian merchants already outnumbered their Old Christian counterparts two-to-one.[24] By the end of the century, the ratio had risen to three-to-one.[25]

The explanation for this apparent contradiction is manifold. Although some wealthy New Christian merchants were absorbed into the nobility and gentry, this was significantly more common for well-to-do Old Christian merchants. The latter's withdrawal from wholesale commerce made this sector, by default, more "Jewish." Indeed, the Portuguese Marxist historian, António José Saraiva, asserted that the New Christians had essentially become the Portuguese bourgeoisie at odds with the nobility, and that the repression of presumed Crypto-Jews obeyed class rather than religious conflicts and interests.[26] The argument may be overly materialistic and more than a bit reductionist, but its sociocultural implications are relevant. Before the proliferation of joint-stock companies and state mercantilism, most long-distance trade worldwide transpired through specific ethno-religious networks, from Punjabi Khatris spread between the Indus and Volga rivers to Syrian-Lebanese Christians in the Levant and the Igbo Aro in the Bight of Biafra. In all these cases, the economic and the sociocultural intertwined in a symbiotic manner. New Christian artisans or professionals, for example, could assimilate completely into Portuguese Catholic society and continue being, say, tailors or apothecaries, but not long-distance merchants, for whom the occupation depended on a system of trust and credit embedded in a particular ethnic, and diasporic, network. The more the non-merchant New Christians assimilated to Luso-Catholic culture, the more homogenous those remaining became as a minority mercantile group, and—as elsewhere with similar cases in the world—the longer they continued to exist as a self-conscious ethno-religious group. Indeed, commerce became a marker of ethnic identity both within and outside the group.

The other explicative factor in the transformation of the newly converted into a quasi-permanent ethnoracial group is external: *limpeza de sangue* (purity of blood in Portuguese), the Old Christians' aspiration to remain "clean" by avoiding mixing with people of Jewish or Muslim ancestry. Historians have usually interpreted this as a form of religious rather than racial prejudice. After all, several historiographical currents have identified racial ideologies with nineteenth and twentieth-century European imperialism and pseudoscientific racism. Already in 1951, Hannah Arendt had explicitly pointed to the "New Imperialism" (1884–1914), race-thinking, and bureaucratic rule as *The Origins of Totalitarianism*. This view also matches a common teleology that perceives a movement from early medieval Christian tolerance of Jews to a late medieval religious anti-Judaism, and then to modern racial antisemitism. Yet, the concept of purity of blood clearly contradicted the tenets of a proselytizing religion that literally means universal and all-embracing, and most Catholic authorities rejected it.[27] To be sure, sixteenth-century Iberians did define their suspicions of conversos in religious terms (that their conversions were not sincere) rather than in the language of biological superiority. Nonetheless, the concept and practice of purity of blood shares at least five main traits with the biologized racial taxonomies that surfaced, particularly in the Americas, two or three centuries later.[28]

The first common trait between *limpieza de sangre* (the original Spanish term for purity of blood) and later racial taxonomies is the obvious use of biological imagery. Racial language continued to employ "blood" as its most recurrent motif until the popularization of genetics. Indeed, a Google N-gram search shows that "in your blood" continues to be a more common expression than "in your genes" or "in your DNA." Tellingly, Iberian conquerors and colonists took the term limpieza de sangre to the Americas, added Amerindians and Afro-descendants to the undesirables list, and continued to use it centuries after both groups had been thoroughly Christianized. A second similarity is the tendency of portraying Jews as physically distinct (with darker skin and hooked noses, for example) in visual representations. Sara Lipton not only noticed an increase of these unflattering images in the late medieval period but also argued that more than "mirroring" preexisting negative Christian attitudes they helped to create such attitudes.[29] At the same time, biblical characters, including those in the Old Testament, were increasingly portrayed as European in both complexion and dress, furthering the separation of Jews from Christianity and Europeanness. A third commonality is the fusion of "natural" and "cultural" categories. Modern racism has never been only, or even mainly, about phenotype but also about all sorts of putative cultural flaws from savagery, criminality, and sloth, to "amoral familism" and the "culture of poverty." A fourth common characteristic relates to a conception of ethnicity as permanent rather than malleable. As in the biblical rhetorical question—"Can the Ethiopian change his skin or the leopard its spots?" (Jeremiah 13:23)—Jewishness became increasingly conceived as some inheritable and thus immutable trait. The fifth similarity is the practice of determining the identity of individuals of mixed origin through hypodescent (the identity of the subaltern group) rather than hyperdescent (the identity of the dominant group). As Daviken Studnicki-Gizbert put it: "To be an Old Christian required a homogeneously Christian ancestry; it required purity. On the other hand, it took but a single converso or Jewish ancestor in an individual's family tree to be designated a converso; Judaism, carried in the blood, was viewed as a taint regardless of its dilution."[30]

Neither the concept nor the *practice* of limpieza de sangre differ significantly, in all these regards, from the "one-drop rule" in the US South, where, at its most extreme, a person with thirty-one white and one black ancestor would be classified as black. Neither does it differ from the racial taxonomies of the Americas in general that classified mulattoes, quadroons, and octoroons as nonwhite although they were equally or mostly of European ancestry. Indeed, the exact same equivalents—half-New Christian, quarter-New Christian, one-eighth-New Christian—can be found in the Inquisition records of 625 Portuguese conversos convicted in autos-da-fé between 1633 and 1746, where 42 percent were only partially New Christian.[31] In all of these cases, the logic, and the apparent lack of it, were the same. Paradoxically, they all presented the dominant group as so naturally feeble that they could not absorb a little blood from presumably inferior people without losing their identity and the subordinate group as so overpowering that just a few drops of their blood would determine the identity of their mixed descendants forever. Equally paradoxical is that a system meant to diminish a particular group ended up enlarging it by the use of hypo- rather than hyperdescent classificatory schema. In all the cases, these taxonomies emerged not just to classify, as in Linnaean botany, but also to rank and exclude with Christianity and whiteness functioning as both default (expressed in the common use of nonwhite or non-Christian as if white and Christians were the norm) and a gatekeeper preventing others from entering the group defined as White or Christian.

The Jewish experience in late medieval Iberia, however, differed from that of Africans in three critical ways. One is slavery. Individual Jews were enslaved in the late medieval and early modern periods—as were Muslims, Christians, pagan Slavs (who were so numerous that their ethnonym became the word for persons in bondage in all Romance and Germanic languages), and many other groups.[32] The enslavement of sub-Saharan Africans, however, is unique in many ways. In terms of volume, Christian traders took 12 million slaves from West Africa across the Atlantic between 1500 and 1850, and Muslim traders took a higher number from the Sahel and East Africa across the Sahara and Indian Ocean between the ninth and mid-twentieth centuries. Over 95 percent of Afro-descendants in the US South and the British and French West Indies were slaves, by far the highest proportion ever recorded in the long history of slavery. Equally exceptional, their status was permanent and inherited ad infinitum.

The two other key differences between the experience of Iberian Jews and Africans in the Americas and the Arab world related to class and phenotype. In a 1940 essay comparing antisemitism in twentieth-century Germany and late medieval Iberia, and referring to the conversos' socioeconomic success, Cecil Roth wrote, "The sudden preeminence of a fraction of the population previously considered inferior not unnaturally gave rise to jealousy. The prejudice which had previously been ostensibly religious became 'racial.'"[33] To what degree the prejudice became "racial" remains a question of debate. Whether it was or not, the combination of ethnophobia and class resentment resembles not the African experience in the Americas and the Arab world but that of what sociologist Edna Bonacich termed *middleman minorities*: economically successful mercantile minority groups that occupy a vulnerable middle ground between the ruling elites and the local peasantries.[34] Indeed, anti-Jewish resentment among the peasantry in Spain and Portugal seems to have intensified as the Jewish and converso population became more urban.[35] Conversos in the Iberian world gained greater access to non-commercial high spheres (including the Catholic Church, as the cases of Torquemada and Hernando de Talavera, the Queen's confessor, indicate), but otherwise their situation paralleled that of Parsis in India, Indians in East Africa, Chinese in Southeast Asia, Armenians in Safavid Iran, and many others. The other key difference was phenotype. Despite depictions of Iberian Jews as physically different, they were in reality indistinguishable from their neighbors. It was obviously easier for Jews to become or pass for Christians than for blacks to become or pass for whites in the Americas and the Arab world.

The New Christians' freedom, inconspicuousness, and integration into non-mercantile realms made it easier for them to blend, assimilate, and eventually disappear as a distinguishable group. The estimated number of New Christians in Portugal declined from 100,000 in 1497 to 60,000 in 1542 and 30,000 in 1604.[36] By the time the Secretary of State, Marquis de Pombal, abolished any distinction between Old and New Christians in 1772, there were very few of the latter left. With the exception of the Chuetas of Mallorca, Spain, and the Marranos of Belmonte, Portugal—who continued to exist as marginalized conversos or Crypto-Jews well into the twentieth century—memories of Jewish origin among Spaniards and Portuguese are limited to isolated families rather than larger collectivities.[37] In the twenty-first century, the notion of Sephardic *bnei anusim* (children of the coercively converted) has gained ground in the US Southwest (particularly New Mexico) and Ibero-America with Hispanics and Latin American families doing genealogical research and DNA testing to search for Jewish origins. The phenomenon contains its share of factitious identity, but it should remind us that the decline of Jewish or converso identity and culture in the Iberian Peninsula also reflected an exodus and the reconstructions of those communities elsewhere.

The Cristãos-Novos' Atlantic Exodus and Beyond

Although Iberian Jews and conversos had been emigrating in visible numbers since the late fourteenth century, several factors increased the outflow from Portugal during the sixteenth and first half of the seventeenth centuries. Some were push factors: the Lisbon 1506 anti-Jewish riots, the establishment of the Inquisition in 1536, and the decrees that followed requiring conversos to wear distinctive signs. Others fell under pull factors, like the opportunities generated by an expanding empire. The empire and the opportunities doubled during the union of the Spanish and Portuguese kingdoms between 1580 and 1640. These opportunities included the chance for the conversos to continue with their religious practices either openly and legally or furtively but in significantly more open environs.

The earliest post-1492 exodus out of Portugal headed mostly for the western African colonies. In 1493, the Portuguese Crown sent 2,000 *moços judeus*, recently arrived Spanish Jewish youths forcefully removed from their parents, along with banished convicts, to the uninhabited island of

São Tomé.[38] Despite their inauspicious beginnings, they did quite well economically. The Crown granted the youngsters land and a couple of African slaves for every five of the youth. They eventually became the richest landowners in the island, the founders of the first sugar mills, and the main slave traders from the African mainland to São Tomé and from there to the Antilles and later Brazil. Along with later New Christian arrivals and investors, they came to dominate the colony's economy to such a degree that "Jews" became a generic term for the non-black early settlers.[39] A papal nuncio, sent to the colony in 1632 to investigate the poisoning of the bishop by a Jew, complained that with that definition alone it would be impossible to find the culprit because "the major part of the people are of that blood."[40] São Tomé came to be known as a place where Crypto-Jews could find refuge and practice their religion in relative freedom.[41]

Jewish and New Christian emigration to Africa continued through the sixteenth century and beyond. When Columbus stopped in the Cape Verde islands in July 1498, he noticed a situation similar to that of São Tomé: convict settlers, black slavery, and large numbers of cristãos-novos, whom a visitor in 1510 described as "Jews without synagogues."[42] The latter worked in similar occupations as those in Portugal—merchants, *rendeiros* (tax collectors), and artisans—plus new ones related to the emergence of an Atlantic economy (slave and sugar traders). Culturally, they experienced processes of both creolization and racialization into a four-fold taxonomy of blacks, Old Christians, New Christians, and Moors.[43] The flow to the northwestern African coast increased exponentially after 1509, when King Manuel I issued a decree assuring Jews living in or moving to Safi, the main Portuguese post in Morocco, "that at no time can they be expelled from the city, nor shall they be made Christians by force or by any other means against their will."[44] In Angola, the presence of New Christians became significant and distressing enough to warrant an inquisitorial visitation in 1626.[45] New Christians could also be found in most, and probably all, of the 113 factories (trading posts) the Portuguese established in Africa and the Persian Gulf in what are today Morocco, Mauritania, Senegal, Gambia, Guinea Bissau, Guinea, Sierra Leone, Benin, Nigeria, Equatorial Guinea, Namibia, Mozambique, Malawi, Madagascar, Tanzania, Kenya, Somalia, Yemen, Oman, the United Arab Emirates, Saudi Arabia, Bahrain, Iraq, and Iran.

New Christians in Africa also headed to places beyond Portuguese jurisdiction.[46] These *lançados* (literally "launched" or individuals that cast their lot among African societies) clustered along the coast of Senegambia,

Guinea, and Sierra Leone, where they traded in kola, salt, iron, blade weapons, hides, malagueta pepper, civet cats (for their musk), and slaves.⁴⁷ A Cape Verdean trader observed their presence in the Petite Côte (south of today's Dakar), noticing they had been born in Portugal and "came here to declare themselves [Jews], because the kings of the land protect them." He added that they had to pay more tribute to rulers than other traders but did so "in order to practice in freedom their own religion and law."⁴⁸ A Portuguese traveler writing about the Wolof Kingdom in 1625 expanded on the topic:

> The Wolofs were heathens [*gentios*] but adopted the law of Mohammed less than eighty years ago. Portuguese Jews and Christians, who go there as adventurers [lançados] to trade, as well as Frenchmen, live in the kingdom. The king will not permit them to argue about whose laws are the best, declaring that each person must please himself and live according to the law they accept. If there is any quarrelling in his Kingdom they will be punished.⁴⁹

The observations demonstrate that lançados included both Old and New Christians, the existence of a high level of both religious and ethnonational pluralism, and that the position of Jews and Christians resembled that in other Muslim societies. The "tribute" may be similar to the *jizya*, the tax religious minorities (the *dhimmi* or "protected persons") paid in exchange for official recognition and protection in the Ottoman Empire.

Portuguese emigration of both Old and New Christians to Asia followed that to Africa and soon surpassed it in volume. In the half-century following 1497, the Portuguese founded scores of colonial outposts in the Arabian Peninsula, India, Ceylon, Indonesia, Southeast Asia, China, and Japan. India, however, became the main magnet. Indeed, between 1500 and 1700, three times more Portuguese headed to India than to Brazil.⁵⁰ As early as 1513, Afonso de Albuquerque, the second governor of Portuguese India, communicated his concern to the king that the influx of Portuguese and Castilian Jews could "damage the new plants" of Christianity. Jesuit dispatches during the middle decades of the century expressed the same alarm about the influence of Iberian Jews on New Christians. The latter, they alleged, were returning to Judaism, practicing circumcision, and even building synagogues.⁵¹

The suspicions had some substance. The presence of a pre-existing Jewish community descended from Yemenite and Arab traders, and of Sephardic Jewish arrivals from the Ottoman Empire, facilitated the recuperation of

Jewish practices among the New Christians. So did the transference of hypodescent notions and practices to the colonies. A French traveler in Goa in the 1680s observed how the "issue [of New Christians] are daily reproached with being in part new, which the Portuguese express by saying, *Tem parte de cristão-novo;* so that though their grandparents and great grandparents may have been Christians, these unfortunates are unable to procure admission into the ranks of the Old Christians."[52] By preserving cristãos-novos as a distinct and separate group, the practice ended up enabling their return to Judaism. Known locally as *paradesi*, "white" or "foreign" Jews, the presence of Portuguese Jews in India outlasted that of the Portuguese Empire. The Paradesi Synagogue in Cochin (now Kochi), founded in 1568, has become the oldest active synagogue in the [British] Commonwealth.

In April of 1500, a Portuguese fleet of thirteen ships and 1,500 men heading for India took an exploratory detour and "discovered" Brazil. The fact that they stayed only eleven days offers an indication of imperial priorities. Unlike the complex, technologically advanced, state societies that the Portuguese had encountered in Africa and Asia, the Tupi and Tapuia of coastal Brazil constituted premetal, prestate, premonetary societies with limited surplus or commercial production, and thus had little to trade. New Christians would play a central role in the introduction of the three resources that made the colonization of Brazil viable during its first two centuries: brazilwood, sugar, and African slaves.

Pau-brasil (a tree related to Indian redwood used mainly to make red dye and known to the Portuguese as "ember wood") provided the first significant resource, the name for the country, and the commodity for the first New Christian enterprise in Brazil. In 1501, Fernão de Loronha, the chief representative for a group of cristão-novo merchants at the Portuguese court, led the first direct official expedition to Brazil—then known as Santa Cruz.[53] Sailing a thousand miles of coastline, they discovered little of commercial use except brazilwood. Loronha's pedigree and experience alerted him to its potential. His grandfather had been part of the flow of Portuguese merchants to English ports in the decades after the Portuguese-English alliance of 1385—the longest standing alliance in history—and he had worked at a Portuguese trading house in Bruges in the 1480s. This helped him realize that the dyewood would find demand among cloth dyers in England and Flanders, and that taking the lumber from Brazil would be much cheaper than importing it from India. After assembling a consortium of Lisbon merchants and receiving a royal monopoly for the brazilwood trade in 1502, Loronha outfitted a new expedition with a largely

New Christian crew of 300, and continued to bring six ships a year until 1515, dominating the economy of Brazil during this period.[54] Some authors have claimed that his reluctance, as a Jew, to call the new land after the True Cross, led him to rename it Brasil. This would have been quite a coincidence because the crew of both expeditions included Amerigo Vespucci, after whom the entire hemisphere would later be named. However, the change most likely just reflected the Portuguese habit of naming the places they discovered after the commodities they found, like Madeira, the Ivory Coast, and the Spice Islands.

The arrival of sugar and slaves in Brazil followed similar connections of Atlantic New Christian networks and royal monopolies. In 1515, when their brazilwood monopoly ended, the Loronha group brought the first sugar cane planted in Brazil from the islands of Madeira and São Tomé. Four years later, Fernão de Loronha became the first person granted a royal contract to supply slaves to Elmina for reexport to São Tomé, where in 1526, his son Duarte and a group of cristão-novo investors bought all the sugar produced in the King's plantations for the next three years. Around the same time, the island became an entrepôt for the export of slaves to Lisbon, the Spanish Antilles, and Cartagena. Around the middle of the century, Brazil entered the list. Many of the Spanish Jewish refugee boys taken from their parents and shipped to São Tomé in 1493, or their offspring, were now exporting not only slaves to Brazil but also the São Tomé model based on plantations and black slavery—rather than that of Madeira which was based on small farms and free, white family labor. From the 1540s onward, they began moving first to Pernambuco, then Bahia, and later São Paulo. One of these New Christian merchants, Diogo Fernandes, built one of the first sugar mills in the country in Pernambuco in 1542. His wife, Branca Dias, would later fall prey to inquisitors as a Judaizer.[55] As in Africa, the process incorporated New Christian traders and investors in places like Lisbon, Seville, Antwerp, Livorno, London, and later Amsterdam, investors who were usually relatives of those in Brazil. Most of the sugar mill mechanics and skilled workers were Jewish or cristãos-novos.[56] New Christians accounted for one-fifth of the early population of Bahia but for one-fourth of its plantation owners.[57] They dominated the slave trade in the South Atlantic "almost in its totality."[58] Those in Brazil had come mainly from São Tomé and Cape Verde in the early years. Later, they also arrived from Angola, Madeira, the Azores, Portugal, and other sites in the New Christian diaspora, usually circulating between these diasporic nodes rather than staying put in one of them. They were thus both widespread and peripatetic.

Not surprisingly then, the association of Portuguese Jews and New Christians with sugar and slavery appears elsewhere. As early as 1472, when sugar production was still limited to Madeira and the Canary Islands, Portuguese merchants were complaining about the monopoly held by Jewish dealers on its trade.[59] In Pernambuco during the Dutch occupation, Jews accounted for one-third of the white population but for two-thirds of those buying sugar plantations at auctions, including the largest one, owned by Moyses Navarro, a noncommissioned officer who arrived with the Dutch army.[60] Sephardic Jews accounted for less than 2 percent of the population of Amsterdam but for 45 percent of all slave-trading contracts at the city's market between 1596 and 1675 and were equally overrepresented in sugar trading.[61] In 1680, the proportion of Jewish families in Port Royal, Jamaica, that owned slaves (90 percent) nearly doubled that of non-Jewish white households (52 percent).[62] In Barbados during the same year, 93 percent of Jewish households owned slaves.[63] Eight years later, the local council prohibited "persons of the Hebrew Nation" from owning "more than one Negro" because their practice of purchasing slaves to hire them out had increased the cost of labor for the local planters.[64] In 1680s Suriname, 40 percent of Jewish heads of households owned slave-run sugar plantations, and each Jewish family lived with four to six slaves.[65] In Curaçao, one-third of Jewish households owned sugar plantations in 1710, even though they were mainly a mercantile group.[66] Of the Portuguese engaged in the slave trade in Lima between 1611 and 1650, at least 67 percent were New Christians suspected of Crypto-Judaism.[67] During the same period, Lusitanian cristãos-novos established a veritable monopoly of the slave trade in Cartagena, the principal port for the traffic to Spanish America at the time.[68]

This spread of Portuguese Jews, New Christians, and sugar and slave trading ensued from two forces. The one pushing the Jews (but not the New Christians) was the Luso-Brazilian reconquest of Pernambuco from the Dutch in 1654. For a quarter of a century, more than 1,500 Jews, who accounted for half of the white civilian population, had lived there openly. Judaism had thrived. The first synagogue in the New World opened in Recife in 1636. The Portuguese-born Isaac Aboab da Fonseca, descendant of the last Jewish Sage of Castile and himself the ḥakham of the Sephardic community in Amsterdam, came over to become "the first American Rabbi." After the defeat of the Dutch, some Jews stayed in Brazil living as

Crypto-Jews. Others returned or moved to Amsterdam, including Aboab da Fonseca, who infamously would excommunicate Baruch Spinoza for heresy. One group headed for Livorno, which had, at the time, the second largest Sephardic community in Western Europe. Most, though, moved to Dutch, British, and French colonies in the Americas where they were usually welcomed because of their knowledge of the sugar industry right when sugar plantations were appearing in those colonies. Joined by Sephardim from the Netherlands and Britain, a group of 1,200 founded Jodensavanne, a semiautonomous Jewish rural colony in Suriname envisioned as "a second Brazil."[69] They came to account for 5 percent of the white population in Barbados, 10 percent in Jamaica, and 35 percent in Curaçao.[70] From Curaçao, some moved to Venezuela in 1715 where they established what may be the only synagogue in colonial Spanish American history.[71] They also headed for Saint Kitts, the French colonies of Martinique and Guadeloupe, Dutch New York, Rhode Island, Savannah, and to Charleston, South Carolina—which by 1800 had a 2,000-strong Jewish community, the largest in the United States at the time.

The spread of Portuguese New Christians (as opposed to Jews), on the other hand, sprung from the union of the Spanish and Portuguese Crowns between 1580 and 1640. This represented a dynastic union. Portugal officially became a sixth kingdom along with the kingdoms of Castile, Aragon, Italy, Flanders, and the Indies, all under the Habsburg monarch but with their own government councils and alien laws so that a national of one kingdom was a foreigner in the others. Yet, it made it easier to migrate because de facto the "natives of the kingdoms of Spain" enjoyed preference over more foreign "foreigners."[72] Besides, as Spanish conversos had done after 1492, the Portuguese cristãos-novos figured myriad ways to circumvent restrictions: faking documents, bribing officials, evading authorities, enlisting as sailors and soldiers, or going as servants of well-heeled passengers and going AWOL. Spanish American archives are full of documents showing Portuguese who disembarked as servants, but began working as merchants soon after arrival.[73] It helped that almost all Portuguese New Christians spoke Spanish. So did the fact that many of them left for the Indies from Seville after having lived for some time in Spain, drawn by the economic opportunities that American silver had generated there.[74] The increase in the African slave trade to Brazil and Spanish America also made it easier for them to leave from the Portuguese and Spanish Atlantic islands. By the early seventeenth century, Portuguese accounted for more than a tenth of the population in Mexico City, Cartagena, Lima, Buenos Aires, and other commercial hubs in the Spanish Indies.

This migratory wave turned "Portuguese" into a synonym of Jew in Spain and Spanish America during the seventeenth century. A contemporary vulgarity had it that "a Portuguese was born of a Jew's fart." The irony may have been undetectable to contemporary observers, but it was still telling. After all, most of *these* Portuguese, including Baruch Spinoza whose family hailed from Burgos, were actually recent descendants of Spaniards since there had been relatively few Jews in Portugal before the 1492 exodus from Spain. Equally ironic was that diasporic nostalgia had engendered in the Portuguese New Christians an emotional attachment to Spain that must have been rare in a country where local and regional identities still predominated. They used Portuguese at home and even in synagogue sermons but Spanish in formal settings and as the language of intellectual and literary expression, partly because of its prominent international status at the time. Additionally, unlike the Sephardim that left for North Africa and the Ottoman Empire—whose Spanish became a more hybrid Ladino, mixed with Arabic, Turkish, and other local languages—the Portuguese New Christians, Crypto-Jews, and Jews spoke and wrote standard Portuguese and Castilian and continued to do so for centuries. The inscriptions on more than 2,500 tombstones in Curaçao's old Sephardic cemetery offer silent but telling evidence. A bit over 71 percent are engraved in Portuguese, 20 percent in Spanish, 4 percent in English, only 1 percent in Hebrew and 1 percent in Dutch (the official languages of the religion and the polity), only one in Yiddish, and none in Ladino (the supposed language of the Sephardim).[75] Similarly, Portuguese Jews in the Netherlands, France, Italy, and Britain usually wrote and published Jewish sacred texts in Castilian rather than Hebrew or the local languages.[76] Cecil Roth referred to Spanish in this context as "a semi-sacred language" through which most conversos rediscovered Judaism, adding that "the Jew of Amsterdam, whether affirming his faith or rebelling, was above all a Spaniard."[77]

The wave of Portuguese migration may have also helped to revive Judaism in Spain and Spanish America. Most historians agree that by the late sixteenth century or earlier, Judaism had become residual in both places after five generations without Jewish texts and institutions, the cumulative effect of even low intermarriage rates and slow but persistent assimilation.[78] Other historians agree but downplay the religious impact of the Portuguese immigrants and reject the automatic assumption that they were

Crypto-Jews.⁷⁹ The latter is incontrovertible. Obviously not all Portuguese immigrants were of Jewish origin and not all, or even most, New Christians were secret Jews. On the other hand, there is plenty of evidence that the number of both New Christians and Crypto-Jews significantly increased toward the end of the sixteenth century and that this reflected the surge of Portuguese arrivals. Data from Portuguese America and Africa show that the migration rates of New Christians doubled or tripled those of Old Christians and it is difficult to think why the gap would be significantly different in the flow to Spanish America. Portuguese migrants to Spanish America did not originate in any particular region of the country in stark contrast to Old Christian Portuguese migrants to Brazil who came overwhelmingly from a few northern districts—an indirect indication that most of the former must have been New Christians. If anything, the migration rate of Portuguese New Christians has been likely underestimated. As María Navarrete has shown, many of the migrants counted as Spaniards were the Spanish-born children of Portuguese cristão-novo migrants in Spain.⁸⁰ The number of Inquisition cases did shoot up during the period both in Spain and in the Spanish Indies, and so did (1) the proportion of the cases that related to Judaism, and (2) the proportion of the latter that concerned a person of Portuguese birth or ancestry. For example, of the penitents in the Lima 1639 auto-da-fé, the largest in Spanish American history, 73 percent were Portuguese and another 20 percent children of Portuguese-born in either Spain or the Indies.⁸¹ Almost all of the thirty-seven suspected Jews sentenced to death by the Lima Inquisition were of Portuguese origin.⁸²

So, there is little question that a disproportionately high number of the Portuguese immigrants to Spanish America were either converted or Crypto-Jews, that to some degree they reenergized a religion that seemed extinct (there is even evidence of proselytizing among the conversos), and that inquisitorial repression targeted them specifically. But we have no way of knowing about the religious beliefs, practices, identities, and the like of the 99 percent of Portuguese immigrants who never had any encounter with the Inquisition. When it comes to Judaism in the Iberian World, the majority is invisible to a greater degree than just about everywhere else.

The Jewish Experience in the Iberian World in a Comparative Perspective

The most obvious trait that distinguishes the Jewish experience in the early modern Iberian world from elsewhere is precisely its invisibility. It is a hidden history. Jews endured discrimination in many other places at the time and often greater violence. They had to pay special taxes and did not have the rights of other subjects in the Ottoman Empire. Cossacks massacred tens of thousands of Jews during the 1648–1657 Khmelnytsky Uprising in the Polish-Lithuanian Commonwealth. The Zaydi Imamate of Yemen expelled them en masse in 1679. The supposedly tolerant Dutch did not allow Jews to settle outside of Amsterdam, and even there, they endured an array of restrictions lifted only with the emancipation decree at the end of the early modern period (1796).[83] Yet, in all of these cases, Jews were completely visible.

For the early modern Iberian world, therefore, we can only see isolated trees, raise questions, and speculate about the hidden forest. The lack of synagogues presumably would be the second-most distinguishing trait of the Jewish experience in the Iberian world. Yet, we know of at least one within Spain's jurisdiction in the Americas founded in the 1690s in the town of Tucacas on the northern coast of Venezuela by a group of Sephardic Jews from Livorno who had settled in Curaçao. It lasted for more than two decades because the local population, including the colonial authorities, found in these Jewish smugglers an optimal outlet for their cacao and a source of well-priced consumer goods.[84] Was this a singular tree? Could there be others in similar cases—peripheral, isolated regions with weak state control and locals that benefit from it? Did New Christians in northeastern Brazil have some way of crossing into Dutch controlled Pernambuco to attend services in the oldest synagogue in the Americas? How much access did cristãos-novos have to the synagogues of non-Portuguese Jews in Cochin and Goa? What about the generational back and forth of lançado New Christians in Senegambia? Living beyond Portuguese jurisdiction, they were able to return to Judaism and even erected a "synagogue" with a self-appointed rabbi who had managed to buy a few copies of the Torah. Their Eurafrican children with African women saw themselves as Jews, and outsiders considered them as such. Yet, French Capuchin missionaries converted them or their descendants to Christianity around the middle of the seventeenth century, turning this into a two- to three-generation return to some form of Judaism.[85]

We also know that there were plenty of "Jews without synagogues," as a traveler described Cape Verde's cristãos-novos in the early 1500s. Crypto-Jews were more than a figment of the distorted imagination of inquisitors. Over 90 percent of the New Christian males condemned by the Inquisition in Spanish America as Crypto-Jews had been circumcised.[86] We do not know if any of them had the procedure done in the Indies. But we know of cases where the condemned had it done in places where Judaism was legal (Amsterdam and Salonica), where colonial control was less tight (Angola), and places that were just beyond imperial jurisdiction (Senegambia and parts of Indian Kerala).

These bits and pieces can help us understand why the Inquisition was so concerned about the Portuguese New Christians. Portugal's Empire had been significantly smaller in terms of territory than that of its Iberian neighbor. But it was more globally spread and infinitely more diverse. It had Spanish-style land occupation in Brazil, the Atlantic islands, and India. It also had hundreds of outposts throughout the Atlantic and Pacific in all sorts of milieus: surrounded by Hindus, Muslims, Buddhists, animists, or all; within state societies like China and India, more dense and complex than Europe; and abutting preagriculturalist groups in Mozambique and the Spice (Maluku) Islands. And then, with the Iberian Union, the global space of the New Christian diaspora doubled. How could the Inquisition—or for that matter the most sophisticated of intelligence agencies, say the Stasi—control a group that is everywhere and invisible at the same time and, to boot, cryptic and hyperconnected, marginal and economically powerful? While the Inquisition attempted to restrict invisible Jews, secular authorities were warning the Crown of the threat New Christians' economic clout posed to their authority, in part because the level of their indebtedness to New Christian bankers.[87]

Historians and observers have had an equally hard time figuring out this elusive group. A Dutch savant described the cristãos-novos as "Roman Catholics without faith and Jews without knowledge, but wishing to be Jews," which does not differ much in essence from the "Jews without synagogues" definition.[88] Israel Salvator Révah, a French Hispanist born in Berlin to a Sephardic family from Salonica, defined conversos as "potential Jews." He then divided them into three groups: sincere Catholics who usually married Old Christians; those without religious convictions who could be one thing or another (or none) depending on circumstances and material interest; and those who practiced a "Marrano religion" in secrecy. The latter could also equate to "Jews without synagogues" because if they had synagogues, it would then just be Judaism rather than a "Marrano religion." The not-so-hidden assumption here is that Jews without institutional Judaism can be potential Jews but not real Jews. This has led others to define New Christians as an ethnic rather than religious group, "cultural Jews" *avant la lettre,* like the thousands of "Jews" from New York to Buenos Aires who have never stepped into a synagogue. New Christians definitely had all the markings of a diasporic ethnic group: shared origins, language, experiences, memories, and transregional social networks. I argue, nonetheless, that the distinctive cultural and socioeconomic features in the making of New Christians in the early modern Iberian world also produced a strong religious component.

The element of class/occupation selection that we noticed in the assimilation process in Portugal continued in the diaspora with important consequences for the religiosity of the New Christians. Anita Novinsky found that the New Christians' assimilation to Luso-Catholic culture and society in Bahia was highest on both ends of the socioeconomic spectrum.[89] Poorer workers and artisans tended to mix with the population of color. Rich landlords and sugar mill owners tended to marry into upper-class Old Christian families. In both cases, they would integrate into local society and drop out of the New Christian community. On the other hand, those in the middle, New Christian merchants who moved back and forth between Brazil, Portugal, and other nodes of the Sephardic commercial diaspora, were the least likely to marry out of the group and the least likely to become actual Christians. As had already happened back in Portugal, the process steadily turned New Christians into a less heterogeneous, more mercantile, and more Jewish group with each generation. Its social structure was not completely horizontal. It included magnates and mariners, wealthy bankers and modest bookkeepers. But it was way flatter than the social structures of the external societies.

In a symbiotic process, trade (particularly maritime trade) became a marker of Jewishness and vice versa. As in most other mercantile diasporas, trading and dealing began to be seen as an inherent group trait, celebrated within the group as a virtue, distrusted by outsiders as a threat, and fodder for popular humor for both. This growing association of trade with Portuguese Jews and New Christians surfaced in linguistic shifts. The term *nação* (nation) historically referred to a collectivity of foreign traders, say the Genoese Nation or the Flemish Nation in Seville or London. The first uses in reference to Lusitanian Jews appeared as "Portuguese of the Hebrew Nation." As the association of Jews with commerce increased, it shortened to "Portuguese Nation," and eventually just "Nation," as if Jews and merchants were one and the same.

The system of trust, insurance, and credit, essential for a trading diaspora before the emergence of international legal structures that could guarantee property and contracts, rested on intra-ethnic cooperation, arbitration, and policing. This also had an impact on religion. Belonging to the group was a requirement for being a long-distance trader, banker, or the like. Jewishness was a requirement for group membership. And Jewishness in turn required some degree of Judaism, even if not in a particularly strict manner. Indeed, in an example of religious syncretism, the veneration of Saint Moses among cristão-novo merchants became so common that outsiders often thought it was a Jewish saint.

Long-distance trade also had an impact on religious practice by expanding the middle spaces between a regular Jewish institutional life and that of "Jews without synagogues." Even if one resided in a city where Judaism was not legal, say Caracas, the odds of spending some time in places where there were synagogues were relatively high given the average level of mobility in the business. In this particular example, it would have taken an eight-hour trip by sail, with two more options within two-day's travel. It would take less for those in Seville to get to Tangier, or for those in Le Havre to reach London. At some point, most of these people would be at a place with a synagogue even if there were none where they normally resided. Occasional access to religious institutions and rabbis, even if rare, could serve to reinforce their Judaism, and even that of their family.

In this context, the connection of New Christians and the Middle Passage acquires an unexpected religious connection. The beliefs and religious practices of Crypto-Jews and African slaves turned colonial Latin America into a de facto multireligious society despite the official lack of religious freedom.

Besides their "Jews without synagogues" condition, cultural homogeneity would have to be the most distinguishing marker of the Jewish/converso experience in the Iberian world. Most Jewish societies were cultural composites. A shtetl in Eastern Europe could include Galician and Bessarabian Jews; Yiddish, Ukrainian, and Moldavian speakers; Haredim and liberal rebels. The twenty-five Jewish families in Famagusta, Cyprus, in the 1560s split into Sicilian, Sephardic, and Levantine congregations. The nomenclature for Jews in sixteenth-century Italy included *vecchi* (old)—those there since Roman times; *theutonic* [sic]—the descendants of those expelled from the Rhineland during the Black Death; *levantini*—arrivals from the Middle East; *spagnoli*—Spaniards that had arrived in 1492 but strongly implied Jewishness; and *portoghesi*—like "Spaniards," ostensibly a national term but, in practice, a synonym for converso.[90]

The double meaning of the term Sephardic and the conceptual Ashkenazic/Sephardic dichotomy has obscured this diversity. The term has a narrow ethnic meaning (those from Sepharad, i.e., Iberia) and a broader one for those using the liturgical tradition that the ethnic Sephardim diffused after 1492. However, a western-centric metanarrative of Iberian Sephardic exiles populating northern Africa and the Middle East has muddled the semantic difference and has erased the largest Jewish group in the early modern period: the *Mustaʿarabim* (Jews from the Arab lands) that included Mizrahi (eastern) Jews and the Maghrebim of Morocco and Algeria. The Sephardic exiles had enough education and prestige to influence religious rituals, but not much beyond that because they represented a small minority of the Jewish population in most destinations. Most *Toshavim* (pre-1492 Moroccan Jews) continued to have their own separate social circles and institutions well into the twentieth century. Tunisians made a strong and enduring distinction between the *Twansa* (the "indigenous" Jews) and *L'grana* (the economically dominant Sephardim who arrived, not directly from Spain, but after a stay of a generation or two in Livorno).

Diversity is apparent even in Salonica, the "Jerusalem of the Balkans" and presumably the most ethnically Sephardic city in the diaspora. In 1430, it had a large Jewish population (17,300) made up of Romaniots (Greek-speaking Jews previously expelled from Thrace, Bulgaria, and Anatolia) and arrivals from the Rhineland, Hungary, Provence, Bohemia, Sicily, and other places. The Spanish exiles arrived not only with education and prestige but also in high enough numbers that it enabled them to Sephardize the rest of the Jewish population, which ended up speaking a hybridized Ladino and touting their "Spanish roots." Greeks and Turks expressed astonishment at the confidence and even haughtiness of the Spaniards because the previous Jewish population had usually tried to keep a low profile. When Spanish scholars visited the city in the late nineteenth century, they were thrilled to find a mini-Iberia. But even in this overseas Sepharad, the process of Sephardization had taken several generations. A century after the arrival of the Sephardim, a local rabbi could still assert: "in Salonika, every [Jewish] man speaks his own native tongue. When the exiled arrived, each vernacular group founded a congregation . . . each [functioning as] an independent city."[91]

The high degree of homogeneity in the cristão-novo diaspora represented the polar opposite of the standard intra-Jewish cultural diversity mentioned above and of the composite character of those communities. They shared the same origins (in Portugal, and their deeper roots in Spain), the same collective memories of forced exile and conversion, the same linguistic combination—Portuguese for quotidian, family use; Spanish for formal occasions and sacred texts; and local languages if, or when, living outside of the Iberian world. They shared the nostalgia of exile and a yearning for a Spain that became more mythical with each generation and a similar emotional longing for the faith of their forebears where they could not practice it openly.

Socioeconomic processes augmented the cohesiveness of the group. Social and business lives overlapped. Partners, agents, and factors were usually family members, in-laws, or close friends, sometimes living close by but more often spread in port cities throughout the world. Families tried to marry their sons and daughters to current or prospective business partners. In the larger cities, the New Christians congregated in specific districts. Some merchants maintained large houses where several related families lived together. Fictive kinship and degrees of separation, or the "cousin of my cousin effect," enabled the system to work at a global scale. If a merchant in, say, Guatemala did not know anyone in Goa, a friend would likely know, and if not, a friend of a friend might help. Indeed, the "potential Jews" of the early modern Iberian world may have been the most culturally homogenous group in the long history of the Jewish people. By the end of the early modern period, however, external economic and political trends would diminish the New Christian as both a mercantile diaspora and an ethnic group.

The Twilight of the New Christians

At its peak during the union of the Iberian Crowns (1580–1640), the New Christian trade and finance network literally girdled the globe. Its major nodes in Europe included Lisbon, Porto, Seville, Madrid, Medina del Campo, Barcelona, Livorno, Antwerp, Amsterdam, Hamburg, Salonica, and Istanbul; in Asia: Goa, Cochin, Malacca, Macau, Nagasaki, and Manila connecting to Acapulco/Mexico and Lima on the other side of the Pacific.

On the Atlantic, one would find New Christian enclaves along the African coast and islands, in Bahia, Pernambuco, Olinda, Recife, Buenos Aires, Cartagena, Curaçao, Barbados, and Jamaica. What explains this is not just the entrepreneurship of the Sephardim. Non-Sephardic Oriental Jews, Melkite Greeks, and Maronite Lebanese were equally enterprising in the Ottoman Empire. German Jews had become synonymous with peddling. Armenian traders had spread from Italy to India. But unlike New Christians, none of these groups were part of the largest and most globally spread ultramarine empire of its time. Timing was equally important. The New Christian mercantile diaspora would have been less mighty a century later, when the growth of stock companies, large non-ethnic shipping, trading, insurance, and banking enterprises, and the expansion of legal mechanisms to assure property and contracts made commercial arrangements based on ethnic trust less important if not obsolete.

During its heyday, the New Christians' commercial diaspora had also occupied a central place in the development of the world economy. Their overrepresentation in slave and sugar trading reflects that fact, plus their particular imperial association, and timing. These two "commodities" were the most important in Atlantic and global trade during the early modern period other than silver, which the Spanish Crown monopolized. The Portuguese dominated the trade in slaves and sugar during the first 150 years of the Atlantic economy, when the entirety of the slave traffic took place within the Iberian world. In turn, New Christians—who comprised three-fourths of the Portuguese merchants—dominated the slave traffic even beyond that proportion due to their overrepresentation in the Lusitanian colonies in Africa, the Atlantic islands, and Brazil, and, after 1580, the Spanish American ports of Cartagena, Veracruz, and Buenos Aires. Yet, they ended up accounting for a small proportion of the entire slave trade because 92 percent of it took place after 1650, when the French and, particularly, the English progressively replaced the Portuguese, and thus the New Christians, as the principal traffickers in the Middle Passage.

The transformation associated with industrial and financial capitalism, nation states, and the concentration of economic power during the nineteenth century left no space for global ethnic mercantile networks in the Atlantic and the West. The best illustration of this shift is another Jewish international trade network: the "white slavery" or international prostitution rings run by Eastern European Jews during the late nineteenth and early twentieth centuries. Its geographic range did not reach the scope of that of the Sephardim, but it was still impressive. It branched into the Middle East,

North and South Africa, the United Kingdom, the United States, Brazil, and, particularly, Argentina. Yet, while the cristãos-novos merchants were at the core of the world-dominant Atlantic economy and at the forefront in the development of mercantile capitalism, the Ashkenazic traffickers could not have been more marginal and inconsequential. Indeed, given the continuous concentration of wealth and power in multinational corporations, it seems impossible that anything remotely resembling the New Christian trade diaspora would ever appear in the West or in any other place for that matter. Except, we should never say never.

The decline of the mercantile diaspora also undermined New Christian identity, and external political changes accelerated the trend. As New Christians became increasingly connected to global commerce and thus occupationally homogeneous, international trading and its related mobility and lifestyle had progressively become a basic marker of collective identity. The withering of the global trading network and its concomitant way of life, therefore, deprived the group of one of its most defining features of affiliation. At the same time, the abolition of legal distinctions between Old and New Christians in the Iberian world in the late eighteenth century, and, soon after, Latin American independence, whose ensuing republican regimes defined membership in the polity by secular citizenship rather than religion, furthered the absorption of an already shrinking group. The emancipation of Jews in France, the Netherlands, and the United Kingdom during the same period had a similar effect on the Sephardim of Western Europe, most of whom were New Christians.

All of this bifurcated the Western Sephardim into Jews and non-Jews, erasing interstitiality and, thus, in-between groups like the New Christians, who were of Jewish origins and felt Jewish but often existed outside of institutional Judaism. Some remained or became observant—or at least fully self-aware—Jews. Over time, however, others became practicing Christians, nonreligious, or even devout atheists, married other like-minded folks, and eventually vanished as a distinct group. In this new binary world, spaces for "Marrano religion," "potential Jews," and "Jews without synagogues" shrank almost to the point of disappearance, diminishing in the process the numbers of the Western Sephardim. Already by the late 1700s, these Sephardim had become greatly outnumbered in Paris, Amsterdam, London, and New York by poorer Ashkenazic arrivals from Central Europe. The outnumbering would reach a new level in the nineteenth century when the Ashkenazic population in Eastern Europe quintupled and large numbers of them began moving westward.

The ethnic Eastern Sephardim, the descendants of Iberian exiles—mainly Spaniards—who had settled in North Africa and the Ottoman Empire after their expulsion, experienced a similar diminution. In a few places, like Salonica, Sarajevo, and Istanbul—where they had arrived in large enough numbers—they had managed to Sephardize the preexisting Jewish population either completely or to a significant degree. Elsewhere, however, their relative numbers were too small to accomplish this, and despite their sense of cultural superiority, ethnic Sephardim became slowly, but progressively, absorbed by the Mizrahi or Musta'arabi majority. They remained Sephardic in the generic sense of religious rituals but not in the ethnic sense of language, culture, awareness of origin, memories, marriage and socializing patterns, identity, and just about anything else that makes an ethnic group. In regions like the former Yugoslavia and Bulgaria, the pressure came from large numbers of Ashkenazic arrivals and assimilation to local cultures. As late as 1895, 80 percent of the Jews in Serbia spoke Ladino as their first language. By 1931, less than 30 percent did so.[92]

Nevertheless, during the two centuries after 1492, the ethnic Sephardim helped shape, for better or for worse, the early modern world, and the twenty-first century has witnessed a Sephardic ethnic revival. In Israel, where the majority of the Sephardim ended up after World War II, the term Mizrahi has steadily become the catch-all rubric for the non-Ashkenazi, freeing "Sephardi" from that role and allowing it to regain its original meaning (Jews from Iberia), making the ethnic Sephardim both more self-aware and more visible in the process. The 2015 Spanish and Portuguese laws granting citizenship to Sephardic Jews had a similar effect because they required proof of Iberian origin and cultural connection. The large presence of Latin American Jews in Israel (even though they are mostly Ashkenazic), and the popularization of Latin American music, telenovelas, football (soccer), and other cultural forms has fomented interest in all things Hispanic. So have the cultural prestige of Spain in design, film, haute cuisine, and as a favorite tourist destination for Israelis.

By the time of the Spanish and Portuguese citizenship laws, the ethnic Sephardim accounted for less than one-tenth of global Jewry. What is striking, however, is that for more than five centuries, so many retained their identity, language, memories, in many cases even the keys to their ancestral houses, and what must have been a bittersweet longing for a homeland that expelled them. Equally striking, they did so while living as a minority of the population and, outside of the Iberian world, mostly as a minority of local Jewry. One does not have to posit Sephardic exceptionalism to admit it is difficult to think of a comparable case in the long history of diasporas and exiles, particularly if one remembers that Hebrew had disappeared as a spoken language by 200 CE, less than two centuries after the Jewish dispersion through the Roman Empire.

Notes

1. William D. Phillips and Carla Rahn Phillips, *The Worlds of Christopher Columbus* (New York: Cambridge University Press, 1992), 145; Norman Roth, *Conversos, Inquisition, and the Expulsion of the Jews from Spain* (Madison: University of Wisconsin Press, 2002), xi.

2. William and Carla Phillips in *The Worlds of Columbus*, 91, assert "the persistent notion that the Colombo family was secretly Jewish or had converted from Judaism has no credible basis in the historical record." Felipe Fernández-Armesto, *Columbus on Himself* (Indianapolis: Hackett, 2010), 34–35, is equally dismissive of these and similar claims about Columbus's non-Genoese origins, and so are most professional historians.

3. The term New Christians is often used as a synonym of *conversos,* Jews who converted to Christianity in Spain in the centuries up to 1492. Here we make a distinction because, unlike conversos, who had a choice between leaving or converting and had converted over centuries, the New Christians, as we will later explain, had no such choice and rather than converting, *were converted* at once and by fiat.

4. Cecil Roth, *A History of the Marranos,* rev. ed. (Philadelphia: Jewish Publication Society of America, 1941), 272.

5. Antonio Domínguez Ortiz, *Los judeoconversos en España y América* (Madrid: Ediciones Istmo, 1971), 129.

6. Domínguez Ortiz, *Los judeoconversos,* 131.

7. Jean-Pierre Dedieu, *L'administration de la foi: L'Inquisition de Tolède, XVIe–XVIIe siècles* (Madrid: Casa de Velázquez, 1989), 31–33, 240.

8. José C. Moya, "The Iberian Atlantic, 1492–2010," in *Theorising the Ibero-American Atlantic,* eds. Harald Braun and Lisa Vollendorf (Leiden: Brill, 2013), 51–73.

9. Calculated from various estimates in Joseph Pérez, *History of a Tragedy: The Expulsion of the Jews from Spain* (Urbana: University of Illinois Press, 2007), 14–15, and other sources.

10. Harry Friedenwald, *The Jews and Medicine: Essays,* vol. 2 (Baltimore, MD: Johns Hopkins University Press, 1944), 695–97.

11. Günter Böhm, "Crypto-Jews and New Christians in Colonial Peru and Chile" in *The Jews and the Expansion of Europe to the West, 1450–1800,* eds. Paolo Bernardini and Norman Fiering (New York: Berghahn Books, 2001), 203–12. Stanley M. Hordes, *To the End of the Earth: A History of the Crypto-Jews of New Mexico* (New York: Columbia University Press, 2005).

12. A.J.R. Russell-Wood, "Before Columbus: Portugal's African Prelude to the Middle Passage and Contribution to Discourse on Race and Slavery," in *Spain, Portugal and the Atlantic Frontier of Medieval Europe,* ed. José Juan Lopez-Portillo (London: Routledge, 2013), 259.

13. Joaquim Mendes dos Remedios, *Os judeus em Portugal*, vol. 1 (Coimbra: F. França Amado, 1895), 211–12 on the migration of Jews from Castile to Portugal after the late fourteenth century.

14. José A. Rodrigues da Silva Tavim, "In the Shadow of Empire: Portuguese Jewish Communities in the Sixteenth Century," in *Portuguese Colonial Cities in the Early Modern World*, ed. Liam M. Brockey (London: Routledge, 2016), 17–40.

15. António de Almeida Mendes, "Portugal, Morocco and Guinea: Reconfiguration of the North Atlantic at the End of the Middle Ages," in *From Al-Andalus to the Americas, 13th-17th Centuries*, eds. Thomas F. Glick et al. (Leiden: Brill, 2018), 401–28.

16. Estimates of the number of Spanish Jews moving to Portugal in 1492 run between 30 and 120 thousand. Maria Ferro Tavares, *Os judeus em Portugal no século XV* (Lisbon: Universidade Nova de Lisboa, 1982–84), 270–71.

17. João Lúcio de Azevedo, *História dos Cristãos Novos Portugueses* (Lisbon: Classica, 1921), 21.

18. E. H. Lindo, *The History of the Jews of Spain and Portugal* (London: Longman, Brown, Green and Longmans, Paternoster Row, 1848), 306. Mendes dos Remédios, *Os judeus em Portugal*, vol. 1, 115–25.

19. Lindo, *The History of Jews*, 321; Cecil Roth, *A History of the Marranos*, 55.

20. Norman Roth, *Conversos, Inquisition, and the Expulsion of the Jews from Spain*, xx, 376. Eva A. Uchmany estimated that "two-thirds of the Hebrew nation [in Spain] had converted to Christianity, by coercion or voluntarily" by 1492. See Eva A. Uchmany, "The Participation of New Christians and Crypto-Jews in the Conquest, Colonization, and Trade of Spanish America, 1521–1660," in *The Jews and the Expansion of Europe to the West, 1450–1800*, eds. Paolo Bernardini and Norman Fiering (New York: Berghahn Books, 2001), 186–202.

21. Miriam Bodian, "Men of the Nation: The Shaping of Converso Identity in Early Modern Europe," *Past & Present* 143 (May 1994): 58–59.

22. Carlos Carrete Parrondo, "Nostalgia for the Past (and for the Future?) among Castilian Judeoconversos," in *Jews, Christians, and Muslims in the Mediterranean World after 1492*, ed. Alisa Meyuhas Ginio (London: Routledge, 1993), 25–43.

23. Cecil Roth, *A History of the Marranos*, 21.

24. Stuart B. Schwartz, "Prata, açúcar e escravos: de como o imperio restaurou Portugal," *Tempo* (January 2008): 201–23.

25. Daviken Studnicki-Gizbert, *A Nation upon the Open Sea: Portugal's Atlantic Diaspora and the Crisis of the Spanish Empire, 1492–1640* (New York: Oxford University Press, 2007), 24.

26. António José Saraiva, *Inquisição e cristãos-novos* (Porto: Editorial Inova, 1969).

27. Bishop Alfonso de Cartagena (1384–1456), himself a descendant of conversos, expressed the normative Catholic position in these terms: "The Israelites, like the gentiles, upon entering the Catholic faith through the gate of sacred baptism endure not as two peoples or two different lineages, but from the offspring of one and the other is created a new people." Cited in Antonio Feros, *Speaking of Spain: The Evolution of Race and Nation in the Hispanic World* (Cambridge: Harvard University Press, 2017), 83.

28. Some historians have ventured into explorations of the place of race in the expul-

sion and conversion of Iberian Jews while trying to avoid dichotomies. David Nirenberg urged his fellow historians to transcend both facile rejections of the racial elements in *limpieza de sangre* and seeing these as a precursor to modern biological racism. "Was There Race before Modernity?" in Miriam Eliav-Feldon, Benjamin Isaac, and Joseph Ziegler, eds., *The Origins of Racism in the West* (Cambridge: Cambridge University Press, 2009), 232-64. Jonathan Elukin warned about the dangers of importing modern language of racism into medieval realities but also acknowledged that ideas about Jews' physical distinctiveness, lineage, and immutability made it easier for Christians to think of Jews as unassimilable. "From Jew to Christian? Conversion and Immutability in Medieval Europe," in *Varieties of Religious Conversion in the Middle Ages*, ed. James Muldoon (Gainesville: University Press of Florida, 1997), 171-89.

29. Sara Lipton, *Dark Mirror: The Medieval Origins of Anti-Jewish Iconography* (New York: Metropolitan Books, 2014).

30. Studnicki-Gizbert, *A Nation upon the Open Sea*, 24.

31. Cecil Roth, *A History of the Marranos*, 397n3.

32. Jonathan S. Ray, *After Expulsion: 1492 and the Making of Sephardic Jewry* (New York: New York University Press, 2003), 64-65.

33. Cecil Roth, "Marranos and Racial Antisemitism: A Study in Parallels," *Jewish Social Studies* 2, no. 3 (1940): 239-48.

34. Edna Bonacich, "A Theory of Middleman Minorities," *American Sociological Review* 38, no. 5 (1973): 583-94.

35. Tobias Oliver Green, "Masters of Difference: Creolization and the Jewish Presence in Cabo Verde, 1497-1672" (Ph.D. diss., University of Birmingham, UK, 2007), 33, 56-59, goes as far as to argue that "Jews were hated in Iberia not as Jews but as a largely urban people."

36. Saul Friedman, *Jews and the American Slave Trade* (London: Routledge, 1998), 57.

37. Tamar Herzog, *Defining Nations: Immigrants and Citizens in Early Modern Spain and Spanish America* (New Haven: Yale University Press, 2003), 124-28, 248. David Augusto Canelo, *The Last Crypto-Jews of Portugal* (Portland: IJS, 1990).

38. Luis de Albuquerque, *A Ilha de São Tomé nos séculos XV e XVI* (Lisbon: Publicações Alfa, 1989), 39, 73. A. Teixeira da Mota, *Some Aspects of Portuguese Colonization and Sea Trade in West Africa in the 15th and 16th Centuries* (Bloomington: Indiana University Press, 1978), 11-12. Paul D. Cohn's novel *São Tomé: Journey to the Abyss, Portugal's Stolen Children* (2005) mentions a 1998 Brandeis Ph.D. dissertation on the topic "An Early History of the Portuguese Inquisition" authored by Ervin Kolbertz. However, this seems like an imitation of, or homage to Jorge Luis Borges's habit of including citations to non-existing scholarly works in his stories because I have not been able to find the dissertation anywhere.

39. Arlindo Manuel Caldeira, "Learning the Ropes in the Tropics: Slavery and Plantation System on the Island of São Tomé," *African Economic History* 39 (2011): 35-71.

40. Robert Garfield, "Public Christians, Secret Jews: Religion and Political Conflict on São Tomé Island in the Sixteenth and Seventeenth Centuries," *Sixteenth Century Journal* 21, no. 4 (1990): 651.

41. José Gonçalves Salvador, *Os cristãos-novos e o comércio no Atlântico Meridional* (São Paulo: Livr. Pioneira Ed., 1978), 261.

42. Hugh Thomas, *Rivers of Gold: The Rise of the Spanish Empire, from Columbus to Magellan* (New York: Random House, 2003), 152. T. Monod, R. Mauny, and A. Texeira da Mota, eds., *Description de la Côte Occidentale d'Afrique: Sénégal au Cap de Monte, Archipels par Valentim Fernandes, 1506–1510* (Bissau: Centro de Estudos da Guiné Portuguesa, 1951), 61.

43. Green, "Masters of Difference: Creolization and the Jewish Presence in Cabo Verde," chap. 5.

44. Malyn Newitt, ed., *The Portuguese in West Africa, 1415–1670: A Documentary History* (New York: Cambridge University Press, 2010), 35–36.

45. Cecil Roth, *A History of the Marranos*, 237, 359.

46. See Peter Mark and José da Silva Horta, *The Forgotten Diaspora: Jewish Communities in West Africa and the Making of the Atlantic World* (New York: Cambridge University Press, 2011) for a detailed study of two communities on Senegal's Petite Côte.

47. George E. Brooks, *Landlords and Strangers: Ecology, Society, and Trade in Western Africa, 1000–1630* (Boulder: Westview Press, 1993), 137–40.

48. George E. Brooks, *Eurafricans in Western Africa: Commerce, Social Status, Gender, and Religious Observance from the Sixteenth to the Eighteenth Century* (Athens: Ohio University Press, 2003), 93.

49. André Donelha, *Descrição da Serra Leoa e dos rios de Guiné do Cabo Verde, 1625* (Lisbon: Junta de Investigações Científicas do Ultramar, 1977), 128.

50. Sanjay Subrahmanyam, *The Portuguese Empire in Asia, 1500–1700: A Political and Economic History* (Chichester: Wiley-Blackwell, 2012), 122–23, 227–36.

51. J. B. Segal, *A History of the Jews of Cochin* (London: Vallentine Mitchell, 1993), 32–35.

52. Gabriel Dellon, *L'Inquisition de Goa, la relation de Charles Dellon, 1687*, ed. Charles Amiel and Anne Lima (Paris: Editions Chandeigne, 1997), 164. Dellon's book became quite popular in Europe and served as part of the basis for Voltaire's *Candide*.

53. John L. Vogt, "Fernão de Loronha and the Rental of Brazil in 1502: A New Chronology," *The Americas* 24, no. 2 (1967): 153–59.

54. John L. Vogt, "Portuguese Exploration in Brazil and the Feitoria System, 1500–1530" (Ph.D. diss., University of Virginia, 1967), 10–13, 67–112.

55. Caldeira, "Learning the Ropes in the Tropics," 67.

56. Gilberto Freyre, *The Masters and the Slaves* (New York: Knopf, 1946), 25. Manoel de Oliveira Lima, "A Nova Lusitânia," in *História da colonização portuguêsa do Brasil*, vol. 3 (Porto: n.p., 1924), 199.

57. Anita Novinsky, *Cristãos novos na Bahia* (São Paulo: Editôra Perspectiva, 1972), 59–75, 88, 176. Lúcia Helena Costigan, *Through Cracks in the Wall: Modern Inquisitions and New Christian Letrados in the Iberian Atlantic World* (Leiden: Brill, 2010), 18, 144, 161. Arnold Wiznitzer, *Jews in Colonial Brazil* (New York: Columbia University Press, 1960).

58. Salvador, *Os cristãos-novos e o comércio no Atlântico Meridional*, 258.

59. Alberto Vieira, *Comercio inter-insular. Séculos XV e XVI, Madeira, Açores e Canárias* (Funchal: CEHA, 1987), 77.

60. Arnold Wiznitzer, "The Jews in the Sugar Industry of Colonial Brazil," *Jewish Social Studies* 18, no. 3 (1956): 189–99.

61. Computed from data in Maarten Prak, *The Dutch Republic in the Seventeenth Century* (New York: Cambridge University Press, 2005), 219, 257; and Catia Antunes and Filipa Ribeiro da Silva, "Amsterdam Merchants in the Slave Trade and African Commerce, 1580s-1670s," *Tijdschirft voor Economisch en Sociale Geschiedenis* 9, no. 4 (2012): 3–30. Yda Schreuder, *Sephardic Merchants and the Atlantic Sugar Trade in the Seventeenth Century* (Cham, Switzerland: Palgrave, 2019).

62. Eli Faber, *Jews, Slaves, and the Slave Trade: Setting the Record Straight* (New York: New York University Press, 1998), 52–53.

63. Faber, *Jews, Slaves,* 45–46.

64. N. Darnell Davis, "Notes on the History of the Jews in Barbados," *Publications of the American Jewish Historical Society* 18 (1909): 137–38, 143–44.

65. Aviva Ben-Ur, *Jewish Autonomy in a Slave Society: Suriname in the Atlantic World, 1651-1825* (Philadelphia: University of Pennsylvania Press, 2020), 47, 66.

66. Calculated from data in Linda M. Rupert, *Creolization and Contraband: Curaçao in the Early Modern Atlantic World* (Athens: University of Georgia Press, 2012), 125–139.

67. Gleydi Sullón Barreto, "Vasallos y extranjeros: portugueses en la Lima virreinal, 1570-1680" (Ph.D. diss., Universidad Complutense de Madrid, 2014), 158.

68. María Cristina Navarrete, "Judeo-conversos en la audiencia del Nuevo Reino de Granada, siglos XVI y XVII," *Historia Crítica,* no. 23 (2002): 73–84.

69. Wim Klooster, "The Essequibo Liberties: The Link between Jewish Brazil and Jewish Suriname," *Studia Rosenthaliana* 42/43 (2010): 77–82.

70. N. Darnell Davis, "Notes on the History of the Jews in Barbados," *Publications of the American Jewish Historical Society* 18 (1909): 137–38, 143–44. Dana Rabin, "The Struggle for Jewish Naturalization from Jamaica to London, 1748–1753," in this volume.

71. Günter Böhm, *Los sefardíes en los dominios holandeses de América del Sur y del Caribe, 1630-1750* (Frankfort: Vervuert, 1992), 203, 214.

72. Herzog, *Defining Nations,* 49–50.

73. Sullón Barreto, "Vasallos y extranjeros," 56.

74. For the migration of Portuguese New Christians and Crypto-Jews to Spain, see James C. Boyajian, *Portuguese Bankers at the Court of Spain, 1626-1650* (New Brunswick: Rutgers University Press, 1983); Julio Caro Baroja, *La sociedad criptojudía en la corte de Felipe IV* (Madrid: Real Academia de la Historia, 1963), 35–128,

75. Computed from numbers in Isaac Samuel Emmanuel, *Precious Stones of the Jews of Curaçao: Curaçaon Jewry 1656-1957* (New York: Bloch, 1957), 111–12.

76. Henry Méchoulan, "The Importance of Hispanicity in Jewish Orthodoxy and Heterodoxy in Seventeenth-Century Amsterdam," in *In Iberia and Beyond: Hispanic Jews between Cultures,* ed. Bernard Cooperman (Newark: University of Delaware Press, 1998), 353–72.

77. Cecil Roth, *A History of the Marranos,* 370.

78. For example, Dedieu, *L'administration de la foi;* Julio Caro Baroja, *Los judíos en la España moderna y contemporánea* (Madrid: Istmo, 1986), 474; Eva A. Uchmany, *La vida*

entre el judaísmo y el cristianismo en la Nueva España, 1580–1606 (Mexico City: Archivo General de la Nación, 1992).

79. For example, Sullón Barreto, "Vasallos y extranjeros"; Susana R. Frías, *Portugueses en Buenos Aires. Mito y realidad, 1600–1699* (Buenos Aires: Academia Nacional de la Historia, 2011).

80. Navarrete, "Judeo-conversos en la audiencia del Nuevo Reino de Granada," 75. DOI:10.7440/histcrit23.2002.04.

81. José Toribio Medina, *Historia del Tribunal del Santo Oficio de la Inquisición de Lima, 1569–1820*, vol. 2 (Santiago de Chile: Imprenta Gutenberg, 1887), 127–56.

82. Teodoro Hampe Martínez, *Santo Oficio e historia colonial: aproximaciones al tribunal de la inquisición de Lima, 1570–1820* (Lima: Ediciones del Congreso del Perú, 1998), 42.

83. J.C.H. Blom et. al., eds., *The History of the Jews in the Netherlands* (Liverpool: Liverpool University Press, 2001), 74, 97–99, 202–208.

84. Mordechai Arbell, "Rediscovering Tucacas," *American Jewish Archives* 48, no. 1 (1996): 35–43.

85. Brooks, *Eurafricans in Western Africa*, 89–93.

86. Eva Uchmany, "The Participation of New Christians and Crypto-Jews in the Conquest, Colonization, and Trade of Spanish America," 198.

87. Huguette and Pierre Chaunu, *Séville et l'Atlantique, 1504–1650*, vol. 4 (Paris: Librairie Armand Colin, 1956), 314.

88. F. J. Dubiez, *The Sephardic Community in Amsterdam* (self-pub., 1965), 90.

89. Anita Novinsky, *Cristãos novos na Bahia*, 60–61.

90. Renata Segre, "Sephardic Settlements in Sixteenth-Century Italy: A Historical and Geographical Survey" in *Jews, Christians, and Muslims in the Mediterranean World after 1492*, 112–37.

91. Mark Mazower, *Salonica, City of Ghosts: Christians, Muslims and Jews, 1430–1950* (New York: Knopf, 2005), 36, 45–63.

92. Harriet Pass Freidenreich, *The Jews of Yugoslavia: A Quest for Community* (Philadelphia: Jewish Publication Society of America, 1979), 216.

Bibliography

Antunes, Catia, and Filipa Ribeiro da Silva. "Amsterdam Merchants in the Slave Trade and African Commerce, 1580s-1670s." *Tijdschirft voor Economisch en Sociale Geschiedenis* 9, no. 4 (2012): 3–30.

Arbell, Mordechai. "Rediscovering Tucacas." *American Jewish Archives* 48, no. 1 (1996): 35–43.

Ben-Ur, Aviva. *Jewish Autonomy in a Slave Society: Suriname in the Atlantic World, 1651–1825*. Philadelphia: University of Pennsylvania Press, 2020.

Bernardini, Paolo, and Norman Fiering, eds. *The Jews and the Expansion of Europe to the West, 1450–1800*. New York: Berghahn Books, 2001.

Blom, J.C.H., R. G. Fuks-Mansfeld, and I. Schöffer, eds. *The History of the Jews in the Netherlands*. Liverpool: Liverpool University Press, 2001.

Bodian, Miriam. "Men of the Nation: The Shaping of Converso Identity in Early Modern Europe." *Past & Present* 143 (May 1994): 48–76.
Böhm, Günter. *Los sefardíes en los dominios holandeses de América del Sur y del Caribe, 1630–1750*. Frankfort: Vervuert, 1992.
Bonacich, Edna. "A Theory of Middleman Minorities." *American Sociological Review* 38, no. 5 (1973): 583–94.
Boyajian, James C. *Portuguese Bankers at the Court of Spain, 1626–1650*. New Brunswick: Rutgers University Press, 1983.
Brooks, George E. *Eurafricans in Western Africa: Commerce, Social Status, Gender, and Religious Observance from the Sixteenth to the Eighteenth Century*. Athens: Ohio University Press, 2003.
———. *Landlords and Strangers: Ecology, Society, and Trade in Western Africa, 1000–1630*. Boulder: Westview Press, 1993.
Caldeira, Arlindo Manuel. "Learning the Ropes in the Tropics: Slavery and Plantation System on the Island of São Tomé." *African Economic History* 39 (2011): 35–71.
Canelo, David Augusto. *The Last Crypto-Jews of Portugal*. Portland: IJS, 1990.
Caro Baroja, Julio. *La sociedad criptojudía en la corte de Felipe IV*. Madrid: Real Academia de la Historia, 1963.
———. *Los judíos en la España moderna y contemporánea*. Madrid: Istmo, 1986.
Carrete Parrondo, Carlos. "Nostalgia for the Past (and for the Future?) among Castilian Judeoconversos." In *Jews, Christians, and Muslims in the Mediterranean World after 1492*, edited by Alisa Meyuhas Ginio, 25–43. London: Routledge, 1993.
Chaunu, Huguette, and Pierre Chaunu. *Séville et l'Atlantique, 1504–1650*. Vol. 4. Paris: Librairie Armand Colin, 1956.
Costigan, Lúcia Helena. *Through Cracks in the Wall: Modern Inquisitions and New Christian Letrados in the Iberian Atlantic World*. Leiden: Brill, 2010.
Davis, N. Darnell. "Notes on the History of the Jews in Barbados." *Publications of the American Jewish Historical Society* 18 (1909): 129–48.
De Albuquerque, Luis. *A Ilha de São Tomé nos séculos XV e XVI*. Lisbon: Publicações Alfa, 1989.
De Almeida Mendes, António. "Portugal, Morocco and Guinea: Reconfiguration of the North Atlantic at the End of the Middle Ages." In *From Al-Andalus to the Americas, 13th–17th Centuries*, edited by Thomas F. Glick, Antonio Malpica, Félix Retamero, and Josep Torró, 401–28. Leiden: Brill, 2018.
De Azevedo, João Lúcio. *História dos Cristãos Novos Portugueses*. Lisbon: Classica, 1921.
De Oliveira Lima, Manoel. "A Nova Lusitânia." In *História da colonização portuguêsa do Brasil*. Vol. 3. Porto: n.p., 1924.
Dedieu, Jean-Pierre. *L'administration de la foi: L'Inquisition de Tolède, XVIe–XVIIe siècles*. Madrid: Casa de Velázquez, 1989.
Dellon, Gabriel. *L'Inquisition de Goa, la relation de Charles Dellon, 1687*. Edited by Charles Amiel and Anne Lima. Paris: Editions Chandeigne, 1997.
Domínguez Ortiz, Antonio. *Los judeoconversos en España y América*. Madrid: Ediciones Istmo, 1971.
Donelha, André. *Descrição da Serra Leoa e dos rios de Guiné do Cabo Verde, 1625*. Lisbon: Junta de Investigações Científicas do Ultramar, 1977.

Dubiez, F. J. *The Sephardic Community in Amsterdam*. Self-published, 1965.
Elukin, Jonathan. "From Jew to Christian? Conversion and Immutability in Medieval Europe." In *Varieties of Religious Conversion in the Middle Ages*, edited by James Muldoon, 171–89. Gainesville: University Press of Florida, 1997.
Emmanuel, Isaac Samuel. *Precious Stones of the Jews of Curaçao: Curaçaon Jewry 1656–1957.* New York: Bloch, 1957.
Faber, Eli. *Jews, Slaves, and the Slave Trade: Setting the Record Straight*. New York: New York University Press, 1998.
Fernández-Armesto, Felipe. *Columbus on Himself*. Indianapolis: Hackett, 2010.
Feros, Antonio. *Speaking of Spain: The Evolution of Race and Nation in the Hispanic World*. Cambridge: Harvard University Press, 2017.
Ferro Tavares, Maria. *Os judeus em Portugal no século XV*. Lisbon: Universidade Nova de Lisboa, 1982–84.
Freidenreich, Harriet Pass. *The Jews of Yugoslavia: A Quest for Community*. Philadelphia: Jewish Publication Society of America, 1979.
Freyre, Gilberto. *The Masters and the Slaves*. New York: Knopf, 1946.
Frías, Susana R. *Portugueses en Buenos Aires. Mito y realidad, 1600–1699*. Buenos Aires: Academia Nacional de la Historia, 2011.
Friedenwald, Harry. *The Jews and Medicine: Essays*. Vol. 2. Baltimore, MD: Johns Hopkins University Press, 1944.
Friedman, Saul. *Jews and the American Slave Trade*. London: Routledge, 1998.
Garfield, Robert. "Public Christians, Secret Jews: Religion and Political Conflict on São Tomé Island in the Sixteenth and Seventeenth Centuries." *Sixteenth Century Journal* 21, no. 4 (1990): 645–54.
Green, Tobias Oliver. "Masters of Difference: Creolization and the Jewish Presence in Cabo Verde, 1497–1672." Ph.D. diss., University of Birmingham, UK, 2007.
Hampe Martínez, Teodoro. *Santo Oficio e historia colonial: aproximaciones al tribunal de la inquisición de Lima, 1570–1820*. Lima: Ediciones del Congreso del Perú, 1998.
Herzog, Tamar. *Defining Nations: Immigrants and Citizens in Early Modern Spain and Spanish America*. New Haven: Yale University Press, 2003.
Hordes, Stanley M. *To the End of the Earth: A History of the Crypto-Jews of New Mexico*. New York: Columbia University Press, 2005.
Klooster, Wim. "The Essequibo Liberties: The Link between Jewish Brazil and Jewish Suriname." *Studia Rosenthaliana* 42/43 (2010): 77–82.
Lindo, E. H. *The History of the Jews of Spain and Portugal*. London: Longman, Brown, Green and Longmans, Paternoster Row, 1848.
Lipton, Sara. *Dark Mirror: The Medieval Origins of Anti-Jewish Iconography*. New York: Metropolitan Books, 2014.
Mark, Peter, and José da Silva Horta. *The Forgotten Diaspora: Jewish Communities in West Africa and the Making of the Atlantic World*. New York: Cambridge University Press, 2011.
Mazower, Mark. *Salonica, City of Ghosts: Christians, Muslims and Jews, 1430–1950*. New York: Knopf, 2005.
Méchoulan, Henry. "The Importance of Hispanicity in Jewish Orthodoxy and Heterodoxy in Seventeenth-Century Amsterdam." In *In Iberia and Beyond: Hispanic Jews*

between Cultures, edited by Bernard Cooperman, 352–72. Newark, DE: University of Delaware Press, 1998.
Medina, José Toribio. *Historia del Tribunal del Santo Oficio de la Inquisición de Lima, 1569–1820.* 2 vols. Santiago de Chile: Imprenta Gutenberg, 1887.
Mendes dos Remedios, Joaquim. *Os judeus em Portugal.* Vol. 1. Coimbra: F. França Amado, 1895.
Monod, T., R. Mauny, and A. Texeira da Mota, eds. *Description de la Côte Occidentale d'Afrique: Sénégal au Cap de Monte, Archipels par Valentim Fernandes, 1506–1510.* Bissau: Centro de Estudos da Guiné Portuguesa, 1951.
Mota, A. Teixeira da. *Some Aspects of Portuguese Colonization and Sea Trade in West Africa in the 15th and 16th Centuries.* Bloomington: Indiana University Press, 1978.
Moya, José C. "The Iberian Atlantic, 1492–2010." In *Theorising the Ibero-American Atlantic,* edited by Harald Braun and Lisa Vollendorf, 51–73. Leiden: Brill, 2013.
Navarrete, María Cristina. "Judeo-conversos en la audiencia del Nuevo Reino de Granada, siglos XVI y XVII." *Historia Crítica,* no. 23 (2002): 73–84.
Newitt, Malyn, ed. *The Portuguese in West Africa, 1415–1670: A Documentary History.* New York: Cambridge University Press, 2010.
Nirenberg, David. "Was There Race before Modernity?" In *The Origins of Racism in the West,* edited by Miriam Eliav-Feldon, Benjamin Isaac, and Joseph Ziegler, 232–64. Cambridge: Cambridge University Press, 2009.
Novinsky, Anita. *Cristãos novos na Bahia.* São Paulo: Editôra Perspectiva, 1972.
Prak, Maarten. *The Dutch Republic in the Seventeenth Century.* New York: Cambridge University Press, 2005.
Phillips, William D., and Carla Rahn Phillips. *The Worlds of Christopher Columbus.* New York: Cambridge University Press, 1992.
Pérez, Joseph. *History of a Tragedy: The Expulsion of the Jews from Spain.* Urbana: University of Illinois Press, 2007.
Ray, Jonathan S. *After Expulsion: 1492 and the Making of Sephardic Jewry.* New York: New York University Press, 2003.
Rodrigues da Silva Tavim, José A. "In the Shadow of Empire: Portuguese Jewish Communities in the Sixteenth Century." In *Portuguese Colonial Cities in the Early Modern World,* edited by Liam M. Brockey, 17–40. London: Routledge, 2016.
Roth, Cecil. *A History of the Marranos.* Rev. ed. Philadelphia: Jewish Publication Society of America, 1941.
———. "Marranos and Racial Antisemitism: A Study in Parallels." *Jewish Social Studies* 2, no. 3 (1940): 239–48.
Roth, Norman. *Conversos, Inquisition, and the Expulsion of the Jews from Spain.* Madison: University of Wisconsin Press, 2002.
Rupert, Linda M. *Creolization and Contraband: Curaçao in the Early Modern Atlantic World.* Athens: University of Georgia Press, 2012.
Russell-Wood, A.J.R. "Before Columbus: Portugal's African Prelude to the Middle Passage and Contribution to Discourse on Race and Slavery." In *Spain, Portugal and the Atlantic Frontier of Medieval Europe,* edited by José Juan Lopez-Portillo, 257–91. London: Routledge, 2013.

Salvador, José Gonçalves. *Os cristãos-novos e o comércio no Atlântico Meridional.* São Paulo: Livr. Pioneira Ed., 1978.
Saraiva, António José. *Inquisição e cristãos-novos.* Porto: Editorial Inova, 1969.
Schreuder, Yda. *Sephardic Merchants and the Atlantic Sugar Trade in the Seventeenth Century.* Cham, Switzerland: Palgrave, 2019.
Schwartz, Stuart B. "Prata, açúcar e escravos: de como o imperio restaurou Portugal." *Tempo* (January 2008): 201–23.
Segal, J. B. *A History of the Jews of Cochin.* London: Vallentine Mitchell, 1993.
Segre, Renata. "Sephardic Settlements in Sixteenth-Century Italy: A Historical and Geographical Survey." In *Jews, Christians, and Muslims in the Mediterranean World after 1492,* edited by Alisa Meyuhas Ginio, 112–37. London: Routledge, 1993.
Studnicki-Gizbert, Daviken. *A Nation upon the Open Sea: Portugal's Atlantic Diaspora and the Crisis of the Spanish Empire, 1492–1640.* New York: Oxford University Press, 2007.
Subrahmanyam, Sanjay. *The Portuguese Empire in Asia, 1500–1700: A Political and Economic History.* Chichester: Wiley-Blackwell, 2012.
Sullón Barreto, Gleydi. "Vasallos y extranjeros: portugueses en la Lima virreinal, 1570–1680." Ph.D. diss., Universidad Complutense de Madrid, 2014.
Thomas, Hugh. *Rivers of Gold: The Rise of the Spanish Empire, from Columbus to Magellan.* New York: Random House, 2003.
Uchmany, Eva A. "The Participation of New Christians and Crypto-Jews in the Conquest, Colonization, and Trade of Spanish America, 1521–1660." In *The Jews and the Expansion of Europe to the West, 1450–1800,* edited by Paolo Bernardini and Norman Fiering, 186–202. New York: Berghahn Books, 2001.
———. *La vida entre el judaísmo y el cristianismo en la Nueva España, 1580–1606.* Mexico City: Archivo General de la Nación, 1992.
Vieira, Alberto. *Comercio inter-insular. Séculos XV e XVI, Madeira, Açores e Canárias.* Funchal: CEHA, 1987.
Vogt, John L. "Fernão de Loronha and the Rental of Brazil in 1502: A New Chronology." *The Americas* 24, no. 2 (1967): 153–59.
———. "Portuguese Exploration in Brazil and the Feitoria System, 1500–1530." Ph.D. diss., University of Virginia, 1967.
Wiznitzer, Arnold. *Jews in Colonial Brazil.* New York: Columbia University Press, 1960.
———. "The Jews in the Sugar Industry of Colonial Brazil." *Jewish Social Studies* 18, no. 3 (1956): 189–99.

III

PERCEPTIONS OF MIGRANTS AND MIGRATION

5

Navigating Citizenship
Consular Practices and the Brazilian Jewish Community in Nineteenth-Century Morocco

LUCAS DE MATTOS MOURA FERNANDES

In an 1879 report to the Brazilian Empire's Ministry of Foreign Affairs, José Daniel Colaço (1831–1907), Brazil's Consul General to Morocco since 1851, succinctly described the significance of consular protection Brazil provided to its nationals in Morocco, specifically to Moroccan Jews returning to their former homelands as naturalized Brazilian citizens.[1] He claimed that not providing this protection to Jews when they returned to their North African country would make Brazil less desirable for Jewish migration. Colaço recognized that the protections that he could offer in his capacity as Brazil's consul to naturalized citizens helped his efforts to guide the migratory flow from Morocco to Brazil. In other words, migrants and Brazil equally benefitted from the system of consular protections.

Before Colaço was appointed to consulship, Brazilian institutions did not guide, let alone advance, migration from Morocco to Brazil, which was in a steady rise since the opening of Brazilian ports to "friendly nations" in 1808 and more, following the declaration of Brazilian independence in 1822. Brazil became the fourth largest country by territory and needed workers willing to face the lack of infrastructure and precarious public services and take advantage of the available land not yet occupied by large estates in regions where the hilly terrain and vegetation made it difficult to engage with agriculture. The settlement of immigrants in border areas answered these economic needs and resolved the central government's geopolitical concerns.[2] The support for the emigration of Moroccan Jews that Colaço urged proved to be an economically rewarding activity not only for Brazil, but also for its consuls given that, from 1891 onward, the Ministry of Agriculture, Commerce, and Public Works began paying consuls on a quarterly basis, according to the number of migrants they "dispatched" to Brazil.[3] However, Colaço's interests in promoting the migration of Moroccan Jews to Brazil went beyond finances. When evaluating possible activities for his consular post, Colaço was resentful of the weak commercial relationship between the Islamic country and Brazil, which reflected poorly on the significance of the Moroccan Consulate General from the perspective of the administration of the Brazilian chancellery.[4] To Colaço's ambitions as the Consul of the Brazilian Empire, it was more important that the protections provided to Moroccan Jews—who returned from Brazil as naturalized citizens—opened an avenue to developing Brazil's political presence in North Africa, comparable to that of European colonial powers, and, thus, raising the young South American country's prestige in the continent.

Only recently, and mainly as a part of Sephardic Jewish Studies, have scholars in Brazil begun to study the history of Moroccan Jews who migrated to the Amazon. Initially, the Sephardic communities appeared in memoir-like accounts that emphasized the spontaneous beginnings of these migratory waves and recorded that these pioneer immigrants founded synagogues and associations. Later works discussed them in relation to the cultural impact of Iberian colonization.[5] Due to the scarcity of sources, relying on documentation provided by the Alliance Israélite Universelle, historians noted that about a thousand Jews from Morocco formed a significant group of immigrants to one of Brazil's more remote areas—the Amazon region.[6] This number is only a fraction of the more than seventy thousand Jewish migrants who entered Brazil in the four decades after 1890.[7] This study focuses on a relatively large number—about six hundred—of those Moroccan immigrants to the Brazilian Amazon who returned to their original homeland and established a Brazilian community in Morocco.[8] This community was formed and maintained by the back-and-forth flow of workers and their families. Moving between Brazil and Morocco, these Jewish migrants remained connected through historical, cultural, and blood ties throughout the second half of the nineteenth century. They formed a part of both the Moroccan Jewish community and the Jewish community in the Amazon region, which were linked together by their Brazilian citizenship, resulting from a relatively easily completed naturalization process.[9]

Collaboration between authorities capable of "opening and closing the country's doors"[10] supported this migration. In his work, Fabio Koifman demonstrates how, through the Ministry of Justice, the Estado Novo (1930–1945) selected the desirable immigrants and allowed them to enter the national territory. In contrast, during the period covered by my research, the role of "gatekeeper" was assumed by the Ministry of International Affairs.

Brazilian diplomatic papers, Colaço's dispatches especially, document how Brazil perceived its citizens living in Morocco while striving for more influence and great power status in the region. They also offer insights into the role Brazilian consular authorities played in the life of the emerging Brazilian Jewish colony in Morocco. As Colaço noted, Moroccan Jews returning to Morocco as Brazilian citizens were well aware of the advantages the Brazilian naturalization provided. The ways in which consular authorities dealt with these Brazilians and the development of the relationship between the Brazilian community and the consulate that served it reveal the ambivalence of identifying as a Brazilian and a Jew in Moroccan cities. These documents also highlight the limitation of this community's Brazilian identification. Following a review of Colaço's vision of the diplomatic potential of his consular post, this study offers a micro-scale analysis of cases found in previously untapped sources, which also permits the reconstruction of everyday life and practices of the Moroccan Jewish community. My goal in this chapter is to analyze how Brazilian citizenship was perceived and used by members of this community in Morocco, and how their citizenship status offered more than just civil identification.

I begin with the examination of the establishment of Brazilian consular offices in Morocco—particularly the office of Consul General of Brazil in Tangier founded by Colaço—in a period of exceptional consular activities in the country that attested to the importance of the Brazilian community there. The aim is to follow the succession of Brazilian representatives in Morocco, under the administrations of Jacob Attias and Adoniram Calimerio—that is, between 1860 and 1903—outlining the ways in which these institutions were routinely used to address legal claims, taking into account the prerogatives of Brazilian citizens. The study concludes with an analysis of the changes in Brazilian politics that led to the closure of consulates in Morocco and the limits set to naturalization and protections of Moroccan immigrants.

José Daniel Colaço, Brazilian Consul in Morocco

During its early years, the Consulate General of Brazil in Tangier, along with all diplomatic services provided by the Brazilian Empire to citizens in Morocco, was under Colaço's authority, the first occupant of this post, officialized by the Brazilian Emperor. In 1851, Colaço was appointed vice-consul of Portugal in Tangier and in 1861 he succeeded his brother, Jorge Colaço, to the post of Portuguese Consul General in Morocco. Due to his assistance to the victims of the Brazilian corvette D. Izabel, shipwrecked in the Bay of Tangier in November 1860, he was also named Consul of Brazil in that country.[11] In Portugal, he was promoted to Chargé d'Affaires and Extraordinary Envoy and Minister Plenipotentiary in 1869, but he was relieved of those duties in 1896 in the interests of Portuguese foreign policy. Colaço's consular mission coincided with one of the most turbulent periods in the history of Morocco, when powers such as Spain and France started to interfere in the country's internal politics. In addition to representing Portuguese and later Brazilian interests, he renegotiated the Peace and Commerce Treaty between Morocco and Portugal in 1880, a treaty that had been in force since 1774.

Born in the Moroccan city of Tangier himself, Colaço was a member of a family of Portuguese orientalists who served the Portuguese chancellery, partly because his publications focused on Islamic history and customs. He, thus, wrote his reports from the perspective of a Portuguese orientalist, who saw in Al-Maghreb Al-Aqsa (Far West in Arabic) of the Muslim world a decadent society, one that had lost the glory of the Islamic caliphs of the past. The use of pejorative terms that depicted the country in terms of cultural asymmetry drew from a language typical of colonialism, in which the colonizer sees in the other only the inverted reflection of their own self-image.[12] His reports, as well as his other works, display a discourse shaped by Portuguese imperialism in Morocco, once established through military means.[13]

Accordingly, Consul Colaço argued in favor of his proposal for the development of relations between Brazil and Morocco and for Brazil to emulate the "gunboat diplomacy" practiced by the great powers in their relationships with North African countries.[14] In a memo dated February 25, 1892, Colaço related the concern of the consular authorities of several countries based in Morocco regarding the consequences that the conflict between villages of the interior and the government of Tangier would have for foreign citizens residing in that country:

> There is no doubt that the presence of these ships calmed the shock that most of the Christians and the Israelite colony felt, believing that the rebel tribes could from one moment to the next attack

the residence of Bachá [the local governor], and compromise public safety. This, however, did not happen, and, consequently, those countries that harbor aspirations of conquest or a protectorate with respect to that African Empire . . . were frustrated in any plan they might have entertained to intervene in the affairs of that country, if an aggression by rebel tribes had justified the landing of armed forces from those ships.[15]

Colaço identified Great Britain, France, and Spain by name as those military forces whose interventions in Morocco were still imminent. Additionally, the memo he sent to the Ministry of Foreign Affairs reemphasized his analysis of the situation by pointing out that while the Sultan of Morocco had resolved the dispute in Tangier simply by replacing the city's governor, news spread among Brazilian citizens in Morocco that Brazil was supposedly in the process of being divided—an international repercussion of the Armada Revolts (1891–1894)—and that precisely for that reason, they would not see any Brazilian ship docking in Morocco in order to protect their compatriots.

Guided by self-interest, Colaço argued that in order to definitively demonstrate that Brazil was not only a unified country, but also a naval power, it should send a warship "to wave the flag of the republic and make a significant public display of its eminent presence here." The Brazilian government should be sure not to send a small ship to Morocco. Instead, Colaço asked for an "imposing ship, because the inhabitants of this country, accustomed to the presence of British, French, and other nations' battleships and cruisers, are not impressed by the sight of small vessels."[16]

It was nearly a year after this request that Tangier was included in the route of the cruiser, *Benjamin Constant*. The ship docked in the bay and greeted those present with a twenty-one gun salute, which was reciprocated by the garrison of the port square. The entire scene was organized in response to Colaço's requests to the commander of the cruiser, as well as to the local authorities.[17]

According to Colaço's reasoning, and supposedly based on how institutional relations worked in Morocco, it was necessary for countries that had citizens to protect in Morocco to maintain an active presence through political and military displays that provided evidence of their sovereignty. The constant call for Brazilian intervention in Morocco or, more correctly, for Brazilian military displays in Morocco, which occupies a large part of the letters sent by the Brazilian representation in Tangier under Colaço's administration, was motivated by his effort to describe and seek solutions for the condition of Jews in Morocco. This can be seen in the letter of March 29, 1880, in which, after a clash between Jewish and Muslim residents of the city of Fez, Colaço warns of the disorder and possible persecution of Jews in Morocco:

> In any case, the fate of the Israelites who inhabit the interior of this Empire is sad and risky, because regardless of the protection that a small number of them enjoy, the aforementioned incident and others that occur throughout the country demonstrate clearly that hatred based on race and religion has been cultivated from ancient times among the Moors against the Hebrews; and if they live in the interior of the country and conduct their trade there, [they suffer] countless forms of humiliation, the most common being that they are forced to walk barefoot through the streets of those cities once they leave their neighborhood, under the risk of being beaten or even killed if they insist on wearing shoes.[18]

Colaço's administration of Brazilian diplomatic institutions in Morocco reveals a particular aspect of the way the Brazilian state related to the Brazilian Jewish community that was established there. Even before being officially recognized by the Ministry of Foreign Affairs as Consul General of Brazil in Morocco, Colaço encouraged support for the migration of Moroccan subjects to Brazil in a dispatch to the Brazilian chancellery from 1864, with the purpose of colonizing fertile lands located in regions that bordered other countries. In a brief memo, dated February 16, 1864, Colaço proposed the migration of Moroccan, mainly Jewish, subjects living in poverty to the country's main cities. He pointed out that:

> These individuals might be predominantly Hebrew subjects of the Sultan, and perhaps some Christians; as for Moors, it is likely that none, or very few would accept the invitation, because they are too fanatical to leave their homeland as emigrants.[19]

Sixteen years later, in a memo sent to the office of the Ministry of Foreign Affairs on October 27, 1880, Colaço stated that Brazil, alongside Portugal and France, would be one of the countries with the largest contingent of protected residents in Morocco that year. He noted that the deterioration of conditions for Jews in the North African country, in addition to the very chaotic situation in which many of the cities in that kingdom found themselves, had influenced many Jews to decide to emigrate. However, geographical proximity and travel routes favored migration to Europe. Colaço emphasized the challenges that the migratory flow faced, especially since migrants were forced to go to Europe first,

> and then travel to Brazilian ports, because there are no direct means. These conditions prevent large-scale emigration, and for the time being, only a limited number of individuals are embarking on this journey, most of whom men who leave their families in Morocco. Some send for their wives later.[20]

According to Colaço, upon returning to Morocco, these migrants increased by at least 50 percent[21] the number of Brazilian citizens to be protected by consular authorities. Relying on an argument characteristic of the period, the consul explained that the migrants were of Jewish and urban origin: "[T]he Moors, shrouded by their indomitable fanaticism and complete lack of education, are, for the time being, resistant to the idea of expatriation."[22] His plan was to encourage the migration of Jews from the interior of Morocco, who "if transportation were facilitated, would not only be willing to form a real emigration current to this Empire,"[23] but they could also form a permanent colony in Brazil and contribute to the development of commercial relations between the two countries, the true interest of the consular authorities.[24]

The extent to which the Moroccan emigration was deemed important can be gauged by the fact that the subject was addressed in every discussion and report filed by the consulate. The process of creating the relationship between the consulate and individuals and families belonging to this Brazilian community also opened a window on a repertoire of practices and strategies that initially aimed to mobilize the community in the interests of the consulate. At the same time, individual members of this community deciphered and utilized legal and behavioral codes that allowed them to exert influence over consular services. The example below will illustrate this point. The documentation produced by the Consulate General of Brazil in Tangier also described the deployment of Brazilian citizenship, which is analyzed in the next section of this chapter.

The Case of Saul Benshaya: Naturalization as a Tactic

Like most of his neighbors and acquaintances, Saul Benshaya, from Rabat, had traveled to Brazil. After residing in Manaus and obtaining Brazilian citizenship, he returned to Morocco with his wife and children, where he worked in trading fabric, the profession that had also supported him in Brazil. He had already been back in Morocco for seven years when one day, while he was away from his shop,

> [His] son who was twelve or thirteen years old sold a cut of fabric to a Moor, and as this individual did not complete the payment, the boy ... went to ask him for money, but the Moor ... mistreated him; a few moments later the father arrived and, as he saw his son crying, he inquired as to the cause and ... publicly insulted the Moor who had beaten his son. This was enough for other Moors, taking sides with their coreligionists, to make noise and bring an accusation against Saul to the territorial judge, who decided to bring the case to the vice-governor, who sent a soldier to bring Saul Benshaya to appear before him, but Saul replied that he was a Brazilian citizen and that if they had anything against him, they should take him to his consular authority.[25]

As the governor of Rabat was absent at the time because he was meeting with the Sultan of Morocco himself, his acting deputy, Vice-Governor Saddek Bargash, sent yet more soldiers who, invading Benshaya's store, dragged him out "without a hat or shoes, barbarously beating him along the way, until he reached the vice-governor," who, upon receiving him, ordered him to be "incarcerated and put in irons," without any sort of investigation of the facts.[26]

In Rabat at the time (1897), there was no established Brazilian vice-consulate and the only person capable of seeking a solution for Benshaya was an unofficial agent who worked for the newly installed Consul in Tangier, Jacob Attias. This agent sent a letter notifying the authorities that Benshaya was a Brazilian citizen and that this gave him the status of Protected Person. The Treaty of Madrid (1880) governed the condition of those protected by foreign powers in Morocco, and in accordance with Article 9 of the treaty, under no circumstances could the authorities arrest a foreign or protected citizen without immediately informing their respective consular authority.[27]

However, two days after the letter was sent, Saddek had neither responded to, nor investigated, Benshaya's situation. When reporting to the consulate in Tangier, the Brazilian Consul wrote to the Sultan's representatives in the City of Tangier. He also corresponded with the Grand Vizier of Morocco in Marrakesh requesting justice in the case of the Brazilian citizen.

Lebaddy, the Sultan's mediator in dealings with foreign legations in Tangier, responded to the Brazilian consul that he had received a letter from the aforementioned vice-governor of Rabat who confirmed his version of the case, stating that "the Hebrew Saul Benshaya was arrested for insulting the religion of the Muslims and because the vice-governor did not know he was Brazilian," but that in light of the correspondence from the consulate in Tangier, he would order the immediate release of Benshaya.[28]

Benshaya was imprisoned for a total of 52 hours. After being released, he filed a request for indemnification, demanding financial compensation for the period he was out of work in the amount of three pounds sterling for each hour he was incarcerated. He made the request following the suggestion of the unofficial consular agent in Rabat, who, at no point in the narrative, is identified by name.

Seeking support from the Brazilian Federal Government to move the litigation forward so that it could serve as an example that Brazilian citizens were effectively protected, the Consul in Tangier reported that in most cases, local authorities respected the status of Moroccan Protected Persons, including individuals associated with the Brazilian Consulate, only if they recognized the power of the nation that provided the protection. Because of that, according to the Consul, two North American cruisers, the *San Francisco* and the *Raleigh*, arrived in Morocco as diplomatic tools of persuasion to advance American interests in relation to the local government. The Consul then advised the Brazilian government to send "Brazilian warships that are closest at hand with respect to Morocco," given that

> The Brazilian colony, like the North American one [. . .] is almost entirely comprised of naturalized citizens of Hebrew religion; exceptionally, a few individuals are Brazilian born. Now, knowing in depth this country and the situation in which it finds itself, as well as the hatred that the Moors, starting with their authorities, profess regarding those who do not share the same belief, and above all regarding the Israelites, who for traditional reasons of race need strong protection in order to be respected, each flag owes this protection to those who belong to it.[29]

The quotation above refers directly to the language that individuals who dealt with this everyday reality used to describe their problems. These problems related to (a) cases of abuse of power by local Moroccan authorities, imposing intolerable conditions on members of the Jewish community and their associates, (b) personal disputes over rights not fully recognized, and (c) adversity of a material nature, which directly prejudiced those who worked in commerce, which characterized many members of this community.

For such situations as the case of Benshaya, Brazilian citizenship was deployed as a defense tactic to confront the precarious guarantees of the rights of Moroccan Jews, especially when dealing with an opponent who was not characterized as an individual or a specific official, but rather as the inherently anti-Jewish nature of the Moroccan government itself. It was to confront this other that members of the Brazilian community in Morocco appropriated the statutes on foreigners and Protected Persons, using the regulations established by the very entity that persecuted them to escape their worst effects.

It is important to note that, like Benshaya and the other cases described below, members of the Brazilian community in Morocco were identified as Brazilian citizens only when their rights were challenged or offended. The documents I analyze serve as an indication that there were no apparent means to distinguish between naturalized Brazilian-Moroccan Jews and their peers who did not have the same life experience, especially with regard to the niche of migrants who are the focus of this research, namely, urban Jews who lived through the period of the westernization of Morocco. In daily life, the difference between Brazilian-naturalized and non-naturalized Moroccan Jews was only perceived by the local authorities in conflictual situations in which jurisdiction distinguished one from another.

Transforming Circumstance into Opportunity

In November 1892, the naturalized Brazilian Jacob E. Muniz, who had returned to Morocco and was living in the city of Larache, saw the lack of Brazilian consular representation in his city as an opportunity. In a letter addressed to Consul General Adoniram Maurity Calimerio, he "humbly" requested to be appointed Vice-Consul of Brazil in Larache.

Jacob Muniz had spent a large part of his life in Brazil, where he held several government positions in the Amazon region, having been First Lieutenant, Artillery Division, in the Solimões River region in the province of Amazonas. He listed each of these positions in chronological order in his correspondence to the Consulate. Elected Vice President of the Chamber of São Paulo do Olivença in 1884, he acquired a parliamentary post when he was named Delegate for Public Sanitation. After leaving that position, he became deputy police chief in July 1886 and, having earned a reputation for respectability, became a member of the Parish Council of the same city in 1888. In addition to telling his life story, Muniz's correspondence included an invoice for 160 pounds of coffee, which would be arriving from Rio de Janeiro.

Alleging that he had come to perceive that Brazilians in Larache lacked the support of a consular office to protect them, Muniz did not hide his primary intention: to set up a commercial enterprise that would "introduce Brazilian products such as coffee, cachaça [cane alcohol], and other items."[30] If he obtained the status of vice-consul in Larache, a post that was at a considerable distance from the Consulate General, Muniz would not only be responsible for ensuring the protection of citizens there, but would also enjoy several benefits that would favor his business. However, the Brazilian government was not interested in establishing a consulate in that city at the time.

With the growth in the number of Brazilians in Morocco from the 1880s onward, the position of consul or vice-consul was increasingly coveted, not only for the prestige inherent in the position, but also because the Treaty of Madrid had determined that consular officials were the major administrative and judicial authorities with jurisdiction over foreigners in Morocco. As the regulatory instrument for the protection system in Morocco, the treaty stipulated that leaders of foreign legations or consular bodies in Morocco would be responsible for recognizing and listing their citizens who resided in the kingdom and then communicating this information to the Moroccan government. In addition, each nation's consular corps in Morocco had the right to place under its protection native individuals who contributed to the diplomatic and commercial operation of the respective legation.[31] In this way, the positions of consul general and vice-consul concentrated very important powers in an environment in which the protection system created a legal social divide between those who were subject to the local justice system and those who were not.

The protection system extended legal status to *mokhalatas* or *mojalatas* (native farmers who associated themselves with foreign traders) and *samsares* (commercial representatives in cities far from the respective business), who were Moroccans of Islamic origin or part of the Jewish community.[32] As the Treaty of Madrid levied an additional fee to be collected by the foreign consular body for each non-Moroccan citizen who acquired productive land in Morocco, it was essential for naturalized individuals to form commercial partnerships with natives.[33]

These developments help explain why citizens such as Jacob Muniz were not entirely satisfied with the benefits of naturalization and wanted to secure them through consular posts. It was the Consul General of Brazil in Morocco who validated the status of Brazilian citizens in the local community for legal purposes in relation to the Moroccan justice system; who named vice-consuls; and who approved Protected Person status for those Moroccans who worked directly with the Brazilian Consul. The Consul General also approved immigrant visas to Brazil and collected fees and emoluments related to consular services. The desire to become part of the consular service was related to its power to control the Moroccan side of the migratory process of the Brazilian community and its descendants.

The Federal Decree 997B of November 11, 1890, established a hierarchical organization of Brazil's consular posts. Eight posts were designated Consulate General First Class; the other eight, Consulate General Second Class, in accordance with reigning foreign policy interests. Within each class, the posts received the status of consulate, as in the case of the Tangier legation, or vice-consulate, which functioned as an extension of the consulate. Positions within the posts were also ranked in the order of consul, vice-consul, commercial agent, chancellor, and first and second secretaries. The position of vice-consul was often exercised unofficially, without registration by the Ministry of Foreign Affairs but with recognition by the local community and support from the Consul General. In 1891, although correspondence circulated among the consulate in Tangier and vice-consulates in Tetuan, Saffi and Rabat, the ministry included in its personnel list only the names of José Daniel Colaço, Consul; Emilio Rey (Reis) Colaço, Vice-Consul in Tangier; and Alexander A. Carara, Vice-Consul in Casablanca.[34]

The most striking measure included in the efforts to reorganize Brazilian consular offices was the stipulation that posts should be primarily occupied by Brazilian citizens,[35] which, in the Moroccan case, placed Colaço in a provisional situation. In posts where it was difficult to fill the position, a foreigner could be retained until the national diplomatic corps could find a Brazilian replacement. Colaço remained Consul General of Brazil in Tangier until 1897. After thirty-seven years of service to Brazilians in Morocco, he was removed from his office due to rising nationalism in Brazil. His successor, Jacob Attias, was directly recruited by the Brazilian Ministry of Foreign Affairs.

There is very little information available about Consul Jacob Attias, even in the reports he produced. Attias was part of the Moroccan Jewish community and, like other migrants, had lived in Brazil and later returned to settle in Morocco. Nonetheless, it is clear that Attias's consulship was a milestone in the history of the Jewish community in Morocco. He represented the community and managed to control the administrative processes that not only validated the status of Brazilian citizens, but also enabled the migration of other individuals. The strategy of becoming naturalized in Brazil and, upon return to Morocco, using the status afforded by the Brazilian naturalization, permitted Attias to navigate through the loopholes of the same regulation that resulted in the dismissal of José Daniel Colaço, who was a foreigner. The difficulty of providing a consular agent who would move to Morocco, and who would be able to deal with cultural differences, made Attias the most competent successor to Colaço in the eyes of the Ministry of Foreign Affairs.

The emphasis my research places on the symbiotic relationship between Brazilian consular institutions in Morocco and the community of returnees from Brazil also highlights that it became the main official link between Brazil and North Africa at the turn of the century. Moreover, as the status of citizen was still under debate even in Brazil under the First Republic, the consular protection alone proved to be insufficient to the community of returnees. Consular posts occupied by peers maximized security conditions and favored business.

The occupation of local consular posts by individuals from the Jewish community who had returned from Brazil became a common practice under Attias's administration. On August 16, 1900, the vice-consulate post that Jacob Muniz had previously been denied was conferred to the naturalized Brazilian Yusuf Abtibol. Two months later, claiming that he had to make a business trip, Abtibol appointed his brother as the vice-consulate's commercial agent,[36] amassing the main consular posts in the city of Larache in the hands of his family.[37]

Assigning family members to consular posts was a common practice at the time. For example, on December 9, 1900, Jacob Benata, Vice-Consul in the important city of Rabat, told the Consul of Tangier that he had to leave his position to take his son for medical treatment in Tangier and appointed his father as the vice-consulate's commercial agent. Benata did this to ensure that the post remained "under control." A key detail is that his father, Mr. Haim R. Benata, already held the posts of Consul of Belgium and Consul of the Austro-Hungarian Empire in Rabat, having the status of Protected Person of both countries. Another important detail is that Jacob Benata had migrated to Brazil in 1875 when he was 27 years old, lived there as a merchant, married a woman named Simy, and had his firstborn David in Pará. While occupying the post of Brazilian Vice-Consul, he continued balancing public service with his business in Rabat, the city where he was born and resided in for over twenty years. Curiously, however, he did not communicate in Portuguese, even in the exercise of his consular function. His correspondence, replete with complex information, was written entirely in French, including ostensible letters answered in Spanish.[38]

The creation of a network of vice-consulates in Moroccan cities that were further away from Tangier and, therefore, from the geographical limits of the consulate's services, corresponds not only to Attias's greater concern with serving the Brazilian communities located in these cities, but also to opening space for the appointment of agents to these important positions, creating an opportunity for more Brazilian citizens in Morocco to occupy positions of power in relation to the protection system. Precisely for this reason, family nominations were very common, especially in positions that did not necessarily require the approval of a higher authority above Attias in order to extend benefits related to consular services. During Attias's period as Consul General, Brazilian consular bureaucracy increasingly came to be controlled by members of the Moroccan Jewish community who were naturalized Brazilians.

Consularization of Everyday Life

Abraham Eleazar was a native of Tangier, Morocco, but like many of his generation, he emigrated to Brazil on a trip that, as in the case of many fellow merchants, was a business opportunity: to accumulate capital and return to make a bigger investment.[39] Eleazar resided in Teffé, in the district of Manaus, where on March 27, 1884, he became a naturalized Brazilian. Four years after his naturalization, he was able to return to his hometown. In Morocco, Eleazar invested in a house that he renovated to make room for a commercial establishment. Two or three months later, Eleazar opened two doors of his establishment for business, employing two masons in the work of adapting the property.

The street where Eleazar had chosen to acquire his property was very busy and, as was the custom at addresses of this type, there were commercial tents in front of the houses, in which itinerant Moroccan traders, both Jews and Muslims, resided temporarily while offering their goods.[40] Upon realizing that Eleazar's investment would soon become a competing store, one of these merchants housed in a tent, Mordokay Casez, a Jew protected by Italy, went to the construction site and warned the masons that in that place, in front of his tent, a door could not be opened, and persuaded them to stop the work.

A few days later, Casez decided to sue Eleazar in court, in an effort to prevent his potential future competitor from opening his business. As the two merchants were protected by foreign nations in accordance with the Treaty of Madrid, their dispute fell under the jurisdiction of either the Brazilian or Italian consular tribunals. However, Casez appealed to the local judge, who would evaluate it by applying *Chraa* (Muslim law). The then-Brazilian Consul who monitored the case claimed that

> The Italian protected person Mordokay Casez was cleverer than Mr. Eleazar, and for that reason he complained that the matter was referred to *Chraa*, since this court, consulted on similar matters, usually orders to close doors and especially windows in front of doors or houses, based on this fanatical principle that Moorish women cannot be seen.[41]

The court passed the sentence against Eleazar's enterprise while he was out of town, tackling a problem with his health. The sentence demanded that the naturalized Brazilian merchant close his doors. To address the problem and try to save his business, Eleazar sent a letter directly to the Brazilian Minister of Foreign Relations, Quintino Bocaiúva.

Bocaiúva's demand for better results in the case infuriated the then-Consul General José Daniel Colaço, in Tangier, who in his response to the minister stated that Eleazar was "so clumsy as an interested party" that it did not even occur to him to go to the Brazilian Consulate and explain the situation, and that it was clear that as the doors opened onto a public street, the case should never have reached this point. As a demonstration of his efforts, even after the sentence was passed, Colaço investigated other possible options and discovered the property of another Italian Protected Person who had his windows open onto the field of a Moroccan Muslim's farm. Appealing to Minister Mohammed Torres, he requested that the judicial order be enforced in either both cases, or neither of them.[42]

The dispute between Eleazar and Casez, which began with a merchant's fear of seeing a possible competitor threaten his business and ultimately reached the highest diplomatic authorities—the Brazilian Minister of Foreign Relations and his Moroccan counterpart—serves as an example of how daily quarrels that were decided by local courts and even by the rabbinical court of the Jewish community prior to European interference, began to involve high-level authorities from other countries. The saturation of official correspondence of the Brazilian offices in Morocco by accusations and arguments over individual conflicts reflects the effect of the Madrid Treaty, which designated Moroccan society as a society of consularization.

According to Mohammed Kenbib, the neologism *m'qûnssô* (consularized) that became popular in the last decade of the nineteenth century in Morocco was an adjective sought by many natives of the country, becoming a symbol of "possessions, power, and arrogance."[43] The expansion of the social groups who could claim Protected Person status—which was nothing more than an extension of the privileges previously inherent in foreign consular functions in Morocco to their respective colony within the country—contributed, in Moroccan eyes, to the dissolution of order and of state institutions. However, in the eyes of the Brazilian Ministry of Foreign Affairs and other institutions that dealt with these Protected Persons, the result was an overload of the consular system.

Trying to meet the demand of their Protected Persons, the consulates installed in Morocco started to solve situations in which the nature or status of Protected Person began to be used in mundane situations. As reported by Colaço in a meeting of the consulates to resolve "municipal issues," examples of these situations included the water supply problems in Tangier, the construction of a breakwater in Casablanca, and the activation of a pier in Tangier.[44]

Demographic Profile of the Morrocan Brazilian Community in 1900

The successor to Portuguese Consul José Daniel Colaço, the Moroccan naturalized Brazilian Jew Jacob Attias remained in office only briefly. Due to his death on February 24, 1900, the cause of which is not reported in the consulate's documentation, the Ministerio decided to send a Brazilian diplomat, oblivious to the modus operandi of exchanging favors and nominations from the Moroccan consular post.

In order to reorganize the Brazilian Consulate in Tangier, the new Consul, Adoniram Maurity de Calimerio, decided to register the Brazilian citizens in the country as a strategy to identify the local community. Consular offices in Tangier, Rabat, Marrakesh, Mogador, Tetuan, Arzila, Casablanca, Mazagão, Larache, and Alcácer thus gathered information about the main Brazilian families residing in the country during the year 1900, and after these data were gathered by the Consulate General in Tangier, Consul

General Calimerio edited the "Livro de Registro de Súditos Brasileiros Residentes no Marrocos em 1900–1901" (Book of Registration of Brazilian Subjects in Morocco in 1900–1901), a source that has allowed me to create a typology of this Brazilian community. The book also documents the progressive movement toward restricting citizenship and the assistance provided by the Brazilian government to the naturalized Brazilian community.

In the consulted sources, there are reports of at least two previous censuses taken in 1880 and 1890.[45] However, the 1901 census is the result of the expansion of Brazilian consular institutions in Morocco, due to the arrival and departure of immigrants between Morocco and Brazil and on account of peak demands on the consulate by the local community. Citizens who presented themselves to local consulates not only sought recognition as Brazilians, but they especially sought the benefits laid out in the Treaty of Madrid, of which they took advantage to obtain protection from the Brazilian government in view of the geopolitical situation of Morocco in the specific North African context of the nineteenth century.

The "Livro de Registro de Súditos Brasileiros Residentes no Marrocos em 1900–1901," prepared by the Consulate General of Brazil in Tangier, required Brazilian citizens who appeared for registration purposes to verify their citizenship through documentation of naturalization, birth, voter registration, or a passport, each of which indicated the geographical origin of the declarant. It also required data such as profession, place of birth, and marital status (including spouse's name and age); name, sex, and age of children; time and place where the person lived in Brazil; and the period of stay in Morocco after being naturalized. The inclusion of this last piece of information in the formal spreadsheet of the data collected might indicate that the census-takers of the Brazilian consular corps expected to deal with a significant number of registrations by citizens who were Brazilian by naturalization.[46] When Adoniram Calimerio occupied the consular post in Morocco, Brazilian intellectuals and legislators during the period were all trying to answer the same question as him: Who can be considered a Brazilian citizen?[47]

The census completed in 1901 reveals that 110 Brazilian citizens presented themselves at the local Moroccan consulates with a certificate of naturalization, seven appeared with a Brazilian voter registration document, and twenty-four registered with a passport—comprising a total of 141 individuals, considered "heads of family" (parents in a restricted family nucleus, financially independent single individuals, or widows). Curiously, in addition to these numbers, the final report issued in this census adds another seventy Brazilian citizens who did not register because they were absent from Morocco at the time the data was collected. It is not clear why these seventy individuals were included in the final number of Brazilian citizens, even without having responded to the census call. A plausible explanation may be personal recognition, and a close relationship between the community and the respective consulate.

The fact that seventy citizens who did not appear at consular posts were still counted in the statistics and their data included in the spreadsheet prepared by the Consulate General, indicates (1) the importance that those responsible for the lists attributed to the number of Brazilian citizens registered, as this might indicate the greater or lesser importance of their consular post, a criterion still used by the Ministry of Foreign Affairs; and (2) the possibility that these seventy citizens had already been included in previous censuses or that they were at least recognized as Brazilian citizens by the local community, having been numerically registered as part of an estimate based on the consular agents' expectations.[48] Geographic mobility was part of the daily lives of the members of this community, and the possibility that many of them were absent from their homes during the census-taking process did not seem to prevent the consular bodies from including them among the citizens they counted.

It is important to remember that the target of the census was "heads of family." In other words, the majority of those who are counted represented not only themselves but also their children and spouses, revealing that during this period in Morocco, there were a total of 211 families in which at least the provider was a Brazilian citizen. It is also important to emphasize that the relevance of this migratory movement should not be analyzed in absolute numbers, in comparison to the numbers of immigrants of other nationalities who came to Brazil during this period, but in relative numbers, as they impacted the economy and culture of the region whose demographic development is among the lowest in South America.

The most common profession among the Brazilian citizens who made up the Brazilian community in Morocco was that of merchants (158 of the citizens), followed by investors (7), and business owners (4). In addition to showing quantitatively that commerce was the most representative occupation among those registered, the data points to the self-identification of these individuals with the profession and suggests that distinctions among their role within commerce—that is, whether the declarant was self-employed, a business owner, an investor, or a salaried employee—was especially relevant to them.

Another data point collected by the census carried out in 1900 that offers objective evidence of the most peculiar aspect of this Brazilian community living abroad is that among the 211 citizens who were registered and who provided information on their family, only one was actually born in Brazil. Myer Azulay[49] presented a birth certificate issued in 1877 in Belém, province of Grão-Pará, in the Amazon region. He declared that at the age of twenty-three, he was still single, a resident of Casablanca for three years, and an employee. The overwhelming majority of the Brazilian citizens who provided information about their birthplaces were Moroccans by birth and naturalized Brazilians. The only exception was Samuel Laredo, who was born in Algeciras, Spain. The numbers are based solely on the birthplace of adults and especially the men who were registered, as the census did not specifically obtain the birthplaces of their children, most likely born in Brazil.

Calimerio's bureaucratic strategy of registering Brazilian citizens to identify them and delimit the consulate's scope of action demonstrates that the status of a Brazilian in Morocco depended on the availability of a consular post. Calimerio and his peers at the vice-consulates were the only ones capable of providing these Moroccan Jews and even those who were born on Brazilian soil the means to access the rights that were legally attributed to them. However, the attractiveness of the status of a naturalized Brazilian was so great that even some individuals who did not fit the requirements tried to access its benefits, as will be addressed next.

Suppression of the Consulate: The End of the Brazilian Jewish Community in Morocco?

A major financial crisis in the early years of the Republican government in Brazil (1889–1894), resulting from the policy of entrenchment, had a major impact on ministerial budgets. The Ministry of Foreign Affairs was one of the most adversely affected due to its constant need to use international financial assets to support its elaborate activities. As a result of this situation, the Ministry of Foreign Affairs reduced the number of Brazilian legations in foreign countries to eight and closed or demoted a number of consular posts.[50]

Responding to this administrative reform, the Brazilian Consulate in Tangier struggled to fight inefficiency. It had reduced the number of its vice-consuls and many of those who held these positions were recognized only at the local level.[51] The large volume of complaints and disputes in which personnel were involved on a daily basis put the legation in a problematic situation, especially in the face of fraudulent activity that was beyond the control of immigration authorities. For example, David Bensimol Bingdom and David Abecassis, who never went to Brazil, falsified the documents needed to register as citizens and were discovered only after Consul José Daniel Colaço contacted the governor of Pará, who, in turn, contacted the sister of one of the individuals who lived there.[52]

Another example is the case of the brothers Abraham and Mier Azulay, who, upon contracting a debt in the amount of seventy-five pounds sterling with the Messrs. J. Cohen and Co. in Pará, tried to embark on the steamboat *Cintra* toward Morocco, leaving their late father's house as payment. Meanwhile, Mier had been captured by police before boarding, and Abraham Azulay, having boarded, presented the Consul in Morocco with a counterfeit passport, declaring himself to be Brazilian. Had he not been warned by the Pará authorities, Adoniram Calimerio probably would have registered the fugitive as yet another Brazilian Protected Person, given that, in the words of the vice-consul in Casablanca, who was responsible for jailing Abraham temporarily, it was "a transcendent fraud."[53]

Information on how Brazilian naturalization and citizenship were being used in Morocco appeared in parliamentary debates and legal settings in Brazil, building political pressure for an administrative resolution of the issue which progressively reduced the government's provisions that favored naturalized citizens. In 1900, an informal rule had been adopted that restricted the status of Brazilian Protected Persons in Morocco to only those who had naturalized prior to the Treaty of Madrid.[54]

The Ministry of Foreign Affairs received exhaustive reports on the recurring problems that the peculiarities of this consular post generated. Unable to overcome these difficulties and due to the scarcity of funds, Calimerio requested funds for his repatriation. Understanding the request as his request for resignation, Minister Baron of Rio Branco ordered the closure of the consular post, dismissing Calimerio by means of a telegram dated February 6, 1903. Following the standard protocol for closing legations,[55] he asked Calimerio to deliver the consulate's archive to the Portuguese representative in Morocco, Count de Martins Ferrão, before returning to Brazil with his wife and daughter.

After the closure of the Brazilian Consulate in Tangier, the Portuguese Consulate unofficially assumed responsibility for the Brazilian citizens residing there. Juan Lapeen, now the former Brazilian Vice-Consul in Casablanca, would return to dedicating himself entirely to his business in the

Canary Islands. In his final report to the Ministry of Foreign Affairs on July 28, 1904, he wrote that the Brazilian community was dispersing, with some seeking the protection of other powers present in Morocco. Mindful of the continuing migratory flow between Brazil and Morocco, in 1913, the Ministry of Justice and Internal Affairs, under the direction of Rivadávia Correia (1866–1920), issued an official warning that Brazil would no longer grant naturalization to Moroccans, Syrians, Arabs, Egyptians or Turks, except on the condition that, if they returned to their country of origin, they would no longer be recognized as foreigners and would no longer have the right to Brazilian protection.[56]

Conclusion

In the period reviewed in this essay, the Brazilian consular documents record the simultaneous development of the Brazilian-Moroccan Jewish communities in both Morocco and Brazil. Moroccan Jewish workers left their homeland to "make America" in the Amazon region and their efforts also resulted in the consolidation of the status of Jews in Morocco returning from Brazil. Taking advantage of the fluidity of the definition of Brazilian citizenry and the fragmentation of the Moroccan judicial system, Moroccan Jews mobilized their Brazilian citizenship in a strategic way to deal with their precarious legal and social condition. However, in addition to the legal status, naturalization also affected the social positioning of families facing privileges and adversities. Sometimes they presented themselves as Brazilians while on other occasions as Moroccans, according to the situation and in order to enhance their social mobility. Rescuing the term used in the period—consularization—to describe daily usage of citizenship, this chapter analyzed the intermediary situation in which naturalized Brazilian Moroccans, who accessed the privileges of the protection of a foreign government, found themselves. The micro-analytical perspective, thus, highlights that the imperialist interference in Morocco, also through the Madrid Treaty, shaped dynamics between the groups that made up Moroccan society, such as the relationship between Jews and the Muslim authorities and those between naturalized Brazilians and consular authorities established in the country.

This essay cannot offer an exhaustive picture of the complex relationship that the Brazilian-naturalized Moroccan Jews established with Brazil, the country which was in the making then and in which today most of their descendants reside. Nor can it document the diversity of naturalized people who sailed across the Atlantic building their networks of sociability. While Moroccan Jews from Brazil represent a small minority of the groups immigrating at the turn of the twentieth century, they demonstrate a collective ability to take advantage of opportunities provided by the Brazilian consular presence in the country.

The activities of the Brazilian Consulate in Morocco as an institution that brought together this community of returnees did not replace the historical construction of Jewish-Moroccan identity that preceded it. Nevertheless, they were considered important in the international arena. Diplomatic relations with African countries became prestigious when European imperialist powers entered into dispute over the establishment of their respective areas of influence.[57] For this reason, the maintenance of consular posts in the North African territory, even if it did not generate commercial benefits, guaranteed the Brazilian state a privileged position in international politics, keeping abreast of the geopolitical maneuvers of the great military powers of the time. Consequently, the everyday problems of the Jewish community in nineteenth-century Morocco were significant to Brazil's international preeminence. The subsequent retreat of the consular presence from the African territory signaled Brazil's weakening role in the global theater.[58]

Editors' Note

Translation from the original Brazilian Portuguese is by Elizabeth Martins.

Notes

1. In the memo, he expressed the following: "[We] have also kept in mind that if the Israelites of this country who are naturalized Brazilian subjects did not count on the protection of the Imperial Government, even in their home country, when they return to it, would prevent others from wanting to go to Brazil." Memo, May 8, 1879, 265-1-10, Arquivo Histórico do Itamaraty (AHI).

2. See particularly the works of José Murilo de Carvalho, ed., *História do Brasil nação. A construção nacional (1830–1889)* (São Paulo: Editora Objetiva, 2012) and Jeffrey Lesser, *A invenção da brasilidade. Identidade nacional, etnicidade e políticas de imigração* (São Paulo: Editora Unesp, 2015).

3. Memo, 265-1-11, Documentação recolhida do Consulado Geral em Tânger, AHI.

4. Memo, March 3, 1876, 265-1-10, AHI.

5. Anita Novinsky and Diane Kuperman, eds., *Ibéria judaica: roteiros da memória* (São Paulo: EDUSP, 1996); Keila Grinberg, *Judeus no Brasil: inquisição, imigração e identidade* (Rio de Janeiro: Civilização Brasileira, 2005); Reginaldo J. Heller, *Os judeus do*

Eldorado. Reinventando uma identidade em plena Amazônia (Rio de Janeiro: E-papers, 2010); and others.

6. Lesser, *A invenção da brasilidade*; Lesser, *Immigration, Ethnicity, and National Identity in Brazil, 1808 to the Present* (New York: Cambridge University Press, 2013), and others.

7. Eva A. Blay, "Judeus na Amazônia," in *Identidades judaicas no Brasil contemporâneo*, ed. Bila Sorj (Rio de Janeiro: Centro Edelstein de Pesquisas Sociais, 2008), 29.

8. The number of "returnees" is based on the census conducted in 1900. Today, descendants of this community are present in every strata of Brazilian society.

9. In the Brazilian imperial period (1822–1889), immigrants were required to reside in Brazil for more than two years (Decree No. 291/1843), form family bonds with Brazilians, acquire property, and demonstrate interest in being a citizen by means of an oath. In addition, they were to cover the fee for the Naturalization Letter in the amount of 12$000. For comparison, in 1908 a weaver in Rio de Janeiro was paid $1 a day and a factory worker just over $2 a day. See Eulalia M. L. Lobo, "Evolução dos preços e do padrão de vida no Rio de Janeiro, 1820–1930," *Revista Brasileira de Economia* 25, no. 4 (October/November 1971): 256. Wives shared their husband's naturalized citizenship while he was alive. With the advent of the Republic (1889–1930), the government decreed (Decree 58-A/1889) that all those residing in Brazilian territory would be considered citizens. José Tavares Bastos, *Naturalização: contendo todos os decretos* (Coimbra: Coimbra Ed., 1925), 10, 27. This republican decree constituted "The Great Naturalization," which resulted in diplomatic problems with some of the countries of origin of the naturalized citizens; this process continued to be debated until the passage of the Brazilian Civil Code (1916). Keila Grinberg, *Código civil e cidadania* (Rio de Janeiro: Jorge Zahar, 2001).

10. The phrase is from Fábio Koifman's *Imigrante ideal: o Ministério da Justiça e a entrada de estrangeiros no Brasil (1941–1945)* (Rio de Janeiro: Civilização Brasileira, 2012).

11. Dispatch, November 21, 1878, 265-1-10, Documentação recolhida do Consulado Geral em Tânger, AHI.

12. One of the basic premises of Cultural Studies is the mobilization of language, especially in Orientalist literary production, for the construction of discourses that legitimize colonial domination and its various forms of violence, including in international relations. See Gayatri C. Spivak, "Can the Subaltern Speak?" in *Marxism and Interpretation of Culture*, eds. Cary Nelson and Lawrence Grossberg (Basingstoke: Macmillan, 1988), 271–313, and Edward Said, *Orientalism* (New York: Vintage Books, 1979).

13. Lucas de Mattos Moura Fernandes, "Caminhando entre mouros: o relato da viagem de D. Fernando II (1856) ao Marrocos por José Daniel Colaço," *XII Jornada de Estudos Históricos Professor Manoel Salgado-PPGHIS-UFRJ* 3 (October 2017): 1138–50.

14. The work of James Cable has been the subject of debate, but foundational to the concept. See James Cable, *Gunboat Diplomacy, 1919–1991: Political Applications of Limited Naval Force*, 3rd ed. (Basingstoke: Macmillan, 1994).

15. Memo, February 25, 1892, 265-1-11, Documentação recolhida do Consulado Geral em Tânger, AHI.

16. Ibid.

17. Memo, July 14, 1894, 265-1-11, Documentação recolhida do Consulado Geral em Tânger, AHI.

18. Letter, March 29, 1880, in ibid. The same discourse on the Jewish condition in Morocco and the Brazilian intervention is adopted by Colaço in the memo of November 30, 1880, pointing to a series of murders of Moroccan Jews in protest of the Moroccan agreement to the terms of the Madrid Convention, of the same year. See AHI, 265-1-10.

19. Memo, February 16, 1864, 265-1-11, Documentação recolhida do Consulado Geral em Tânger, AHI.

20. Memo, October 27, 1880, 265-1-11, Documentação recolhida do Consulado Geral em Tânger, AHI.

21. Ibid.

22. Ibid.

23. Memo, October 8, 1889, 265-1-10, Documentação recolhida do Consulado Geral em Tânger, AHI.

24. In a memo dated October 8, 1889, Colaço asked the government to communicate with the Genoese company La Velvo, which had steam ships transiting between the coast of Italy and South America, suggesting the possibility that they could make a stopover in Tangier. See Memo, October 8, 1889, 265-1-10, Documentação recolhida do Consulado Geral em Tânger, AHI.

25. Memo, July 28, 1897, in "Despachos da Secretaria de Estado para o Consulado Geral em Tânger (1894–1897)," Documentação recolhida, Consulado Geral do Brasil em Tânger, AHI.

26. Memo July, 28, 1897, 265-1-10, Documentação recolhida do Consulado Geral em Tânger, AHI.

27. *Right of Protection in Morocco. Convention Signed at Madrid July 3, 1880*, accessed July 15, 2018, https://www.loc.gov/law/help/us-treaties/bevans/m-ust000001-0071.pdf.

28. Ibid.

29. Dispatch from Minister Dionísio de Castro Cerqueira to Consul in Tanger, Jacob Attias, containing in the annex the case report by Colaço, September 9, 1897, "Despachos da Secretaria de Estado para o Consulado Geral em Tânger (1894–1897)," Documentação Consular recolhida—Consulado Geral do Brasil em Tânger, AHI.

30. Memo, 265-1-11, Documentação recolhida do Consulado Geral em Tânger, AHI.

31. See *Right of Protection in Morocco*.

32. In the Brazilian Vice Consulate of Casablanca alone, eighty-five *samsars and mojalatas* were listed linked to eighteen naturalized Brazilian merchants. In addition to the city in which the *mojalata* resided, the list also included the Islamic jurisdiction to which he was subjected, pointing to the normality of the litigious situation with local justice. April 15, 1900, CB Tânger 9, AHI.

33. See Art. 12 in *Right of Protection in Morocco*.

34. 374-4-671, packet 4, folder 2, Documentação recolhida do Consulado Geral em Tânger, AHI.

35. Article 7, Decree 997B of November 11, 1890, accessed March 22, 2022, https://www2.camara.leg.br/legin/fed/decret/1824-1899/decreto-997-b-11-novembro-1890-553452-publicacaooriginal-71415-pe.html.

36. Memos from August 16, 1900, and October 10, 1900, 265-1-15, Documentação recolhida do Consulado Geral em Tânger, AHI.

37. Despite its small population and minor political importance, the city of Larache (*Al Araishi*) is prominently located on the northwest coast of Morocco, on the bank of the Lucos River, offering access to mountainous regions in the interior of the country.

38. Memo, July 10, 1900 et seq., 265-1-13, Documentação recolhida do Consulado Geral em Tânger, AHI.

39. Memo, July 26, 1891, 265-1-11, Documentação recolhida do Consulado Geral em Tânger, AHI.

40. Memo, January 8, 1891, 265-1-11, Documentação recolhida do Consulado Geral em Tânger, AHI.

41. Ibid.

42. Memo, July 7, 1891 et seq., 265-1-11, Documentação recolhida do Consulado Geral em Tânger, AHI.

43. Mohammed Kenbib, *Juifs et musulmans au Maroc* (Paris: Editions Tallandier, 2016), 69.

44. Memo, April 5, 1887, 265-1-10, Documentação recolhida do Consulado Geral em Tânger, AHI.

45. See Annex to Memo of March 29, 1880, 265-1-10, Documentação recolhida do Consulado Geral em Tânger, AHI.

46. I consider the fact that the model of the Brazilian registry books in Morocco already included the requirement for the registration of an individual, providing information such as "place of residence in Brazil" and "how long has the person been in Morocco since naturalized"—items on the questionnaire that would never apply if the majority of individuals to be interviewed were expected to be native-born Brazilians. See "Livro de Registro de Súditos Brasileiros Residentes no Marrocos em 1900–1901," Documentação Consular recolhida—Consulado Geral do Brasil em Tânger, AHI.

47. On the debate about the need to elaborate a Brazilian civil code and the development of different definitions of who would be the "people" in Brazil, see Grinberg, *Código civil e cidadania;* José Murilo de Carvalho, "Cidadania: tipos e percursos," *Estudos Históricos* 9, no. 18 (1995): 337–59; and de Carvalho, *Cidadania no Brasil. O longo caminho* (Rio de Janeiro: Civilização Brasileira, 2001).

48. See "Livro de Registro de Súditos Brasileiros Residentes no Marrocos em 1900–1901," Documentação Consular recolhida—Consulado Geral do Brasil em Tânger, AHI, 40–50.

49. A fundamental technical consideration is that the Sephardic community has a tradition of honoring living male relatives by naming their children after them. This and other specificities of this community make the repertoire of names limited and there are many namesakes, making biographical research very difficult. Valuing accuracy, I avoid affirming the identification between people based only on the name and surname information, as in the case of the two "Mi (y) er Azulay" mentioned in this article. Other personal data must be available to verify identification.

50. Dispatch, 374-4-671, Documentação recolhida do Consulado Geral em Tânger, AHI.

51. In a dispatch dated October 1903, Juan Lapeen discovers that the Vice-Consulate under his responsibility in Casablanca had been missing from the personnel list since 1889 (!). 250-2-4, Documentação recolhida do Consulado Geral em Tânger, AHI.

52. Memo, November 18, 1885, 265-1-10, Documentação recolhida do Consulado Geral em Tânger, AHI.

53. Memo, August 31, (1900) et seq., CB Tânger 9, AHI.

54. Lesser, 171.

55. Decree No. 3248, April 7, 1899, accessed March 22, 2022, https://www2.camara.leg.br/legin/fed/decret/1824-1899/decreto-3248-7-abril-1899-539116-publicacaooriginal-37013-pe.html.

56. Bastos, *Naturalização*, 164.

57. See Eric J. Hobsbawm, *A era dos impérios (1875–1914)*, 21st ed. (São Paulo: Paz e Terra, 2016), 427; and more specifically, Mohammed Nadir, "Em torno da viagem diplomática do Rei D. Fernando II de Portugal a Marrocos, em 1856," *Revista de História da Sociedade e da Cultura* 8 (January 2008): 281–306.

58. Frederico Antonio Ferreira, "Diplomacia do Império Brasileiro na África entre 1850 e 1860: abolicionismo, liberalismo e civilização," *Revista Discente do Programa de Pós-graduação em História da UFJF* 3, no. 5 (January/July 2017): 1–22.

Bibliography

Primary Sources

Archive

Arquivo Histórico do Itamaraty (AHI, Rio de Janeiro)

Electronic Source

Right of Protection in Morocco. Convention signed at Madrid July 3, 1880. Accessed July 15, 2018. https://www.loc.gov/law/help/us-treaties/bevans/m-ust000001-0071.pdf.

Secondary Sources

Bastos, José Tavares. *Naturalização: contendo todos os decretos*. Coimbra: Coimbra Ed., 1925.

Biguelman, Paula. *A crise do escravismo e a grande imigração*. São Paulo: Brasiliense, 1982.

Blay, Eva A. "Judeus na Amazônia." In *Identidades judaicas no Brasil contemporâneo*, edited by Bila Sorj, 25–57. Rio de Janeiro: Centro Edelstein de Pesquisas Sociais, 2008.

Cable, James. *Gunboat Diplomacy, 1919–1991: Political Applications of Limited Naval Force*. 3rd. ed. Basingstoke: Macmillan, 1994.

de Carvalho, José Murilo. "Cidadania: tipos e percursos." *Estudos Históricos* 9, no. 18 (1995): 337–59.

———. *Cidadania no Brasil. O longo caminho*. Rio de Janeiro: Civilização Brasileira, 2001.

―――, ed. *História do Brasil nação. A construção nacional (1830–1889)*. São Paulo: Editora Objetiva, 2012.

Fernandes, Lucas de Mattos Moura. "Caminhando entre mouros: o relato da viagem de D. Fernando II (1856) ao Marrocos por José Daniel Colaço." *XII Jornada de Estudos Históricos Professor Manoel Salgado-PPGHIS-UFRJ* 3 (October 2017): 1138–50.

Ferreira, Frederico Antonio. "Diplomacia do Império Brasileiro na África entre 1850 e 1860: abolicionismo, liberalismo e civilização." *Revista Discente do Programa de Pós-graduação em História da UFJF* 3, no. 5 (January/July 2017): 1–22.

Grinberg, Keila. *Código civil e cidadania*. Rio de Janeiro: Jorge Zahar, 2001.

―――. *Judeus no Brasil: inquisição, imigração e identidade*. Rio de Janeiro: Civilização Brasileira, 2005.

Heller, Reginaldo J. *Os judeus do Eldorado. Reinventando uma identidade em plena Amazônia*. Rio de Janeiro: E-papers, 2010.

Hobsbawm, Eric J. *A era dos impérios (1875–1914)*. 21st ed. São Paulo: Paz e Terra, 2016.

Kenbib, Mohammed. *Juifs et musulmans au Maroc*. Paris: Editions Tallandier, 2016.

Koifman, Fábio. *Imigrante ideal: o Ministério da Justiça e a entrada de estrangeiros no Brasil (1941–1945)*. Rio de Janeiro: Civilização Brasileira, 2012.

Lesser, Jeffrey. *Immigration, Ethnicity, and National Identity in Brazil, 1808 to the Present*. Cambridge: Cambridge University Press, 2013.

―――. *A invenção da Brasilidade. Identidade nacional, etnicidade e políticas de imigração*. São Paulo: Editora Unesp, 2015.

Lobo, Eulalia M. L. "Evolução dos preços e do padrão de vida no Rio de Janeiro, 1820–1930." *Revista Brasileira de Economia* (Rio de Janeiro) 25, no. 4 (October/November 1971): 235–65.

Nadir, Mohammed. "Em torno da viagem diplomática do Rei D. Fernando II de Portugal a Marrocos, em 1856." *Revista de História da Sociedade e da Cultura* 8 (January 2008): 281–306.

Novinsky, Anita, and Diane Kuperman, eds. *Ibéria judaica: roteiros da memória*. São Paulo: EDUSP, 1996.

Said, Edward. *Orientalism*. New York: Vintage Books, 1979.

Spivak, Gayatri C. "Can the Subaltern Speak?" In *Marxism and Interpretation of Culture*, edited by Cary Nelson and Lawrence Grossberg, 271–313. Basingstoke: Macmillan, 1988.

6

A *Yanqui's* Gaze

Maurice Schwartz's South American Travelogues from 1930

Zachary M. Baker

Historically, Yiddish-speaking Jews were largely concentrated in the western provinces of the Russian Empire (the Pale of Settlement and Congress Poland), the neighboring regions of Austrian Galicia and Bukovina, and portions of Hungary and Romania. With the mass emigration of Eastern European Jews, from the 1880s to the 1930s, sizable communities of Yiddish speakers set down roots in many countries worldwide. That period also experienced the proliferation of new political movements and ideologies among Jews of Eastern European backgrounds, including different—and sometimes overlapping—strains of Zionism, modern religious orthodoxy, anarchism, socialism, communism, and Yiddish cultural nationalism, or Yiddishism. The historian Mariusz Kałczewiak writes that Yiddishist ideology "focused on the advancement of Yiddish as a language of high and popular culture and scholarship," giving rise to "the transnational space of Yiddishland as an imagined diasporic nation, inhabiting old and new centers of Eastern European Jewishness."[1] Yiddish theater occupied an important position in this transnational cultural system.

Modern Yiddish theater emerged in Romania and Russia during the late 1870s. From its very beginnings, troupes of Jewish actors who performed in Yiddish wandered from city to city and across boundaries and oceans, throughout the expanding diaspora of Yiddishland.[2] The major stars brought along scripts of original and translated plays, stage instructions, costumes, sets, and sometimes even stage equipment.[3] Argentina was a node in an international network comprising locally based theater owners, impresarios, actors, musicians, and crews, plus the guest stars and directors

Figure 6.1. Photograph of Maurice Schwartz's family dated 1948. It was a gift to the family of the renowned graphic artist Leon Poch, illustrating that during his many visits, Schwartz, the North American celebrity actor and director, built lasting relationships with Argentinian artists. The handwritten dedication in Yiddish accompanying the photograph says: "With friendship to the Poch family from the family of Maurice Schwartz." Courtesy of Dina and Susana Poch, daughters of Leon Poch.

from abroad. At the same time, the Argentine Yiddish theater functioned within the diverse and multilingual theatrical ecosystem of Buenos Aires.[4]

In the second half of May 1930, Maurice Schwartz (1889–1960)—Yiddish actor, director, impresario—embarked upon a seventeen-day sea voyage that took him from New York to Buenos Aires. This was his first trip to South America, and also the first time that he traveled abroad as an individual guest star on the international Yiddish theater circuit.[5] Although Schwartz was a Yiddish-speaking Jew who was born in Ukraine, by 1930 he had long since become a fixture of New York City's theatrical scene. Schwartz was accompanied by his wife Anna; when they reached Argentina, they met up with Joseph Schwartzberg, a New York actor who served as advance man and stage manager for Schwartz's tour.

The international repertory of Yiddish plays—whether popular (*shund*, meaning "trash") or literary (*beser*, i.e., "better") in their orientation—was familiar to audiences wherever Yiddish theater was performed. Having led New York's Yiddish Art Theatre since its founding in 1918, Schwartz enjoyed a worldwide reputation as one of the leading exponents of the highbrow, "better" repertory. His was the only Yiddish theater in New York to offer its audiences a steady diet of literary plays, both those originally written in Yiddish (many of which Schwartz himself adapted for the stage) and those in Yiddish translation. Many of the plays that Schwartz staged in Buenos Aires in 1930 had been performed there previously, some of them multiple times.

At no point during its thirty-plus years of existence was Schwartz's Yiddish Art Theatre ever on secure financial grounds—not even after the company had built its own theater on New York's Second Avenue in the mid-1920s. Following the Wall Street crash of October 1929, it was in notably dire straits, so the invitation to perform in Argentina came at an opportune time, since it would enable Schwartz to pay off some of his company's debts. As the Buenos Aires–based actor-impresario Leon Brest put it in a letter to Schwartz: "The chief purpose of your tour is to make money—and that will be an absolute, 100 percent certainty."[6] During the course of his ten-week stay in Buenos Aires, Schwartz mounted a dozen plays at two centrally located venues: the Teatro Nuevo and the Teatro Argentino. He then toured Jewish communities in the Argentine provinces and, on his way home, in Montevideo, São Paulo, and Rio de Janeiro. Subsequently, Schwartz would regularly return to South America.

Apart from his stage performances, the South American tour offered Schwartz another way to augment his income. The New York Yiddish daily *Forverts* (*The Jewish Daily Forward*) commissioned him to write a series of ten travelogues, which were published in that newspaper between June 28 and October 11, 1930. After spending a few weeks in Buenos Aires, his journalistic horizons expanded to include both of that city's Yiddish dailies, *Di Presse* (also transliterated as *Di Prese*) and *Di Idishe Tsaytung* (*Diario Israelita*), as well as the weekly magazine *Der Shpigl* (*El Espejo*).[7] His articles were conversational in tone and peppered with amusing anecdotes. Schwartz's observations were informed by his extensive involvement with the Yiddish theaters of New York City during his nearly three decades of life in the United States, since his arrival there in 1901 at the age of twelve. As his dispatches reveal, he shared his impressions of Brazil, Uruguay, and Argentina very much through the lens of a "Yanqui" tourist.

In his South American travel journalism, Schwartz not only discussed the theater at length, but also offered his observations concerning political and social conditions in each of the places that he was visiting and prospects facing Jewish immigrants to these countries. Schwartz's travel series thus provided potentially useful information to his North American readers, almost all of whom were immigrants from Eastern Europe, many with relatives there who wished to relocate overseas. With immigration to the United States almost completely closed by the Johnson-Reed Act of 1924, South American countries offered a potential destination for Eastern European Jews. Indeed, while in Buenos Aires, Schwartz visited an uncle and a cousin who had recently emigrated to Argentina.

Yiddish Travel Narratives

Schwartz's South American travelogue fit into "the prolific genre of Yiddish travel writing," which was quite familiar to the global Yiddish reading public of 1930.[8] Yiddish travel accounts of the late nineteenth and early twentieth century ran the gamut from the fictional to the factual. Publications like *The Travels of Benjamin the Third* (*Masoes Binyomen ha-shlishi*),by Mendele Moykher Sforim (the authorial alter ego of Sholem-Yankev Abramovitsh [1836–1917]), *Travel Scenes* (*Bilder fun a provints-rayze*) by I. L. Peretz (1852–1915), and the *Railroad Stories* (*Ayznban geshikhtes*) of Sholem Aleichem (1859–1916) are all classics of Yiddish literature and have travel as their main motifs.[9] Nonfiction travel narratives and guidebooks in Yiddish reported on remote and exotic locales (such as equatorial Africa, India, China, Japan, and the Hawaiian Islands), outstanding geographical features (e.g., Niagara Falls), polar expeditions, political utopias, and of course, countries that were prospective magnets for immigrants. A minority of these publications were translations into Yiddish from other languages. Some travel writing was expressly addressed to children, be they inside or outside the classroom.[10]

Yiddish newspapers and magazines in the United States and elsewhere serialized travel accounts, some of which were later issued in book form.[11] Most Yiddish travel books published before 1940 dealt either with Palestine (both traditional pilgrimages and descriptions of the rapidly growing Zionist *Yishuv*), the United States (especially before 1914), or Soviet Russia (after 1918 with an increasing emphasis on Birobidzhan during the 1930s). Travel writing about South America also existed in Yiddish, though to a lesser extent than works devoted to these other destinations. Two topics stood out in works dealing specifically with Argentina: the agricultural colonies on the Pampas and Argentina as a magnet for sex traffickers and a trap for their victims. Writers such as the peripatetic Peretz Hirschbein and H. D. Nomberg dwelt extensively on the colonies in their South American travelogues,[12] while Schwartz's travel journalism (with the exception of his account of the Moisés Ville agricultural settlement) had an almost exclusively urban focus.

Given his insider perspective as a Yiddish-speaking cultural figure visiting an outpost of the expanding diaspora of Yiddishland, Schwartz's South American travelogue "can be considered a form of autoethnography or native ethnography," to use anthropologist Tamar Lewinsky's label. She writes: "As lay-ethnographers, the travel writers were interested in the mores, stories, material culture, and language of the Jews in Argentina. . . . The writers' use of tropes and images underscores their notion of a transnational East European Jewish Diaspora connected through language, cultural traditions, and memories." Like Hirschbein, Schwartz "paraphrase[d] conversations and interviews with members of the immigrant community" in Argentina and "directe[d] readers' attention to specific differences, linguistic and cultural, that [had] emerged as a result of migration and cross-cultural influences."[13] In Mariusz Kałczewiak's words, "Jewish travel writers and their subjects shared a common language, an Eastern European background, and the experience of travel or migration."[14] In contrast to non-Jewish writers from Western Europe and the United States, "the cultural, social, and political contexts of Jewishness placed Jewish travelers on the margins of the classic travel discourse of the era."[15]

In contrast to Hirschbein and (especially) Nomberg, Schwartz came to his topic having lived most of his life in New York City, at one diasporic remove from the Eastern European heartland where those two Polish-Jewish authors grew to maturity.[16] Amenities that he took for granted were not always present, even in a modern city like Buenos Aires. Schwartz implicitly accepted the premise that the economic development of the countries of the Southern Cone hinged upon the involvement of Anglo-American capital, which he amended by advocating the continued immigration of Eastern European Jews. Even so, Schwartz's travel writing shared many of the themes, large and small, elaborated by the two Eastern European authors. As Kałczewiak writes, "Nomberg's and Hirschbein's travel books both exoticized and objectified the people of Argentina."

Relations between the sexes, Jews' participation in the underworld of sex trafficking, assumptions concerning indigenous populations, and contrasts between Argentina's relative underdevelopment with the "modern, urban experience of immigrants in the United States"[17] figure in all three writers' travel narratives. If, in their descriptions of non-Jewish spaces, Hirschbein's and Nomberg's "gaze" was Eurocentric, the underlying objective of their narratives was to depict the remote expansion of the East European Jewish Diaspora, as opposed to "serv[ing] as an intellectual and scientific arm of colonization and conquest." By contrast, Schwartz's perspective was that of a longtime resident of the North American imperium, a Yiddish-speaking New Yorker who was also completely fluent in English. Nevertheless, all three writers "acted as cultural mediators . . . or as good entertainers" for their readers, a role for which the actor Schwartz was especially suited.[18]

Brazil and Uruguay

Schwartz's travelogues conveyed his sense of wonder at the sights and sounds of South America, while also holding up a mirror to his readers— Yiddish-speaking immigrants living under rather different conditions in New York and other large North American cities. Most of them would have undergone an ocean voyage from Europe to the Americas. However, they were traveling as emigrants and not as tourists or on business. Emigrants' trips were one-way, from east to west, across the Atlantic, often in the cramped quarters of steerage. By contrast, the north-to-south sea route in the Western Hemisphere was not a major migration path in 1930. Like Hirschbein and Nomberg on their own South American voyages, Maurice and Anna Schwartz traveled first-class, joined in that section by just forty-eight other passengers. The SS *Southern Cross* made several calls along the way to pick up and drop off cargo and passengers.[19]

Schwartz populated his South American travelogue with theatrical comparisons, commencing with his depiction of the scene aboard the boat at the New York pier just before its departure. Friends and relatives mingled with passengers during the frenzied moments before the ship's whistle signaled the non-passengers to come ashore. Schwartz likened the festive mood of that moment to "the most powerful and theatrical crowd scenes" and invoked the German director Max Reinhardt's production of Romain Rolland's play *Danton*.[20]

Schwartz described the breathtaking approach to Rio de Janeiro at sunrise as "the gate of Paradise," likening the clouds to "the production of a heavenly spectacle, and the performers are the amazing colors [that] change so quickly." Rio struck Schwartz as a "dreamy dollhouse," a seductive and "flirtatious" city with its "wonderful, idiosyncratic houses and mansions," sidewalk mosaics, and open-air shops. The mountains surrounding the city's harbor, among them the famous Sugar Loaf, added to the theatrical tableau.

Schwartz felt compelled to comment on the seeming absence of racial segregation in restaurants, theaters, and schools, drawing an implicit contrast with conditions prevailing in the United States. He observed people of numerous backgrounds—many of them brown or black—on the city's streets.[21] Blacks (those who could afford it) sat alongside whites in restaurants and at the theater, he wrote, and their children were able to attend the same schools. The "Spanish [sic] and the Italians" intermarried with blacks, bringing about a racially "mixed generation." However, the only well-dressed individuals he spotted were foreign tourists, and he noticed barefoot children along the main thoroughfares. He reported that a skilled artisan earned 16 million inflationary reais a day—about two dollars—and an ordinary laborer earned only about eighty cents a day. Working-class Brazilians subsisted on a diet of rice and black beans; their thirst was quenched with Cerveja Fidalga.

Schwartz was met at the pier by local Yiddish journalists and a committee of young men and women "with pioneering spirit." In the day or so that he spent in Rio, he transmitted what these Yiddish-speaking immigrants told him about their new country's vastness and natural resources: coffee and sugar were the country's main products, but mineral deposits were being neglected and economic development was slow. The illiteracy rate was high and there was no opera or serious theater in Rio—just American movies and a revue theater. The imposing Theatro Municipal was open only a few days each year.

About 15,000 Jews lived in Rio, Schwartz reported, and immigration levels were low; what Brazil needed, he asserted, was a million "worker bees." Rather than squander its budgetary resources on airplanes, the government of President Washington Luís Pereira de Sousa ought to foster the country's economic development by publicizing the benefits of Jewish immigration. Brazil needed to "import" Jewish magnates and philanthropists the likes of Nathan Straus (1847–1931; co-owner of Macy's) and Julius Rosenwald (1862–1932; he ran Sears, Roebuck), "a few good union organizers," and Jews who would support newspapers, young Yiddish poets, literary critics, and "ambitious actors." Entire regions, inhabited by "savage Indian tribes," were untouched by civilization. "The Jews would even civilize [*gemakht far mentshn*] the Indians," he condescendingly remarked.[22]

Montevideo was the penultimate port of call before Buenos Aires. Schwartz was welcomed by the editors of a local Yiddish newspaper and magazine, and also by Yiddish actors visiting from Buenos Aires who hoped to set up a permanent theater company in the Uruguayan capital. Aboard ship, Schwartz had heard Uruguay's praises sung by two of his fellow passengers, the philosemitic Dr. Trewitt from Dallas, and a Father Kelsey, who resided in Montevideo—and he was curious to learn more.

Schwartz offered his readers an excursus about Uruguay's geography ("about the size of New Jersey" [sic; actually, it is roughly the size of Missouri]), history, and politics. Channeling his local informants, Schwartz communicated an upbeat précis of political, economic, and social conditions in Uruguay: "Though I wasn't there for very long, it was hard to leave behind the freedom that is in the air." Schwartz approved of the fact that the country's constitution mentioned political refugees, one of whom, the Ukraine-born anarchist Simón (Shimen) Radowitzky (1891–1956), had recently been admitted to Uruguay after serving more than 20 years in an Argentine prison for assassinating a government official.[23]

In contrast to Brazil, Uruguay's currency was stable, and the standard of living was higher. The country's main exports were wool, meat, grain, and marble. To Schwartz's approbation, international capital dominated the economy; the tram franchise, telegraph agency, and hotels were all in foreign hands and operated according to "European" standards. Chicago's Swift meatpacking company obligingly supplied the US market with expensive Uruguayan steaks.

The government's main office building, by the Plaza de la Independencia, was a little smaller than Cooper Union (i.e., not large at all), Schwartz wrote, and was guarded by three armed soldiers who reminded him of extras in a play. They yawned and wondered when it would be time for lunch. All of the city's businesses shut down during the two-hour lunch break. A restaurant in Montevideo was a "factory" where the "labor" consisted of consuming liquor, appetizers ("sufficient for the pre–Yom Kippur meal," referring to the Jewish Day of Atonement, a fast day), soup, meats accompanied by wine and beer, and Brazilian coffee, in that order.

The Jewish population of Uruguay was still small—between "7,000 and 8,000 Jewish families." Most of Uruguay's Jews earned their livelihoods as peddlers, selling everything on credit ("from the suit to the bed") to their Christian customers. Though the immigration rate was low, Schwartz reported that the prospects for Jewish immigrants were excellent, better even than in North America.[24]

Arrival in Buenos Aires—Impressions of the City

Schwartz proceeded from Uruguay to Argentina, where he would remain for three months. North American Yiddish readers of Schwartz's articles were doubtless eager to learn more about conditions in this distant Latin American land which had become a destination for many of their relatives and *landslayt* (compatriots) who were still living in Eastern Europe. "Immigration is flowing as if from a spring," Schwartz wrote, with a dash of exaggeration, "The gates are open. Everyone can bring his relatives and friends here without impediment." (In fact, by 1930 Argentina, too, was beginning to restrict immigration.) Seven of his travel articles dealt exclusively with Argentina—five with Buenos Aires alone.

Schwartz's comings and goings were accorded blanket coverage by the Yiddish press of Buenos Aires. He was ferried about town, wined and dined, and feted by cultural organizations. His theatrical productions were reviewed by the two Yiddish dailies and in a few instances also by Spanish- and German-language newspapers in the Argentine capital.

Schwartz was dazzled by the sounds, gesticulations, speech, restaurants, cafés, and sartorial habits of this "world metropolis"—the "Paris of America"—starting with the ubiquitous expression *sí-sí*, which Jewish immigrants, including his "still green" uncle, quickly picked up: "He kisses me and weeps and shouts [in Yiddish], 'My Moyshele, *sí-sí*, I've missed you for so long, *sí-sí!* How's your father? *sí-sí!* What's doing in North America? You make a better living there, *sí-sí!*'" The city's many Spanish-language newspapers, Schwartz wrote, blared headlines, and featured large photos like the New York *Daily News*. Some printed four to six editions each day, "just as in New York."

The narrowness of the streets and sidewalks of Central Buenos Aires caused pedestrians to brush up against one another, which reminded Schwartz of scenes in the Abraham Goldfaden play *The Sorceress* (*Di kishefmakherin*). He compared Calle Florida, with its cramped sidewalks, big businesses, clubs, and galleries, to New York's Fifth Avenue. It offered an open-air fashion show, where wealthy women flaunted their finery and their jewels: "The couples proudly promenade, like Adam and Eve in Paradise." Schwartz also commented on the ethnic mix—what he called the "national colonies"—of Buenos Aires. In addition to the very large Spanish and Italian "colonies," he mentioned the city's sizable communities of English-, French-, and German-speaking inhabitants.

Early in his visit to Argentina, Schwartz was an inadvertent witness to a political rally of the Partido Socialista Independiente (PSI), which took place one afternoon inside one of the theaters where he was performing. About 5,000 people crammed into an auditorium with just 2,000 seats. The dramatic oratory reminded him of demonstrations that he had witnessed as a teenager at Rutgers Square on New York's Lower East Side: "I was practically carried away by the crowd's fire and temperament." Speaker after speaker denounced and mocked President Hipólito Yrigoyen—who would soon be overthrown by the Argentine military (with support from the PSI). Schwartz was returning to Buenos Aires from his tour of the Argentine provinces when the coup took place on September 6th.

He was shown around one affluent residential district by his "cousin, a greenhorn, just two years in the country, [who] speaks of Palermo like a religious Jew about Jerusalem." The cousin compared Palermo and its public gardens to Versailles—but "there is one Versailles and one Versailles flower garden." Still, Schwartz felt reassured that such comparisons reflected Jewish immigrants' growing sense of at-homeness. Already, he continued, Argentina's Jews had made distinguished contributions to the country's mainstream culture. There were people like "[Samuel] Eichelbaum, [who] is considered one of the country's finest playwrights"; Alberto Gerchunoff, the "Argentine Anatole France" with his impeccable Spanish style ("he also speaks a genuine 'Sholem Aleichem Yiddish'"); and the Singerman sisters, Berta and Paulina, who had become famous for their recitations and acting throughout Latin America and Spain.[25]

The constant influx of immigrants had led to a housing shortage in this city of 2.5 million inhabitants. North American forms were beginning to overtake European influences, though with "little consideration for beauty or comfort," Schwartz wrote. The majority of houses, and also "many hospitals, restaurants, and theaters lack 'steam' [central heating] and must make do with electrical and oil [space] heaters." This became a leitmotif of his travelogue, one that doubtless resonated with his North American readers. Only the newer houses were equipped with "steam" ("which is unusual throughout South America"). Hotels with "steam" cost as much as, or more than, New York's Commodore Hotel next to Grand Central Station. In contrast to North Americans, who insisted on their "steam" inside and out, "it's very easy to satisfy the Argentine, which is why he lives in uncomfortable houses." At any rate, people live on the streets more than in their houses, because the air is good (*"buenos aires"*), Schwartz glibly added.[26]

The Status of Women in Buenos Aires

In the first of his Buenos Aires travel pieces, Schwartz had written about what he considered to be the atmosphere of freedom that prevailed on the streets and in public places. Later, however, he amended this by considering relations between the sexes and the status of women in the public sphere. In terms of commonplace etiquette, "Buenos Aires is very backward," he remarked; men don't remove their hats in elevators unless they're hot. More to the point was his observation that social mores demanded that women's public movements be closely supervised and circumscribed, an observation that was shared by Nomberg, Hirschbein, and other contemporary observers.[27]

Despite—or rather, as historian Mir Yarfitz and others have argued, *because* of—its reputation as "sin city," Buenos Aires seemed quite the opposite.[28] Married women left their houses only when accompanied by their husbands or friends. A mother kept watch on her engaged daughter until she married—which might be a matter of years. Schwartz attended a ball at the Sociedad Hebraica, a social and cultural club with about 1,500 younger, mostly Spanish-speaking members, among them some of the most prominent Jewish doctors, lawyers, journalists, and artists. Yet, even there he observed young men dancing with their future mothers-in-law rather than with their fiancées. Whereas, "with us, it often happens that the daughter must look after the mother, because her father demands it." Women in the United States enjoyed greater personal autonomy; consequently, in Schwartz's view, "it's better to be a mother in North America than in South America."

Schwartz's 1930 visit coincided with a major crackdown on the Sociedad Zwi Migdal, the fraternal organization of Jewish procurers and sex traffickers in Argentina. The arrests were a topic of everyday conversation, and the newspapers were replete with stories about the ongoing operation. Schwartz could not avoid commenting on this. Prostitution was officially legal in Argentina, he wrote, but Buenos Aires was actually a very "pious" city. Jews were accused of running the traffic in women, but the accusation was quite exaggerated: "I spoke with many Jews from all sorts of classes" about this; French, Spanish, and Argentine procurers were actually the main factors behind the sex trade. What made the Jewish procurers distinctive, he (and others) wrote, was that they were organized into a *hevrah* (a voluntary, mutual-aid society) with its own cemetery, synagogue, cantor, and *shohet* (ritual slaughterer).[29] Fear of antisemitism combined with a desire for respectability drove the organized Jewish community's opposition to the *tme'im* (literally, its "ritually impure" elements).

The Theater Scene in Buenos Aires

Naturally, Schwartz devoted a considerable amount of attention to theater in general and the Yiddish theater in particular: actors, repertory, productions, audiences, and finances. Buenos Aires was a city of theaters, opera, and cinema, Schwartz reported, with more theaters, per capita, than New York City. "Here, in Buenos Aires, the audience hungers after theater. They run to the theater and love theater," he wrote. The comparisons between North and South America began at the box office and continued through the hall onto the stage and, from there, into the wings. One element of culture shock for Schwartz was that evening performances began as late as 10:00 p.m., and often wound up after 1:00 a.m.[30]

The box-office cashiers hoarded the best tickets, he commented, and to get a good seat in the *platea* (orchestra) or the *palcos* (boxes) the cashiers needed to be tipped. Close and reciprocal relationships prevailed between audience members and the cashiers, "but friendship is friendship and tips are tips." Schwartz's depiction of box-office operations in Buenos Aires likely struck his New York readers as odd because, by contrast, New York's Yiddish theater operations were heavily unionized.[31] Ticket sales for Schwartz's productions were brisk; he compared the scenes around the box offices to the pandemonium on the trading floor at the New York Stock Exchange.

Schwartz claimed that audiences were befuddled by stage practices that he had instated at the Yiddish Art Theatre and followed in Argentina, such as raising the curtain and taking bows only at the conclusion of the final act (rather than at the end of each act), and not singing encores of songs. "Ensemble performance ... is unknown here," he commented, "People come to see the star." Schwartz encountered complaints in Buenos Aires when he played secondary roles—rather than starring—in a couple of plays. On balance, he considered his tour to have met with an extremely appreciative reception. Audiences were easily "ignited"; a few of his productions, including *God of Vengeance* by Sholem Asch and *Bloody Laughter* (*Hinkemann*) by Ernst Toller, elicited some of the strongest applause that he had ever received.

There were some negative aspects to performing there, however. "In the strongest dramatic scenes, crying can suddenly burst out in the theater."

Sometimes, the bawling of infants resonated between dueling palcos. Nor were the aural distractions limited to the youngest members of the audience. The stagehands, actors, extras, and musicians all "talk and talk, and they don't permit the show to go on."[32]

The plays that Schwartz put on in Buenos Aires were staples of his Yiddish Art Theatre's repertory: literary works by classic and modern Yiddish and European authors. "I wanted to mount complete productions," he wrote. But, at the rate of at least one play per week, each production was granted only eight rehearsals (two per day), so he recognized that his ambitions were unrealistic. Nevertheless, Schwartz felt that the local actors gained a lot through his presence; they "speak Yiddish for hours on end and are serious about applying their makeup for even the smallest roles."[33]

Schwartz's Buenos Aires tour coincided with visits by the celebrated Russian bass Fedor Chaliapin (who was singing at the Teatro Colón) and Aleksandr Tairov's Moskovskii Kamernyi Teatr' (Moscow Chamber Theater, performing at the Teatro Odeón).

Chaliapin was visiting Buenos Aires after a twenty-two-year absence. He had been "banished" from Argentina, Schwartz related, because he offended opera patrons by showing up half-naked on stage in the role of Mephistopheles. Now, for ten performances in Mussorgsky's *Boris Godunov*, he was guaranteed the princely sum of $50,000 (the equivalent of over $770,000 in 2020 US dollars). Schwartz complained that Chaliapin's presence had a dampening effect on ticket sales at the Yiddish theater, since Jews who might otherwise have attended some of his own performances "pawned their clothes" in order to purchase expensive tickets at the grand opera house of Buenos Aires, the Teatro Colón. Although Schwartz could not attend Chaliapin's performances, he managed to tour the Colón during its off-hours, proclaiming it almost as beautiful as the Garnier Opera in Paris. Schwartz was especially impressed by its red carpeting, up-to-date electrical installations, and the support that it received from the Argentine government—"plus, the theater also possesses *calefacción* ('steam')!"

Schwartz did attend three of the Tairov company's *vermouth* (late afternoon) performances and offered his thoughts on the Kamernyi Teatr' briefly in his *Forverts* travelogue and at greater length in a separate article in *Di Presse*. Most Yiddish stars, like Schwartz in 1930, traveled to Buenos Aires alone or were accompanied only by a manager and/or an acting partner.[34] In contrast, Tairov's traveling company comprised fifty-two actors and stagehands, plus sets. Evidently, the Kamernyi Teatr' did not come close to covering its tour's enormous costs. Schwartz was impressed with this "very interesting troupe," its dedicated and versatile performers, and its modernist productions.[35]

Two other Yiddish stars from New York, Samuel Goldenberg and Stella Adler, were performing in Buenos Aires at precisely the same time as Schwartz. They were playing at the Teatro Excelsior, yet their names and that theater passed completely unmentioned in Schwartz's travelogues. He made only the vaguest allusion to the existence of a second Yiddish troupe in Buenos Aires when he gently chided the city's Yiddish newspapers for their (in his view) overly indulgent reviews of shund productions.[36] Since Schwartz did not consider his own repertory to fall into that territory, it was left to the reader to infer that shund plays were being put on elsewhere in Buenos Aires.

The Provinces and Moisés Ville

After completing their engagements in Buenos Aires, Yiddish guest stars typically performed in cities and agricultural colonies outside of the Argentine capital, and Schwartz followed suit. While the vast majority of Argentina's Jews resided in Buenos Aires, there were sizable numbers in the country's smaller cities and in the agricultural colonies that had been established by Baron Maurice de Hirsch and the Jewish Colonization Association (JCA). Schwartz performed in the cities of Santa Fe, Rosario, and Córdoba, and in the Moisés Ville colony. He devoted the final two installments of his *Forverts* travelogue to his tour of the provinces, supplementing this with a couple of articles for *Der Shpigl*.[37]

The Yiddish critic Samuel Rollansky once observed that "The Yiddish theater in Argentina is a hotel with a large office [providing] transit visas" for the overseas stars. The impresarios offered ship passage and suitable accommodations, along with a percentage of the box-office take.[38] Schwartz was a beneficiary of this "hospitality"; while the other members of his traveling troupe made the overnight train journey to Santa Fe in the overcrowded second-class carriages, he traveled in the comparative comfort and privacy of a first-class compartment. Schwartz claimed that he preferred to join the troupe in second-class but elected instead to suppress his "sentiments of humanity" and remain in his compartment.

Schwartz was inspired by the young people whom he encountered in Santa Fe, a city of some 60,000 inhabitants (including 500 Jewish families), and by the evidence of an active Yiddish cultural life there, with books being imported from all over and lectures held in a large hall erected by the Jewish community. The troupe put on two productions in that hall: *Shabetai Zvi* and *God of Vengeance*. "Everyone came," he recounted, but news of a woman's death caused some families to leave the *salón* (auditorium) early. "A pity, such a young woman," his impresario lamented. "So much income lost."[39]

Schwartz reserved his only negative comments about an Argentine locality in an article intended for local consumption. Rosario was a "theatrically dead city" where the crowd's indifference to *Shabetai Zvi* sapped the actors' energies. Silence reigned in the hall as the curtain was raised and silence reigned again as it was lowered. Nor was this unresponsiveness limited to just that one performance; the troupe encountered a similar coldness at its productions in Rosario of *God of Vengeance* and *Jud Süss*. His spirits revived only somewhat at the banquet in his honor: "The guests smiled, did their best to create the appropriate atmosphere for an encounter with the director of a Yiddish art theater." But the barbecue conjured up unpleasant historical associations, which resonated with Yiddish readers' collective memory—and tallied with Schwartz's unhappy experience in Rosario. The *asado* (barbecue) "reminded me of the Spanish Inquisition, where flesh was also roasted—Jewish flesh."[40]

By contrast, when Schwartz arrived in Córdoba, the sun began to shine again—literally and figuratively. He spent three happy and memorable days in that city—"this is not Córdoba, Spain," whose Jews were expelled in 1492, along with the rest of Spain's Jewish population. The audience was young and cheerful; every moment was filled with pleasure, he recalled. The audience was enthusiastic, as in New York during the heyday of the Yiddish theater back in the early 1900s. (The Yiddish theater in Argentina reached its apogee during the 1920s and 1930s.) "Even the gentiles on stage who changed the sets were dear gentiles."[41]

Finally, there was Moisés Ville, the first and "most important Jewish colony in Argentina" (as the *Forverts* headline put it), dating back to 1889. The prominence of this and other agricultural settlements offered one of the main contrasts between the Jewish communities of Argentina and the United States. Schwartz's *Forverts* article was calibrated to appease his New York readers' natural curiosity about Jewish life on the Pampas, at a time when many Jews considered it an existential need to "productivize" Jewish labor through settlement on the land in Palestine, the Soviet Union, and also Argentina. Even before he traveled to Moisés Ville, Schwartz sensed the powerful hold that the colonies had on the country's urban Jewish imagination. The colonists' children filled the ranks of doctors, lawyers, and community leaders in Buenos Aires and the provincial cities.

When the actors arrived at the train station, several miles distant from Moisés Ville, they were greeted by representatives of various organizations, including the president of the Kadima cultural center, Dr. Malamut. Theater performances took place in Kadima's building, which impressed Schwartz as both beautiful and modern, with a good stage and seats for 600 to 800 spectators. Elsewhere, Schwartz rhapsodized about cultural life in the settlement: Not only were the Jewish colonists helping to feed the nation and the world, "but they haven't forgotten that they are a People of the Book and [also] built auditoriums and libraries."[42]

Although the ostensible purpose of Schwartz's visit to Moisés Ville was to perform there—and his troupe did so within hours of arriving—he devoted most of his attention to the colony's physical plan and its economic prospects, and to establishing the colonists' Yiddish bona fides. "I have seen Moisés Ville," he wrote, "and for that alone my trip to South America was worthwhile.... It's been a long time since I heard little children speaking a clear, healthy Yiddish as in Moisés Ville—not pretentiously, as the boast goes, but simply; they speak a natural Yiddish." He spent a total of four days there, which afforded him the time to absorb the colony's ambience and meet many of its residents.[43]

Schwartz shared some of the frustrations that his interlocutors had with the JCA, in Paris. By their reckoning, the JCA's leadership was indifferent to the colonists' conditions and prospects. No new colonists were arriving, and Moisés Ville had fallen far short of Baron de Hirsch's ambitions of settling 75,000 Jews on the Pampas. Schwartz expressed the view that the JCA's activities in Argentina might be invigorated through the involvement of North American Jewish philanthropists and an infusion of Yankee capital and know-how. At the same time, he took a sober view of the colony's future prospects; while the original colonists possessed enough land to sustain the next generation, he predicted that their grandchildren would drift off to the cities.

Reflections on Schwartz's South American Tour

As Schwartz's stay came to an end, he offered some reflections about what, for him, was the fulfillment of a dream. He accurately foresaw that Buenos Aires would occupy an increasingly prominent position in the Yiddish theater world, while also expressing the view that the ranks of performers there required better and more serious acting talent. His productions "confirmed the fact" that there was an audience in Buenos Aires for the "better," more literary plays. His experience there also persuaded him that he needed to travel around and share his repertory with actors everywhere, and not just in New York City. That would vindicate his twelve years of work with the Yiddish Art Theatre.[44]

In practice, Schwartz *did* travel more during the following three decades, including numerous trips to South America, and Buenos Aires became one of the last redoubts of the "better" Yiddish repertory. This was true both in terms of the other guest actors who also performed there (such as Jacob Ben-Ami, Joseph Buloff, and Luba Kadison) and with respect to local developments—in particular, the independent, leftist Teatro IFT or Idisher Folks-Teater, which flourished from the mid-1930s into the mid-1950s, when it shifted to performing in Spanish.[45]

Contemporaneous readers in North America must have appreciated Schwartz's colorful depictions of street scenes, everyday life, and the Buenos Aires Yiddish theater. Both explicitly and implicitly, his travelogues underscored parallels and divergences in the conditions facing their fellow Jewish immigrants in Latin American cities (large and small) and in the Argentine colonies. Given the timing of his visit, Schwartz might not have been able to foresee the shifts in government policies that were placing obstacles to immigration resembling those that were already in place in the United States.

If Schwartz's series in the New York *Forverts* held up a mirror to his North American readers' experiences, then the decision of *Di Presse* to reprint three of the articles in effect bounced a reflection off of that mirror.[46] By assigning the headline "How Maurice Schwartz Views Our Communities" to two articles, that newspaper highlighted Schwartz's exalted status as an international celebrity and he responded in kind, though not without a degree of bemusement: "I was proclaimed the 'Conqueror of the World,' 'the Genius of the Twentieth Century,' the 'Most Famous,' the 'Greatest.' Napoleon is a blade of straw compared to [me]."

Today, Schwartz's South American autoethnography can be profitably read from a variety of perspectives. His observations concerning theatrical repertory, performance practices, stagecraft, and economic factors (something that he often mentioned in his articles) are of interest to theater historians and scholars of performance studies in general. For Yiddish theater specialists, Schwartz remains an iconic personality, the preeminent North American male Yiddish actor and director of his era. His comparisons between the theater scenes of New York and Buenos Aires are significant for Yiddish theater scholarship, given his position as the leading advocate of the literary repertory and his participation in the international star system that dominated the Yiddish stages of those times. For Yiddish Studies in general, Schwartz emerges as a talented raconteur with an ear for piquant and amusing anecdotes and an eye for details that the ordinary tourist might have overlooked. His voice comes through as clearly as Sholem Aleichem's in that author's monologues. And for Latin Americanists, Schwartz's impressions of the countries and cities that he visited must be understood as those of a first-time visitor from the metropole of New York City's Broadway, Second Avenue, and Wall Street of 1930.

Like any journalistic travelogue, Maurice Schwartz's articles presented a snapshot of a time and a place. They can be fruitfully compared with other travel journalism of the period—not only for the sights, sounds, smells, and flavors that they conveyed, but also for the distinctively Yiddish perspective that Schwartz brought to bear as an internationally connected theater personality. After all, this "intermediary and cultural translator"[47] had himself once been as "green" as many of the audience members who attended his plays—and read his articles—in North and South America alike.

Notes

1. Mariusz Kałczewiak, *Polacos in Argentina: Polish Jews, Interwar Migration, and the Emergence of Transatlantic Jewish Culture* (Tuscaloosa: University of Alabama Press, 2020), 17–18. Fairly extensive literature has arisen concerning the concept and concrete manifestations of Yiddishland. A good starting point is Jeffrey Shandler's book *Adventures in Yiddishland: Postvernacular Language & Culture* (Berkeley: University of California Press, 2006).

2. For a historical overview, see Nahma Sandrow, *Vagabond Stars: A World History of Yiddish Theater* (New York: Harper & Row, 1977; an updated edition was published by Syracuse University Press, 1996). *The Rise of the Modern Yiddish Theater*, by Alyssa Quint (Bloomington: Indiana University Press, 2019) is a pathbreaking study of the formative years of the Yiddish theater in Romania and Russia. Debra Caplan's book *Yiddish Empire: The Vilna Troupe, Jewish Theater, and the Art of Itinerancy* (Ann Arbor: University of Michigan Press, 2018) provides a case study of the ways in which transnationalism was

baked into the Yiddish theatrical endeavor. The Digital Yiddish Theatre Project blog is a platform for current scholarship on the Yiddish theater: https://web.uwm.edu/yiddish-stage/, accessed February 26, 2020.

3. The Argentine Yiddish actor-impresario Leon Brest advised Maurice Schwartz to bring along his costumes and a few "spots" (spotlights). Brest to Schwartz, March 18, 1930, box 6, folder 55, Maurice Schwartz Papers (RG 498), YIVO Institute for Jewish Research Archives, New York. In 1939, Herman Yablokoff brought along "large crates with costumes for my productions, microphones, amplifiers, a record player, crates with projectors, reflectors, dimmer-boards, 'gelatin' (colored reflector paper), special curtains, and painted canvas decorations. I had been informed that these things were not available in Buenos Aires." See Herman Yablokoff, *Arum der velt mit idish teater* (*Around the World with Yiddish Theatre*), vol. 2 (New York: Workmen's Circle, 1969), 368, 386–87, 399–400.

4. Beatriz Seibel's book, *Historia del teatro argentino*, 2 vols. (Buenos Aires: Corregidor, 2002–2010), provides chronological, annotated documentation of the theater scene in Argentina from its beginnings to 1956, covering "national" (Argentine) companies, troupes specializing in peninsular Spanish repertory (e.g., zarzuela), French- and Italian-language companies, variety and cabaret troupes, and even circuses. The Yiddish theater and its connections to the "national" theater of Argentina are also mentioned.

5. In the mid-1920s, Schwartz toured Western Europe together with his company, the Yiddish Art Theatre.

6. Brest to Schwartz, March 18, 1930, box 6, folder 55, Maurice Schwartz Papers (RG 498), YIVO Institute for Jewish Research Archives, New York.

7. As Mariusz Kałczewiak observes, "Emigration from eastern Europe created a new diasporic Jewish world and diasporic Yiddish literature, while the Yiddish press evolved to a major platform linking the communities in Europe and the Americas." See *Polacos in Argentina*, 107. Three of Schwartz's *Forverts* travelogues were picked up by *Di Presse* and in *Der Shpigl* he published a couple of travel pieces to supplement those that were appearing in the New York paper. In addition, Schwartz wrote articles on other theater-related topics for these publications.

8. Tamar Lewinsky, "Eastern Europe in Argentina: Yiddish Travelogues and the Exploration of Jewish Diaspora," in *Writing Jewish Culture: Paradoxes in Ethnography*, eds. Andreas B. Kilcher and Liliane Weissberg (Bloomington: Indiana University Press, 2016), 252.

9. In *Journeys Beyond the Pale: Yiddish Travel Writing in the Modern World* (Madison: University of Wisconsin Press, 2003), Leah Garrett discusses Yiddish literary works in which travel is a central feature.

10. A search in the WorldCat database, in December 2019, using keyword "travel" and limiting by format "book, -book, and microform," language "Yiddish," and date range "1800–1940" yielded a result list of 641 items. There was a considerable amount of internal duplication within this list, and moreover it included some titles that are

A *Yanqui's* Gaze: Maurice Schwartz's South American Travelogues from 1930 · 195

in languages other than Yiddish. Nevertheless, even a cursory analysis led to overall conclusions concerning the breakdown of topics covered in Yiddish travel books.

11. For example, in July 1930 the Argentine Yiddish daily *Di Presse* published a Canadian travelogue by Leib Malach in three parts. The longtime editor of the *Forverts*, Abraham Cahan, visited the Soviet Union and British Mandate Palestine (twice) during the 1920s. His serialized travelogues focused primarily on political and social conditions in those lands. Abraham Cahan's travel narratives about Palestine were eventually published in book form: *Palestine: a bazukh in yor 1925 un in 1929* (New York: Forward Association, 1934). Alongside Hirschbein, Henry Shoshkes was probably the champion Yiddish travel writer. However, most of his travel books came out after World War II.

12. Peretz Hirschbein, *Fun vayte lender: Argentine, Brazil, yuni November 1914* (New York: 1916); H. D. Nomberg, "Argentinishe rayze in yor 1922," part 3 in *Gezamlte verk*, vol. 6, *Amerike* (Warsaw: Kultur-lige, 1928). Nomberg's visit made a lasting impression on the growing Yiddish literary community of Argentina; in the wake of his death in 1927, the Yiddish Writers' and Journalists' Association of Argentina was named after him. After World War II, that organization published Marcos Paryszewski's two volumes on Amazonia, *Dzhungls un shtet: rayze-ayndrukn* (Buenos Aires: aroysg. fun Yidishn literatn un zhurnalistn fareyn "H. D. Nomberg," 1951). Kałczewiak discusses Hirschbein's and Nomberg's travels in *Polacos in Argentina*, chapters 3 and 4.

13. Lewinsky, "Eastern Europe in Argentina," 253, 258, 265.

14. Kałczewiak, *Polacos in Argentina*, 103.

15. Kałczewiak, *Polacos in Argentina*, 103.

16. Schwartz emigrated from the Russian Pale of Settlement at the age of 11 and, after spending one year in England, joined his family in New York in 1901, when he was 12.

17. Kałczewiak, *Polacos in Argentina*, 87, 89, 100–102, 104, 107–8.

18. Kałczewiak, *Polacos in Argentina*, 87, 89, 100–102, 104, 107–8.

19. On Hirschbein's and Nomberg's accounts of their ocean voyages, see Kałczewiak, *Polacos in Argentina*, 92. A fair number of middle-class North American Jews would recross the Atlantic during the interwar decades, both on business and to visit relatives in Europe. "Going Home" is the theme of volume 21 of the *YIVO Annual*, edited by Jack Kugelmass (Evanston: Northwestern University Press; New York: YIVO Institute for Jewish Research, 1993).

20. Maurice Schwartz, "Moris Shvarts bashraybt zayn rayze keyn Argentine," *Forverts*, June 28, 1930, 4.

21. Nomberg, too, "was amazed by the ethnic diversity of Rio de Janeiro"; see Kałczewiak, *Polacos in Argentina*, 97.

22. Maurice Schwartz, "Moris Shvarts bashraybt di vunder-shehne shtodt Rio de zhaneyro fun Brazil," *Forverts*, July 5, 1930, 4. Schwartz's remarks about "savage Indian tribes" echoed Nomberg's comments on the same subject; see Kałczewiak, *Polacos in Argentina*, 89.

23. The Spanish Wikipedia article about Radowitzky notes that he subsequently fought with the International Brigades in the Spanish Civil War, following which he settled in Mexico City: "Wikipedia: Simón Radowitzky," Wikimedia Foundation, accessed December 26, 2019, https://es.wikipedia.org/wiki/Sim%C3%B3n_Radowitzky. There is also a brief Wikipedia article about him in English: https://en.wikipedia.org/wiki/Simón_Radowitzky (accessed February 26, 2020).

24. Maurice Schwartz, "Moris Shvarts bashraybt di kleyne zid-amerikanishe land Urugvay," *Forverts*, July 12, 1930, 4.

25. Maurice Schwartz, "Oyf di gasen un in di teaters fun Buenos Ayres," *Forverts*, August 28, 1930, 3, 5. Berta Singerman's performing career began on the Yiddish stage.

26. Maurice Schwartz, "Moris Shvarts shildert Buenos Ayres, di 'Pariz' fun Amerike," *Forverts*, July 19, 1930, 4, 6.

27. Kałczewiak, *Polacos in Argentina*, 100.

28. Mir Yarfitz, *Impure Migration: Jews and Sex Work in Golden Age Argentina* (New Brunswick: Rutgers University Press, 2019).

29. Maurice Schwartz, "Stsenes un bilder fun idishen leben in Buenos Ayres," *Forverts*, August 2, 1930, 4, 7. For a recent treatment of Jews and the sex trade in Argentina, see Yarfitz, *Impure Migration*.

30. Herman Yablokoff wrote that evening performances in Buenos Aires ran from 10:00 p.m. to 1:00 a.m. (versus 8:30 to 11:30 in New York); and *vermouth* (matinées) from 6:00 to 9:00 p.m. (versus 2:30 to 5:30 in New York). This meant that on weekends, when there were two performances each day, actors had only an hour of down time between 6:00 p.m. and 1:00 a.m. See Yablokoff, *Arum der velt mit idish teater*, vol. 2, 392.

31. However, according to Yablokoff, the cashiers in Buenos Aires were tipped in lieu of receiving salaries. See Yablokoff, *Arum der velt mit idish teater*, vol. 2, 389–91.

32. When the young prima donna Miriam Kressyn visited Buenos Aires in 1931, she published a magazine article in which she implored theatergoers to show up at the theater punctually, maintain better decorum, and especially keep their small children under control. See "Meynungen vegn hign teater bazukher," *Der Shpigl* (Buenos Aires), September 11, 1931. Yablokoff noted that his theater's crews were Spanish-speaking Argentines (except for the electrician, who spoke only Portuguese). See Yablokoff, *Arum der velt mit idish teater*, vol. 2, 387.

33. Maurice Schwartz, "Moris Shvarts vegen idishen teater in Nyu York un in Buenos Ayres," *Forverts*, August 21, 1930, 4–5.

34. In 1933, Schwartz would return to Buenos Aires, together with half a dozen actors plus supporting crew from the Yiddish Art Theatre. During that tour the company staged its greatest hit, *Yoshe Kalb*, adapted from the novel by Israel Joshua Singer.

35. Schwartz, "Oyf di gasen un in di teaters fun Buenos Ayres"; "Moris Shvarts vegn Tairovs trupe: fun a briv tsum 'Forverts,'" *Di Presse*, October 3, 1930, 8 [?].

36. See Maurice Schwartz, "Moris Shvarts bashraybt zayne letste forshtelungen in Buenos Ayres," *Forverts*, September 4, 1930, 3, 6. And yet, it is quite likely that Schwartz was in touch with one of the rival actors, Stella Adler, during their parallel tours in Buenos Aires. Shortly after they both returned to New York, Adler served as Schwartz's co-star in *The Witch of Castile*, based on the novel by Sholem Asch. See Abraham Cahan,

"Sholem-Ash's 'Di kishef-makherin fun Kastilyen' in Shvarts's kunst teater," *Forverts*, October 31, 1930, 4. Schwartz did not name any of the Yiddish plays that were being produced by a rival actor-director in a different theater in Buenos Aires at the same time as his own performances were taking place. I discuss this in an article that appeared online in November 2020, in two installments. See: Zachary Baker, "Ven Moysh iz geforn: Maurice Schwartz on the Yiddish Theatre in Argentina in 1930," Digital Yiddish Theatre Project, November 2, 2020, https://web.uwm.edu/yiddish-stage/ven-moysh-iz-geforn-maurice-schwartz-on-the-yiddish-theatre-in-argentina-in-1930, and November 11, 2020, https://web.uwm.edu/yiddish-stage/ven-moysh-iz-geforn-maurice-schwartz-on-the-yiddish-theatre-in-argentina-in-1930-part-ii.

37. In his *Forverts* series he wrote about only the first and last of these localities.

38. Samuel Rollansky [Shmuel Rozhanski], "Dos idishe gedrukte vort un teater in Argentine," in *Yoyvl-bukh: sakh-haklen fun 50 yohr idish leben in Argentine; lekoved "Di Idishe Tsaytung" tsu ihr 25-yohrigen yubileum (Cincuenta años de vida judía en la Argentina: homenaje a "El Diario Israelita" en su vigesimoquinto aniversario)* (Buenos Aires: 1940), 412, 415. Rollansky's essay was subsequently issued as a monograph, under the title *Dos yidishe gedrukte vort un teater in Argentine* (Buenos Aires: n.p., 1941).

39. Maurice Schwartz, "Moris Shvarts shildert stsenes un bilder in di shtetlakh fun Argentine," *Forverts*, September 27, 1930, 3.

40. Maurice Schwartz, "Ayndrukn fun idishn lebn in Argentine," *Der Shpigl*, October 16, 1930, 8–9.

41. Maurice Schwartz, "Ayndrukn fun idishn lebn in Argentine," *Der Shpigl*, October 23, 1930, 6–7.

42. Schwartz, "Ayndrukn fun idishn lebn in Argentine," *Der Shpigl*, October 23, 1930, 6–7. Transnationalism in Yiddishland was marked as much by its libraries as by its theaters.

43. Maurice Schwartz, "Mozesvil, di vikhtigste idishe kolonye in Argentine," *Forverts*, October 11, 1930, 6.

44. Schwartz, "Moris Shvarts bashraybt zayne letste forshtelungen in Buenos Ayres." *Forverts*, September 4, 1930, 3, 6.

45. For background on the Teatro IFT or Idisher folks-teater, see: Karina Wainschenker, "Antecedentes, surgimiento y desarrollo del teatro IFT," *VII jornadas de Jóvenes Investigadores, Instituto de Investigaciones Gino Germani*, Facultad de Ciencias Sociales, Universidad de Buenos Aires, 2013, accessed January 11, 2019, https://www.aacademica.org/000-076/338); Paula Ansaldo, "El teatro como escuela para adultos: un recorrido por la historia del IFT en su tránsito del ídish al español," in *Teatro ídish argentino (Argentiner yidish-teater)*, eds. Susana Skura and Silvia Glocer (Buenos Aires: Editorial de la Facultad de Filosofía y Letras, Universidad de Buenos Aires, 2016), 143–60, accessed November 29, 2019, http://publicaciones.filo.uba.ar/sites/publicaciones.filo.uba.ar/files/Teatro%20%C3%ADdish%20argentino%20%281930-1950%29_interactivo_0.pdf.

46. The travel pieces by Schwartz in *Di Presse* were: "Vi Moris Shvarts zet undzere yishuvim," August 15, 1930 (published in the *Forverts*, July 12, 1930); "Vi Moris Shvarts zet undzere yishuvim," August 19, 1930 (published in the *Forverts*, July 19, 1930); and "Moris Shvarts vegn idishn teater in Buenos Ayres," September 15, 1930 (published in the

Forverts, August 21, 1930). In addition, his article in *Di Presse* about the Tairov troupe from October 3, 1930, apparently was intended for the *Forverts* but may not have been run in that newspaper.

47. Kałczewiak, *Polacos in Argentina*, 91.

Bibliography

Primary Sources

Archives

YIVO Institute for Jewish Research Archives (New York), Maurice Schwartz Papers (RG 498)

Journalism by Maurice Schwartz (Ordered Chronologically)

"Moris Shvarts bashraybt zayn rayze keyn Argentine." *Forverts*, June 28, 1930.
"Moris Shvarts bashraybt di vunder-shehne shtodt Rio de zhaneyro fun Brazil." *Forverts*, July 5, 1930.
"Moris Shvarts bashraybt di kleyne zid-amerikanishe land Urugvay." *Forverts*, July 12, 1930. Republished in *Di Presse*, under the title "Vi Moris Shvarts zet undzere yishuvim," August 15, 1930.
"Moris Shvarts shildert Buenos Ayres, di 'Pariz' fun Amerike." *Forverts*, July 19, 1930. Republished in *Di Presse*, under the title "Vi Moris Shvarts zet undzere yishuvim," August 19, 1930.
"Stsenes un bilder fun idishen leben in Buenos Ayres." *Forverts*, August 2, 1930.
"Moris Shvarts vegn idishen teater in Nyu York un in Buenos Ayres." *Forverts*, August 21, 1930. Republished in *Di Presse*, under the title "Moris Shvarts vegn idishn teater in Buenos Ayres," September 15, 1930.
Maurice Schwartz, "Oyf di gasen un in di teaters fun Buenos Ayres." *Forverts*, August 28, 1930.
"Moris Shvarts bashraybt zayne letste forshtelungen in Buenos Ayres." *Forverts*, September 4, 1930.
"Moris Shvarts shildert stsenes un bilder in di shtetlakh fun Argentine." *Forverts*, September 27, 1930.
"Moris Shvarts vegn Tairovs trupe: fun a briv tsum 'Forverts.'" *Di Presse*, October 3, 1930.
"Mozesvil, di vikhtigste idishe kolonye in Argentine." *Forverts*, October 11, 1930.
"Ayndrukn fun idishn lebn in Argentine." *Der Shpigl*, October 16, 1930; October 23, 1930.

Printed Sources

Cahan, Abraham. *Palestine: a bazukh in yor 1925 un in 1929*. New York: Forward Association, 1934.
———. "Sholem-Ash's 'Di kishef-makherin fun Kastilyen' in Shvarts's kunst teater." *Forverts*, October 31, 1930.
Hirschbein, Peretz. *Fun vayte lender: Argentine, Brazil, yuni November 1914*. New York: [P. Hirschbein], 1916.

Kressyn, Miriam. "Meynungen vegn hign teater bazukher." *Der Shpigl*, September 11, 1931.
Nomberg, H. D. *Gezamlte verk*. Vol. 6, *Amerike*. Warsaw: Kultur-lige, 1928.
Rollansky, Samuel. "Dos idishe gedrukte vort un teater in Argentine." In *Yoyvl-bukh: sakh haklen fun 50 yohr idish leben in Argentine; lekoved "Di Idishe Tsaytung" tsu ihr 25-yohrigen yubileum (Cincuenta años de vida judía en la Argentina: homenaje a "El Diario Israelita" en su vigesimoquinto aniversario)*. Buenos Aires: Comité de homenaje a "El Diario israelita," 1940.
———. *Dos yidishe gedrukte vort un teater in Argentine*. Buenos Aires: n.p., 1941.

Secondary Sources

Baker, Zachary. "Ven Moysh iz geforn: Maurice Schwartz on the Yiddish Theatre in Argentina in 1930." Digital Yiddish Theatre Project. November 2, 2020. https://web.uwm.edu/yiddish-stage/ven-moysh-iz-geforn-maurice-schwartz-on-the-yiddish-theatre-in-argentina-in-1930; November 11, 2020. https://web.uwm.edu/yiddish-stage/ven-moysh-iz-geforn-maurice-schwartz-on-the-yiddish-theatre-in-argentina-in-1930-part-ii.
Caplan, Debra. *Yiddish Empire: The Vilna Troupe, Jewish Theater, and the Art of Itinerancy*. Ann Arbor: University of Michigan Press, 2018.
Garrett, Leah. *Journeys Beyond the Pale: Yiddish Travel Writing in the Modern World*. Madison: University of Wisconsin Press, 2003.
Kałczewiak, Mariusz. *Polacos in Argentina: Polish Jews, Interwar Migration, and the Emergence of Transatlantic Jewish Culture*. Tuscaloosa: University of Alabama Press, 2020.
Lewinsky, Tamar. "Eastern Europe in Argentina: Yiddish Travelogues and the Exploration of Jewish Diaspora." In *Writing Jewish Culture: Paradoxes in Ethnography*, edited by Andreas B. Kilcher and Liliane Weissberg, 251–70. Bloomington: Indiana University Press, 2016.
Paryszewski, Marcos. *Dzhungls un shtet: rayze-ayndrukn*. Buenos Aires: Aroysg. fun Yidishn literatn un zhurnalistn fareyn "H. D. Nomberg," 1951.
Quint, Alyssa. *The Rise of the Modern Yiddish Theater*. Bloomington: Indiana University Press, 2019.
Sandrow, Nahma. *Vagabond Stars: A World History of Yiddish Theater*. New York: Harper & Row, 1977. Updated edition. Syracuse: Syracuse University Press, 1996.
Seibel, Beatriz. *Historia del teatro argentino*. 2 vols. Buenos Aires: Corregidor, 2002–2010.
Shandler, Jeffrey. *Adventures in Yiddishland: Postvernacular Language & Culture*. Berkeley: University of California Press, 2006.
Skura, Susana, and Silvia Glocer, eds. *Teatro ídish argentine (Argentiner yidish-teater)*. Buenos Aires: Editorial de la Facultad de Filosofía y Letras, Universidad de Buenos Aires, 2016. http://publicaciones.filo.uba.ar/sites/publicaciones.filo.uba.ar/files/Teatro%20%C3%ADdish%20argentino%20%281930-1950%29_interactivo_0.pdf.
Wainschenker, Karina. "Antecedentes, surgimiento y desarrollo del teatro IFT." *VII jornadas de Jóvenes Investigadores, Instituto de Investigaciones Gino Germani*. Facultad

de Ciencias Sociales, Universidad de Buenos Aires, 2013. https://www.aacademica.org/000-076/338.

Yablokoff, Herman. *Arum der velt mit idish teater* (*Around the World with Yiddish Theatre*). 2 vols. New York: Workmen's Circle, 1969.

Yarfitz, Mir. *Impure Migration: Jews and Sex Work in Golden Age Argentina*. New Brunswick: Rutgers University Press, 2019.

7

Going Where?
The Trope of Migration in Yiddish Movies from the Year 1939

Elisa Kriza

Due to the importance of migration in Jewish culture and the extreme existential dangers Jews had to face in the late 1930s and in the 1940s, studies about Jewish migrant cultures and the topic of displacement have offered multiple perspectives on these issues.[1] However, studies about Yiddish cinema are rare and studies about migration patterns from Eastern Europe in general are also underrepresented, despite the relevance of Eastern European mass migration in the twentieth century.[2] In this chapter I discuss the way three Yiddish-language movies shot in 1939 touched on the subject of migration. *Tevye the Milkman* by Maurice Schwartz, *The Light Ahead* by Edgar Ulmer, and *The Yiddishe Mama* by Henry Lynn were produced in the United States and they depict the perils and opportunities of migration, even though references to the political events of their day are largely indirect. Lynn's movie was screened before the war began, and Schwartz's and Ulmer's films were premiered after the invasion of Poland.

There are several reasons why sources from this year are particularly interesting, though Yiddish-language films of the 1930s were not the first Jewish movies to discuss issues of migration. In the United States, Jewish silent films from the 1920s tapped this subject dozens of times and offered their own perspectives. In the 1930s, the Yiddish film industry was a transnational endeavor with movies made in coproductions that involved US producers filming in Poland and European actors performing for films shot on US soil.[3] Migration and travel were part of the movie narratives and of the personal lives of these filmmakers. But by 1939, Yiddish culture was facing rapidly growing threats to its existence in the months leading up to World War II. Increasing threats were debated directly and indirectly in Yiddish print and film culture on both sides of the Atlantic. Whereas films from previous years represented diverse—often optimistic—perspectives on migration, those shot in early 1939 appear increasingly somber. But their engagement with this question remains complex, and their answers often ambivalent, mirroring the confusion of their time.[4]

This was the last batch of movies produced before the Yiddish film industry was truncated. Eric Goldman writes that in 1939, plans to make more than a dozen pictures in Yiddish were thwarted by the Nazi invasion of Poland. Immediately after the invasion of Poland, the Nazis took over local movie theaters, reopening them once they had placed Germans in the management positions.[5] Only German productions and Nazi propaganda newsreels were permitted. Not only could Yiddish movies no longer be produced, but most of the Yiddish speakers in Poland were murdered by the Nazis.[6] Moreover, during the war, movie export between other countries became more difficult. The world of Yiddish cinema changed radically after September 1939.

The choice of sources for this chapter is based on Goldman's overview of all Yiddish movies that have been preserved until today, and on previous studies about migration in Yiddish film.[7] Among these studies are James Hoberman's book about the transatlantic cooperation in movie production and Chantal Michel's monograph about the "American Dream" in Yiddish film.[8] Michel's emphasis is on movies that discuss migration as a means of social mobility. Michel offers a detailed overview of theoretical approaches to immigration and how movies may be studied under this prism, but this overview neglects the individual historical background of the movies and their sources.[9] This lack of context leads to misleading or idiosyncratic terminology in her analysis that appears inappropriate, especially in her discussion of films from the late 1930s.[10] Another previous work I refer to is my own book on Yiddish movies, which focuses on their cultural context and their religious motifs.[11] My current analysis takes a different approach by studying these film productions in their historical environment and studying how they engaged with it, reinterpreted it, and even neglected it.[12] The underlying sense of rivalry between Jewish life in Europe and America is examined in this context. The films I chose for this analysis were all made in the United States by filmmakers with European roots in order to highlight the juxtaposition between these two regions. All three films discuss the implications of migration from different viewpoints. The overlapping themes of danger and displacement contrast with the question of religion as a means to secure or lose a future.

Films convey an illusion of reality through an active re-creation of life.[13] But I do not study them as sources of ethnographic information; I examine them as cultural artifacts representing a web of narratives that can be interpreted in multiple ways. I study the narratives, the symbolisms, and the visual elements of these movies in order to interpret their core ideas. A narrative analysis takes into consideration not only the events, agents, and actions of the story, but how these are arranged and how they relate to each other.[14] According to David Bordwell, "Films . . . display a dynamic of semantic implications."[15] My purpose is to study the "semantic fields suggested by the film" in order to interpret them.[16] In this study of visual and narrative symbols, I draw from Jurij Lotman's theory of film semiotics. Lotman sees film as a "carrier of meaning."[17] This meaning is expressed through signs in the form of words, music, or images.

This chapter analyzes how the events, agents, and actions of the story discuss the subject of migration through images, dialogue, and plot. The term migration is defined here as a "move across a specified border or boundary from one location to another, usually with the aim of redefining one's main place of residence."[18] Historian Frank Wolff has studied Jewish migration patterns in the interwar period and he regards this period as a time in which a "new diaspora" emerged.[19] Eastern European Jews were "marked and identified as such."[20]

The Yiddish films I study offer a cultural discussion of migration from a complicated viewpoint—as it stems from the minority Yiddish speakers themselves. These films broach issues of displacement including the possibilities or threats of assimilation, acculturation, and segregation.[21] Michael LeMay describes how some groups or individuals opt to separate themselves from the majority population physically, by living in separated quarters, or psychologically or both.[22] According to LeMay, assimilation is a process that involves "the gradual cultural and legal integration of an individual into a new culture/society" to the point that the person who assimilates cannot be identified as belonging to a subculture.[23] In this chapter I use the term acculturation solely to define a process of adoption of certain traits from a majority population while maintaining one's original culture or blending both of these cultures.[24] When discussing marriage between Jews and non-Jews, I use the term intermarriage only when one of the partners remains Jewish, either because this is legally possible or because Judaism is primarily defined as a nation or culture and not a religion.[25]

Historical Background

Watching Yiddish films after the Shoah gives viewers a different perspective from that of the original audiences. Joel Rosenberg warns of the danger of "backshadowing" these movies, specifically of interpreting them with the events of World War II in mind.[26] This is no trivial matter, as, for instance, the DVD version of *Tevye the Milkman* includes a new prologue from the distributor informing the viewer that this film shows an antisemitic pogrom and that the threat of Nazism "looms in the horizon"—although the movie is set in Tsarist Russia. The Polish production *A Letter to Mother*, which was shot in 1938 and is set during World War I, is described by its distributor as "a metaphor for the displacements facing European Jews in 1939."[27] Rosenberg suggests that one should "sideshadow" these movies instead of "backshadowing":

> This involves taking into account how conflicting interpretations of present and future, manifest in an artistic work of the past, are partly rooted in earlier cultural expression and interact with it.[28]

It is important to remember the historical setting in which these movies were made and originally shown. This can help us avoid judging these films in hindsight, expecting them to assess their time with the knowledge we have today.

So, what was the world like in 1939? Financial meltdown still affected the United States, Germany, Poland and many other states since the late 1920s, causing social unrest that included antisemitic violence. Famine endangered the livelihood of millions in Ukraine and other parts of the Soviet Union (USSR) in the 1930s. The Show Trials in the USSR threatened the local population. The Nuremberg Laws had been in place in Germany since the mid-1930s, robbing Jewish Germans of their rights, and the Pogrom Night on the 9th of November 1938 was a portent of the terror the German population was capable of. Germany invaded Czechoslovakia and Austria in 1938. All these events created an environment of uncertainty in Europe and the United States, directly affecting significant parts of the Yiddish-speaking diaspora. These threats led to increased migration away from Europe and they heightened a sense of insecurity in the United States. Until then, migration from Eastern Europe had mostly led not to America but to Western European countries. This option became less and less viable as the threat of Nazi invasion affected the entire continent.[29] The White

Paper issued in mid-1939 in Great Britain was to drastically reduce Jewish immigration to Palestine in order to bring it to a full stop. Migration from the USSR was characteristically difficult. Migration numbers from Europe remained relatively small as the option of where to go was in itself a challenging question. Discussing these threats in film in the United States was also complicated.

The US film industry enjoyed many liberties, but producers were not entirely free. Criticism of Nazi Germany in movies was considered a problem until the United States entered World War II in 1941.[30] Since the early 1930s pre-vetting of films according to the Production Code, also known as the Hays Code after its creator, meant that certain subjects or images were essentially off-limits to the film industry. The Code resulted from Catholic efforts to purge movies of perceived immoral content, but in practice, the Hays Office often intervened when movies touched contemporary political subjects.[31] The Hays Office prevented criticism of Nazi Germany or Mussolini's Italy in the prewar years, arguing that US movies should remain neutral toward these countries.[32] But self-censorship and police censorship further curtailed the inclusion of references to the contemporary dangers posed by European fascism. In 1938, for example, the Chicago Police Board of Censors banned "the first commercially released anti-Nazi American motion picture,"[33] a short documentary called *Inside Nazi Germany 1938* produced by Louis de Rochement. The Censors argued "on the grounds that it was unfriendly to the Hitler Government and likely to create public resentment against a nation friendly with the United States."[34] The ban was lifted after a court injunction, but the Warner Brothers Theaters across the country withdrew it from their screens. Another prominent example is the shelving of the film adaptation of Sinclair Lewis's novel *It Can't Happen Here* in mid-production because "the film might displease Hitler and Mussolini."[35] An exception to this attitude of appeasement was the movie *Confessions of a Nazi Spy*, but the producer was threatened by the German Consul in Los Angeles and the film was banned in several countries, including Argentina.[36] Yiddish filmmakers were aware of the struggles of their non-Jewish and Jewish colleagues working in Hollywood, and they had to devise indirect ways to address thorny issues in their own work.

Narratives of Migration in Three Yiddish Films

The Light Ahead: Poverty and Disease

The Light Ahead (aka *Di Klatshe* or *Fishke der Krumer*) was the work of the Austrian Jewish director Edgar Ulmer (1904–1972). Ulmer had settled in the United States in 1930. *The Light Ahead* was Ulmer's third film in Yiddish, a language he did not speak. Ulmer's incursion into Yiddish culture began with a visit to the theater. According to his biographer, he was so touched by Peretz Hirshbein's play *Griner Felder* that he decided to bring it to the silver screen.[37] *Green Fields* was filmed and released in the United States in 1937 and Ulmer went on to shoot three other works in Yiddish.

Ulmer's contribution to Yiddish cinema was central to the artistic development of this industry. As opposed to other Yiddish filmmakers, he was a director—a professional filmmaker—and not an entrepreneur who made movies, like Henry Lynn, or a theater director who wished to reach a different audience, like Maurice Schwartz. His films brought a new level of sophistication and professionalism that set new standards in the Yiddish film world.[38] Helen Beverley (1916–2011), the female protagonist of *The Light Ahead*, was a stage actress who also appeared in Ulmer's earlier film *Green Fields*. She describes her first collaboration with Ulmer as a valuable lesson in the differences between stage and screen acting.[39] This professionalism was part of Ulmer's aim of bringing "dignity" to the Yiddish screen, by overcoming cheap and low-quality productions known as *shund* (garbage) and overly theatrical works produced by Yiddish theater directors.[40] Ulmer and his wife Shirley (née Kassler, 1914–2000) wrote the screenplay of *The Light Ahead* based on stories by the Yiddish writer Mendele Moicher Sforim (Sholem-Yankev Abramovich, 1835–1917) that had been adapted by the writer Chaver Paver (Gershon Einbinder, 1901–1964). Their literary adaptation managed, nonetheless, to achieve a genuinely cinematic quality. This means that they took full advantage of the means of film (image, sound, editing, narrative, dialogue, etc.) to create a work of art imbued with meaning.[41]

As opposed to the two other films I discuss later, this movie is set in an entirely Jewish context in the Russian Empire. The name of the village depicted in the film is Glupsk, which alludes to the villagers' ignorance and foolishness.[42] Glupsk is part of the Jewish Diaspora in Eastern Europe, but the non-Jewish rulers and inhabitants are absent. The movie focuses on the tender love story of the blind orphan, Hodl, and Fishke, who has a mobility disability. The social criticism of the narrative focuses on poverty and disease as the main threats to the protagonists' existence. But the corruption and mismanagement that aggravate these issues are the result of the Jewish self-administration organizations known as the *havurot* and not the non-Jewish authorities.[43] The diegesis is thus self-critical and this self-criticism is voiced mainly by Hodl's and Fishke's elderly friend, the book-peddler Mendele. The shtetl (village) is almost always dark, allowing for light and shadow to emphasize the angular architecture of the expressionist set. In fact, the expressionist aesthetics of the set, the pathos of the narrative, and the emotional performances make the film even more poignant in its message.[44]

The central element of the plot is a cholera epidemic that engulfs Glupsk after the village girls go for a swim on a Sabbath evening, a forbidden act according to Jewish custom.[45] The synagogue usher's wife had discovered the girls swimming and warned them that their sin would bring God's punishment upon the village. The visual imagery of the tree-lined river engulfed in fog gives the scene a fairy-tale atmosphere which contrasts sharply with the dire consequences of the swim.

Mendele explains that filth in the river is the origin of the ensuing epidemic, but the village is convinced of a connection between the transgression and the disease. The community decides to make an act of appeasement toward God: they will sponsor the wedding of the poorest villagers and these happen to be Fishke and Hodl. They are forced to marry in a spooky ceremony in the cemetery, in a so-called *mageyfe khasene* (plague wedding) to avert the cholera epidemic. The protagonists are devastated, as they had longed to marry—but not as a cholera-couple! They decide to accept to take part in the wedding, but then leave the village so as to not be stigmatized henceforth as the cholera-couple or to endure the foolishness of the village any longer. The film sequence of the wedding focuses on the couple with their ambivalent emotions and the grotesque villagers surrounding them. The camera frame often conveys a sense of claustrophobia and entrapment during the wedding.

Noah Isenberg, Sylvia Paskin, and James Hoberman agree in their judgment that this was the "only overtly negative representation of the shtetl in an American-made film."[46] When it premiered, it was not well received. To be sure, the film shows a corrupt environment that is beyond improvement: the young couple's only hope for the future is starting a new life elsewhere. However, the movie's heroic representation of two handicapped young people is remarkable for its time. Isenberg writes: "Ulmer renders

Figure 7.1. Fishke and Hodl encroached by death and darkness during their wedding. Courtesy of the National Center for Jewish Film. Edgar Ulmer, dir., *The Light Ahead* (USA: Carmel Productions, 1939).

the town pariahs . . . almost heroic."[47] The fact that, despite their physical constraints, Hodl and Fishke are almost the only inhabitants of Glupsk who are reasonable and prepared to embrace an enlightened form of faith and move to a better place offers a ray of hope for those in a weak position who find themselves surrounded by an adverse environment. It is no wonder, then, that Vincent Brook sees them as a metaphor for the Jewish people in 1939.[48] In this sense, the English and the (alternative) Yiddish titles of the movie complement each other: *The Light Ahead* presents itself as a ray of hope in the life of *Fishke der Krumer* (Fishke the Cripple) and Hodl, his blind bride. Ulmer's decision to portray the protagonists in a positive manner is a deviation from the literary source it is based on, as is the much less dismal portrayal of the shtetl and its inhabitants.[49]

The protagonists learn a lot from Mendele, the visiting book-peddler, but also from a couple of other citizens who question the corrupt ways of the ḥavurot and the consequences of this corruption: the different ḥavurot donated the money originally intended for the hospital and for the cleaning of the city to each other,[50] preparing the way for the catastrophe that took

Figure 7.2. A beard and a tallit do not define a good Jew. Courtesy of the National Center for Jewish Film. Edgar Ulmer, dir., *The Light Ahead* (USA: Carmel Productions, 1939).

place. One of Mendele's beardless friends complains to the ḥavurot that it is better to be a "Jew without a beard, than a beard without a Jew" as they are.[51] True Judaism is not defined by one's appearance or by empty rituals.

Ulmer, the director, grew up as a secular Jew in Austria. He worked as set builder and art director in theaters in Vienna and Berlin until he got involved in filmmaking in Berlin in the late 1920s.[52] He left mass unemployment and rising antisemitism in Berlin before Hitler's rise to power, and the United States became his home until his death in 1972.[53] According to one of his biographers, Noah Isenberg, Ulmer's life can be regarded as a perennial exile. Isenberg explains how this influenced Ulmer's movies from the late 1930s and 1940s:

> His handling of characters, regardless of setting and social milieu, tended to reveal the complexity and ambivalence of identity, the internal strife individuals face, and the external battles against corrupting and exploitative forces. These dynamics shaped Ulmer's ethnic films of the late 1930s and early 1940s, an intensely personal phase,

as Krohn suggests, that enabled Ulmer "to explore his own condition of exile and his mixed feelings about being an inheritor of an alien tradition."[54]

Ulmer had experienced poverty during World War I in Europe and he went through several phases of hardship while establishing himself as director in the United States. Perhaps, as Isenberg suggests, this experience influenced his choice of subject in *The Light Ahead*. Eve Sicular argues that Ulmer's work making public health movies commissioned by the National Tuberculosis Association warning against this illness in the 1930s may have also played a role in his decision to depict a cholera epidemic in this movie.[55] But regardless of Ulmer's personal concerns, the movie makes exile a natural and indeed necessary choice for the protagonists. During Fishke's and Hodl's wedding, which was a purported act of charity, the *badḥan*, the MC of the wedding, announces the gifts the couple are given: all the presents consist of old junk or a few kopecks.[56] Glupsk has nothing good to offer and the only reasonable reaction is to leave.

The Light Ahead was shot in New Jersey in 1939 and it came out in cinemas in the United States shortly after Germany invaded Poland.[57] Ulmer's biographer, Stefan Grissemann, criticized the indirect and indeed abstract way in which existential danger was represented in *The Light Ahead* given the threats Jews were facing at the time.[58] In contrast, Maurice Schwartz's *Tevye the Milkman* broached the subject of antisemitism directly—although it was also set in a shtetl in the Tsarist Empire. As we shall see, this was not necessarily a coincidence.

Tevye the Milkman: Place and Displacement

Maurice Schwartz (1890–1960) was undoubtedly one of the best-known stars of the Yiddish stage in New York during the first half of the twentieth century. He was born in Zidichov (Zhydachiv), which is now in Ukraine, and he migrated to the United States as a little boy. He became the acclaimed director of the Yiddish Art Theater, which he had founded in 1918. Schwartz was active as theater director and actor until his death in Israel, his last home, in 1960. He performed in several silent films and in a few talkies, including in Sidney Goldin's talkie *Uncle Moses* (1932), one of the most successful Yiddish movies. His best-known role is that of the milkman Tevye in the movie he directed himself in 1939. The plot of the movie is based on a stage play that had adapted a series of short stories by Sholem Aleichem (Sholem Rabinovitz, 1859–1916), one of the most prominent Yiddish writers. In an analysis of multiple adaptations of the Tevye stories, Ken Frieden explains that "each version conveys an ideology" that differs from earlier ones.[59] The deviations from Aleichem's original stories and their stage adaptation reveal an emphasis on Jewish identity and survival.[60]

Judith Goldberg explains how Schwartz, who had previously directed only one silent film, had long wished to make a movie about Tevye. During a theater tour in Poland in 1936 Schwartz discussed this idea with producer Joseph Green, but Green considered the topic matter too controversial for Poland.

> Green thought that, although *Tevya* would make a good movie, this was not the time, nor was Poland the place. The story would be too touchy because of Tevya's daughter marrying a gentile, and the family sitting *shiv'a* (mourning) over her.[61]

Indeed, the plot of *Tevye the Milkman* (aka *Tevya*) does not beat about the bush when it comes to confronting the issues of antisemitism, marriage outside the faith, and assimilation. As in Ulmer's film, the story is set in a poor village in prerevolutionary Ukraine. But here non-Jews play a key role in the protagonists' misfortunes: the sunny and bucolic countryside is juxtaposed with the coarseness and abusiveness of the local population. Schwartz's decision not to include any other Jewish characters on-screen apart from Tevye's family members is a poignant deviation from Sholem Aleichem's short stories.[62] This choice underlines the isolation and existential danger Tevye's family find themselves in. It also makes them the symbolic Jews of the narrative.

Two main leitmotifs lead the narrative of the movie, strengthening the impact of its antiassimilation message. The association of death and marriage outside the faith is one of them. Tevye and Golde are an elderly couple with a young and single daughter, Chave, and a young married daughter, Tseytl. Soon after the movie begins, a sequence in Tevye's farm presents us with the main conflict of the movie. Tevye and his family are enjoying a nice day eating outside on the farm when the priest stops by. The priest tells Tevye about a young Jewish woman who recently converted in order to marry a non-Jew. The montage sequence then alternates between Tevye's, the priest's, and Chave's reactions. Tevye announces that he would rather die and see his daughter die than see her do the same. The priest confronts

Figure 7.3. The Ukrainian wedding dress is a symbol of Chave's apostasy. Courtesy of the National Center for Jewish Film. Maurice Schwartz, dir., *Tevye the Milkman* (New York: Maymon Films, 1939).

Tevye, and Chave cries out and faints. Later, Tevye asks Chave if she would ever do anything that would "send her parents to the grave." She says no, but she knows exactly what he means and breaks into tears.

Despite her family's warnings that non-Jews cannot be trusted and that she should break up with Fedya, her Ukrainian (i.e., Christian) suitor, Chave converts to Christianity and marries him. (In the Tsarist Empire, intermarriage between Christians and Jews was forbidden, and the only option for the couple was that the Jewish partner would convert to Christianity.) The sequence that follows emphasizes the separation marked by the marriage: the movie shows Tevye, Tseytl, and Golde perform the *havdalah* ceremony—the ritual separating the Sabbath from the week—immediately after. This ceremony includes a prayer in which God is blessed for making certain distinctions, such as the distinction between Israel (i.e., Jews) and the nations (i.e., other nations). Then they mourn Chave as if she were dead.

In an ideologically revealing deviation from Aleichem's short stories, we see Golde agonizing in her bed shortly after. Superimposed is an image of

Chave in her Ukrainian wedding dress. Golde dies and Chave witnesses this through the window, unable to be with her mother. Chave's apostasy had severed the ties to her family and hence to her people, and the closed window and her inability to enter the home is a cinematic means to visualize this segregation between Jews and non-Jews.

According to Annamaria Orla-Bukowska, conversion and marriage outside the faith in the Tsarist Empire were regarded by the Jewish community as clean breaks from Judaism both as a faith and as an ethnicity.[63] She explains that this viewpoint was a result of the perceived need to have boundaries, mainly from other groups' religion:

> Living primarily in the very center of town, Jews were nevertheless able to build and maintain the strongest border possible between themselves and the others, the non-Jews. Under these conditions their separate cultures could and did bloom and grow; ignoring or destroying the boundaries would mean self-destruction.[64]

A second leitmotif of the movie that simmers in the background dominates in the last scenes: the notion of property and belonging. Who belongs to Tevye's family? Where do Tevye's family members—as symbolic Jews—belong? Multiple scenes set Tevye's family members in the landscape that surrounds them—long shots show us how much they are a part of this place. Yet, non-Jews also belong to this environment and interaction with them is presented as a threat. These threatening encounters initially take place outside, but once danger becomes graver it moves into Tevye's home and robs him of it.

The first sequence that places the issue of belonging center stage is when Chave is about to marry. Tevye and Golde reach the priest's quarters, where Chave awaits the ceremony. They are not allowed inside, but the priest is prepared to drink tea with them outside. Tevye and Golde reject the tea, and Tevye asks the priest to return his daughter to him, reminding him of the biblical story of the rich man who steals a lamb from a poor man.[65] He calls Chave his "lamb" and asks the priest to return her. The priest drives Tevye and Golde off his property, reminding them that he is the servant of the Tsar.

In the film's climax, the *khromada*, the Ukrainian administration of the village, announces that Jews—Tevye's family—shall be expelled from the village. The members of the khromada, as are all Ukrainians in the film, are unkempt and uncouth, and some are even drunk. Chave's father-in-law is among the most enthusiastic about evicting the Jews. By expelling Tevye's

Figure 7.4. Tevye and his family seem rooted in the Ukrainian countryside. Courtesy of the National Center for Jewish Film. Maurice Schwartz, dir., *Tevye the Milkman* (New York: Maymon Films, 1939).

family, the local population has decided that they do not belong there—albeit some claim that they are only obeying the orders of the Tsar. The notion that the Ukrainians are stealing Tevye's home is underlined by the scenes that follow. By now, the widowed Tseytl and her children live with Tevye, and the family must choose which belongings they will take with them and which they will sell. Once they open their home to sell the rest, their neighbors gladly take everything they can. One remarks to another that it is nice of Tevye to sell everything so cheap, and his friend responds that they would otherwise steal everything anyway. And indeed, one of Fedya's relatives steals Golde's Sabbath dress and a Hanukkiah[66] and brags about it in Fedya's home in Chave's presence. Chave decides then and there to leave, taking Golde's dress.

Tevye takes his dusty religious books from the shelf and sadly exclaims that these are the only possessions they will take from *galut* (exile) to *Eretz Israel* (the land of Israel), where they plan to go.[67] Tevye had briefly considered going to the United States or to Argentina, ultimately prioritizing Eretz Israel over these options. While he justifies this choice with religious arguments such as the importance of praying at the Western Wall (HaKotel), it is important to note that Tevye is taking this step only after being forced out of his home. This choice is therefore thrust upon him; it did not merely grow out of spiritual longings. And what about the blatant rejection of going to America? Tevye says that people in America and he do not speak the same language—a statement that appears awkward, as this movie was made for a US audience in that very language. He does not explain why they should not go to Argentina.

The movie ends with a reconciliation between Chave and her family when she decides to abandon her Ukrainian husband and regain her Jewishness. At that point, she explains to her husband that they live in two different worlds. She tells her father that she had left thinking that "among them" (i.e., among the non-Jews) things were better, but she has realized her mistake: "Your faith is truer and deeper," she says. But it was not only that. After her controversial marriage, Chave essentially becomes a maid for her husband's family. Michel interprets the sequences showing Chave toiling for her in-laws as an intentional disavowal of the notion of conversion as a form of social advancement.[68] Michel argues that conversion generally helped Jews escape the stigma of being considered "subhuman" (*Untermenschen*) in antisemitic societies.[69] Alas, given the way that Jewish converts to Christianity often continued to be stigmatized in numerous Christian countries, it is difficult to accept this view as a norm.[70] But I agree with Michel's view that the scenes depicting Chave's difficult life after marriage are transparent attempts to discourage viewers from following a similar path.[71] Once Chave is readmitted to the family, she tells them "*mayn neshume gehert aykh*"—my soul belongs to you. The Jewish family is restored, but homeless.

Tevye's delimitation of where he and his family belong is influenced by outside forces, but it is also determined by a strong sense that the bonds of Judaism must remain strong. This is important because the entire narrative is focused on showing why, on the one hand, Eastern Europe was a dangerous home to the Jews. On the other hand, by touching upon the topic of marriage outside the faith, which was becoming rarer in Europe in the 1930s due to racial laws,[72] it is obvious that the movie is addressing its audience in America, where this type of marriage was more likely.[73]

The movie builds up an argument in favor of segregation from non-Jews and against assimilation. As Schwartz carefully chose the plot elements of the film and the movie invests so much of its focus and pathos on the topic of marriage to non-Jews, it is plausible to assume that he shared the view that this type of marriage was a path to the loss of Jewish identity and religious affiliation.[74]

Yiddish movies like *Tevye* offer a viewpoint on intergenerational conflict, assimilation, and romantic relationships with non-Jews that contrasts with the representation of intermarriage in non-Yiddish-language movies of the 1920s.[75] Friedman explains that "The various films of the silent era about Jews stress intermarriage, economic success, freedom, and accommodation to middle-class American values. Religious scholarship, parochialism, duty, and ethnic uniqueness represent outworn notions associated with foreign countries and bygone times."[76] According to Rosenberg, Jewish film studio moguls producing non-Yiddish films were "architects of acculturation" in the first half of the twentieth century.[77] The plot of *The Jazz Singer* (1927) was paradigmatic in its upbeat portrayal of a young man who leaves behind his traditional Jewish home and the role of cantor in order to join a non-Jewish woman in his pursuit of a career in jazz.[78] But for films like *Tevye*, the United States—a country that had become home to millions of immigrants—was no longer the *goldene medina* (golden country) of previous Jewish films, but rather a *treifene medina* (non-kosher country), which is rejected in the movie even by the victims of a Ukrainian pogrom.

Schwartz's *Tevye the Milkman* engages with the topic of migration as a result of antisemitism in a way that may seem surprising today: instead of including the obvious threats of Nazism and fascism in 1939, the film is set in the Tsarist Empire and focuses on marriage outside the faith as an existential threat. Schwartz's choice to use the Tsarist Empire as a metaphor seems more plausible when we recall that the Hays Office regulations suppressed discussions of contemporary antisemitism in Hollywood films in the name of purported neutrality.[79] Similarly, Jews in Poland were afraid to make openly anti-Nazi movies in the 1930s—they wished to avoid being accused of provocation.[80] This curtailment of direct criticism of Nazi Germany very likely also affected Edgar Ulmer's *The Light Ahead*. But choosing to set the film in Ukraine had other reasons, too.

There is no evidence that Schwartz, who was born in Ukraine and left the country as a boy, might have set the film there for autobiographical reasons. It is more likely that this choice mirrored the setting of the literary source of the film. One of the stories in the *Tevye* series that was written in 1914 depicts a Ukrainian pogrom, although it is not associated with the story of Chave's marriage, Golde's death, or Tevye's decision to go to Eretz Israel. Adaptations are always interpretations that translate literary works into a new medium for a new audience, leaving enough room for creative license—and the film already starkly deviates from Aleichem's original stories.[81] Choosing to set the film in Ukraine was likely influenced by this country's symbolic notoriety for antisemitism; as late as the 1920s it had been the setting of particularly violent anti-Jewish pogroms.[82] The negative representation of Ukrainians in the movie was nonetheless heavily criticized by Jewish and non-Jewish intellectuals when the film was released in 1939.[83] But later reviewers show more understanding. Marat Grinberg plausibly explains that this cinematic representation might have been "a reaction to the situation the Jews began to experience in Europe."[84]

The portrayal of marriage outside the faith as an existential threat in films like *Tevye* was more in tune with its time, but it is less fathomable for today's audiences. Today in the United States around 58 percent of Jews choose to marry a non-Jew, as opposed to less than 10 percent in the first half of the twentieth century.[85] Later adaptations of the Tevye story in the United States and Russia have chosen to represent this motif in a positive light.[86]

The Yiddishe Mama: Not Going Anywhere?

The Yiddishe Mama (aka *Hayntike Mames*) illustrates Tevye's fears regarding the luring dangers of assimilation in the United States in many ways. The director, Henry Lynn (1895–1984), was born in Bialystok, which is now in Poland. He migrated to the United States as a young man, where he lived until his death. Lynn directed several Yiddish-language movies, and he is one of the main representatives of the so-called shund filmmakers. Shund was what low-quality cultural output (movies, plays, etc.) was called at the time, and it referred mostly to melodramatic tearjerkers or people-pleasing comedies shot or staged with minimum technical and artistic efforts. Shund might have been a nightmare for critics, but these films tended to be very successful commercially.[87] As this was a strongly audience-oriented form of cinema, its cultural significance should not be ignored, despite its conspicuous artistic faults. Another important reason to include this film in this chapter's analysis is the fact that the narrative takes place in a contemporary setting, and it is not a literary adaptation, adding a new perspective to this study.

The Yiddishe Mama is set in New York City. The Yiddish-speaking family and their neighbors are immigrants, but they are staying put: leaving the city is out of the question. Nonetheless, the movie presents us with a world full of threats: crime, poverty, and assimilation. The protagonist and her family are not moving anywhere, but they are going back to the ways and traditions of the Old World. Early in the film, the protagonist, a mother of two adult children, tells her daughter that she evokes her happy memories of the old country to gather strength for the difficult life they have in America. Her daughter responds that the old country has nothing to offer them. As in *Tevye*, the danger of assimilation is played out as an intergenerational conflict. The plot shows us how misfortune coaxes those who assimilate to separate themselves once more from the "modern" ways of New York. In a paradoxical manner, religion and tradition are presented as the means to secure a future in this dangerous modern world. The plot and the heavily emotional performances carry the narrative most of the time, as Lynn does not make good use of the means of cinema. He relies too much on repetitive frames and a limited amount of aesthetic means of expression.

Excessive acculturation is presented as foreshadowing the loss of faith and identity. The film begins with an extreme long shot, setting the film in New York City; subsequent long shots approach our protagonist until—at the end of the sequence—a close-up of a woman's head and hands are shown above the Sabbath candles on a table in a living room. Throughout the film, what is on the table often determines a person's priorities. The table shows us that the Jewish mother and widow Esther Waldman is perfectly prepared to welcome the Sabbath. The Sabbath table is so symbolic that there is even a song praising it later in the movie.

The main conflict of the plot is addressed immediately in the following scenes. Esther's adult daughter Anna comes home with a diamond ring on her hand. It is a present from Hymie, the new neighbors' son. Getzel Boxer, the new neighbor, enters the apartment and immediately expresses his surprise and joy to see a family ready to celebrate the Sabbath properly. Salomon, Esther's son who works as a cantor, comes home from the synagogue. Getzel explains that his wife Breindl (alias Beatrice) never lights the candles, as she is a modern person and plays cards instead of celebrating the Sabbath. He sadly confesses that his two children take after their mother. Getzel is a self-confessed "old-fashioned" man and tells Esther, "How happy I would be if I were a widower, just like you." Everyone laughs, but the link between bad behavior and death soon becomes seriously real.

In Ulmer's film, we saw exemplary Jews with and without a beard, and in Schwartz's film Tevye's beard and his religious clothing emphasize his faith and identity,[88] but in Lynn's movie, we are presented with a new situation: the son of the protagonist is a cantor—but he has no beard, no visible religious garments, and his name is Salomon, instead of Shlomo (like Tevye's

Figure 7.5. A proper Sabbath table. Courtesy of the National Center for Jewish Film. Henry Lynn, dir., *The Yiddishe Mama* (USA: Lynn Productions, 1939).

grandson, for instance).[89] The protagonist and her children pepper their Yiddish with English words. But this acculturation is only one step away from genuine danger: as Esther's children get involved with Getzel's secularized, gambling, naughty children, they are drawn into the underbelly of crime. Getzel's son Hymie is a criminal gang member who frames Salomon and then tries to kill him. Getzel's daughter Evelyn seduces Salomon, elopes with him, and convinces him to become a singer instead of a cantor. Hymie seduces Anna, elopes with her, and makes her his accomplice, landing both in prison.

The entire narrative is centered on the role of the mother and how a good Jewish mother is rewarded in the end. Breindl, Getzel's wife, serves as a foil representing the opposite. The trope of the mother as the keeper of tradition and the guardian of her children is not unique to this Yiddish film, but this is one of the most hyperbolic examples.[90] In the second part of the twentieth century, a lot was written about cultural notions of the Jewish mother, and this is one interesting example of how a movie defines what this should be in an openly moralizing manner.[91]

Again, just by looking at the tables in front of Esther or Breindl, the audience knows what kind of person each of them is: Breindl sits in front of playing cards, a tobacco box, or a makeup set—indicating vice and vanity. Esther's table reflects her prioritization of religion and family: the challah, a braided bread traditionally eaten on the Sabbath, lies under a cloth on the table next to the wine used for the *kiddush* (blessing of the Sabbath). Breindl is shunned by Esther and Getzel, with Getzel often asking her to leave the room, saying aloud, "wherever she enters the devil follows." Getzel constantly repeats the phrase, "When you throw God out, the devil moves in." The outside represents threat: street scenes are full of shadows, the streets are filthy, and there is sinister music on the soundtrack. As in *Tevye*, whoever enters the home from outside can bring destruction.

Like *Tevye*, this film offers a crescendo of catastrophes, and, as in *Tevye*, a direct reference to the biblical Job is made.[92] In Lynn's movie, as in the biblical story, there is a twist toward a happy end. Anna proves her innocence and leaves prison. Esther, who had suddenly become blind, is told that doctors say this was probably just a temporary shock and that she will recover her eyesight. Salomon returns to being a cantor and apologizes to his mother.[93]

The movie's ideological and narrative climax is reached when Hymie is about to face his execution in prison. Hymie prays in his cell that parents will not allow their children to be "independent" and that they will not indulge them—because that "leads to crime." This hyperbolic pathos is further underlined by the whining tunes of the instrumental music in the background. Getzel and Breindl arrive in order to say goodbye. Hymie lectures Breindl about how her gambling ruined their home and adds, "Now you will lead me to the electric chair, instead of the altar." Hymie apologizes to his father for having disobeyed him.

The film's black-and-white perspective offers mild acculturation—such as the adoption of modest modern clothing—and segregation as a possible model for life in the United States. Esther is the perfect woman described by the biblical Salomon in Mishlei (Proverbs) 31: a woman who is successful in her business and her home and who maintains tradition. In contrast, Breindl introduces her children to the ways of non-Jews and brings the filth of the city streets into the home.[94] Bad behavior is referred to as "modern," but its depiction makes it clear it is more related to being non-Jewish. For instance, Hymie's gang is marked as non-Jewish because it uses the English words "synagogue" and "reverend" instead of the Yiddish word *shul* for the house of prayer and *khazn* for cantor. In this movie, Jewish identity is faith, and faith is obedience.

In the final sequence of the movie, Breindl comes into Esther's apartment and sadly claims, "I paid my price." The movie ends with a surprisingly cheerful rendition of *Kol Nidre*, the most important prayer of Yom

Figure 7.6. Hymie's gang illustrates a view of non-Jews as leading a life of vice. Courtesy of the National Center for Jewish Film. Henry Lynn, dir., *The Yiddishe Mama* (USA: Lynn Productions, 1939).

Kippur (the Day of Atonement). This is in tune with the film's use of singing to lighten the mood while praising tradition.

The symbolic last scene, in which all gather in Esther's home, emphasizes the traditional Jewish perception of the home as the center of Jewish religious life—the place where religion and identity are nurtured.[95] By creating a hyperbolic happy end for those who repent and those who maintain the faith, the narrative conveys the notion that only with faith and obedience is the future secure—only then will crime, death, and disease be avoided. Patricia Erens explains the meaning of happy endings such as the one of *The Yiddishe Mama:*

> Generally this [the happy end] is accomplished by a reconciliation scene which restores family unity. Sometimes members have died or are missing, but the continuation of the line is always assured. In this microcosm this no doubt served to reaffirm the continuation of the race as well. For a people so constantly uprooted, reunification took on special significance, particularly during one of the largest migrations in their history.[96]

Subtlety is missing from the movie's narrative. And the film lacks sophistication in its composition, editing, and framing—but it is an interesting representation of existential fears that were very likely shared by numerous viewers in the United States in 1939. In its lack of nuance, *The Yiddishe Mama* recorded a pious answer to the question of how to overcome the danger of post-migratory assimilation that Tevye was so fearful of in the eponymous movie. The threats it portrays are independent of the historical context in which the film was produced in its apparent attempt to provide an all-round solution to existential dangers.

Conclusion

Tevye the Milkman by Maurice Schwartz, *The Light Ahead* by Edgar Ulmer, and *The Yiddishe Mama* by Henry Lynn are three examples of cinematic perspectives on the topics of migration, assimilation, and survival in Yiddish cinema in 1939. In all three, Jewish identity is connected to religion, but its geographical links are loose. Schwartz and Ulmer represent migration as an acute necessity: in *Tevye* this is prompted by antisemitic violence and in *The Light Ahead* by inherent problems in the shtetl. In Lynn's movie, the reason for the family's migration to the United States is unknown; the mother's yearning for the old country is based on family ties there and on the lack of temptations for her children. But the movie does not advocate either assimilation or migration back to Europe or elsewhere. None of the movies mention the changes in migration policy in the United States or Palestine that made it more difficult for Jews to flee there. These movies themselves had difficulties reaching wider audiences abroad, not just in Poland. Because all three were made by small production companies owned, at least in part, by their directors, the studios lacked the resources to export and promote movies abroad in war time.[97]

These movies' narratives engage with the concerns and fears that their creators considered relevant at the time they made them. On the surface, it might seem that they do not sufficiently engage with their historical surroundings. Like many US films of their time, they did not risk setting their stories in a contemporary environment that would incur direct political criticism and possible censorship. Yet, danger was not far from the lives of the cast and crew. For example, the Jewish actor Leon Liebgold, who plays Chave's husband in *Tevye*, missed his ship back to Poland at the end of August 1939, due to delays in shooting the film. This saved him from experiencing the war in Poland. The heightened sense of urgency to migrate that Schwartz and Ulmer added to their literary adaptations and the choice of topics by all three directors reflect worries shared by their audiences. It would be unrealistic to expect more decisiveness and more clarity in their message in a time during which most Jews in America and Europe (with the exception of Germany) continued to largely trust that their governments and the non-Jewish population around them—despite a growing sense of suspicion—would not allow the worst to happen to them.[98]

These movies are like time capsules that grew out of a social environment that is different from our own. Poverty, disease, crime, and antisemitism might still be threats to rural and urban communities today. Superstition and religious bigotry continue to challenge contemporary societies and individuals, but not in the same way as back then. Some of the solutions offered by the narratives of these films—a return to tradition and faith or migration to Israel—continue to be weighed out by some Jewish families. In April 2020, newspapers worldwide reported that a plague wedding was conducted in an Israeli cemetery, a rare event but perhaps not the only wedding ceremony carried out to purportedly avert the coronavirus pandemic.[99] Yet other aspects of these films, such as the fear of intermarriage, have lost much of their resonance. Ultimately, what these film narratives show us are horizons of possibilities in confronting life's challenges and threats: religious observance, new interpretations of faith, apostasy, migration, assimilation, acculturation. In this sense, Ulmer was right in saying that Yiddish culture touched upon universal themes—topics that could be relevant to any nation or culture—despite the specific problems that Jews had and continue to face.[100]

Notes

1. Amy Colin and Elisabeth Strenger, eds., *Bridging the Abyss. Brücken über dem Abgrund* (Munich: Wilhelm Fink Verlag, 1994).

2. Elisa Kriza, *Jiddische Filme verstehen: Religiöse Symbolik und kultureller Kontext*, 2nd ed. (Bamberg: University of Bamberg Press, 2018), 19; Anika Walke, introduction to *Migration and Mobility in the Modern Age: Refugees, Travelers, and Traffickers in Europe and Eurasia*, eds. Anika Walke et al. (Bloomington: Indiana University Press, 2017), 2.

3. Eric Goldman, *Visions, Images, and Dreams: Yiddish Film Past and Present* (Ann Arbor: UMI Research Press, 1983), 109.

4. Jehuda Reinharz writes about the situation in Europe: "In the course of 1939 the level of fear, anxiety, and hope fluctuated." Jehuda Reinharz and Yaacov Shavit, *The Road to September 1939: Polish Jews, Zionists, and the Yishuv on the Eve of World War II* (Waltham: Brandeis University Press, 2018), 224.

5. "Propaganda Films Fed Poles as Nazis Take over Theaters in Poland," *Jewish Telegraph Agency*, December 3, 1939, 4.

6. Goldman, *Visions*, 132.

7. Ibid.

8. James Hoberman, *Bridge of Light: Yiddish Film between Two Worlds* (New York: Dartmouth College Press, 2010); Chantal Michel, *Das jiddische Kino. Aufstiegsinszenierungen zwischen Schtetl und American Dream* (Berlin: Metropol, 2012).

9. Michel's theoretical musings in *Das jiddische Kino* encompass large sections of chapters 2–4.

10. An example of Michel's lack of consideration of a larger context is her use of the term *identitär* (identitarian) to criticize Yiddish movies shot in the late 1930s which depict antisemitic non-Jews in a negative manner. The term "identitarian" is closely connected with right-wing nationalist movements—using this term to denounce these Yiddish perspectives on antisemitism makes it even more inadequate. Michel, *Das jiddische Kino*, 356.

11. Kriza, *Jiddische Filme*.

12. Roland Gruschka notes that a close look at the political environment in which Yiddish films of the late 1930s were made would contribute to a better understanding of them. Gruschka, review of *Das jiddische Kino: Aufstiegsinszenierungen zwischen Schtetl und American Dream*, by Chantal Catherine Michel, *East European Jewish Affairs* 44, no. 1 (2014): 110–11.

13. Jurij Lotman, *Semiotics of Cinema* (Ann Arbor: University of Michigan Press, 1976), 4.

14. Kent Puckett, *Narrative Theory: A Critical Introduction* (Cambridge: Cambridge University Press, 2016), 2.

15. David Bordwell, *Making Meaning: Inference and Rhetoric in the Interpretation of Cinema* (Cambridge: Harvard University Press, 1991), 259.

16. Ibid.

17. Jurij Lotman, *Semiotics of Cinema*, 14.

18. Walke, introduction to *Migration and Mobility in the Modern Age*, 2.

19. Frank Wolff, "Global Walls and Global Movement: New Destinations in Jewish Migration, 1918–1939," *East European Jewish Affairs* 44, no. 2–3 (2014): 189.

20. Ibid.

21. Michael C. LeMay, "Assessing Assimilation: Cultural and Political Integration of Immigrants and Their Descendants," *In Defense of the Alien* 23 (2000): 164–65.

22. Ibid., 165.

23. Ibid., 167. This process requires tolerance on the part of the majority population and adaptability on the part of the members of the minority group.

24. Pamela J. Hickey, "Lingua Anglia: Bridging Language and Learners: One of These Things Is Not Like the Others: Assimilation, Acculturation, Education," *English Journal* 104, no. 5 (2015): 108.

25. Jews were regarded as a nation in the Soviet Union (USSR).

26. Joel Rosenberg, "The Soul of Catastrophe: On the 1937 Film of S. An-Sky's *The Dybbuk*," *Jewish Social Studies* 17, no. 2 (2011): 3–4.

27. Quotation from: http://jewishfilm.org/Catalogue/films/alettertomother.htm. The film was produced in 1938 and released in the United States in September 1939. Goldman, *Visions*, 104.

28. Rosenberg, "The Soul of Catastrophe," 4.

29. Saul Friedländer, *Die Jahre der Vernichtung* (Munich: C. H. Beck, 2006), 33.

30. William Bruce Johnson, *Miracles and Sacrilege. Robert Rossellini, the Church, and Film Censorship in Hollywood* (Toronto: University of Toronto Press, 2016), 165–66.

31. Ibid., 108–10.

32. Ibid., 160.

33. This is how the movie was marketed.

34. "Film Company Criticized for Dropping 'It Can't Happen Here,'" *Jewish Telegraph Agency*, July 6, 1939, 5.

35. Ibid.; Johnson, *Miracles*, 160.

36. Johnson, *Miracles*, 161; "'Nazi Spy' Film Banned in Argentina," *Jewish Telegraph Agency*, June 16, 1939.

37. Noah Isenberg, *Edgar G. Ulmer—A Filmmaker at the Margins* (Berkeley: University of California Press, 2014), 95.

38. Ibid., 96.

39. Ibid.

40. Ibid., 96, 105.

41. Lotman, *Semiotics*.

42. *Glupsk* alludes to the Yiddish *glomp* and the Russian *glupiy*, words that mean stupid or fool. The name Glupsk is a reference to the fictional town of Glupov in the satirical novel *The History of a Town* (1870) by Russian writer Mikhail Saltykov-Shchedrin.

43. The ḥavurot, the plural of ḥavura, were originally religious organizations that helped organize burials or prayer circles, but since the middle of the nineteenth century in the Russian Empire they were responsible for carrying out administrative duties in the Jewish communities in the Pale of Settlement. Kriza, *Jiddische Filme*, 100–101.

44. Goldman, *Visions*, 121.

45. Kriza, *Jiddische Filme*, 91.

46. Quotation from Isenberg, *Edgar G. Ulmer*, 127; cf. also: Paskin, "The Light Ahead," 127–8; Hoberman, *Bridge*, 302.

47. Isenberg, "Perennial Detour," 13.

48. Vincent Brook, "Forging the 'New Jew'": Ulmer's Yiddish Films," in *The Films of Edgar G. Ulmer*, ed. Bernd Herzogenrath (Lanham: Scarecrow Press, 2009), 81.

49. For a detailed discussion of the movie's relationship to the literary source, cf., Kriza, *Jiddische Filme*, 108–14.

50. The different ḥavurot distributed the money to each other.

51. Kriza, *Jiddische Filme*, 100.

52. Noah Isenberg, "Perennial Detour: The Cinema of Edgar G. Ulmer and the Experience of Exile," *Cinema Journal* 43, no. 2 (2004): 3–4.

53. Brook, "Forging the 'New Jew,'" 72.

54. Isenberg, "Perennial Detour," 15. Apart from Yiddish movies, Ulmer also made

Ukrainian-language movies and a film with almost exclusively African American actors in this period.

55. Eve Sicular, "In a Horror Master's Rare TB films, Warnings for a Future Pandemic," *Forward*, July 6, 2020, https://forward.com/culture/450007/in-noir-master-edgar-ulmers-rare-tuberculosis-films-warnings-for-a-future/.

56. Kriza, *Jiddische Filme*, 98.

57. Ibid., 87.

58. Stefan Grissemann, *Mann im Schatten. Der Filmemacher Edgar G. Ulmer* (Wien: Zsolnay Verlag, 2003), 138.

59. Ken Frieden, "A Century in the Life of Sholem Aleichem's Tevye," *Religion* 46 (1993): 24, http://surface.syr.edu/rel/46.

60. These issues will be discussed below, but for a detailed comparison see Frieden, "A Century"; Kriza, *Jiddische Filme*, 143-51.

61. Goldberg, *Laughter*, 105.

62. Cf. Aleichem, *Tevye*.

63. Annamaria Orla-Bukowska, "Maintaining Borders, Crossing Borders: Social Relationships in the Shtetl," in *The Shtetl: Myth and Reality*, ed. Antony Polonsky, vol. 17 of *Polin: Studies in Polish Jewry* (Liverpool: Liverpool University Press, 2004): 171-96.

64. Ibid., 191.

65. He refers to biblical prophet Nathan's allegory as told to King David in 2 Samuel 12. Cf. Kriza, *Jiddische Filme*, 126.

66. A *hanukkiah* is a candelabrum with nine branches used to light the candles to celebrate the Jewish holiday of Hanukkah.

67. *Galut* is the Hebrew word for exile and it is used here in the understanding that the Jewish Diaspora was in exile as long as it did not inhabit the land of Israel (the territory before the State of Israel was founded in 1948).

68. Michel, *Das jiddische Kino*, 99.

69. Ibid., 98-99.

70. Friedländer, *Die Jahre*, 29-31.

71. Michel, *Das jiddische Kino*, 99.

72. This refers to both marriage after conversion and marriage in which one partner remains Jewish. Milton Barron, "The Incidence of Jewish Intermarriage in Europe and America," *American Sociological Review* 11, no. 1 (1946): 7-10.

73. Kriza, *Jiddische Filme*, 126-127. Michel, *Das jiddische Kino*, 277-81. Intermarriage was common in the USSR, but in the 1930s US movies were banned from release in that country, so this movie was unlikely to have been addressed to this audience.

74. Kriza, *Jiddische Filme*, 126-36.

75. In the 1930s, there was a deficit in Jewish characters in non-Yiddish movies, so the films of the silent era are more representative in their discussion of the subject. Joseph Greenblum, "Does Hollywood Still Glorify Jewish Intermarriage? The Case of 'The Jazz Singer,'" *American Jewish History* 83, no. 4 (1995): 445-69; Patrick Mullins, "Ethnic Cinema in the Nickelodeon Era in New York City: Commerce, Assimilation and Cultural Identity," *Film History* 12, no. 1 (2000): 115-24; Joel Rosenberg, "Jewish Experience on Film—An American Overview," *American Jewish Year Book* 96 (1996): 3-50.

76. Lester D. Friedman, "Celluloid Assimilation: Jews in American Silent Movies." *Journal of Popular Film and Television* 15, no. 3 (1987): 135.

77. Rosenberg, "Jewish Experience," 9–11.

78. Greenblum, "Does Hollywood," 452–55.

79. Rosenberg, "Jewish Experience," 19. It is not unlikely that antisemitism played a part in this policy, as the 1930s saw a surge in antisemitism in the United States as well. Michel, *Das jiddische Kino*, 282.

80. Goldman, *Visions*, 107. As mentioned previously, a Polish Jewish producer rejected making the film in Poland for political reasons.

81. Kriza, *Jiddische Filme*, 143–51.

82. Sheila Fitzpatrick, "Annexation, Evacuation, and Antisemitism in the Soviet Union, 1939–1946," in *Shelter from the Holocaust: Rethinking Jewish Survival in the Soviet Union*, eds. Mark Edele, Sheila Fitzpatrick, and Atina Grossman (Detroit: Wayne State University Press, 2017), 135.

83. It is worth mentioning that the ludicrous portrayal of the Ukrainians is often a source of comic relief which includes scenes of slapstick comedy. Alas, humor can indeed be cruel, too.

84. Marat Grinberg, "Rolling in Dust: Maurice Schwartz's *Tevye* (1939) and Its Ambiguities," *Shofar* 32, no. 2 (2014): 52.

85. Pew Research Center. *A Portrait of Jewish Americans. Findings from a Pew Research Center Survey of U.S. Jews* (Washington, DC: Pew Research Center, 2013), 9; Greenblum, "Does Hollywood," 450.

86. Frieden, "A Century," 21–23.

87. Patricia Erens, "Mentshlekhkayt Conquers All: The Yiddish Cinema in America," *Film Comment* 12, no. 1 (1976): 49.

88. Grinberg, "Rolling in Dust," 53.

89. Michel notes that clothing and outward appearance are important clues in the interpretation of assimilation or acculturation represented in Yiddish films. Michel, *Das jiddische Kino*, 285.

90. Zehavit Stern, "The Idealized Mother and Her Discontents: Performing Maternity in Yiddish Film Melodrama," in *Choosing Yiddish: New Frontiers of Language and Culture*, ed. Lara Rabinovitch (Detroit: Wayne State University Press, 2012), 163.

91. Riv-Ellen Prell, *Fighting to Become Americans: Jews, Gender, and the Anxiety of Assimilation* (Boston: Beacon Press, 1999), 85; Gary Gerstle, "Liberty, Coercion, and the Making of Americans," *Journal of American History* 84, no. 2 (1997): 547; Erens, "Mentshlekhkayt," 49–50.

92. Tevye quotes Job 1:21, "God gave and God took away," as a way of coping with his troubles.

93. Here we have another good example of an inverted version of the trope also seen in *The Jazz Singer*: temptation is averted.

94. Kriza, *Jiddische Filme*, 163.

95. Louis Finkelstein, "The Jewish Religion: It's Beliefs and Practices," in *The Jews: Their History, Culture, and Religion*, edited by Louis Finkelstein, vol. 2 (New York: Harper, 1949), 1329.

96. Erens, "Mentshlekhkayt," 51.

97. An online search of movie releases in the Mexican Yiddish newspapers *Der Weg und Di Shtime* revealed no evidence that these three films were shown in this neighboring country in 1939 and 1940. For providing access to these newspapers, I would like to thank the Jewish Research and Documentation Center in Mexico, CDIJUM, and the George A. Smathers Libraries at the University of Florida.

98. Friedländer, *Die Jahre*, 35.

99. "Las bodas negras—o bodas de la peste—que se celebran en los cementerios durante las pandemias," *Enlace Judío México*, May 9, 2020, https://www.enlacejudio.com/2020/05/09/las-bodas-negras-o-bodas-de-la-peste-que-se-celebran-en-los-cementerios-durante-las-pandemias/.

100. Isenberg, *Edgar G. Ulmer*, 95.

Bibliography

Primary Sources

Archives

George A. Smathers Libraries (University of Florida)
Jewish Research and Documentation Center (Mexico City)
National Center for Jewish Film (Brandeis University)

Films

Crosland, Alan, dir. *The Jazz Singer*. USA, 1927.
Glenn, Jack, dir. *Inside Nazi Germany—1938*. USA, 1938.
Green, Joseph, dir. *Letter to Mother* or *A Brivele der Mamen*. Poland, 1938.
Lynn, Henry, dir. *The Yiddishe Mama* or *Hayntike Mames*. USA, 1939.
Litvak, Anatole, dir. *Confessions of a Nazi Spy*. USA, 1939.
Schwartz, Maurice, dir. *Tevye the Milkman* or *Tevya*. USA, 1939.
Ulmer, Edgar, dir. *The Light Ahead* or *Di Klatshe; Fishke der Krumer*. USA, 1939.

Printed Sources

Aleichem, Sholem. *Tevye der Milkhiker*. Warsaw: Kultur-Lige, 1921.
"Film Company Criticized for Dropping 'It Can't Happen Here.'" *Jewish Telegraph Agency*, July 6, 1939.
"'Nazi Spy' Film Banned in Argentina." *Jewish Telegraph Agency*, June 16, 1939.
"Propaganda Films Fed Poles as Nazis Take over Theaters in Poland." *Jewish Telegraph Agency*, December 3, 1939.
"'Time' Film on Reich Impressive; Nazi Censor Efforts Rebuffed; Chicago Police Ban Picture." *Jewish Telegraph Agency*, January 20, 1938.

Secondary Sources

Barron, Milton. "The Incidence of Jewish Intermarriage in Europe and America." *American Sociological Review* 11, no. 1 (1946): 6–13.

Bordwell, David. *Making Meaning: Inference and Rhetoric in the Interpretation of Cinema.* Cambridge: Harvard University Press, 1991.

Brook, Vincent. "Forging the 'New Jew': Ulmer's Yiddish Films." In *The Films of Edgar G. Ulmer,* edited by Bernd Herzogenrath, 71–85. Lanham: Scarecrow Press, 2009.

Colin, Amy, and Elisabeth Strenger, eds. *Bridging the Abyss. Brücken über dem Abgrund.* Munich: Wilhelm Fink Verlag, 1994.

Erens, Patricia. "Mentshlekhkayt Conquers All: The Yiddish Cinema in America." *Film Comment* 12, no. 1 (1976): 48–53.

Finkelstein, Louis. "The Jewish Religion: It's Beliefs and Practices." In *The Jews: Their History, Culture, and Religion,* edited by Louis Finkelstein, 1327–90. Vol. 2. New York: Harper, 1949.

Fitzpatrick, Sheila. "Annexation, Evacuation, and Antisemitism in the Soviet Union, 1939–1946." In *Shelter from the Holocaust: Rethinking Jewish Survival in the Soviet Union,* edited by Mark Edele, Sheila Fitzpatrick, and Atina Grossman, 133–60. Detroit: Wayne State University Press, 2017.

Frieden, Ken. "A Century in the Life of Sholem Aleichem's Tevye." *Religion* 46 (1993): 1–25. http://surface.syr.edu/rel/46.

Friedländer, Saul. *Die Jahre der Vernichtung.* Munich: C. H. Beck, 2006.

Friedman, Lester D. "Celluloid Assimilation: Jews in American Silent Movies." *Journal of Popular Film and Television* 15, no. 3 (1987): 129–36.

Gerstle, Gary. "Liberty, Coercion, and the Making of Americans." *Journal of American History* 84, no. 2 (1997): 524–58.

Goldberg, Judith. *Laughter through Tears. The Yiddish Cinema.* Rutherford/Madison: Fairleigh Dickinson University Press, 1983.

Goldman, Eric. *Visions, Images, and Dreams: Yiddish Film Past and Present.* Ann Arbor: UMI Research Press, 1983.

Greenblum, Joseph. "Does Hollywood Still Glorify Jewish Intermarriage? The Case of 'The Jazz Singer.'" *American Jewish History* 83, no. 4 (1995): 445–69.

Grinberg, Marat. "Rolling in Dust: Maurice Schwartz's *Tevye* (1939) and Its Ambiguities." *Shofar* 32, no. 2 (2014): 49–72.

Grissemann, Stefan. *Mann im Schatten. Der Filmemacher Edgar G. Ulmer.* Wien: Zsolnay Verlag, 2003.

Gruschka, Roland. Review of *Das jiddische Kino: Aufstiegsinszenierungen zwischen Schtetl und American Dream,* by Chantal Catherine Michel. *East European Jewish Affairs* 44, no. 1 (2014): 109–11.

Hickey, Pamela J. "Lingua Anglia: Bridging Language and Learners: One of These Things Is Not Like the Others: Assimilation, Acculturation, Education." *English Journal* 104, no. 5 (2015): 107–9.

Hoberman, James. *Bridge of Light: Yiddish Film between Two Worlds.* New York: Dartmouth College Press, 2010.

———. "Der ershter Talkies: 'Uncle Moses' and the Coming of Yiddish Sound Film." *Film Comment* 27, no. 6 (1991): 32–39.
Isenberg, Noah. *Edgar G. Ulmer—A Filmmaker at the Margins.* Berkeley: University of California Press, 2014.
———. "Perennial Detour: The Cinema of Edgar G. Ulmer and the Experience of Exile." *Cinema Journal* 43, no. 2 (2004): 3–25.
Johnson, William Bruce. *Miracles and Sacrilege. Robert Rossellini, the Church, and Film Censorship in Hollywood.* Toronto: University of Toronto Press, 2016.
Kriza, Elisa. *Jiddische Filme verstehen: Religiöse Symbolik und kultureller Kontext.* 2nd ed. Bamberg: University of Bamberg Press, 2018.
Laczó, Ferenc, and Joachim von Puttkamer, eds. *Catastrophe and Utopia: Jewish Intellectuals in Central and Eastern Europe in the 1930s and 1940s.* Berlin: Walter de Gruyter, 2017.
"Las bodas negras—o bodas de la peste—que se celebran en los cementeros durante las pandemias." *Enlace Judío México,* May 9, 2020. https://www.enlacejudio.com/2020/05/09/las-bodas-negras-o-bodas-de-la-peste-que-se-celebran-en-los-cementerios-durante-las-pandemias/.
LeMay, Michael C. "Assessing Assimilation: Cultural and Political Integration of Immigrants and Their Descendants." *In Defense of the Alien* 23 (2000): 163–76.
Lotman, Jurij. *Semiotics of Cinema.* Ann Arbor: University of Michigan Press, 1976.
Michel, Chantal. *Das jiddische Kino. Aufstiegsinszenierungen zwischen Schtetl und American Dream.* Berlin: Metropol, 2012.
Mullins, Patrick. "Ethnic Cinema in the Nickelodeon Era in New York City: Commerce, Assimilation and Cultural Identity." *Film History* 12, no. 1 (2000): 115–24.
Orla-Bukowska, Annamaria. "Maintaining Borders, Crossing Borders: Social Relationships in the Shtetl." In *The Shtetl: Myth and Reality,* edited by Antony Polonsky, 171–95. Vol. 17 of *Polin: Studies in Polish Jewry.* Liverpool: Liverpool University Press, 2004.
Pew Research Center. *A Portrait of Jewish Americans. Findings from a Pew Research Center Survey of U.S. Jews.* Washington DC: Pew Research Center, 2013.
Paskin, Sylvia. "The Light Ahead." In *When Joseph Met Molly. A Reader on Yiddish Film,* edited by Sylvia Paskin, 119–29. Nottingham: Five Leaves, 1999.
Prell, Riv-Ellen. *Fighting to Become Americans. Jews, Gender, and the Anxiety of Assimilation.* Boston: Beacon Press, 1999.
Puckett, Kent. *Narrative Theory: A Critical Introduction.* Cambridge: Cambridge University Press, 2016.
Reinharz, Jehuda, and Yaacov Shavit. *The Road to September 1939: Polish Jews, Zionists, and the Yishuv on the Eve of World War II.* Waltham: Brandeis University Press, 2018.
Rosenberg, Joel. "Jewish Experience on Film—An American Overview." *American Jewish Year Book* 96, (1996): 3–50.
———. "The Soul of Catastrophe: On the 1937 Film of S. An-Sky's *The Dybbuk.*" *Jewish Social Studies* 17, no. 2 (2011): 1–27.
Sicular, Eve. "In a Horror Master's Rare TB films, Warnings for a Future Pandemic." *Forward,* July 6, 2020. https://forward.com/culture/450007/in-noir-master-edgar-ulmers-rare-tuberculosis-films-warnings-for-a-future/.

Stern, Zehavit. "The Idealized Mother and Her Discontents: Performing Maternity in Yiddish Film Melodrama." In *Choosing Yiddish: New Frontiers of Language and Culture*, edited by Lara Rabinovitch, 163–78. Detroit: Wayne State University Press, 2012.

Walke, Anika. Introduction to *Migration and Mobility in the Modern Age: Refugees, Travelers, and Traffickers in Europe and Eurasia*. Edited by Anika Walke, Jan Musekamp, and Nicole Svobodny, 1–31. Bloomington: Indiana University Press, 2017.

Wolff, Frank. "Global Walls and Global Movement: New Destinations in Jewish Migration, 1918–1939." *East European Jewish Affairs* 44, no. 2–3 (2014): 187–204.

8

Deforestation and Jewish Settlement in Fazenda Quatro Irmãos

A History of the Jewish Colonization Association's Activities in Rio Grande do Sul, Brazil

Isabel Rosa Gritti

Two agents of colonization were involved in the settlement of European immigrants and/or their descendants as farmers in the state of Rio Grande do Sul: the state government and private immigration and colonization companies. The intense campaign and the implementation of an immigration and colonization policy initiated by the Imperial government, and later by the Republican government, directed toward the arrival of European immigrants, must be understood in the context of the replacement of slave labor for the work of immigrants, especially in coffee plantations in southeastern Brazil, and in the formation of small food-producing properties, based on family work in the South Region of Brazil. This is how we should understand the Land Law of 1850, which made land a commodity. The only way to acquire land was through purchase, which prevented freed blacks and squatters from becoming landowners. Immigrants were able to purchase land under the conditions created by the immigration policy.

Fernando Carneiro explains that the entry of immigrants into a country, and their settlement, owes much less to the propaganda and expenses created by public authorities than to the nation's social, political, and economic situation.[1] He argues that the increase in the flow of immigrants in Brazil was due to the expansion of the coffee industry, which created demand for labor, in addition to the range of opportunities presented by growing urban centers.

The commodification of land, combined with the desire of the federal and provincial governments to populate areas that were considered unpopulated—although they were, in fact, already occupied by indigenous and mixed-race populations. These inhabitants became "invaders" as a result of the Land Law, as they were unable to buy the land from the government. It was this context that enabled the colonizing companies to operate.

One of these companies was the Jewish Colonization Association, better known as the JCA. The Association was created in 1891 by Baron Maurice Hirsch (1831–1896) with the purpose of freeing Jews from persecution and discrimination in Eastern Europe. Hirsch believed that the only way to help them was to support their emigration to regions where they could live freely. This study focuses on the JCA's activities in the colony Fazenda Quatro Irmãos, located in the Erechim region, home of European immigrants, indigenous people, and *caboclos* (a term usually referring to Brazilians of mixed indigenous and European descent). It explores the JCA's support for Jewish immigration to Brazil and its economic operations in the south of Brazil. The Association's philanthropic ends were met through profitable means: the JCA was heavily involved with intense deforestation and the timber industry in this area. The influx and settlement of immigrants, at the same time, was key to the launch and success of the JCA's economic enterprise. The state immigration and colonization policies, to a large extent, advanced the JCA's interests to the detriment of local populations and the environment. The chapter also examines the criticism directed toward the JCA for the ecological impact of the deforestation driven by its economic activities in the area, which, beginning from the 1930s, became disconnected from the Association's involvement with Jewish immigration to Brazil.

The Jewish Colonization Association

Since its foundation, the JCA was registered as a limited liability company by Baron Hirsch and other wealthy members of the Jewish communities in Brussels, London, Berlin, and Frankfurt, with startup capital of two million pounds sterling. According to the Memorandum of Association of the Jewish Colonization Association, the JCA's stated objective was "to assist and promote the emigration of Jews from any part of Europe or Asia, and principally from countries in which they may for the time being be subjected to any special taxes or political or other disabilities, to any part of the world, and to form and establish colonies in various parts of North and South America and other countries, for agricultural, cultural, commercial and other purposes."[2]

According to Kennee Switzer-Rakos, to achieve these goals, the JCA was authorized "to purchase, or acquire, any territory outside of Europe from governments, states, municipal or local authorities, corporations or persons."[3] The Association was also given the power to establish emigration agencies in various parts of the world and to build, rent, charter, and equip steamships and other vessels, in order to facilitate emigration.

Upon the death of Baron Hirsch, in 1896, JCA directors and administrators had at their disposal the grand total of £8,830,116, almost entirely invested in bank deposits and other investments. However, after more than ten years of activity, the Association had earned about £300,000 from the enormous capital invested in several financial companies in Europe. Added to that were the significant assets acquired, over time, in the New World. Compared to the income and capital of other organizations, this was a huge sum. For example, the Keren Kayemet Leisrael (Jewish National Fund), the main instrument of the Zionist movement for land acquisition and development, reported in 1905 that over a three-year period, worldwide it had managed to collect only £45,589.[4]

Haim Avni argues that the JCA's possession of significant capital gave board members complete independence, and that, at the start of their activities, they decided not to provide information to the public about the Association's capital and earnings, or its decisions. Public opinion thus had very little influence on the JCA's decisions, which was not the case for other institutions providing support to Jewish emigrants. This explains why the campaign that the Jewish press in Eastern Europe and elsewhere launched against these JCA policies did not, for the most part, provoke any public response by the Association.

After the death of Baron Hirsch, a new council was elected, composed of S. H. Goldschmidt, Narcise Leven, Salomão Reinach, Alfred L. Cohen, Herbert Lousada, Zadoc Kahn, Claude J. G. Montefiori, Leopold Schioss, Julius Plotke, Dr. Edmund Lachmann, and Franz Philipson. According to Jeffrey Lesser, the new council of the JCA retained very little of the Baron's generous spirit. In 1900, they decided "to expand the organization's scope, always with the idea that a coincidence of interests might be found between charity and capitalism."[5] Canada was one of the newest nations chosen by the JCA. In 1901, the JCA sent its Argentine director, David Cazés, together with Eusébio Lapine, agronomist and chief administrator of the Argentine colony of Entre Ríos, to assess the conditions for expansion in southern Brazil. The information they collected was positive and the Company "decided that Rio Grande do Sul, because of its proximity to the Argentinian colonies, its constitutionally mandated religious toleration, and its desire for new colonists, would be a good home for Russian Jews."[6]

The Brazilian Colonies

The JCA began its long history of activities in Brazil and, more specifically, in Rio Grande do Sul, in 1902. That year, the JCA purchased its first property, an area of 5,500 hectares (approximately 13,591 acres), in Pinhal, in the municipality of Santa Maria, where, in 1904, the settlement of Jewish immigrants began. This original Jewish nucleus was called Filipson, in honor of Franz Philipson, the then-vice president of JCA and president of Compagnie Auxiliaire de Chemins du Fer au Brésil, a Belgian leasing company that was, at the time, a part of the network of the Rio Grande do Sul railroad company.

The authorization for the JCA to operate in Rio Grande do Sul was granted by the state government in 1903 and published in the newspaper *A Federação*, on July 20:

> Considering that the Company called the Jewish Colonization Association, based in England, was organized to promote the immigration of Hebrews from various parts of Europe and Asia to different regions of the Americas; whereas, in accordance with its institutional purposes, the same Company intends to found colonial centers dedicated to the work of agriculture, commerce, and industry in this state; considering, therefore, that the purposes of the Company are of public benefit, helping to promote immigration and material progress; I resolve, by decree 434, of July 4, 1891, Articles 47, 51, 52, 53 and 54, to grant the authorization requested by engineer Eusébio Lapine, so that said Company may operate in this state.[7]

In 1904, the JCA began its colonization work. Initially, it settled thirty-seven Jewish families in Filipson, comprising a total of 267 people from Bessarabia, on plots of 25 hectares (62 acres) of forest and fields. In addition, when they arrived, the immigrants received housing, agricultural implements, two teams of oxen, two cows, one horse, and a cash allowance that varied according to the number of family members until they could live off the crops. Lassance Cunha believes that the Filipson colony's location in the vicinity of the railroad managed by Philipson was an important factor in its prosperity, as "this certainly motivated his interest in the prosperity of this and any other colonies that would be created, because of the financial benefits that would result from transporting the colonies' products by the railroad."[8] However, the long anticipated and much-discussed prosperity of the Filipson colony did not materialize. This did not prevent the JCA from acquiring new properties in the state. Not accidentally, they were mostly located in the vicinity of the railway.

When the JCA purchased Fazenda Quatro Irmãos[9] in 1909—a property with an area of 93,985 hectares (232,241 acres), in what was then the municipality of Passo Fundo—the Filipson colony was practically empty. The location of the new area acquired by JCA in the state was similar to the Filipson colony. It was near the São Paulo–Rio Grande railway line, still under construction by the Compagnie Auxiliaire de Chemins du Fer au Brésil. If, on the one hand, the state government saw the JCA's work as a means of achieving objectives, such as populating sparsely inhabited regions through immigration, on the other hand, the JCA and the Compagnie Auxiliaire de Chemins du Fer au Brésil clearly shared common economic interests. From 1909 to 1962, only 436 Jewish immigrants were settled on the property, which was one of the reasons JCA's performance in relation to Quatro Irmãos was constantly criticized. This criticism was voiced even by the settlers themselves, who were concerned about the fate of their European countrymen and women in the period leading up to World War II. The deforestation of Quatro Irmãos was also a cause for concern and complaint, as will be discussed next.

Finding a Gold Mine: The Pine Forest of Fazenda Quatro Irmãos

The JCA's interest in the Quatro Irmãos forests demonstrates its economic drive. Six months after the purchase of the land, that is, in January 1910, the JCA board of directors wrote to the director of the Filipson colony, announcing "the visit by a special envoy of Mr. Teixeira Soares to study the forest issue on our property, with the purpose of presenting you a detailed report on its value."[10] This was not the only occasion that the JCA appraised the land; in fact, four appraisals of the forests on the property were completed by different people in 1911. One of these appraisals was done by the forestry engineer at Bromberg and Company of Porto Alegre. According to JCA correspondence, "This man was amazed, and commended me for the high quality of the wood. He gave me his expert opinion that we should not yet begin to harvest the wood, because the industry will not reach it true value for a few years."[11]

Figure 8.1. Map of Quatro Irmãos. From *Atlas des colonies et domaines de la Jewish Colonization Association en République Argentine et au Brésil* (Paris: Jewish Colonization Association, 1914). Courtesy of the Isser and Rae Price Library of Judaica, Special and Area Studies Collections, George A. Smathers Libraries, University of Florida.

The importance that the JCA attributed to the wealth of forest products in the domain of Quatro Irmãos was confirmed by the fact that it was the company's general manager who went to Rio Grande do Sul in 1911 to gather information on the timber market. In July 1911, the director of the Filipson colony wrote to the board of directors in London:

> Accompanying Mr. Oungre, in different centers, such as Porto Alegre, Rio Grande, Pelotas, and Rivera, I took care to gather information about the wood. Mr. Oungre was able to see, everywhere, great enthusiasm for this industry, especially on the day when all the necessary information was brought together for exporting the timber to the Argentine Republic and Uruguay.[12]

The value of the forest on the newest property of the JCA is evident in the enthusiasm of the director of the Filipson colony. On February 6, 1911, Leibovich exclaimed: "The calculations regarding the value of wood prove sufficiently the great wealth that remains to be exploited, and there is no better comparison than calling it a gold mine."[13] It is after this series of promising appraisals of the forest lands and feasibility of their development that the Jewish colonization began in 1912.

There was constant concern on the part of JCA with the exploitation of the forests on 93,985 hectares (232,241 acres) of Fazenda Quatro Irmãos. In 1915, when Mr. Forbes planned to travel to Brazil to evaluate the Brazil Railway properties, the JCA board of directors asked the Quatro Irmãos administrators to be aware of how the railway intended to exploit its property, Três Barras. Similarly, it also asked the director of Quatro Irmãos to keep up with the news regarding the navigability of the Uruguay River, because "this issue is of utmost interest to the development of trade in our colonies."[14]

Due to its interests in the commercialization of timber, the JCA was careful to include a clause in the purchase and sale agreements made with Jewish settlers that prohibited them from deforesting the acquired lot without the Association's prior authorization. Similarly, the land was only sold to non-Jews after the JCA had extracted the timber from the respective lots through a forestry contract, in which the Association leased a certain wooded area to loggers, Jewish or not, so that they could extract timber. The exploitation of forest products in Fazenda Quatro Irmãos intensified during World War I, a favorable period for the timber industry because during this time it did not suffer competition from European producers and could thus export to the neighboring countries of Argentina and Uruguay.

Both the value of the forest lands belonging to Fazenda Quatro Irmãos and the goal to exploit them were the determining factors in the construction of the nineteen-kilometer-long Quatro Irmãos–Erebango railway line. It had already been planned by 1911 to support the commercialization of timber, the main activity developed by the JCA on its Quatro Irmãos property. Although it was completed in 1915, the railway line was only opened in 1917. The line linked the headquarters of Quatro Irmãos to the Viação Férrea do Rio Grande do Sul line, thus providing the means to transport the products from Quatro Irmãos to the Viação Férrea do Rio Grande do Sul railway.

The JCA's long-term and continuous engagement with deforestation and activities related to the timber industry in the area began in the 1920s. The following three decades—the 1930s, 1940s, and 1950s—witnessed the peak of forest exploitation and wood exports. In 1960, after about forty years, the JCA discontinued its timber enterprise because no forests remained to explore and no more land was available for purchase. The Association's philanthropic activities evolved in a different direction. In 1931, the JCA ceased its colonizing activities in Quatro Irmãos—that is, it stopped helping new immigrants settle in this colony. Nonetheless, the JCA pledged to continue supporting Jewish immigration to Brazil.

Because of the continued deforestation resulting from its timber production, the JCA faced serious complaints at midcentury. In a 1951 letter to state governor Ernesto Dornelles, the representative of the Labor Party of Vila Campinas in the District of Quatro Irmãos accused the JCA of indiscriminate deforestation and failing to fully utilize felled pine trees. The complaint presented to the state governor was challenged by the Rio Grande do Sul Forestry Officer, Henrique Luiz Roessler, who stated that it was "unfortunate that once again the JCA is being harassed with proceedings of this nature, when it is known to be one of the few to fulfill its obligations to the Forestry Service."[15] The JCA was informed of the complaint to the governor by Roessler. In addition to sending a copy of the complaint to administrators in Quatro Irmãos, Roessler also provided them his response to the governor's request for information, before submitting it to the governor: "I am handing these copies over to you confidentially so that you can examine the motives for the complaint and the appropriate measures to be taken, without reprisals, solely for preventive purposes."[16]

In response to the state governor's request for information, Roessler reported that the JCA was the target of constant denunciations to public authorities for destroying the pine forests on its property, arguing:

The company [the JCA] regularly and annually requested licenses to fell the pines for its commercial purposes from the Forest Service. They initially reforested with eucalyptus, hardwood, and pine in the required proportion. Beginning in 1948, it planted mostly pine: five seedlings for each tree felled above 40 cm in diameter. The JCA is perfectly compliant with the provisions of the Forest Code, and its reforestation obligations are up to date, as the signatory of this letter has personally verified in several inspections carried out at Fazenda Quatro Irmãos.[17]

Roessler closed his response to the governor by saying: "To balance the observation of the devastation of the JCA's native pine forests, the complainant also paid a visit to the Company's reforestation areas, where several hundred thousand new pines attest to its leaders' commitment to the perpetuation of hardwood on the [forested] lands on their property, which are not sold as lots."[18]

Although the Forestry Officer confirmed that the JCA was repopulating the deforested areas by planting new trees and that "since 1948, it planted mostly pine,"[19] the results of the reforestation, observed in 1959, were totally different from what he reported. The director of Quatro Irmãos evaluated the result of reforestation to replace the felled pine:

> As a result of reforestation, we currently have an area of approximately 200 hectares [494 acres] of eucalyptus aged between one and ten years. This area of land is included in our reserves. Unfortunately, this eucalyptus does not add commercial value to the land. The eucalyptus [trees] were planted to meet our legal obligation to reforest the land.[20]

The JCA's very "close" relationship with the Rio Grande do Sul forestry officer, evident in the case reported above, was confirmed in 1949, when he annulled the decision of the Erechim Forestry Officer Antônio Pereira de Souza, who had denied the JCA's request to cut down 11,350 pine trees. De Souza claimed that the petitioner was under the obligation to reforest 153,706 pine trees, and that the forests it owned were subject to the restrictive clause of Article 15 of the Forestry Code, as they constituted a forest reserve, which was declared a public utility by State Decree number 658 of March 10, 1949.[21]

It is interesting to note that although Roessler overturned de Souza's denial of the JCA's request to cut down 11,350 pine trees in 1949, a year later, Roessler praised the Erechim Forestry Officer's work, including even his efforts to promote reforestation in Fazenda Quatro Irmãos, calling him the state's best Forestry Officer. Roessler's laudatory remarks appear on the certificate issued in São Leopoldo on April 4, 1950:

> I attest, by [the authority of] my position, that Mr. Antônio Pereira de Souza has been carrying out the work of Forestry Officer with rare intelligence and ability, energy and impartiality since 1942, acting with calm and equilibrium and imposing respect for the Forest Service throughout the northeast of the state, whose center is Erechim, the Forest Service headquarters. An uncompromising protector of our forests and a passionate promoter of reforestation, he managed to create a new mentality regarding the forest among loggers in his area. His initiatives include the campaign against illegal exploitation of the forests in indigenous settlements of this state, and those belonging to the public patrimony, as well as halting the devastation of the extensive pine forests, without reforestation, by the colonizing company, [that is] the Jewish Colonization Association, and so many other important actions. As hunting and fishing inspector, he managed to discipline and moralize these sports, preventing the further destruction of fauna in the vast region under his jurisdiction. As an organizer he has demonstrated unusual qualities, being considered by us as our best officer.[22]

The situation in which Quatro Irmãos found itself after half a century of JCA activity confirms that the Association's interest was primarily economic. It dedicated itself to the exploitation of forest products and the sale of land, which was not consistent with the advertised philanthropic principles of the colonizing company.

The Legion of Good Will appealed to these philanthropic principles in April 1962. They asked the JCA to donate a building and a small area of land for the creation of a juvenile recovery facility in Quatro Irmãos. In response, the JCA director of Quatro Irmãos argued:

> Thanks to a band of disinterested and selfless men, our Association, collaborating with this idea, would conclude its long years of activities in Quatro Irmãos with a flourish. Despite our inglorious task of colonization, it is regrettable and undeniable that after the activity surrounding exploitation of the pine trees that existed on our land was completed, Quatro Irmãos became a village with negligible economic

activity and a cluster of humble people without work, where absolute misery prevails. A childhood of abandonment and hunger proliferates in the semi-deserted streets of the village. Adults live off odd jobs, unable to find steady work. Quatro Irmãos today is not even a shadow of that promising settlement of eight or ten years ago, when the extraction of timber provided work to dozens of families. This project to provide support to those most lacking in protection and luck is, therefore, praiseworthy and, from all points of view, decent.[23]

Even when describing their philanthropic activities, the JCA director of Quatro Irmãos still emphasized the profitability of the timber industry in the colony. He saw that the key to the success of the colony was in its economic gains and rationalized its decline accordingly, pointing out the termination of forestry. The JCA ended up withdrawing from the colony that same year, when logging had completed and sale of plots to Jews and non-Jews was concluded.

Conclusion

What sets the JCA apart from other companies that focused their activities on obtaining profits from immigration and colonization was its philanthropic mission and nature. It propagated its humanitarian action with the help of Jewish immigrants from Eastern Europe. This study shows that the JCA's for-profit activities overshadowed the philanthropic ones in Quatro Irmãos. The JCA documents held at the Jewish Historical Archive of São Paulo attest to the JCA's primary interest in the exploitation of its forest. Contrary to what it claimed, the Association was not concerned with the reforestation of the devastated areas, but rather ignored the legislation regulating forest lands. To do so, it relied on the complicity of the Regional Forestry Officer of Rio Grande do Sul. It must be said that there were several moments when the performance of the JCA relied on the apparatus of state government agencies: when ensuring the continuation of foresting and the timber industry and particularly during periods (and there were several) in which the estate was occupied by squatters and caboclos in search of land. Together with the state, the JCA contributed to their marginalization and deforestation while helping settle migrants from across the ocean.

Editors' Note

Translation from the original Brazilian Portuguese is by Elizabeth Martins.

Author's Note

Earlier versions of this essay in the original Brazilian Portuguese were presented at the Third World Congress of Environmental History, held at the Universidade Federal de Santa Catarina in 2014, and published as "Os pinais da Fazenda Quatro Irmão-RS e a Jewish Colonization Association," in *História ambiental e migrações: dialogos*, eds. Marcos Gerhardt, Eunice Sueli Nodari, and Samira Peruchi Sueto (São Leopoldo, Rio Grande do Sul: Editora Universidade Federal da Fronteira Sul, 2017), 95–108.

Notes

1. J. Fernando Carneiro, *Imigração e colonização no Brasil* (Rio de Janeiro: Universidade do Brasil, 1950), 69.

2. Kennee Switzer-Rakos, "Baron de Hirsch, the Jewish Colonization Association and Canada," *Leo Baeck Institute Yearbook* 32, no. 1 (1987): 391.

3. Ibid.

4. Switzer-Rakos, "Baron de Hirsch, the Jewish Colonization Association and Canada," (version of Switzer-Rakos' article without publishing information located in the library of Instituto Cultural Judaicò Marc Chagall in Porto Alegre), 203.

5. Jeffrey H. Lesser, "Pawns of the Powerful: Jewish Immigration to Brazil, 1904–1945" (Ph.D. diss., New York University, 1989), 25.

6. Ibid.

7. *A Federação*, July 20, 1903.

8. Ernesto Antonio Lassance Cunha, *O Rio Grande do Sul: contribuição para o estudo de suas condições econômias* (Rio de Janeiro: Imprensa Nacional, 1908), 254.

9. As the name implies, the Quatro Irmão lands belonged to these four men: Colonel David dos Santos, later Barão dos Campos Gerais, Judge José Gaspar dos Santos Lima of the district of São Borja, who lived in Cruz Alta until 1854, Antônio dos Santos Pacheco, and Clementino dos Santos Pacheco. The latter lived on the estate and was murdered by the indigenous residents in 1856. The murder resulted from the indigenous residents' dissatisfaction, because "Clementino had taken possession of that great extension of land, which was part of the Indians' patrimony, or at least, was considered to be, as there were those who say that he purchased it from them for a laughable sum." *O Erechim*, July 2, 1930, private collection of Ely Parenti.

10. JCA Correspondence from Filipson to Paris on June 10, 1910, no. 235, reprinted in *Pesquisas Regionais* 5, no. 7 (November 1982).

11. JCA Correspondence from Filipson to Paris, on June 5, 1911, no. 263, in Ibid.

12. JCA Correspondence from Filipson to Paris, on July 6, 1911, no. 283, reprinted in *Pesquisas Regionais* 7, no. 15 (July 1985).

13. JCA Correspondence from Filipson to Paris, on February 6, 1911, no. 268, reprinted in *Pesquisas Regionais* 5, no. 7 (July 1985).

14. JCA Correspondence from Paris to Quatro Irmãos, on March 4, 1915, no. 418, box 8, bundle 1, Arquivo Judaico Histórico Brasileiro-São Paulo (AHJB-SP).

15. Memo 3689 from June 30, 1951, sent by Ministry of Agriculture's Regional Forest Service Office in São Leopoldo, Rio Grande do Sul, to Herbert Schall, JCA Central Administration in Quatro Irmãos, box 17, bundle 3, AHJB-SP.

16. Ibid.

17. Memo n. 3.688 from June 15, 1951, sent by Forestry Officer Henrique Luiz Roessler to the Illustrious Mr. Dr. Director of Land and Colonization at the State Secretariat of Agriculture in Porto Alegre, box 17, bundle 3, AHJB-SP.

18. Ibid.

19. Forest Delegate of Rio Grande do Sul Henrique Luiz Roessler, letter no. 3.688, June 15, 1951; box 17, bundle 3, AHJB-SP.

20. Correspondence from Paris to Quatro Irmãos, on May 23, 1959, no. 1.524, box 19, bundle 4, AHJB-SP.

21. See *A Voz da Serra*, May 20, 1949.

22. Certificate from April 4, 1950, sent by the Ministry of Agriculture's Regional Forest Service Office in São Leopoldo, Rio Grande do Sul, to Antônio Pereira de Souza, Arquivo Particular Antônio Pereira de Souza in Erechim, Rio Grande do Sul.

23. JCA Correspondence from Quatro Irmãos to London, on April 16, 1962, no. 1777, box 19, bundle 2, AHJB-SP.

Bibliography

Primary Sources

Archives

Arquivo Judaico Histórico Brasileiro-São Paulo (AHJB-SP)
Arquivo Particular Antônio Pereira de Souza (Erechim, Rio Grande do Sul)
Private collection of Ely Parenti
Instituto Cultural Judaico Marc Chagall (Porto Alegre)

Periodicals

A Federação (1903)
A Voz da Serra (1949)
O Erechim (1930)
Pesquisas Regionais, Erechim (1982 and 1985)

Printed Sources

Cunha, Ernesto Antonio Lassance. *O Rio Grande do Sul: contribuição para o estudo de suas condições econômias.* Rio de Janeiro: Imprensa Nacional, 1908.

Secondary Sources

Avni, Haim. *Argentina y la historia de la inmigración judía (1810–1950).* Buenos Aires: Editorial Universitaria Magnes, 1983.

Carneiro, J. Fernando. *Imigração e colonização no Brasil.* Rio de Janeiro: Universidade do Brasil, 1950.

Gritti, Isabel R. *Imigração no Rio Grande do Sul: A Jewish Colonization Association e a colonização de Quatro Irmãos.* Porto Alegre: Martins Livreiro Editor, 1997.

———. "O reflorestamento na Fazenda Quatro Irmãos." *Perspectiva* 20, no. 80 (December 1998): 111–18.

———. "Os pinais da Fazenda Quatro Irmão-RS e a Jewish Colonization Association." In *História ambiental e migrações: diálogos,* edited by Marcos Gerhardt, Eunice Sueli Nodari, and Samira Peruchi Sueto, 95–108. São Leopoldo, Rio Grande do Sul: Editora Universidade Federal da Fronteira Sul, 2017.

Lesser, Jeffrey H. "Pawns of the Powerful: Jewish Immigration to Brazil, 1904–1945." Ph.D. diss., New York University, 1989.

Radin, José Carlos. "Companhias colonizadoras em Cruzeiro: representações sobre a civilização do sertão." Ph.D. diss., Universidade Federal de Santa Catarina, Florianopólis, 2006.

Switzer-Rakos, Kennee. "Baron de Hirsch, the Jewish Colonization Association and Canada." *Leo Baeck Institute Yearbook* 32, no. 1 (1987): 385–406.

IV

GLOBAL STRUGGLES AND COMMUNITY ORGANIZING

9

Antifascist Jewish Women in Argentina and Uruguay

Inclusion and Identities, 1941–1945

SANDRA MCGEE DEUTSCH

Dr. Rosa Scheiner, a dental surgeon and veteran leftist of Jewish origin, addressed the audience at the inauguration of the Junta de la Victoria, or JV (Victory Board)—a women's antifascist group which arose in Argentina in September 1941—several months after the German invasion of the Soviet Union. Soviet, British, and other European women's pleas for help, she said, had stirred Argentine hearts. Equally distressing were local Nazi incursions against Argentine sovereignty and freedom. The Board realized "how intimately linked the struggles unfolding on distant Russian steppes, and the no less distant British front, are with our own struggles for liberty and democracy."[1]

Inspired by goals resembling those of the Board, and similarly aligned with the Communist Party, Acción Femenina por la Victoria, or AF (Feminine Action for Victory) was founded in Uruguay in May 1942. Both became Popular Front associations, with thousands of diverse members throughout their respective countries who produced clothing and supplies for Allied soldiers, defended democratic ideals, and supported women's rights. The JV mentored AF, and they collaborated with and supported each other.

Influenced by leftism, ties to Europe, and concern for relatives left behind, Jewish women in Argentina and Uruguay shared Scheiner's views. They played critical roles in the Board and Feminine Action, yet their pattern of participation differed markedly, indicating both the international links and local circumstances that guided their actions. In this study, I compare Jewish activism in these two organizations that contributed to the Allied victory over fascism.[2] First I describe the two movements. Then I discuss their Jewish components and explain the distinctions between them, focusing on variations in Jewish migration and settlement, Jewish experiences in the two countries, the national political and social contexts, and the two associations' organizational patterns and rhetoric. I analyze these groups' degrees of inclusion and how this affected Jewish women and their identities.

Including the AF and JV in studies of Jews in the Americas is important for several reasons. Many Jews have engaged with antifascism and international solidarity in this hemisphere in modern times. Immigration to Argentina and Uruguay, the leftist ideologies some Jews brought from Europe, and their embrace of the Allied cause demonstrate the global connections that have shaped Jewish lives in the Americas. At the same time, Jewish adaptations to varying conditions in the two nations illustrate the tensions between the global and the local. Furthermore, rather than taking Jewish women's opposition to fascism for granted, it is critical to understand how they opposed it and how they cooperated with non-Jews in such efforts. In part this essay responds to Jeffrey Lesser's and Raanan Rein's call for studies of Jewish participation in the wider society, outside the bounds of communal institutions.[3] Furthermore, antifascism has emerged as a significant topic of historical inquiry in recent years, but the literature is heavily slanted toward men in Europe.[4] We need to learn more about antifascist women—including Jews—in the Americas in order to better comprehend these complex movements.[5]

The Victory Board

Disheartened with their government's official neutrality in World War II and its authoritarianism, many Argentines pursued means of opposing fascism and defeating the Axis. These efforts were magnified with the German invasion of the Soviet Union in June 1941, which shattered the German-Soviet Non-Aggression Pact of 1939 and revived the Popular Front strategy. Determined to aid the Allies, and particularly the Soviet Union, two Communist women called upon feminist and antifascist colleagues to construct a new organization. On September 13, these women officially inaugurated the Victory Board. Its president, Ana Rosa Schlieper de Martínez Guerrero, an aristocrat tied to the centrist Radical Party and chair of the Inter-American Commission of Women (IACW), declared that Board members would contribute to the democratic cause overseas by supplying the Allies, and at home they would reinforce the nation's independence and free institutions.⁶

The Board enlisted a broad spectrum of women throughout Argentina along Popular Front lines. By June 1943, it claimed chapters in 135 localities and Buenos Aires neighborhoods, and 45,000 adherents.⁷ While these numbers seem exaggerated, the Board became what was probably the largest women's political organization before Peronism.⁸ Professionals, writers, artists, workers, women engaged in family businesses, farmers, and ranchers formed part of the movement, yet working- and middle-class homemakers probably comprised the majority in rural and urban areas alike. Women who were foreign- and native-born; Catholics, Protestants, Jews, Spiritists, and non-believers; and of varied incomes, ethnicities, and political allegiances joined the Board. Its officers included socialites, intellectuals, artists, and union members.⁹

These diverse women supported the Allied struggle against fascism in many ways. They collected hospital items, foodstuffs, fabric, thread, and used apparel, and made clothing, bedding, and medical supplies in Board workshops and their homes. First aid courses helped prepare Board members for civil defense. They raised money to purchase materials and other goods by paying dues; selling magazines, flowers, badges, and tickets to benefits; and soliciting contributions door-to-door, on the streets, and through collection boxes. The Board coordinated some of its campaigns and events with other antifascist solidarity groups.¹⁰

These duties accorded with customary gender roles, as did the JV's maternalistic appeals, yet they also opened new horizons for women. Fighting fascism meant strengthening and defending democracy, and, as Board orators observed, without women there was no democracy. Argentine women did not yet exercise the vote at the national level. Feminists numbered among the Board's core activists, and they saw the incorporation of women into the political system as part of its democratic mission. To advance toward these goals, the JV publicized its members' engagement with its democratic procedures and its national conventions in 1942 and 1943. Often for the first time in their lives, women prepared themselves for citizenship by organizing chapters, managing budgets and fundraising, giving speeches, and discussing political issues. Moreover, the Board highlighted its pluralism and egalitarianism, which are also ingredients of democracy.

This modeling of democracy contrasted with the authoritarianism of the government and the local fascist movement, known as the Nationalists. Opposed to feminism, Jews, immigrants, and the Allies, the Nationalists attacked antifascist organizations, including several Board chapters. Following the coup of 1930, which ousted a democratic administration, conservatives ruled through electoral fraud, persecution of dissidents, and military backing. In December 1941, after the United States' entry into the war, conservative Ramón Castillo (acting president 1940–1942, president 1942–1943) limited freedom of assembly and the press, and suspended habeas corpus to prevent open disagreement with the official neutrality policy.[11] The military dictatorship that seized power in June 1943 imposed even harsher measures. Heavily influenced by Nationalists, this regime imprisoned and tortured leftists and union militants, fired democratic teachers, dismissed Congress, and installed Catholic education in public schools. Officially neutral, yet including officers sympathetic to the Axis, it outlawed the JV and all other pro-Allied antifascist organizations.[12] However, this was not the end of the Board.

Feminine Action and the Board

One can also trace the origins of Feminine Action back to the German invasion of the Soviet Union. It began as the Ladies' Commission of the largely male-dominated Anti-Nazi Action for Aid to the Soviet Union and Other Peoples in the Struggle (ANA). These groups were more obviously connected to the Communist Party than the Board, since they grew out of efforts to supply only the Soviet Union, and their leaders were Communists or close to the Party. The Commission invited members of democratic parties, Catholics and Protestants (it did not mention Jews), native- and foreign-born, workers, students, professionals, housewives, and mothers to its first assembly on August 30, 1941. Uruguay was transitioning from Gabriel Terra's right-wing dictatorship (1933–1938) to democracy, unlike Argentina, which was moving toward military rule. To reinforce this shift and demonstrate opposition to the right and fascism at home and abroad, the Commission asked its adherents to participate in a march through Montevideo on October 25, and thousands did so. By early November, the Commission's twenty-five chapters were making clothing for the Allies.[13]

In late 1941 the Commission and the Board established contact. Two Commission leaders formed part of the ANA delegation that delivered Uruguayan contributions to a Soviet ship in the Buenos Aires harbor. They used this occasion to question Board dignitaries on their operations. Board officer Scheiner visited the Commission in Montevideo to exchange ideas on women's *ayudismo* (aid activism). ANA and Commission representatives attended the Board's first national convention in April 1942.[14] These encounters enabled the Commission to study its Argentine counterpart.

Using the Board as a model, in May 1942 the Commission transformed itself into Feminine Action. It hoped to create a movement resembling the Board that would bring together diverse women to help the Allies and defeat Nazism.[15] AF exhorted Uruguayan women to protect national independence, democracy, culture, and well-being against the fifth column and possible foreign aggression. It was women's duty to defend the nation, insisted Feminine Action, since this task was an extension of defending the home. The group would engage the global front by making and sending goods overseas and the national front by mobilizing democratic women throughout the country and collaborating with the Ministry of National Defense's civil defense measures.[16] AF proceeded to organize activities that echoed those of its Argentine mentor.

Its maternalism notwithstanding, AF, like the Board, opened new spaces for women. Both groups supported feminism and insisted that they were engaging in an egalitarian political struggle rather than women's top-down philanthropy. AF claimed citizenship, which had rested on military service, by calling its members anti-Nazi "combatants" who wielded sewing needles instead of rifles. Terra's dictatorship had restricted freedom of expression, and many women protested by abstaining from elections. They could vote but lacked political experience. AF—and JV—trained women for political activism by following democratic practices, organizing aid and other programs, speaking in public, and holding conventions.[17]

Feminine Action differed from the Board in some respects. The most crucial was the context in which the two groups operated. The democratic pro-Allied Alfredo Baldomir (1938–43) and Juan José de Amézaga (1943–47) administrations and the armed forces supported AF and permitted it to operate freely. In contrast, under President Castillo, the JV faced growing restrictions and harassment, which turned to outright prohibition under the military dictatorship.

Benefiting from the climate of freedom, Feminine Action grew both in size and diversity throughout the republic. Branches waxed and waned, but as of September 1944 AF had seventeen chapters in the interior and twelve neighborhood chapters in Montevideo, as well as affiliated Yugoslavian, Hungarian, Jewish, and worker committees in the capital, with a total membership of 6,400. Meatpacking plant personnel and commercial, telephone, and municipal employees comprised the worker committees. Industrial laborers joined neighborhood chapters in Montevideo, and textile workers at one time formed an affiliated committee.[18] Working-, middle-, and mixed-class *barrios* (neighborhoods) spawned chapters.[19] AF included teachers, white-collar employees, farmers, ranchers, and women who worked in family enterprises. However, matching the Board's profile, most probably were lower- to middle-sector homemakers.[20] Intellectuals and professionals numbered among the officers, who ranged from Communist to conservative political affiliations; there were more of the former, however, than of any other party. The Communist presence, and political and social heterogeneity resembled the Board.

Board and Feminine Action leaders frequently crossed the Río de la Plata. They spoke at each other's events, and JV officers continued to mentor AF.[21] As the Uruguayan group established itself, however, the relationship shifted to one of equals. The Board approved the Uruguayan delegates' proposal to conduct a joint campaign,[22] but the Argentine coup of June 1943 halted this effort. The Board notified its Uruguayan counterpart that the police had sacked its headquarters, hauling off monies and goods. Feminine Action's attempts to exert diplomatic pressure on the Argentine regime were fruitless.[23]

Yet the Board began to work underground with Uruguayans. It remitted hidden funds to Feminine Action, which used them to finance the making of bandages and garments for Allied soldiers.[24] AF women expressed their solidarity with the besieged Board in celebrations honoring its dedication to freedom and democracy.[25] After Allied forces achieved victory in Europe, the Argentine democratic opposition, including the JV, protested the military regime. AF delegates traveled to Buenos Aires to accompany the Board in its resistance to dictatorship and police brutality.[26] Their partnership kept the Board alive and enabled Feminine Action to finance its ayudismo.

One similarity between AF and JV was that Jewish women provided disproportionate support to both organizations, considering their percentage of the overall population. Feminine Action's Jewish affiliate contributed over one-half of the goods shipped to the Soviet Union in August 1943 and half of total AF aid to this country.[27] It was also the highest producer by far of any AF committee in the campaign to make clothing for European children in late 1945.[28] This was at a time when Jews formed merely 1.71 percent of the Uruguayan population—and 2.56 percent of the Argentine.[29] Since Argentine Jewish women did not affiliate en masse with the Board, it is more difficult to measure their contributions to this group, but one example may suffice. The agricultural center of Moisés Ville in the 1940s contained between 5,000 and 7,000 inhabitants, mostly Jews. Its chapter contributed more to the Board's Campaign for the Stalingrad Heroes of 1943 than any other, including branches located in the largest cities.[30]

In part, Jewish women's antifascist activism in Argentina and Uruguay represented a continuation of experiences in their countries of origin. Those who were politically engaged generally chose leftist parties, since many had favored such groups in Europe, and they welcomed women's participation. In contrast, conservative parties tended to curtail democratic rights and, in Argentina, denied women suffrage. Local fascists shared these sentiments, and also embraced antisemitism and a reactionary brand of Catholicism.

Jewish-Argentine Participation

Jews in rural localities like Moisés Ville played significant roles in the Board. Argentina's vibrant Jewish agricultural communities were shrinking by the 1940s, but they still fostered women's activist networks.[31] In 1942 at least a third of the JV's chapters in the interior were located in Jewish colony zones sponsored by the Jewish Colonization Association (JCA) or in districts populated by both Jewish and other farmers.[32] Most of their Jewish members were Yiddish speakers, along with some German speakers.[33]

Ladino- and Arabic-speaking Jews lived in municipalities in the interior, but I only found them in the Resistencia and Tucumán chapters. While Sephardic men participated in efforts to help Holocaust victims, it is unclear whether women took part in these activities; if they did, some may have joined the JV in places other than these two cities.[34] However, it is difficult to distinguish Sephardim with Spanish surnames from Catholics.

We do not know the precise number of Jews in the Board, since membership lists have not survived. Yet, some qualitative and quantitative data indicate their important presence. For example, virtually all adult women in various Jewish agricultural settlements joined the Board.[35] Some of these chapters were disproportionately sizable, given the small populations of these rural centers. By 1942 Moisés Ville boasted 400 members, Basavilbaso 426, and Rivera 208. This compared favorably with the metropolises of Córdoba (500) and Bahía Blanca (270). Jewish women led the chapters in two agricultural hubs and six Jewish colony communities. Three rural chapters had Jewish vice presidents, and others had Jewish officers.[36]

Ashkenazim, Central Europeans, and perhaps Sephardim joined women of other backgrounds in urban chapters. These branches in Buenos Aires and several large cities were organized by neighborhood. In 1942, sixteen of the eighteen chapters in the capital, known as secretariats, had Jewish officers. Jews served as presidents of two secretariats and vice presidents of four others, which were located in neighborhoods with appreciable Jewish minorities.[37] In addition, three other barrios with thriving secretariats had significant numbers of Jews. Two industrial suburbs with many Jewish-owned textile factories, and Jews who labored in them, also hosted secretariats.[38] Jews figured prominently in the chapters of La Plata, Rosario, Resistencia, Santa Fe, Córdoba, and Tucumán as well. Two of these, along with Bahía Blanca, had Jewish vice presidents.[39]

Jewish women formed part of the Board's leadership. Over time, as many as five pertained to its commission that supervised the secretariats of Buenos Aires, including Rosa Scheiner, human rights activist Dalila Saslavsky, and Fanny Edelman, all of them close to or in the Communist Party. Women of Jewish origin also formed part of the Board's national-level workshop, as well as finance, press, propaganda, and collection committees. As of 1942, the president of the Moisés Ville chapter served in the JV's national commission.[40] Moreover, the roughly fifteen chapters in areas of the countryside populated by Jews sent delegates to the national conventions, demonstrating that the Jews' rural base was a springboard to the Board's center stage and leadership.

Jewish Participation in Uruguay

Jews engaged with AF in a different and less visible manner. First, they lacked a strong foundation in the countryside. Jews established three colonies, two of which were ephemeral, while the other, founded in Paysandú department in 1915, lasted into the 1930s.[41] Perhaps some of the Jewish population of Paysandú, which reached a height of almost one hundred families between 1931 and 1948, came from the former colony. Building upon widespread pro-Spanish Republican sentiments, the Antifascist Committee of this small city attracted much support from Jews and other inhabitants. Given this fertile ground, Jewish women may have joined the Paysandú AF committee.[42] Jews in other provincial municipalities might have belonged to their respective AF committees, but I spotted only one such woman, in the Tacuarembó chapter.[43]

In Montevideo, in 1944, *Diario Popular* reported that some Jews were involved in its AF barrio committees, yet I found only a handful of possible Jewish members mentioned in the press.[44] Sephardim tended to live in the Ciudad Vieja neighborhood. If they participated in Feminine Action, they may have joined its Puerto chapter. Ashkenazim settled in Goes (Ruis) and Villa Muñoz, which did not have AF barrio committees, although some also resided in Barrio Sur and Cerro, which had the committees. Close to Barrio Sur, Palermo had hosted a committee of the AF's predecessor, the Ladies' Commission, with Jewish members. Jewish Germans and Hungarians moved slowly into Pocitos, perhaps too late to join its AF committee.[45] Commonly working in the needle trades, Jews may have belonged to the women's aid committee of the Union of Textile Workers, which, for a while, aligned with AF.[46] Perhaps the Yugoslavian and especially the Hungarian AF affiliates contained Jewish women who identified more with their birthplace than with their ethnicity/religion.

The AF's Jewish affiliate appears to have been the main vehicle for Jewish participation. The Jewish group that adhered to Feminine Action was called the Feminine Central Israelite Committee (CCFI), and its roots are obscure. It may have originated as the women's auxiliary of the Communist-linked Central Israelite Anti-Nazi Committee of Aid to the Soviet Union (CICA), which collaborated with ANA. In 1942 the CICA joined other community groups in a united Jewish pro-Allied aid organization established by the Central Israelite Committee of Uruguay (CCIU). The CCIU had formed in 1940 and soon included all the Jewish communities—Sephardic, Yiddish-speaking, German-speaking, and Hungarian. Like the Argentine Delegation of Israelite Argentine Associations (Delegación de Asociaciones Israelitas Argentinas [DAIA]), it defended Jews against antisemitism, denounced Nazism, and lobbied for admitting Jewish refugees. The CCIU also collected goods for the Allies. A federation of eight groups with a total membership of 800, the CCFI seemed to represent a spectrum of Jewish women in Montevideo.[47] If the CCFI was indeed tied to the CCIU, it may have included Sephardim and Central Europeans.

One of CCFI's chapters was the feminine commission of the antifascist Zhitlovsky Cultural House. Founded in 1935 in Goes—the neighborhood with the largest number of Jewish residences and stores—it promoted leftist Yiddish culture and grounded it in Uruguayan reality through its school, library, and cultural programs. Its feminine commission had contributed its handmade garments to the Ladies' Commission, the AF's precursor, in March 1942.[48] It seemed to be the most active component in the CCFI affiliate. Unfortunately, no membership lists are available for this group or for AF at large.

As an immigrant committee affiliated with Feminine Action, the CCFI exercised less influence in AF than the committees of Montevideo neighborhoods and towns in the interior, each of which had two representatives in AF's monthly assembly. The affiliates only had one apiece.[49] Moreover, initially there was no Jewish representative in the AF board. As the Jewish committee donated ever larger amounts of materials, however, the AF invited some of its leaders to address its national conventions of 1943 and 1944.[50] In the process, they gained visibility. This was especially true for Raquel P. de Svirsky, whom *Diario Popular* described as this committee's "dynamic activist." Relatively well-off and probably a leftist, she joined the AF board in 1943 and became one of its deputy treasurers in 1945. Svirsky gave speeches at the opening ceremonies of the new AF headquarters and the AF convention, both in 1944.[51] A Señora Paikes spoke at the inauguration of the Jewish committee's exposition of its contributions to an AF drive to assemble gift bags for children in Allied countries in March 1944.[52] Another Jewish committee member, Rebeca Requik, was among the speakers at an AF forum in November 1945.[53] Yet, Feminine Action's integration of Jews into its main body was slower and less sweeping than the Board's.

Comparisons

Jewish involvement in the JV and AF differed markedly. Many JV branches around the country contained Jews, unlike in Uruguay, where they concentrated in one urban committee that affiliated with AF. Jews had an equal voice in Board governance, contrasting with the CCFI's lesser status in Feminine Action as an affiliate. Jewish Argentines were officers of many chapters, which enhanced contacts with the Board's national leaders. Thus, they participated to a much greater extent in JV organizational life than their Uruguayan peers in AF, and they were more likely to enter the Board's ruling circles.

Jewish-Argentine women picked from a variety of antifascist groups. Particularly in cities, the Board tended to attract those who were accustomed to interacting with Christians. Among these Jewish members were well-educated homemakers, teachers, and professionals. In the countryside, Yiddish- (and, to a lesser degree, German-) and Spanish-speakers joined the Board. Nevertheless, because of the language difference, in both rural and urban settings, Yiddish speakers often belonged instead to Jewish solidarity groups, some of them tied to the Communist Party.[54] Women who were politically disengaged or oriented toward charitable or conservative Zionist activism joined ladies' auxiliaries of organizations promoted by mainstream Jewish institutions such as the DAIA.[55] Sometimes these women's contingents, along with *ayudistas* (activists) of other ethnicities, collaborated with the Board. Its statutes offered groups the possibility of formally linking to the JV, but only one Jewish entity seems to have done so.[56]

Jews, Yugoslavs, and Hungarians, however, took advantage of this opportunity to affiliate with Feminine Action. Why did Jewish women choose this means of attaching themselves to the organization? Demographic patterns offer at least a partial explanation.

Most Jewish participants in antifascist organizations probably were Eastern and to a lesser degree Central Europeans. Eastern European Jews arrived in Uruguay in the 1920s and 1930s, joined by Central Europeans in the latter decade. In Argentina, however, Ashkenazim were already entering the country in sizable numbers by the 1890s. By 1909, there were over 16,000 Jews in the capital, most of them Russians, and about 50,000 in the nation as a whole; in Uruguay, there were about 1,700 Jews in 1917, mostly living in Montevideo, and only 25 percent of them were Eastern Europeans.[57] As a result of these varied migrations, Ashkenazic institutions formed earlier in Argentina than in its neighbor. Ashkenazic burial societies arose in Buenos Aires in 1894 and in Montevideo in 1916; Ezra aid societies in 1900 and 1909, respectively; and beneficent ladies' societies in 1892 (reconstituted in 1908) and 1916, respectively. Ashkenazic men's and women's involvement in labor organizations and leftism began in the late 1800s in Argentina and twenty years later in Uruguay.[58] As of the 1940s, probably most Jewish adults of Eastern and Central European extraction in Uruguay were foreign-born, whereas many in Argentina were native-born.

Most Jewish women in Montevideo who were of the age and likely backgrounds to join antifascist movements in the 1940s had settled there in the previous two decades. While they lived among non-Jews in their neighborhoods, relatively few had interacted with them in schools or organizations, except perhaps in unions and the Communist Party, although even there they may have belonged to the Yiddish-speaking section. Ester Sutz, however, was a militant who worked alongside, and helped organize, laborers of Catholic backgrounds, and there may have been others.[59] Unlike in Argentina, in the 1940s, few adult Jewish women could have been professionals. Dr. Victor Soriano, who graduated in 1934 as a medical doctor, was the first Sephardic and the fourth Jew (all men) in Uruguay to obtain a professional degree, and women must have lagged behind them.[60] Given their relatively recent arrival, women probably clustered in the CCFI because it offered them camaraderie and the ease of conversing in their native tongues. Even Sutz participated exclusively in Jewish leftist ayudismo, although her union activity took her outside the Ashkenazic community.

Inclusion and Identities

Other factors may have led Jews to adhere to Feminine Action rather than join it. How inclusive were the AF and JV? To what degree did they encourage Jewish participation?

According to one study, Jewish immigrants who looked back on their experiences in interwar Uruguay generally agreed that locals were welcoming, yet some admitted encounters with antisemitism.[61] There were antisemitic newspapers, anti-Jewish immigration restrictions, and pro-Nazi German inhabitants and local politicians.[62] Young Jewish men even formed self-defense groups to prevent attacks on Jewish residences and stores.[63] After the Terra dictatorship, extreme rightist beliefs may not have threatened Uruguayan institutions, as they did in Argentina, but some Jews feared them nonetheless.

In the 1930s, Jews in Uruguay formed organizations to oppose German Nazism and help their German coreligionists. The Spanish Civil War reinforced their antifascist sentiments, leading to Jewish solidarity with Spanish Republicans. Jews worked alongside non-Jews in several groups opposed to racism and antisemitism.[64] Whether women participated in these movements is uncertain. We know, however, that the Zhitlovsky feminine commission made garments for the Spanish Republic and attended antifascist events.[65] Such attitudes eventually ushered its members and other Jewish women into the CCFI and a few AF committees. Jewish-Argentine women followed a similar yet more robust and better documented trajectory.[66]

In Uruguay, the small but vexatious fascist presence, along with European events, heightened insecurity among Jews and may have strengthened desires to reinforce their identity. Scholars Daniela Bourat, Álvaro Martínez, and David Telias claimed that as local Jews felt intimately connected to their European peers, "they fortified their Jewish specificity, and they defined themselves and wanted to be recognized in these terms."[67] This fit within an existing pattern of creating Jewish political and cultural groups rather than joining broader Uruguayan entities, according to historian Rosa Perla Raicher.[68] Not all Jews may have felt this way,[69] but the CCFI seemingly indicated it did by organizing separately. Tellingly, it held its own expositions of handmade goods for the Allies, but in the same places and on the same dates as those held by AF.[70]

CCFI also appropriated and renamed an important Feminine Action initiative. For its Christmas Bags campaign of 1943-1944, AF residential and adhering committees filled empty sacks with clothing, shoes, toys, notebooks, and other gifts for Allied children. The CCFI assembled many more bags than any other committee—but it called them Winter Bags, removing the religious label,[71] thereby asserting that not all antifascists and recipient children were Christian.

In December 1945, Raquel de Svirsky observed that the end of war should have made "us" happy, but "we are not." Whether "we" referred to AF members, all antifascists, and/or Jews was unclear; what was clear was her anger. An eye for an eye was a better means of treating Nazi officials than "the law of Christ" embodied in the Nuremberg trials, a law she regarded as inappropriate given the degree of Nazi crimes. The survivors of Nazi persecution, she noted, were tortured and damaged individuals. Svirsky urged Uruguayan women to clothe these victims and help them rebuild their lives through the AF.[72] While she did not specifically mention Jewish sufferers, Svirsky distanced herself from Christian doctrine, and spoke for many Jews in her desire for revenge.

How non-Jewish AF members and affiliates reacted to these expressions of Jewish antifascism is unclear, but they gave Svirsky a platform to voice her opinions. AF officer and respected educator, Elia Rodríguez Belo de Artucio, praised the CCFI for its "outstanding participation" in the Christmas Bags campaign, while ignoring that it had changed the name.[73] Did this mean an acceptance of Jews, or, instead, an unwillingness to consider their distinct identities?

From its beginnings, the AF seemed hesitant to mention Jews. As indicated above, its predecessor, the Ladies' Commission, had invited Catholics and Protestants to its first assembly, but not Jews. Once AF came into existence, its officers proudly called attention to members of different social classes, neighborhoods, political persuasions, and pursuits, seldom referring to ethnicity or creed.[74] In a rare reference to faith, treasurer Carmen Garayalde, a prominent Communist educator, described AF as a union of Uruguayan and foreign women of varied political affiliations, classes, and religions united by their shared ideals.[75] When the Argentine dictatorship permitted the Board to reopen in 1945, an AF delegate at its assembly in Buenos Aires advised listeners to unite all political, social, and religious sectors behind the transition to democracy.[76] Her recommendation was ironic, given Feminine Action's usual elision of religious and ethnic origins.

While Feminine Action frequently denounced fascism for its dictatorial nature, denial of women's rights, and labor exploitation, I saw only one specific reference to the Holocaust. A neighborhood committee declared that helping the "combatants of antisemitism" overseas was its mission.[77] A Jewish woman's presence in its governing board may have influenced this statement, suggesting that greater Jewish participation in residential chapters could have enhanced mutual understanding.

Perhaps the broader society's limited acquaintance with these relatively new immigrants led Feminine Action to overlook them, or made it feel uneasy about reaching out to them. Did AF try to recruit Jewish women or establish a chapter in Goes? When they displayed their handmade goods simultaneously, did AF and CCFI members converse with each other? We do not know. In 1945, Rodríguez Belo de Artucio acknowledged that as Feminine Action had grown and evolved, members had learned much from women with whom they had had little contact previously.[78] Perhaps, this sharing involved Jews. Once it realized the magnitude of CCFI's contributions, AF praised and publicized this group, and it added Svirsky to its leadership in December 1945.[79] Still, the contact between the two groups' ranks seems limited.

While Board spokeswomen also tended to emphasize their embrace of all classes and political parties, from early on, they alluded to ethnic/religious pluralism. Two months after the JV's inaugural ceremony, Secretary General Cora Ratto, a Communist mathematician, observed that it contained "women of the most diverse sectors." It was easier for people of the same beliefs and backgrounds to work together than for women of distinct social, political, religious, and educational circumstances, she admitted, but acquiring knowledge from each other was the hallmark of a "true democracy," in which "all have acquired the right to not be left excluded."[80] In effect, she celebrated the inclusion of Jews, along with other minorities, the impoverished, and women, in the polity. At the JV's first national convention in April 1942, President Schlieper claimed that the Board had united persons of different "creeds" and ideologies under its antifascist banner. Two delegates of Jewish origins approvingly echoed her remarks.[81] At this same meeting, when Ratto described members' occupations throughout the country, she called special attention to the first Jewish teacher educated in Argentina.[82] In Montevideo a few months later, Ratto told AF that its Argentine sister organization included Jews, Catholics, and atheists.[83]

Christian members demonstrated awareness of the Holocaust. Schlieper had participated in a failed effort to bring thousands of Jewish refugee children to Argentina.[84] The non-Jewish president of a secretariat declared that the crimes against Jews, among other human rights abuses, aroused her hatred of Nazism and urge to destroy it.[85]

The Board offered Jews in the organization more visibility than the AF. It applauded the Moisés Ville chapter, whose largely Jewish identity was obvious, and celebrated the oldest JV member, who was one of its most productive knitters: ninety-five-year-old Señora de Malajovich.[86] Saslavsky, Scheiner, and Edelman were among the leaders of Jewish origin who often spoke for the Board. The famed Jewish entertainers Berta and Paulina Singerman performed in JV fundraisers and wrote in its magazine. Another contributor to this publication was Rosa Vainberg, a member and former teacher in a Jewish agricultural colony, who asserted that as a woman and "a Jew, I suffer doubly a vile injustice."[87] These examples showed that the Board welcomed Jews, including those who spoke as candidly as Svirsky.

Board chapters in Jewish agricultural colonies resembled the CCFI in that they implicitly fostered Jewish identities. Still, they provided their Jewish members with opportunities to work with non-Jews, since these branches usually included at least a few women of other backgrounds, and they sent delegates to the national conventions, as opposed to the CCFI's single representative. Jewish women in the countryside—and beyond—tied themselves to the nation through the Board. Jews in Uruguay lacked these foundational rural experiences.

Conclusion

Jews contributed disproportionately to Victory Board and Feminine Action, but the resemblance largely ends there. They were found in many Board chapters throughout Argentina, where they worked with women of other backgrounds. In Uruguay they concentrated in a single all-Jewish committee in Montevideo that adhered to AF, rather than form a part of it. The CCFI promoted Jewish identities and independence, but could do little to affect AF's inner workings or facilitate mutual comprehension within the ranks. In contrast, Jewish Board members were more noticeable and influential, but they did not unite around their Jewish identities except to a certain degree in the rural chapters. Having arrived later than their Argentine peers, adult Eastern and Central European women in Uruguay had blended less into local society and had less organizational experience with non-Jews. Feminine Action's hesitance also may have deterred them. They found safety and comfort in their own community and mobilized accordingly. Their coreligionists across the Río de la Plata faced a greater fascist threat, but as more Jews had lived longer in Argentina, except for many Central Europeans, they were more likely to have professional credentials and move smoothly in the broader society. Such women joined the Board, while urban dwellers who mainly spoke Yiddish tended to join separate antifascist groups. As Lesser and Rein would put it, Jewish Board members, especially in the cities, were Jewish-Argentines, whereas the CCFI consisted of Uruguayan Jews.[88] These terms highlight how Jewish women created or reinforced their Argentine identities through the JV, whereas their Uruguayan counterparts largely strengthened their Jewish identities through the AF. Neither the Board nor Feminine Action explicitly recruited Jews, but the Board's positive references to them and to religious diversity, and the visibility of Jews in the ranks and leadership, were powerful, albeit tacit, appeals.

The notion of homogenizing newcomers through a melting pot was hegemonic in both societies. Some have seen Uruguay as a model of integration, whereas many observers have perceived Argentina in the 1930s and 1940s as inhospitable toward Jews.[89] Yet the Board's incorporation of Jews at all levels of the organization signified integration (without, however, erasing their identities), and Feminine Action's use of ethnic affiliates seemed to belie it.

Migratory patterns, the leftist allegiances that many carried from Europe, and antifascism were global connections that shaped Jewish women's lives in the Southern Cone and the Americas as a whole. Scheiner and many other Jewish women experienced the war and Holocaust close at hand, as if they were local matters. The Uruguayan Jews' demographics, limited involvement in the rural setting, and lack of organizational and educational ties with non-Jews at this time, in comparison to Argentina, conditioned Jewish engagement with antifascism and affected non-Jewish Uruguayans' reception of them. By 1945, AF was more accepting of its Jewish affiliate, indicating that the relationship between the international pro-Allied cause and local circumstances was complex and fluid.

International solidarity and antifascism were vital for Jewish women in these two countries. Antifascism politicized some of them or furthered their militancy, usually on the left. Participating in solidarity work brought them into contact with women of other backgrounds, particularly in Argentina, and helped prepare those in Uruguay for future engagement with the wider society. This practice also enlarged their understandings of world affairs and trained them in organizational skills, administrative tasks, and internal governance. Uruguayan women could vote, but lacked political experience; Argentine women could not cast ballots until 1947. International solidarity and antifascism were instrumental in converting these Jewish-Argentines and Uruguayan Jews into citizens.

Acknowledgments

I thank Alex Borucki, Magdalena Broquetas, Mischa Klein, Laura Leibman, Gerardo Leibner, Ema Massera, Rodolfo Porrini, Teresa Porzecanski, Adriana Valobra, Nerina Visacovsky, and especially Ana Laura de Giorgi for their comments and assistance. I also appreciate Katalin Rac's and Lenny A. Ureña Valerio's kind support and valuable suggestions.

Notes

1. *La Hora* (LH), September 13, 1941, 4. I sometimes refer to Jewish-Argentine women as "women of Jewish origins." Argentine leftists commonly use this phrase to refer to those who do not practice the religion. This paper ends in 1945 because after this year the JV and AF faded away and new organizations absorbed some of their members and goals. See Sandra McGee Deutsch, "Hands Across the Río de la Plata: Argentine and Uruguayan Antifascist Women, 1941–1945," *Revista Contemporánea* 8 (2017): 29–54.

2. On the pitfalls and benefits of comparative and transnational history, as well as the possible advantages of combining these approaches, see Deborah Cohen and Maura O'Connor, eds., *Comparison and History: Europe in Cross-National Perspective* (New York: Routledge, 2004). On the JV and its Jewish members see Sandra McGee Deutsch, *Crossing Borders, Claiming a Nation: A History of Argentine Jewish Women, 1880–1955* (Durham: Duke Univiversity Press, 2010), 185–89; Eleonora Ardanaz, "Con el puño en alto: Sara Fradkin y la lucha antifascista judía," in *Mujeres en espacios bonaerenses*, ed. Adriana Valobra (La Plata: Edulp, 2009), 111–24. On the JV in general see Sandra McGee Deutsch, "Argentine Women Against Fascism: The Junta de la Victoria, 1941–1947," *Politics, Religion, and Ideology* 13, no.2 (2012): 221–36, and "Gendering Antifascism: Women's Activism in Argentina and the World, 1918–1947" (book manuscript in progress); Adriana María Valobra, "Formación de cuadros y frentes populares: relaciones de clase y género en el Partido Comunista de Argentina, 1935–1951," *Revista Izquierdas*, no. 23 (April 2015): 127–56. Also see Andrés Bisso, ed., *El antifascismo argentino. Selección documental y estudio preliminar* (Buenos Aires: Buenos Libros and CeDinCI editores, 2007), for JV documents. Ana Laura de Giorgi discusses the AF in "Entre la lucha contra la carestía y por los derechos de la mujer. Las comunistas uruguayas durante la segunda mitad del siglo XX (1942–1973)," in *Queridas camaradas. Historias iberoamericanas de mujeres comunistas, 1935–1975*, eds. Adriana Valobra and Mercedes Yusta Rodrigo (Buenos Aires: Miño y Dávila, 2017), 218–19.

The literature on Jewish participation in Latin American and U.S. women's antifascist movements is scanty. Works on German exiles of Jewish origin include Fernando Morais, *Olga* (São Paulo: Companhia das Letras, 1994), and Gisela Cabral Reyes, "Mujeres alemanas exiliadas en México," paper delivered at the Latin American Jewish Studies Association meeting, Universidad Iberoamericana, México, 5 July 2017. Eva Alterman Blay discusses Jewish antifascist women in Brazil in *O Brasil como destino. Raízes da imigração judaica para São Paulo* (São Paulo: UNESP, 2013). Natalia Gurvich Peretzman, "La judía ashkenazí en México: cambios y permanencias, 1920–1945," 55, mentions a leftist Jewish women's group that sent aid to Russia during World War II, and Ana Lau Jaiven and Roxana Rodríguez, "'Ciudadanas mexicanas conscientes y agradecidas': el Consejo Mexicano de Mujeres Israelitas," 259, notes that the women's section of the Israelite Central Committee of Mexico raised money for the British war effort, both in *Tejidos culturales: las mujeres judías en México*, ed. Natalia Gurvich, Liz Hamui, and Linda Hanono (México, D.F.: Editorial Universidad Iberoamericana, Departamento de Historia, 2016). Alicia Gojman, email communication, December 18, 2019, explained that a group of Jewish women collaborated with the Mexican Acción Democrática Internacional, which organized anti-Nazi events. On the U.S. see Melissa R. Klapper, "'Those by Whose Side We Have Labored': American Jewish Women and the Peace Movement between the Wars," *Journal of American History* 97, no. 3 (December 2010): 636–58. According to Klapper, email communication, December 19, 2019, these women were antifascist but might not have identified themselves as such.

3. Jeffrey Lesser and Raanan Rein, "New Approaches to Ethnicity and Diaspora in Twentieth-Century Latin America," in *Rethinking Jewish-Latin Americans*, eds. Jeffrey Lesser and Raanan Rein (Albuquerque: University of New Mexico Press, 2008), 23–40.

4. See, for example, Hugo García et al., eds., *Rethinking Antifascism: History, Memory and Politics, 1922 to the Present* (New York: Berghahn, 2016). Only two chapters out of seventeen are devoted to women, and only in Europe.

5. On antifascist Argentine women, aside from the sources mentioned in note 2, see Clara del Franco, *Mujeres, ese fuego, esas luchas: 1930–1960* (Buenos Aires: Cuadernos Marxistas, 2011); Nerina Visacovsky, "Herencias de 1947. Di idische froi y el sufragio femenino," in *Sufragio femenino. Prácticas y debates políticos, religiosos y culturales en Argentina y América Latina*, ed. Carolina Barry (Buenos Aires: Eduntref, 2011), 91–111. On Uruguay see Gerardo Leibner, "*Nosotras* (Uruguay, 1945–1953), las contradicciones de la escritura femenina comunista y sus significados sociales," in *Escritura femenina y revindicación de género en América Latina*, eds. Roland Forgues and Jean-Marie Flores (Paris: Mare & Martin, 2005). For Chile and Mexico see Karin Rosemblatt, *Gendered Compromises: Political Cultures and the State in Chile, 1920–1950* (Chapel Hill: University of North Carolina Press, 2000); Corinne A. Antezana-Pernet, *El MEMCH hizo historia* (Santiago: Fundación Biblioteca y Archivo de la Mujer Elena Caffarena, 1997); Jocelyn Olcott, *Revolutionary Women in Postrevolutionary Mexico* (Durham: Duke University Press, 2005); Esperanza Tuñón Pablos, *Mujeres que se organizan: el Frente Único Pro Derechos de la Mujer, 1935–1938* (México, D.F.: Universidad Nacional Autónoma de México, 1992). For Latin America see Valobra and Yusta Rodrigo, eds., *Queridas camaradas*.

6. María Rosa Oliver, *Mi fe es el hombre* (Buenos Aires: C. Lohlé, 1981), 41–42, and

interview with Leandro Gutiérrez, May 6, 1971, Proyecto de Historia Oral del Instituto Torcuato di Tella, Buenos Aires; *LH*, September 13, 4, September 14, 1941, 5 (Schlieper). The Communist-linked press, particularly *La Hora* in Buenos Aires and *Diario Popular* in Montevideo, provided the most extensive coverage of the JV and AF, respectively.

7. Ana Rosa Schlieper de Martínez Guerrero, letter to President Pedro Pablo Ramírez, June 30, 1943, Centro de Documentación e Investigación de la Cultura de Izquierdas en la Argentina (CeDInCI), Buenos Aires.

8. The Comité Argentino de Mujeres Pro Huérfanos Españoles (CAMHE), which sent goods to Republican Spain, may have been larger than the Board. Yet membership numbers are unavailable, and the few sources do not indicate the extent of its political mission. See Fanny Edelman, *Banderas, pasiones, camaradas* (Buenos Aires: Dirple, 1996), 45–47.

9. *Argentina Libre*, September 18, 1941, 12. There are no surviving membership lists for the JV or AF. My research is based on names found in periodicals and JV and AF publications. Information on individuals came from these sources, as well as biographical dictionaries, social registers, local histories, and interviews.

10. For more details on the Board's aid and activities, as described in this and the following paragraphs, see Deutsch, "Gendering."

11. Federico Finchelstein, *Transatlantic Fascism: Ideology, Violence, and the Sacred in Argentina and Italy, 1919–1945* (Durham: Duke University Press, 2010), 57, 167; James Cane, *The Fourth Enemy: Journalism and Power in the Making of Peronist Argentina* (University Park: Penn State University Press, 2011), 86.

12. Laurence Duggan, 26 June 1943, 835.00/1575, U.S., Department of State, Records of the Department of State Relating to the Internal Affairs of Argentina, 1940–1944, General Records, Decimal File, National Archives Microfilm Copy M1322; Schlieper, letter to Secretary General of the Federación Obrera Nacional de la Construcción, July 12, 1943, and letter to Ramírez, CeDInCI, June 30, 1943; Andrés Bisso, *Acción Argentina. Un antifascismo nacional en tiempos de guerra mundial* (Buenos Aires: Prometeo, 2005), 235–36.

13. *Diario Popular* (DP), August 23, 4, August 29, 8, September 5, 8, September 15, 7, September 17, 7, October 24, 7, October 25, 7, October 27, 7, November 7, 1941, 7 (statistic).

14. *DP*, December 14, 7, December 22, 1941, 7; January 29, 1942, 7; Junta de la Victoria, *Primera convención nacional* (Buenos Aires: n.p., 1942), 21–22. The convention records listed the two women delegates as officers of a Comité Femenino Uruguayo, which seems to have referred to the Commission.

15. *Justicia*, July 17, 1942, 4.

16. *Justicia*, July 3, 1942, 8; *DP,* July 3, 5, July 4, 1942, 16.

17. *DP,* October 10, 5, November 16, 4, November 29, 1942, 4; May 3, 1943, 2; March 27, 2 (quotation), April 9, 2, May 9, 1944, 2.

18. *DP*, September 2, 5, October 24, 1942, 5.

19. *DP*, September 30, 1944, 2; "Empleadas y obreras trabajan para la causa de la Victoria," in *Acción Femenina por la Victoria. Campaña argentino-uruguaya sanitaria y de abrigo, 1943–1944* (Montevideo: n.p. 1944), n.p. Rodolfo Porrini provided useful information on neighborhoods. Also see Aníbal Barrios Pintos, *Montevideo: los barrios I* (Montevideo: Nuestra Tierra, 1971); *DP,* April 9, 1944, 2.

20. *DP,* June 23, 2, July 24, 1944, 2.

21. *DP,* July 24, 6, September 20, 1, September 21, 1, September 25, 3, October 2, 5, October 5, 1942, 5; *LH,* May 8, 6, May 9, 1943, 6; *Orientación,* May 13, 1943, 5. Uruguayan and Argentine antifascist men also collaborated.

22. *LH,* May 10, 1943, 2.

23. *Justicia,* July 30, 3, and August 13, 1943, 2; *DP,* June 30, 1943, 1, March 30, 1944, 2; Bisso, *Acción Argentina,* 238.

24. *Acción Femenina,* n.p., detailed this joint campaign.

25. *DP,* April 27, 2, July 3, 2, July 4, 2, July 5, 2, July 6, 1944, 4.

26. Deutsch, "Hands Across," 47–48.

27. "Entregas efectuadas por Acción Femenina por la Victoria," n.d. (1944?); *Acción Femenina por la Victoria. Periódico de Ayuda a las Naciones Liberadas por los Fascismos,* no. 1 (March 1946): 4.

28. *DP,* November 16, 1945, 4.

29. In 1946 there were approximately 37,000 Jews in Uruguay and 350,000 in Argentina. For statistics see *American Jewish Yearbook* 48 (1946–1947): 603, accessed April 7, 2017, http://www.ajcarchives.org/main.php?GroupingId=40. Uruguayan national censuses apparently did not specify Jews as a category.

30. *LH,* February 8, 1943, 5. Simón Romero, "Outpost in the Pampas Where Jews Once Found Refuge Wilts as They Leave," *New York Times,* June 9, 2013, estimated a population of 5000; "Moises Ville Argentina. Jewish Gauchos," accessed April 18, 2017, http://www.scatteredamongthenations.org/agentina, estimated 7000 Jewish inhabitants.

31. Among many other sources on these agricultural settlements, see Judith Laikin Elkin, *The Jews of Latin America,* 3rd. ed. (Boulder: Lynne Rienner, 2014), 101–13; Deutsch, *Crossing Borders,* 13–41 and passim.

32. Junta, *Primera convención,* 39; *Mujeres en la Ayuda, 1941–1942* (Buenos Aires: n.p., 1942), 14. Later the Board reported more branches in the interior. The press and Board publications supplied the names of officers and delegates to the group's conventions, as well as occasional descriptions of the chapters' composition.

33. Argentines define Ashkenazim as Yiddish speakers, and they consider German speakers as another category.

34. The press supplied names of Sephardic Board members, and I confirmed this information through consultations with local residents. Regarding Sephardic aid efforts, see Adriana Brodsky, *Sephardi, Jewish, Argentine: Community and National Identity* (Bloomington: Indiana University Press, 2016), 129.

35. *LH,* May 8, 1943, 6.

36. *Mujeres en la Ayuda,* 14, 16, 47–48, 62–64.

37. Ibid., 47; Junta de la Victoria, *Ayuda de las mujeres argentinas a los países que luchan contra el nazismo. 13 septiembre 1941–13 enero 1942* (Buenos Aires: n.p., 1942), n.p.; Junta, *Primera convención,* 39. *LH,* November 27, 1941, 5, reported that Scheiner presided over the secretariat of Ciudadela, just outside the Federal Capital.

38. *LH,* February 17, 1943, 5. Also see Nerina Visacovsky, *Argentinos, judíos y camaradas. Tras la utopía socialista* (Buenos Aires: Biblos, 2015).

39. *Mujeres en la Ayuda,* 48, 62–63.

40. Ibid., 11–13; *LH*, August 28, 1941, 4, May 10, 1943, 3; Junta, *Primera convención*, 5.

41. Ramón Oxman, "Una experiencia de colonización agraria judía: la colonia '19 de abril' de Paysandú. Primera parte," *Hoy es Historia*, no. 13 (December 1985–January 1986): 31–42. I cannot locate Oxman's "Segunda parte," *Hoy es Historia* no. 14 (February–March 1986). Also see Feldman, *Tiempos difíciles*, 190–91; Daniela Bourat, Alvaro Martínez, and David Telias, *Entre la matzá y el mate. La inmigración judía al Uruguay: una historia en construcción* (Montevideo: Ediciones de la Banda Oriental, 1997), 15, accessed April 18, 2017, https://www.jewishvirtuallibrary.org/uruguay.

42. Jaime Sznajder, "Reacciones a conflictos internacionales en una ciudad del interior uruguaya. Paysandú de los años cuarenta," in *Historia viva. Memorias del Uruguay y de Israel*, eds. Haim Avni, Rosa Perla Raicher, and David Bankier (Jerusalem: Instituto de Judaísmo Contemporáneo, Universidad Hebrea de Jerusalem, 1989), 51–54 (statistic on 52). For another testimony of a Jewish inhabitant in the interior, see "Moisés: siempre trabajando por las estancias," in *Historias de vida de inmigrantes judíos al Uruguay*, ed. Teresa Porzecanski (Montevideo: Kehilá, Comunidad Israelita de Uruguay, 1986), 91–83, 91–95 (pages misnumbered in text).

43. *DP*, July 24, 1944, 2.

44. *DP*, October 24, 1942, 5; March 16, 2, June 6, 1944, 2.

45. *DP*, December 17, 1941, 7. On Jewish residential patterns see Miguel Feldman, *Tiempos difíciles. Inmigrantes judíos en Uruguay, 1933-1945* (Montevideo: Universidad de la República, Facultad de Humanidades y Ciencias de la Educación, Departamento de Publicaciones, 2001), 16, 18, 24, 39, and Bourat, Martínez, and Telias, *Entre la matzá*, 60. On German Jewish immigrants and their participation in other local antifascist groups, see Silvia Facal Santiago, "Vida comunitaria de los judíos alemanes y los republicanos españoles en Uruguay," *Revista de Historia de América*, no. 130 (January–June 2002): 41–55.

46. Esther Sutz, interview, in Avni et al., eds., *Historia viva*, 31–32. She was a likely member of the textile workers committee.

47. *Justicia*, October 27, 1944, 2 (statistic); D. D., interview with author, Montevideo, 2015; Rosa Perla Raicher, *Uruguay, la comunidad israelita y el pueblo judío* (Montevideo: Universidad Hebrea de Jerusalén Instituto Avraham Harman de Judaísmo Contemporáneo; Universidad de la República, Facultad de Humanidades y Ciencias de la Educación, 2003), 145–146; Feldman, *Tiempos difíciles*, 192–200. D.D.'s mother was a CCFI member. Mendel Jaikin was a Polish Communist immigrant and officer of ANA, with which AF was affiliated. He noted that there were centers of Jewish women who worked for the aid effort but did not specify the CCFI or AF. See his interview in Avni et al., eds., *Historia viva*, 33, 35. Feldman, *Tiempos difíciles*, 200, mentions a (Jewish) Feminine Central Committee of Aid to the Allies, which contributed to ANA.

48. *DP*, March 9, 1942, 5; Dieter Schonebohm, "Judíos de izquierda en Montevideo (II): la 'Comunidad progresista,'" *Hoy es Historia*, no. 44 (March–April 1991): 59–70, esp. 62–63; Teresa Porzecanski, "Los inmigrantes judíos al Uruguay. Transculturación e ideologías de izquierda," in *Ensayos sobre judaísmo latinoamericano. V Congreso Internacional de Investigadores sobre Judaísmo Latinoamericano* (Buenos Aires: Milá, 1990), 89–90.

49. Acción Femenina por la Victoria, "Estatutos," in *Acción Femenina*, n.p.

50. *Justicia*, August 27, 1943, 3, October 27, 1944, 2.

51. Acción Femenina por la Victoria, "Autoridades emanadas de la Primera Convencion Nacional, agosto 27–29 de 1943," in *Acción Femenina*, n.p.; *DP,* March 16, 2, June 3, 2, October 4, 1944, 2.

52. *DP,* March 16, 1944, 2.

53. *DP,* November 4, 1945, 1.

54. *LH,* May 27, 1942, 5. It is unclear whether Uruguayan Jewish women joined antifascist groups other than the CCFI.

55. For examples see Comité Central Pro-Socorro a las Víctimas de la Guerra y Refugiados, *Memoria y balance 1941–1942* (Buenos Aires: n.p, 1942); *Israel* (Buenos Aires), May 24, 1942, 4.

56. Junta de la Victoria, "Comités adheridos a la Fiesta por la Libertad," flier, n.d., box 1070, Instituto Científico Judío (IWO), Buenos Aires; Junta de la Victoria, *Estatutos* (Buenos Aires: n.p., [1941?], n.p.); Caja Mujeres, Archivo del Partido Comunista, Buenos Aires. Junta, *Primera convención,* 60, mentions a Jewish *seccional* in Rosario.

57. Harry O. Sandberg, "The Jews of Latin America," *American Jewish Yearbook* 19 (1917–1918): 68–69, accessed June 9, 2017, http://www.ajcarchives.org/main.php?GroupingId=10050; Elkin, *The Jews of Latin America,* 59, 73; Feldman, *Tiempos difíciles,* 11–13, 15, 17. We know little about Sephardim in Uruguay.

58. See, among other sources, Haim Avni, *Argentina & The Jews: A History of Jewish Immigration,* trans. Gila Brand (Tuscaloosa: University of Alabama Press, 1991), 44, 69; Rosa Perla Raicher, "Obreros judíos en el Uruguay. Entre los años diez y la época de la Segunda Guerra Mundial," *Hoy es Historia,* no. 26 (March–April 1988): 41–45; Dieter Schonebohm, "Judíos de izquierda en Montevideo I: los bundistas," *Hoy es Historia,* no. 41 (October–November 1990): 21–29, and "Judíos de izquierda . . . II"; Bourat et al., *Entre la matzá,* 17; Feldman, *Tiempos difíciles,* 34; Deutsch, *Crossing Borders,* 153, 165, 167, 206–7.

59. Avni et al., eds., *Historia viva,* 31–32.

60. Soriano interview in ibid., 9–11. I found no studies of Jewish women's education and professionalization in Uruguay.

61. Bourat et al., *Entre la matzá,* 91–98.

62. Feldman, *Tiempos difíciles;* Clara Aldrighi et al., *Antisemitismo en Uruguay, raíces, discursos, imágenes (1870–1940)* (Montevideo: Trilce, 2000); María M. Camou, *Resonancia del nacional-socialismo en el Uruguay* (Montevideo: Facultad de Humanidades y Ciencias, Universidad de la República, 1988).

63. Raúl Blustein, interview in Avni et al., eds., *Historia viva,* 80–86; Bourat et al., *Entre la matzá,* 97.

64. Dieter Schonebohm, "Alemanes, judíos, y judíos alemanes en el Uruguay de los años 1920 y 1930," in *Encuentro y alteridad: vida y cultura judía en América Latina,* eds. Judit Bokser de Liwerant et al. (Mexico: Universidad Nacional Autónoma de México, Universidad Hebrea de Jerusalem, Asociación Mexicana de Amigos de la Universidad de Tel Aviv, and Fondo de Cultura Económica, 1999), 193–196; José Kierszenbaum, "Repercusiones del episodio del 'Conte Grande' en las instituciones judías del Uruguay," in *Vida y muerte en comunidad. Ensayos sobre judaísmo en el Uruguay,* ed. Abel Bronstein (Montevideo: Kehilá, Comunidad Israelita del Uruguay, 1990), 131; Raicher, *Uruguay,*

68, 108, 135–135; Bourat et al., *Entre la matzá*, 115, 122, 126, 128, 132; Feldman, *Tiempos difíciles*, 78, 108, 122.

65. D.D., interview.

66. Deutsch, *Crossing Borders*, 175–84; Raanan Rein, "A Transnational Struggle with National and Ethnic Goals: Jewish-Argentines and Solidarity with the Republicans during the Spanish Civil War," *Journal of Iberian and Latin American Research* 20, no. 2 (2014): 171–82.

67. Bourat et al., *Entre la matzá*, 124.

68. Raicher, *Uruguay*, 31.

69. Gerardo Leibner, *Camaradas y compañeros. Una historia política y social de los comunistas del Uruguay* (Montevideo: Trilce, 2011), 71, claims that immigrants appreciated the security and freedom they experienced in Uruguay, and the general local sympathy for antifascism and pro-Allied government stance gave them a sense of comfort. Feldman, *Tiempos difíciles*, 44–45, emphasizes Jewish integration more than Raicher.

70. For example see *DP*, March 4, 1943, 2.

71. *DP*, February 15, 2, March 16, 1944, 2.

72. *DP*, December 23, 1945, 2.

73. *DP*, September 30, 1944, 2.

74. See, for example, *DP*, July 3, 1942, 5; May 5, 2, June 15, 1943, 2; June 5, 1944, 3. One could argue that Uruguayan secularism precluded mention of religion, but that does not explain why the Ladies' Commission explicitly invited Catholics and Protestants to its first meeting.

75. *DP*, July 31, 1942, 5.

76. *DP*, September 8, 1945, 2.

77. *DP*, June 6, 1944, 2. However, Raicher, *Uruguay*, 155–56, noted that the Uruguayan public repudiated the Holocaust.

78. *DP*, August 30, 1945, 4.

79. *DP*, December 30, 1945, 4.

80. *Orientación*, November 6, 1941, 9.

81. *LH*, April 15, 1 (Schlieper), April 16, 1942, 5.

82. *Orientación*, April 23, 1942, 1.

83. *DP*, July 23, 1942, 5.

84. Deutsch, *Crossing Borders*, 185.

85. *LH*, February 26, 1942, 5.

86. Deutsch, *Crossing Borders*, 187.

87. *Mujeres en la Ayuda*, 1941–1942, 20, 21, 32, 50.

88. Lesser and Rein, "New Approaches," 24–25.

89. There is a substantial literature on these issues for Argentina. On Uruguay, see, for example, Hugo Achugar and Gerardo Caetano, eds., *Identidad uruguaya: ¿mito, crisis o afirmación?* (Montevideo: Trilce, 1992).

Bibliography

Primary Sources

Archives

Archivo del Partido Comunista (Buenos Aires)
Centro de Documentación e Investigación de la Cultura de Izquierdas en la Argentina, CeDInCI (Buenos Aires)
Instituto Científico Judío, IWO (Buenos Aires)
U.S. National Archives (Washington, DC)

Interviews

D. D. Interview by author, Montevideo, 2015
Oliver, María Rosa. Interview with Leandro Gutiérrez. May 6, 1971. Proyecto de Historia Oral del Instituto Torcuato di Tella, Universidad Torcuato di Tella, Buenos Aires

Periodicals

American Jewish Yearbook 19 (1917–1918). Accessed June 9, 2017. http://www.ajcarchives.org/main.php?GroupingId=10050
American Jewish Yearbook 48 (1946–1947). Accessed April 7, 2017. http://www.ajcarchives.org/main.php?GroupingId=40
Argentina Libre, 1941
Diario Popular (DP), 1941–1944
Israel, 1942
Justicia, 1942–1943
La Hora (LH), 1941–1943
Orientación, 1941–1943
Acción Femenina por la Victoria. Periódico de Ayuda a las Naciones Liberadas por los Fascismos, 1946

Books and Pamphlets

Acción Femenina por la Victoria. *Acción Femenina por la Victoria. Campaña argentino-uruguaya sanitaria y de abrigo, 1943-1944*. Montevideo: n.p., 1944.
———. "Entregas efectuadas por Acción Femenina por la Victoria." N.P.: n.p., [1944?].
Comité Central Pro-Socorro a las Víctimas de la Guerra y Refugiados. *Memoria y balance 1941-1942*. Buenos Aires: n.p, 1942.
Junta de la Victoria. *Ayuda de las mujeres argentinas a los países que luchan contra el nazismo. 13 septiembre 1941-13 enero 1942*. Buenos Aires: n.p., 1942.
———. *Estatutos*. Buenos Aires: n.p., probably 1941.
———. *Primera convención nacional*. Buenos Aires: n.p., 1942.
Mujeres en la Ayuda, 1941-1942. Buenos Aires: n.p., 1942.

Other Sources

Achugar, Hugo, and Gerardo Caetano, eds. *Identidad uruguaya: ¿mito, crisis o afirmación?* Montevideo: Trilce, 1992.
Aldrighi, Clara, María Camou, Miguel Feldman, and Gabriel Abend. *Antisemitismo en Uruguay, raíces, discursos, imágenes (1870-1940).* Montevideo: Trilce, 2000.
Antezana-Pernet, Corinne A. *El MEMCH hizo historia.* Santiago: Fundación Biblioteca y Archivo de la Mujer Elena Caffarena, 1997.
Ardanaz, Eleonora. "Con el puño en alto: Sara Fradkin y la lucha antifascista judía." In *Mujeres en espacios bonaerenses,* edited by Adriana Valobra, 111-24. La Plata: Edulp, 2009.
Avni, Haim. *Argentina & The Jews: A History of Jewish Immigration.* Translated by Gila Brand. Tuscaloosa: University of Alabama Press, 1991.
Avni, Haim, Rosa Perla Raicher, and David Bankier, eds. *Historia viva. Memorias del Uruguay y de Israel.* Jerusalem: Instituto de Judaísmo Contemporáneo, Universidad Hebrea de Jerusalem, 1989.
Barrios Pintos, Aníbal. *Montevideo: los barrios I.* Montevideo: Nuestra Tierra, 1971.
Bisso, Andrés. *Acción Argentina. Un antifascismo nacional en tiempos de guerra mundial.* Buenos Aires: Prometeo, 2005.
———, ed. *El antifascismo argentino. Selección documental y estudio preliminar.* Buenos Aires: Buenos Libros and CeDinCI editores, 2007.
Blay, Eva Alterman. *O Brasil como destino. Raízes da imigração judaica para São Paulo.* São Paulo: UNESP, 2013.
Brodsky, Adriana. *Sephardi, Jewish, Argentine: Community and National Identity.* Bloomington: Indiana University Press, 2016.
Bourat, Daniela, Álvaro Martínez, and David Telias. *Entre la matzá y el mate. La inmigración judía al Uruguay: una historia en construcción.* Montevideo: Ediciones de la Banda Oriental, 1997. Accessed April 18, 2017. https://www.jewishvirtuallibrary.org/uruguay.
Cabral Reyes, Gisela. "Mujeres alemanas exiliadas en México." Paper delivered at the Latin American Jewish Studies Association Meeting, Universidad Iberoamericana, México, July 5, 2017.
Camou, María M. *Resonancia del nacional-socialismo en el Uruguay.* Montevideo: Facultad de Humanidades y Ciencias, Universidad de la República, 1988.
Cane, James. *The Fourth Enemy: Journalism and Power in the Making of Peronist Argentina.* University Park: Penn State University Press, 2011.
Cohen, Deborah, and Maura O'Connor, eds. *Comparison and History: Europe in Cross-National Perspective.* New York: Routledge, 2004.
De Giorgi, Ana Laura. "Entre la lucha contra la carestía y por los derechos de la mujer. Las comunistas uruguayas durante la segunda mitad del siglo XX (1942-1973)." In *Queridas camaradas. Historias iberoamericanas de mujeres comunistas, 1935-1975,* edited by Adriana Valobra and Mercedes Yusta Rodrigo, 215-34. Buenos Aires: Miño y Dávila, 2017.
Del Franco, Clara. *Mujeres, ese fuego, esas luchas: 1930-1960.* Buenos Aires: Cuadernos Marxistas, 2011.

Deutsch, Sandra McGee. "Argentine Women Against Fascism: The Junta de la Victoria, 1941-1947." *Politics, Religion, and Ideology* 13, no. 2 (2012): 221-36.
———. *Crossing Borders, Claiming a Nation: A History of Argentine Jewish Women, 1880-1955*. Durham: Duke University Press, 2010.
———. "Gendering Antifascism: Women's Activism in Argentina and the World, 1918-1947." Book manuscript in progress.
———. "Hands Across the Río de la Plata: Argentine and Uruguayan Antifascist Women, 1941-1945." *Revista Contemporánea* 8 (2017): 29-54.
Edelman, Fanny. *Banderas, pasiones, camaradas*. Buenos Aires: Dirple, 1996.
Elkin, Judith Laikin. *The Jews of Latin America*. 3rd. ed. Boulder: Lynne Rienner, 2014.
Facal Santiago, Silvia. "Vida comunitaria de los judíos alemanes y los republicanos españoles en Uruguay." *Revista de Historia de América*, no. 130 (January-June 2002): 41-55.
Feldman, Miguel. *Tiempos difíciles. Inmigrantes judíos en Uruguay, 1935-1945*. Montevideo: Universidad de la República, Facultad de Humanidades y Ciencias de la Educación, Departamento de Publicaciones, 2001.
Finchelstein, Federico. *Transatlantic Fascism: Ideology, Violence, and the Sacred in Argentina and Italy, 1919-1945*. Durham: Duke University Press, 2010.
García, Hugo, Mercedes Yusta Rodrigo, Xavier Tabet, Cristina Clímaco, eds. *Rethinking Antifascism: History, Memory and Politics, 1922 to the Present*. New York: Berghahn, 2016.
Gurvich Peretzman, Natalia. "La judía ashkenazí en México: cambios y permanencias, 1920-1945." In *Tejidos culturales: las mujeres judías en México*, edited by Natalia Gurvich, Liz Hamui, and Linda Hanono, 33-75. Mexico, D.F.: Universidad Iberoamericana, Departamento de Historia, 2016.
Kierszenbaum, José. "Repercusiones del episodio del 'Conte Grande' en las instituciones judías del Uruguay." In *Vida y muerte en comunidad. Ensayos sobre judaísmo en el Uruguay*, edited by Abel Bronstein. Montevideo: Kehilá, Comunidad Israelita del Uruguay, 1990.
Klapper, Melissa R. "'Those by Whose Side We Have Labored': American Jewish Women and the Peace Movement between the Wars." *Journal of American History* 97, no. 3 (December 2010): 636-58.
Lau Jaiven, Ana, and Roxana Rodríguez. "'Ciudadanas mexicanas conscientes y agradecidas': el Consejo Mexicano de Mujeres Israelitas." In *Tejidos culturales: las mujeres judías en México*, edited by Natalia Gurvich, Liz Hamui, and Linda Hanono, 239-73. Mexico, D.F.: Editorial Universidad Iberoamericana, Departamento de Historia, 2016.
Leibner, Gerardo. *Camaradas y compañeros. Una historia política y social de los comunistas del Uruguay*. Montevideo: Trilce, 2011.
———. "*Nosotras* (Uruguay, 1945-1953), las contradicciones de la escritura femenina comunista y sus significados sociales." In *Escritura femenina y reivindicación de género en América Latina*, edited by Roland Forgues and Jean-Marie Flores, 507-21. Paris: Mare & Martin, 2005.
Lesser, Jeffrey, and Raanan Rein. "New Approaches to Ethnicity and Diaspora in Twenti-

eth-Century Latin America." In *Rethinking Jewish-Latin Americans*, edited by Jeffrey Lesser and Raanan Rein, 23–40. Albuquerque: University of New Mexico Press, 2008.

Morais, Fernando. *Olga*. São Paulo: Companhia das Letras, 1994.

Olcott, Jocelyn. *Revolutionary Women in Postrevolutionary Mexico*. Durham: Duke University Press, 2005.

Oliver, María Rosa. *Mi fe es el hombre*. Buenos Aires: C. Lohlé, 1981.

Oxman, Ramón "Una experiencia de colonización agraria judía: la colonia '19 de abril' de Paysandú. Primera parte." *Hoy es Historia*, no. 13 (December 1985–January 1986): 31–42.

Porzecanski, Teresa, ed. *Historias de vida de inmigrantes judíos al Uruguay*. Montevideo: Kehilá, Comunidad Israelita de Uruguay, 1986.

———. "Los inmigrantes judíos al Uruguay. Transculturación e ideologías de izquierda." In *Ensayos sobre judaísmo latinoamericano. V Congreso Internacional de Investigadores sobre Judaísmo Latinoamericano*, 84–103. Buenos Aires: Milá, 1990.

Raicher, Rosa Perla. "Obreros judíos en el Uruguay. Entre los años diez y la época de la Segunda Guerra Mundial." *Hoy es Historia*, no. 26 (March–April 1988): 41–45.

———. *Uruguay, la comunidad israelita y el pueblo judío*. Montevideo: Universidad Hebrea de Jerusalén Instituto Avraham Harman de Judaísmo Contemporáneo; Universidad de la República, Facultad de Humanidades y Ciencias de la Educación, 2003.

Rein, Raanan. "A Transnational Struggle with National and Ethnic Goals: Jewish-Argentines and Solidarity with the Republicans during the Spanish Civil War." *Journal of Iberian and Latin American Research* 20, no. 2 (2014): 171–82.

Romero, Simón. "Outpost in the Pampas Where Jews Once Found Refuge Wilts as They Leave." *New York Times*, June 9, 2013.

Rosemblatt, Karin. *Gendered Compromises: Political Cultures and the State in Chile, 1920–1950*. Chapel Hill: University of North Carolina Press, 2000.

Sandberg, Harry O. "The Jews of Latin America: Including South and Central America, Mexico, the West Indies, and the United States Possessions." *American Jewish Year Book* 19 (1917–18): 35–105.

Scattered among Nations. "Moisés Ville Argentina. Jewish Gauchos." Accessed April 18, 2017. http://www.scatteredamongthenations.org/agentina.

Schonebohm, Dieter. "Alemanes, judíos, y judíos alemanes en el Uruguay de los años 1920 y 1930." In *Encuentro y alteridad: vida y cultura judía en América Latina*, edited by Judit Bokser de Liwerant, Alicia Gojman Backal, and Hellen B. Soriano, 182–198. México: Universidad Nacional Autónoma de México, Universidad Hebrea de Jerusalem, Asociación Mexicana de Amigos de la Universidad de Tel Aviv, and Fondo de Cultura Económica, 1999.

———. "Judíos de izquierda en Montevideo I: los bundistas." *Hoy es Historia*, no. 41 (October–November 1990): 21–29.

———. "Judíos de izquierda en Montevideo II: la 'Comunidad progresista.'" *Hoy es Historia*, no. 44 (March–April 1991): 59–70.

Sznajder, Jaime. "Reacciones a conflictos internacionales en una ciudad del interior uruguaya. Paysandú de los años cuarenta." In *Historia viva. Memorias del Uruguay y de Israel*, edited by Haim Avni, Rosa Perla Raicher, David Bankier. Jerusalem: Instituto de Judaísmo Contemporáneo, Universidad Hebrea de Jerusalem, 1989.

Tuñón Pablos, Esperanza. *Mujeres que se organizan: el Frente Único Pro Derechos de la Mujer, 1935-1938*. Mexico, D.F.: Universidad Nacional Autónoma de México, 1992.

Valobra, Adriana María. "Formación de cuadros y frentes populares: relaciones de clase y género en el Partido Comunista de Argentina, 1935-1951." *Revista Izquierdas*, no. 23 (April 2015): 127-56.

Valobra, Adriana María, and Mercedes Yusta Rodrigo, eds. *Queridas camaradas: historias iberoamericanas de mujeres comunistas*. Buenos Aires: Miño y Dávila Editores, 2017.

Visacovsky, Nerina. *Argentinos, judíos y camaradas. Tras la utopía socialista*. Buenos Aires: Biblos, 2015.

———. "Herencias de 1947. *Di idishe froi* y el sufragio femenino." In *Sufragio femenino. Prácticas y debates políticos, religiosos y culturales en Argentina y América Latina*, edited by Carolina Barry, 91-111. Buenos Aires: Eduntref, 2011.

10

Out of the "Ghetto" and into the World
Argentine Sephardi Youth, 1940s–1950s

ADRIANA M. BRODSKY

In the Argentine summer of 1949, a group of young Sephardim with very little formal education in the ideals of *halutziut* (the Zionist pioneer movement) organized and led fifty young children in their first summer camp.¹ Considering it a success, leader Shabetay Bahbout explained that the raison d'être of the activity was "to identify with life in Eretz Israel."²
"Contact with nature, work, the enticing adventures," he added, "have contributed for *javerim* [friends or members] to elevate their thoughts towards our longed-for Israel."³ "They have returned [from this experience]," he added, "ready to march towards Sion [*sic*], to catch up with our Ashkenazic comrades, so we can tell them: *javerim, anajnu po* [*sic*] [friends, we are here]." Without help from institutions, these older teenagers had created a Sephardi movement that wished to inculcate pioneering ideals and Jewish and Zionist history to young children in order to inspire them to imagine themselves as part of the new Jewish state.

In his study of European Jewish youth after the Holocaust, historian Avinoam Patt sought to understand why those young people in Displaced Persons' (DP) camps were intent on working on kibbutzim and planning their *aliyah* (immigration to Palestine).⁴ Like him, I pursue similar questions. Why would Sephardim in Argentina, most belonging to middle-class families, choose to create Sephardi Zionist groups? Why would they contemplate leaving their families behind to work on kibbutzim in Palestine/Israel, engaging in very different activities than those they would have pursued in the country their parents (or grandparents) had chosen to move to? Unlike those DPs whose lives had been completely uprooted from their local communities and nations, young Sephardim in Argentina were living in much better conditions and had, in some measure, assimilated into Argentine culture. What could explain their resolution to live in Israel as pioneers?

Scholars have discussed Zionist youth movements in Latin America, and many have provided answers to some of the questions I ask.[5] Silvia Schenkolewski-Kroll, for example, a historian of Zionism in Argentina, noted the lack of studies on Zionist youth movements in this historiography, but focused her essay on the similarities and differences between the development of Zionist youth movements in different parts of the word.[6] Schenkolewski-Kroll was mostly interested in the ideologies of the movements, in their relations to other Zionist institutions and groups, and not so much in the actors themselves. Beatrice Gurwitz, in her work on Jewish Argentine youth from 1955 to 1983, argued that these young men and women had "constructed Zionism as a revolutionary national liberation movement" and therefore insisted that aliyah was the only way of realizing that objective.[7] Young people, immersed in the "leftist ferment" that engulfed all of Latin America, and seeking to confront the challenges posed by the New Left, found in aliyah a way to merge their leftist ideology and their Jewish identity. Adrián Krupnik, in his study of one Zionist youth group in particular in the late 1960s and early 1970s (Baderej), explored the ways in which the members navigated their desire to participate in Argentine local political struggles while also declaring themselves Zionist.[8] Unlike Gurwitz, who highlighted how the Latin American reality shaped their Jewish activism, Krupnik suggested that their participation in a Zionist youth group acted as a catalyst for their desire to become involved in local struggles. Other scholars focused on the persecution suffered by left-wing activists during the dictatorship years, many of whom had started their activism in Zionist youth movements but later left them behind.[9]

All these works share some similarities: most weave the experiences of these young people with those of youth in general, merging Jewish and Argentine historiographies very successfully; many also focus on the 1960s and 1970s, during the post–Cuban Revolution context, the rise of Third-Worldism, and the repression suffered during the late 1970s and early 1980s. Yet overall attention to Sephardim has been lacking. My work proposes to chart the history of Sephardi youth from the early 1940s, to show that the Sephardi groups of the 1960s and 1970s were the product of the activism forged beginning in the 1940s and could not have existed without the path made by their predecessors. In this chapter, then, I attempt to answer the question that drove Patt's study of post–World War II young people, in order to understand why such a different context also generated a strong desire, among some, to move to Palestine/Israel. The study would also further our understanding of the history of Zionist youth movements and the role these groups played among Sephardim. Sephardi young men and women chose to create their own Zionist youth groups in a post-Holocaust context that assigned youth an important role in the reconfiguration of Jewish life. Especially in the late 1940s and early 1950s, young Sephardim wished to be involved alongside other young men and women in the construction of a state whose vision they began to learn about and share with others. And while many *halutzim* (pioneers) did not ultimately move to the new State of Israel, the work they engaged in, and what they learned in the process, also impacted the communities they belonged to in Argentina. Zionist youth contributed to break down barriers among Sephardim from different origins, between Sephardim and Ashkenazim, and between youth in Israel and the Diaspora. Sephardi young women were also greatly impacted by their activism in these groups, engaging in activities that pushed them into the public sphere in ways that departed importantly from traditional practices.

Avinoam Patt sought to understand the intentions of the young survivors he focused on by listening to their own voices and not relying exclusively on sources produced by outside observers. This chapter is, likewise, mostly based on interviews with the members of the Zionist Sephardi youth groups created in the late 1940s, and on the materials these young people themselves created: magazines, minute books of the organizations they founded, activities they organized, and interviews they gave to press outlets. I have also consulted the Jewish Argentine press (mostly, but not exclusively, Sephardi) to gauge the impact of these young people's activism and the minute books of the Centro Sionista Sefaradí (CSS), one of the institutions that accompanied the creation of these groups.

The chapter begins with a description of the calls made to Jewish Argentine youth to regenerate Jewish life. Violent antisemitism required that young Jews reconnect with their pride and identity to find solutions to the problems European Jews were facing. I, then, discuss how Sephardim in particular responded to that call, as well as the Sephardi Zionist institutions' role in encouraging youth participation. The Sephardi youth groups that grew out of these calls developed an important fundraising and educational agenda, seeking to bring down barriers that, in their eyes, prevented bringing Zionism to the Sephardi communities they belonged to. In particular, I introduce the work done by the Jewish National Fund's (Keren Kayemet Leisrael, or KKL) Young Women's Commission and the ways in which their participation broke with tradition. The last section focuses on how some young Sephardim came to think of themselves as future pioneers, imagining kibbutzim as their destiny. To that end, they created groups that sought to bring those ideas to other young Sephardim and began to train for that life in Israel.

"If our people are not saved by the youth, they won't be saved at all"

Within the Jewish Argentine community, youth was openly chastised for their perceived desire to assimilate to the local society, and for their apathy toward the project of Jewish nationalism, all in the context of increased anti-Jewish sentiment. In 1937, *La Luz*, a bimonthly Sephardi magazine, published a call to wake the Jewish youth up. "Our [Jewish] youth [in Argentina]," wrote contributor Mary de Rabinovich, "should not be passively observing how their brothers and sisters in Palestine are offering up their lives to their ideals, or how their brethren are oppressed in Germany, Poland or Romania."[10] Stressing that youth were needed to give voice to "our people's rights and demands," Rabinovich ended the essay hoping for a "quick and favorable reaction" from the youth. The unease about the future of Judaism was further made evident in a survey carried out by the Jewish Argentine weekly *Mundo Israelita* in 1941. Titled "Problemas e inquietudes de la juventud judía" (Problems and Concerns of Jewish Youth), the survey gave voice to a variety of "young" guests who were asked to answer questions that sought to understand where Jewish Argentine youth stood and what they should do in the face of antisemitism. Over a period of four months, the weekly periodical published the responses of sixteen members of the Jewish community, including the voices of those from the city as well as from the countryside, female and male, and Sephardim and Ashkenazim. These diverse voices agreed that Argentine youth was not fully committed to battling antisemitism *and* assimilation.[11] These young Argentine Jews were characterized in contrast to the youth in Europe and in Palestine, who *were* imagined to be deeply involved in the future of Judaism, like the partisans and the pioneers, for example. The respondents also agreed that education (Zionist history, but also the history of Jews and their participation in music, art, and even science) was necessary to bring Jewish youth to actively participate in the rebirth of the Jewish people. "If our people are not saved by the youth," pronounced a young Zionist leader, "they won't be saved at all."[12]

Young Sephardim joined young Jews in Argentina in thinking about the role they should play in revitalizing Jewish life. Julieta Camji, an active member of the Sephardi youth, was interviewed by the newspaper in connection with the series mentioned above. Noting the seeming contradiction faced by Jews between becoming recognized members of Argentine society and retaining their identity as an ethnic minority, Camji strongly assured young Jews that "Jewish Argentines were those who live[d] in the country and love[d] it, regardless of where they [were] born." She understood that young people were driven by their desire to become visible Argentines, but went on to add that there were some who "although living in Argentina and being children of Israel, should not be called [Jewish Argentines]."[13] In order to show they were Argentines, Camji explained, these young people had "renounce[d] their Jewish condition, their traditions, religion, customs, and the national language." One way to strengthen their weak Jewish identity was to get youth involved in Zionism. To that end, they had to "learn Jewish history, learn about the benefits Jews brought to humankind, and the principles for which our forefathers fought: justice, individual freedom, and the betterment of social classes." Through this knowledge, she claimed, "they will learn that we were not always a persecuted people, but had a home where we created our own culture and social legislation that has served as a model to other people."[14] Antisemitism had instilled fear, and many Jews, especially young ones according to Camji, had reacted by hiding away from an image tarnished by defeat.

While Camji understood why many had sought to abandon identification with Judaism, and pointed to ways to solve the problem, Shabetay Bahbout, the Sephardi young man introduced at the beginning of the essay, further elaborated on the role that youth—Sephardi youth in particular—should play in bringing Zionism to their coreligionists.[15] Zionism was not only absent from the young, but from Sephardim in general. Bahbout suggested that, unlike Ashkenazim, Sephardim were not considering Zionism as a response to antisemitism, or assimilation. A son of a prominent Sephardi Zionist activist, Bahbout believed that Sephardim needed to follow a different trajectory: they needed to open up their horizons and embrace change. "Only when young people have opened themselves up and seen what is outside the walls of their Oriental ghetto," he argued, "can they bring [Zionism] to those [asleep] inside."[16] Zionism would only be able to be understood and accepted once Sephardim left old ways and traditions behind. Beyond their different takes, both Camji and Bahbout saw young people as educators and facilitators of the change they thought was needed;

both understood that the idea of Israel as a modern nation could only be brought to the Sephardi community via the work of education, and with Sephardi leaders. It was *Sephardi* youth who could break the bounds of religiosity and foster a new relationship with Israel that was concrete, educational, and national. Sephardim needed to modernize, and youth would lead the way.

The "Oriental ghetto" boundaries that needed to be brought down were not only those that separated Sephardim and Ashkenazim, but also those that existed *among* the Sephardi groups in Argentina. In Buenos Aires, Sephardim from Morocco, Syria, and Turkey had settled in different parts of the city, founded their own political, social, and religious institutions, and initially had very little contact with other Sephardi groups.[17] The CSS was one such attempt at bringing all these groups together. Initially founded in 1925 and reorganized in November 1932, this was the organization that came to be in charge of Zionist education and fundraising for Zionist purposes. The CSS represented an important step in breaking down the "Oriental ghetto" boundaries and was a collective effort (even if only very few Sephardim actively participated in Zionist circles) at bringing Zionism to the various communities.

But many Sephardim questioned if the Zionist institution that had been created among Sephardim was doing the job of preventing assimilation and ensuring commitment to the nationalist project. One criticism leveled at the CSS was that it exclusively focused on fundraising and not much on educational work. David and Nissim Elnecavé, editor-in-chief and writer of *La Luz* respectively, resigned from the executive board of the Centro because they disagreed about the lack of educational programming. Nissim Elnecavé, a member of the Zionist youth movement Hashomer Hatza'ir who had lived on a kibbutz in Hedera prior to settling in Argentina where his parents resided, penned a piece titled "Zionist Fundraising, or Fundraising for Zionism?" in which he criticized the organization for only being interested in mere fundraising. "We Sephardim have failed to help the national *political* rebirth of Zionism," he claimed (my emphasis).[18] Insisting that Sephardim were still immersed in traditional practices that only connected them to Palestine on a religious basis, Nissim Elnecavé stated that it was the youth who needed to be more proactive about inculcating the idea of Zionism as a national and political regeneration project. Sephardi Zionist institutions, according to the Elnecavés, needed to be better at educating all Sephardim about what political Zionism meant, and the youth had to help to bring about that nation to fruition.

The criticism leveled at the CSS by the Elnecavés was slightly unfair. The CSS had been central in facilitating the contribution of young Sephardim to the work at hand, and at creating a space for these young people (from a variety of origins) to come together. Nissim Elnecavé, whose experience in Hashomer Hatza'ir back in Bulgaria had involved preparation for—and ultimately the making of—aliyah, sought to promote the idea that young men and women should move to kibbutzim in Palestine and "redeem" the land by settling and working on it, ideas that the CSS was not advancing at this point. And while the CSS fundraised for the KKL and the Keren Hayesod (United Israel Appeal), which sought to purchase land for the construction of, among other things, kibbutzim, this fundraising work was not enough for Elnecavé. His ideas would eventually find echo in the CSS and in the youth groups founded within it after the creation of the State of Israel.

It is true that the CSS mainly "utilized" the youth for fundraising purposes, but once they were brought into the folds of the CSS, these young men and women got involved in various ways. In May 1940, the CSS committee of the KKL founded Comité Juvenil Sionista Sefaradí (Sephardi Zionist Youth Committee), whose aim was to aid in the KKL campaigns.[19] At the end of June of the same year, the Juventud Sionista Sefaradí (Sephardi Zionist Youth or JSS) was finally founded, not exclusively linked to the work of the KKL, although many of the members participated in both groups. And by 1944, a Young Women's Committee of the Sephardi branch of the KKL (Young Women's Committee) came into existence, and their members also participated actively in the JS. The JSS, which was reorganized in 1943 as the Departamento de Juventud del Centro Sionista Sefaradí (CSS Youth Department), took up the call of educating Sephardim: they organized a variety of cultural events, just like Julieta Camji had requested in her 1941 interview for the Jewish weekly, and would later support the ideals of ḥalutziut and aliyah.

The involvement of youth brought about important changes. One important objective achieved by the CSS Youth Department (which included the Young Women's Committee) was to concretely bring a number of existing youth groups in the various Sephardi communities together, furthering the breakdown of the barriers that existed between the different communities and to organize Zionist work.[20] They carried out two initiatives to fulfill this objective. One, they invited representatives of the youth groups to help organize the Baile de la Colectividad (Community Ball). At this event, a jury composed of leaders from various Sephardi communities selected beauty queens (Miss Sefaradí and Queen Esther) from among the many representatives previously elected by the Sephardi clubs and organizations in which the youth groups were active. The ball itself—which continued through the decades—helped to make visible the work that Sephardim were doing for the Zionist project, as all proceeds were donated to the KKL.[21] Another important task they tackled was the organization of a Convención de la Juventud Sefaradí (Sephardi Youth Convention), which sought to "unify all Sephardi youth groups in the country in order to coordinate all Zionist activity; define the position of the Sephardi youth regarding the current Jewish problem; and organize joint activities."[22] The CSS Youth Department kept close contact with many Sephardi youth institutions in Buenos Aires and in other parts of the country and publicized their activities in *Hanoar Hasefaradí* (The Sephardi Youth), the magazine they published between 1948 and 1950. And while the convention did not take place until 1948, the work of bringing together the various youth groups was in their minds since the beginning of their activities.

The CSS Youth Department organized a variety of events of their own, and they were also invited to participate in many meetings and community gatherings. For example, in August 1940, they put together an Acto Cultural y Artistico (Cultural and Artistic Event) in the premises of the Chalom youth organization, located in the Buenos Aires neighborhood of Colegiales.[23] In November of that year, they organized an event commemorating the Balfour Declaration, together with the Union Juvenil Israelita de Flores (Jewish Youth Union of Flores [neighborhood]).[24] In it, members of the CSS Youth Department (male and female) gave speeches on Theodor Herzl (Emma Cabouli) and on the history and significance of the Balfour Declaration itself (José Camji).[25] In 1941, they organized an event to celebrate the Argentine Independence Day on July 9 and three cultural events in the months of October, November, and December.[26] In these monthly meetings young men and women members lectured on "The Meaning of Jewish Holidays," "Imitation and Assimilation," and on "Jewish Women throughout History." Many other events, organized by the members of the CSS Youth Department, combined educational as well as entertainment objectives: teaching about Jewish history many times ended with a dance or a community meal. The events served to connect the young people from various Sephardi congregations of different origins and carry out an educational agenda aimed at bringing Zionism to Sephardim.

Many of the female members of the JSS who founded the Young Women's Committee in 1944 had been working for the CSS KKL subcommittee.[27] Many, but not all, were the daughters of the adult leaders of the CSS, and they came from all the major Sephardi groups—from Syria (Aleppo and Damascus), Turkey, Rhodes, and Morocco. They contributed, then, to many of the Zionist organizations founded by Sephardim. And they did much more than fundraising by placing tin boxes in homes, institutions, and organizations.[28] In fact, creating their own group gave them the ability to devise a very creative cultural plan, to "not only widen the circle of young women, but also to teach about the wonderful meaning of the redemption of the land."[29] About thirty-six young women met weekly in 1945 to develop a cultural plan in which each member would be in charge of preparing the educational portion of one event.[30] The organizer of each event, their founding document explained, "would be forced to research a topic in books and fliers," becoming, in practice, an "*autodidacta* (self-taught)."[31] In September 1945, for example, Julieta Camji gave a presentation on "The Jewish Problem and its Solution," while Regina Barcimanto and Nené Weiltraub showed slides of Eretz Israel while discussing the geography of the region. In December 1946, Elisa Sarano discussed the meaning of Hanukkah at the gathering in which they also celebrated the anniversary of the creation of the commission.[32] The commission was also one of the organizers of the Baile de la Colectividad and their members were asked to speak at important community events, as well as in other non-exclusively Sephardi meetings. On March 1949, for example, Matilde Bensignor lectured on "the concepts of people, nation, civilization and state," at the Zionist organization Libre Israel (Free Israel). In fact, their participation and public speaking served to showcase Sephardi Zionists' commitment to the Zionist project and their dedication to involve the young in keeping Jewish identity alive.[33]

Getting Closer to Israel: Ḥalutziut

While the work of these young men and women sought to "redeem the land" of Israel, and teach about the history and the need for the creation of a Jewish nation, the Land of Israel did not yet figure as a place for *Argentine Sephardim* to live in. Argentine Sephardim publicly discussed their role in contributing to a project that would provide help for *other Jews* who were in need of such a home. Since the beginning of antisemitic persecutions in Germany in the 1930s, the CSS had been very active in raising funds to aid those victims of World War II. The campaigns organized by Jewish Argentines to bring help to those who had been affected by antisemitism and by the war included the participation of important Sephardi men in leadership positions. These campaigns stressed that a permanent solution to the persecution of Jews in Europe could only be solved by the creation of a national home for Jews. Israel, then, came to be seen as the place where displaced Jews could live the rest of their lives. Sephardi youth organizations, like the Sephardi Zionist Youth Committee and the Young Women's Committee, participated in many events organized by the CSS, making clear that Eretz Israel would help those in Europe. Regina Menahem, speaking on behalf of the Young Women's Committee in an event in 1945, reminded people that they were "rais[ing] funds to buy land in Palestine where more refugees from the European inferno could settle in."[34] "We will continue to organize dances," she stressed, "with the hope that we will be able to buy one, two, three more pieces of land so that those still alive can escape to Eretz Israel."[35]

The idea that young Argentine Sephardim had a role to play in Palestine (and later Israel) was first brought up in the early years of the decade but got traction after the creation of the State of Israel. In 1942, Nissim Elnecavé published an article in *La Luz* suggesting that Sephardim in America should emulate the coreligionists who, from their countries of origin, had decided to take up pioneer life and settled in Palestine.[36] Elnecavé brought up the presence of young Sephardim from Greece, Yugoslavia, and Bulgaria on kibbutzim in Palestine, spurred by their participation in youth movements in those countries. He explained that that presence had started in the 1930s and therefore was the result of ideology and not of the need to escape persecution. Elnecavé wanted to show that the young Sephardim who were in kibbutzim in Palestine had not decided their move because of the occupation of invading armies in 1942. Not so subtly, Elnecavé extolled Argentine Sephardim to also follow the example of these ideologically driven young Sephardim; their situation before the war was similar to the situation Argentine Sephardim found themselves in—not in danger for their lives but immersed in the political nationalist project of the new state. And in the preparation of youth for that task, Zionist youth groups were essential.

The ideals of ḥalutziut meant not only different types of activities but also required a different conception of what the new nation meant. Knowledge about the history of the Jewish people was important—the reason why a lot of energy was spent on education—and fundraising was needed in order to contribute financially to that project, but most central to the times at hand, ḥalutzim believed, was the need to *build* a new nation with their bodies and sweat. That new nation would also be based on communal ideals exemplified by the kibbutz. Very few Sephardim, prior to their arrival in Argentina, had been exposed to these ideas. And it was not only the young people who needed to be introduced to those ideas but adults as well, including community leaders who made decisions about what young Sephardim would do in their institutions.

There was a lot of resistance to the participation of children in these types of activities. Most of the young Sephardim who attended the events in which the principles of ḥalutziut were introduced were from families who were Zionist and who were involved in Zionist groups and institutions. And the publicity of these activities was initially somewhat disguised so as not to clearly explain that the objective was to train young Sephardim to make aliyah. In March 1948, for example, the Sephardi magazine *Israel* announced the creation of the group Hejalutz—described below—but suggested that ḥalutziut was only about dances and songs. "The leaders of this group," the magazine explained, "wish to inculcate these ideals, evident in the Hebrew songs they sing, in the Palestinian dances they perform, and in the *'haflagot'* [outings] they organize in appropriate spaces."[37] The text, highlighting innocuous activities, and hiding concrete objectives, suggests what many adult Sephardim would not have approved: talk of aliyah, and communal activities in which young men and women came together away from parental supervision.

Ḥalutziut came to Sephardi youth through two groups: Hejalutz (The Pioneer) and Acción Sionista (Zionist Action).[38] Hejalutz was created in the mid-1940s, and it remained independent of organized Zionist youth movements until they began to train for aliyah. The move to Israel usually required the support of larger institutional structures to make that happen (for example, which kibbutz they would go to once in Israel, where they would train before leaving Argentina, etc.).[39] Acción Sionista was a Zionist collective that formed in the neighborhood of Flores around the same time, which organized many activities alongside Ashkenazim also living in that neighborhood. They supported the creation of a "pioneering group" within it and organized the youth of the area. The youth group of Acción Sionista helped create Lamerjav in the late 1940s, a Zionist youth movement that was not tied to any political party, like Mapai, Mapam, and others.[40] There is evidence that Hejalutz and Acción Sionista helped each other, even when they ended up belonging to different Zionist youth movements.[41]

Hejalutz began with the decision of Iosef Duek to create a Zionist youth group among Sephardim. Duek, whose family had come to Argentina from Aleppo, had begun attending the Macabi sports club in 1943, in particular the activities organized by the Argentine branch of the Hano'ar Hatzioni

(Zionist Youth).[42] These included weekly meetings, and summer camps in the province of Córdoba, which Duek attended for the first time in 1945.[43] He noticed, however, that his Sephardi friends had not been drawn to any of those activities. After learning of the existence of the JSS (a detail which suggests that the JSS did not reach many young Sephardim), he approached them and found support for creating a group that initially gathered in his own house, where they taught themselves *rikudim* (Israeli folk dances) and *canciones jalutzianas* (ḥalutzi songs). This group brought together young Sephardim from Buenos Aires' Once neighborhood but, in their desire to promote unity, they also reached out to Sephardim of other origins in other parts of the city: Villa Crespo, Boca and Barracas, San Fernando, Tigre, and, over time, even in other provincial cities such as Rosario and Córdoba.

After deciding that Hejalutz would not join any political party (see above), and finding a home in which they could carry out their activities (thanks to a family that allowed them the use of one of their properties), they began the work of introducing the ideals of ḥalutziut. In July 1948, for example, they organized the first outdoor event in which forty-five young men and women participated. They practiced how to set up a tent, build a fire, and prepare the food. They also "rested, played some easy games, [while] others talked about Zionist topics."[44] Before returning to the city, the "javerim and *javerot* [feminine form of javerim] sang the 'Hatikva.'"[45] Their first overnight camp took place in the summer of 1949. Declared a success by the organizers, the *moshava* (camp site) "shone brightly in the jalutzi education imparted [to the fifty participants], in the spirit of non-partisanship, in the tents, showers, and tables set up."[46]

While the coverage of these activities said nothing about aliyah, these events were important because, according to the organizers, they made young people feel closer to those young men and women in Israel. The first outdoor event in 1948 was meritorious, the organizers told *Hanoar Hasefaradí*, "because [these young people] are not familiar with the discomfort of traveling on flat seats, eating food prepared by themselves, and the difficulties of putting up a tent."[47] They sang "songs from Eretz" and talked "about Zionism and topics of general interest."[48] They "surely felt like our brothers in Israel must feel." Besides learning how to set up tents, the participants were made to experience the inconveniences, the need to provide for themselves, and life in a difficult place. In the first overnight camp, Rebeca Memun again highlighted how her participation deepened the connection with those in Israel. While standing guard at night, she "recalled my brothers and sisters in Eretz... in my mind; thinking of those who are fighting for our beloved land gave me the strength to [myself] become one more soldier [in Argentina]."[49] "Our *javerim* [sic]," pronounced their leader Shabetay Bahbout, "have returned... transformed... evolved." "All those who have returned," he concluded, "will fight for the spreading of the pioneer ideal, the wonderful means of realization available to the Jewish youth for its national resurrection."[50] He also noted how these experiences contributed to bringing Israel closer to these Argentine young Sephardim. "Is there any other way to get to understand life in the Yishuv," he asked, "than to live it, even when it is without the tragic consequences that our brothers in the Israeli colonies are experiencing?" These events, as shown by these participants' descriptions, served to bring them closer to a very concrete Israel, one that was being built on kibbutzim, in discomfort, and standing guard against possible enemies. These initial activities sought to now break down the walls dividing the young Sephardim in Argentina and those in Israel. Still, the idea that these Argentine Sephardim would make aliyah was not openly discussed in the press; the general public remained reluctant to imagine this possibility.

Moving toward aliyah was undoubtedly an objective that Israel wished to encourage. Preparation of young Sephardim as future pioneers became more organized after Duek was selected, in 1949, to attend the Makhon Lemadrikhei Ḥutz Laaretz, a program that brought young leaders to Israel.[51] They trained in Jerusalem for six months (where they learned Jewish history and Hebrew, among other topics); they also spent six months in various kibbutzim, and they were expected, at their return to their countries of origin, to create *gar'inim* (literally "seeds," but used to describe the group preparing their move to Israel) and prepare for aliyah. These future group leaders, then, were made to experience life in kibbutzim alongside other pioneers who were committed to the project and came back prepared to spread these ideals among the young. Duek, who had initially learned the ropes by participating in Macabi, completed his education in Israel, where the new state sought to channel that energy to organize the diaspora youth more effectively.

Hejalutz also broke barriers between nations by joining similar Sephardi youth from Uruguay. Tejezakna, founded in June 1948 among young Sephardim in Montevideo, sought to "actively awaken Sephardi youth [who have been so] lethargic because of assimilation."[52] The leaders of the organization described Tejezakna as a "bridge between [Sephardi] institutions who had not, until now, pursued the preparation of pioneers, and the pioneer ideal [seen in Israel]."[53] As well, they claimed that their intention was not to highlight differences between Sephardim and Ashkenazim. They wished "to prepare [Sephardi youth] to be able to join the ḥalutzi movements already in existence."[54] In 1951, members of these two groups decided to merge and founded the Hejalutz-Tejezakna collective, beginning to work toward preparing the first groups for aliyah. They joined Gordonia, and many lived for a year on the training farm that this youth movement owned in the province of Buenos Aires. Hejalutz-Tejezakna's older leaders went to Israel in early 1953 (to kibbutz Giv'ot Zaid, and later went on to found kibbutz Or Haner), and the organization continued to prepare members for aliyah, which they did in the late 1950s.[55] After all those members who had been trained by the founders of Hejalutz-Tejezakna made aliyah, Sephardi specificity disappeared as they de facto came to be integrated into a larger movement (Gordonia and Ijud Habonim) with whom they started sharing a house for their activities. There was no longer an exclusive Sephardi group, with Sephardi leaders that worked in Sephardi neighborhoods and institutions.[56]

Surviving material from Acción Sionista is more limited and does not allow for a detailed picture of their activities. But one can point to similarities and differences between the two groups. Acción Sionista, founded in December 1947, was not an exclusive youth group entity (and not exclusively of Sephardi origin) but rather, a Zionist center that supported and encouraged the formation of a youth group in 1948.[57] *Nueva Sión*, the biweekly publication of the Zionist Socialist Youth, favorably announced that the organization had attracted 700 members in its first sixteen months of existence.[58] Its young leaders, fighting against "the laziness and prejudice, the two parasites existing among Sephardim," sought to bring "ideological preparation" which would move Sephardim away from simple economic participation in the movement.[59] To that end, they carried out a variety of activities. For example, in 1948, we learn through *Nueva Sión* that they organized courses on Hebrew language and on "Palestinian Geography"; a lecture on the "possibilities of development in Eretz Israel"; a show on the work of German-born Jewish sculptor Pablo Hannemann, who had emigrated to Argentina in 1937, and whose work depicted the suffering of the Holocaust; an event during which they projected movies about life in Israel and discussed news about the war; and young children presented "Palestinian allegories."[60] Among the leaders were Sion Cohen Imach (a future leader of the Delegación de Asociaciones Israelitas Argentina, DAIA),

Leon Perez, Nissim Elnecavé, and Ashkenazim Jaime Derechinsky and Nehemias Resnitzky (a future leader of DAIA too).[61]

Acción Sionista sought to break down barriers by interacting and working with and among Ashkenazim. "From the start, Acción Sionista has instilled the idea . . . that there is no difference between Ashkenazim and Sephardim," *La Luz* stated.[62] For example, the organization of the youth was placed under the direction of Jaime Derechinsky. As well, and through the connections of Derechinsky, they brought *madrijim* (youth leaders; sing. *madrij*) who worked in Club Macabi (the institution which I also mentioned in connection with Hejalutz) to lead activities in their center. Eventually, however, in an effort to prepare Sephardi young leaders to work among the young, Acción Sionista sent a young man, Simón Dayan, and a young woman, Victoria Saal, to Israel to train as madrijim in 1949, to the same program that Duek from Hejalutz attended. At their return, they organized groups among young Sephardim with the intention to make aliyah.[63]

The story of Raquel Saal, whose sister was the first young Sephardi woman to be sent to Israel to train as a leader, serves as an example of the work done by Acción Sionista. She was "trained" by an Ashkenazic *madrijá* (feminine form of madrij; plural *madrijot*) from Macabi. At age 14, she herself became a madrijá and went from door-to-door trying to get Sephardi parents to agree to send their kids to the activities they organized. They organized summer camps in an outdoor space in Paso Del Rey (in Buenos Aires province). In Raquel's words, their objective was to "inculcate knowledge about Israel the country, and when the [children] were older, promote *aliyah*."[64] After occupying leadership positions in various groups, she chose to make aliyah, and as part of her preparation, she spent a year on the training farm that belonged to the Lamerjav movement (situated in the JCA colony of Moisesville).[65] Another similarity that Acción Sionista and Hejalutz shared was that both groups decided to remain outside of political parties. Sephardim had, according to Raquel, enough difficulty thinking about Zionism; politics would have further complicated the chances to convince parents to let their children become members of these groups.

In the early 1950s, a split within Lamerjav caused a slowdown in the development of the movement, especially among Sephardim, as the Sephardi group that split had to start anew without much help from the Jewish Agency. But eventually, in the late 1950s and early 1960s, Sephardim from Flores increased their participation in the movement, many of whom eventually moved to the kibbutzim Neot Mordekhai and Alumot.[66] In interviews with members of this group, they all referred to the marriages between Sephardim and Ashkenazim as further signs of the "ghetto barriers" that they helped to break down.[67]

Many parents were suspicious of the pioneering activities organized by these Sephardi young men and women of Hejalutz and Acción Sionista. Participation in outdoor activities, specifically in overnight events, was especially difficult for young women. On the one hand, many young women leaders recall that families would make it hard for girls to leave their homes to meet with their group members. The leaders would have to pick the female participants up individually from their homes, so that families would know exactly who their daughters would be with and that they would not be walking alone to their destinations. Young men in these groups also recall escorting young women members to their homes when they finished their activities late at night. When it came to overnight camps, their participation was even more complicated. Letting especially young girls be away from home for a few days (and nights!) was something many families refused to do. The solution these young men and women found was asking a female adult to act as a chaperone. A surviving photograph of the event shows a group of young women (and a slightly older Shabetay Bahbout) who attended the overnight training camp in Adela, in Buenos Aires province, in early 1949, organized by Hejalutz. Among them is an older woman, Bucas Levy, who traveled with the group and remained there for the duration of the summer camp; she was the grandmother of several of these young girls and was related to many other young participants as well. Because she attended this event, many parents were willing to let their daughters participate. Her willingness to be the chaperone could likely be explained by her own life. Bucas Levy had been married off at age thirteen and a half without any input on her part, an experience she recalled bitterly and wrote about in her diary.[68] Could she have wished to help young Sephardi girls have more opportunities that were denied to her earlier in the century? Could she have wished to change traditions that did not allow young Sephardi girls to leave their homes until their wedding day?

In order to continue the path set by these pioneering movements, many young women had to get married; participating in many of these activities as single young women was more complicated for Sephardim than for Ashkenazim. For example, Judit Labatón, a member of Hejalutz who was one of the granddaughters of Bucas Levy, married her fiancé Shabetay Bahbout, also a member of Hejalutz, before starting the year-long training on a farm in Verónica, in Buenos Aires province. Attending the agricultural training with several other pioneers (including Bahbout) and living in a house with no adults (she was seventeen years old at the time) would not have been possible.[69] The need for young Sephardi women to marry before being allowed to make aliyah (or to prepare for aliyah) continued well into the 1970s; only as married women could they leave their parents' home.

But while young Sephardi women had to make compromises and accept some traditional practices if they wished to become involved, they also broke down important barriers that propelled them into the public sphere, and into activities they had never engaged in before. Through their participation in Zionist institutions like the Young Women's Committee and the CSS Youth Department, these young women learned much more than Jewish history and culture. They practiced how to look for information, distill it, and present it to a larger audience; in many cases, young women spoke at large events that were attended not just by young people, or by Sephardim.[70] Women's roles in public events, until then, had usually included giving piano concerts, singing, or reciting poetry (which they still continued to do). As mentioned earlier, the work on behalf of the KKL involved placing tin boxes in people's homes and requesting donations. But the types of activities they engaged in as members of the Young Women's Commission reveals that they were pushing the boundaries of what was accepted behavior for (Sephardi) young women in public events, and addressing some of the concerns that had been leveled at youth in general. They also helped to dismantle the "Oriental ghetto walls," by bringing together young women from all Sephardi communities and by interacting with Ashkenazic Zionist groups like the Women's International Zionist Organization (WIZO).[71] Julieta Camji, many years later, recalled: "I shiver to think about these young adolescent girls who made history when many of the young daughters of wealthy Sephardi families only aspired to show themselves off in salons and dances."[72] These Sephardi young women were educating themselves in order to be able to educate those around them, and through their work, they transformed their own lives while also pushing women into the Sephardi public sphere.

Belonging to *pioneer* groups, and the preparation for pioneer life in particular, also helped push the boundaries of what had defined women's roles. Judit Labatón, who had married Shabetay Bahbout in order to be able to attend the mandatory training on the farm in Buenos Aires province, recalled much physical and emotional hardship. Her husband was asked to lead groups in the city, so he spent most of the week in Buenos Aires while she, alongside the other members in training, worked the land and attempted to produce something to eat. She lost a significant amount of weight—she only ate matzo meal, sent by her family, mixed in with powdered cocoa and milk from the farm cow, and the only adult who visited the farm once a month—an engineer—was afraid she would not be able to conceive children given how undernourished she was. As I interviewed her, she wondered out loud how she had been able to do what she did. "I remember taking the horse-drawn wagon alone and go to pick Shabetay up late at night when he returned from Buenos Aires," she told me. "Alone, at night, in the middle of the empty countryside . . . I don't know how we did it."[73] The experience on the farm, without her family close by, and the engagement in very hard physical labor were certainly very different from the experiences young Sephardi women were used to.

While "leading" young people might seem like a nurturing activity in line with traditional female roles, women recall not being prepared for those roles either. For example, the material covered in these pioneering groups meant that these young Sephardi women ended up discussing issues that did not pertain to Zionism, or even to Jewish history. Judit Labatón and Raquel Saal both recalled talking about topics like sex education, and free love.[74] These topics were not part of what young Sephardi women discussed with their families or even with other friends, and while they had learned those topics from their own madrijot, talking openly about these issues was a break with tradition. They also recall not being ready for many of the situations they faced. "We became the psychologists [of our *janijim*—students]," Judit Labatón remembered, "helping them navigate adolescence." Judit recalled a very young boy who climbed up the windmill tower and threatened to commit suicide during one summer camp. She stressed the fact that the leaders (including herself) did not have much formal training and were not ready to assume the responsibilities they nonetheless assumed, especially when it came to summer camps, in remote places, with little access to medical or emergency support. Looking back at what they achieved, she still marveled at how they managed to do it. Her awe and surprise at what they did reminds us of Julieta Camji's similar words when assessing the activities the Young Women's Commission had organized.

While the preparation for life in Israel on a kibbutz among Sephardim was done by these pioneer groups, the Youth Department of the CSS also contributed to breaking down the barriers between Israel and Argentina. *Hanoar Hasefaradí* sought to give voice and visibility to the work of Hejalutz and their desire to prepare young Argentine Sephardim for life in Israel as

Table 1. Translation of Hebrew words that appeared in *Hanoar Hasefaradí*, March–April 1949, 5

Moshavá	campamento
moshavá Harishoná	primer campamento
Hejalutz	el pionero
javer (javera, javerim, javerot)	compañero
jalutziut (jalutz)	pionerismo
janij (janijim)	educando
menahel (menahelim)	guía, instructor, director
jevraiut	compañerismo
hora	baile palestino
kibutz (kibutzim)	colonial colectiva
kitá	compañía
kvutzá	grupo, patrulla
schmirá	guardia
meshek	depósito
hasjhará	preparación
maskir	secretario
Tanaj	los libros de la ley
michlatim	trincheras
olé (olim)	inmigrante
dir	casa donde ordeñan las vacas
sabra	niño nativo de Eretz Israel
jaial	soldado
tiul	paseo
mishmarut	guardia
madrij	dirigente

pioneers. They also organized weekly Hebrew classes taught by Rabbi Amram Blum. *Hanoar Hasefaradí* summoned young people to "identify with your brothers in Eretz [sic] . . . and register for a Hebrew course."[75] "Hebrew interprets Jewish thought, tradition and ethics, art, political science, sociology, history, and folklore," *Hanoar Hasefaradí* pronounced. Those who attended the course "have understood the importance of learning the national language," they continued.[76] *Hanoar Hasefaradí* also included, in their pages, printed lessons about Hebrew grammar, in the hopes of bringing the language to other youth who did not join the classes. The magazine, importantly, also introduced the "language" of Zionist youth movements, whose use became a marker of belonging to these very groups (see table 1). Through these initiatives, modern Hebrew came to be understood as a language that was creating a nation out of many, and not as exclusively the language of religious practice. Learning it meant belonging to the project of nation building.

Conclusion

In the early 1930s, Sephardi Zionists imagined Eretz Israel as the land that would provide a haven to European Jews persecuted by the rampant European antisemitism. Most Sephardim, however, still saw Israel as a religious center, and many saw in Zionism an important challenge to that religious understanding. Sephardi Zionist institutions, then, focused on the need for land to save other Jews from persecution and death, but not as a national state for all Jews, and certainly not as a home for Argentine Sephardim. Contributing to the KKL became a concrete way in which the "redemption of the land" could be achieved. In the early days of Sephardi youth activism, they were tasked to contribute to that objective, but they took it upon themselves to also carry out an educational agenda that introduced the notion of a Jewish nation as central to the reconfiguration of Jewish life. The youth commission and the Young Women's Committee of the Sephardi branch of the KKL raised funds but also gave lectures about history, art, and about Israel as a place for the rebirth of Jewish life. The introduction of the principles of ḥalutziut also meant that Sephardi youth began thinking about the possibility of leaving Argentina and settling in the newly created State of Israel. The young Sephardim who founded Hejalutz and Acción Sionista learned from madrijim in Macabi but decided to create their own group in order to reach Sephardi youth. Acción Sionista was, unlike the Centro Sionista Sefaradí, and like Hejalutz, not about fundraising but about educating Sephardim about the meaning of Zionism. They carried out a vigorous educational agenda and supported the organization of the youth in the principles of ḥalutziut. The Sephardi group created in Flores, Peulah, joined other nonpolitical youth groups (like Macabi) to form Lamerjav and trained members for life in kibbutzim.

Young Sephardim hoped to break down the many barriers that existed: among different Sephardi groups, between Sephardim and Ashkenazim, among Sephardim living in different countries, between youth in Israel and in Argentina, and between traditional and modern practices. And for these objectives, the young people were imagined to be the only group that would be able to affect these departures from the past. Sephardi youth accepted the difficult tasks of bringing modern ideas about Jewry, about Hebrew, about the Jewish state, and about women's role. They tried very hard to accomplish all these objectives, and with very little institutional help, they achieved much.

Returning to the question posed by Avinoam Patt, the Argentine Sephardi youth who joined in the ranks of the groups outlined above did so out of the conviction that they had a role to play in the regeneration of the Jewish people, and in the construction of the Jewish nation. They were aware of the times they lived in, and felt they were the ones to bring Zionism closer to those in their communities. And on the way to achieving those objectives, they educated about, and modernized, not only their understanding of Israel, but changed their present in Argentina too. These Zionist youth groups did not merely create Israeli pioneers, but, perhaps more importantly, more modern Argentine Sephardim as well.

Notes

1. The phrase "out of the ghetto" was used by Shabetay Bahbout in an article that appeared in *Hanoar Hasefaradí*. In this essay, I use Sephardim to mean not exclusively Jews whose ancestors had been expelled from Spain, but all those who chose to identify themselves as such in Argentina. This included Ladino as well as Arabic speakers. Shabetay Bahbout, "La segunda moshavá del Hejalutz y los problemas de la juventud sefaradí," *Hanoar Hasefaradí*, January, February, March 1950, 13, 15.

2. Shabetay Bahbout, "Realizaciones de la moshavá del Hejalutz," *Hanoar Hasefaradí*, March–April 1949, 2.

3. Ibid.

4. Avinoam Patt, *Finding Home and Homeland: Jewish Youth and Zionism in the Aftermath of the Holocaust* (Detroit: Wayne State University Press, 2009).

5. For works documenting the aliyah of Latin Americans to Israel, see Shlomo Bar-Gil, *Juventud, visión y realidad: movimientos jalutzianos en Argentina, de Dror y Gordonia a Ijud Habonim, 1934–1973* [translation of Ne'urim, hazon u-metsiút], Colección Testimonios (Buenos Aires: Editorial Milá, 2008); Florinda Goldberg and Iosef Rozen, eds., *Los Latinoamericanos en Israel: antología de una aliá* (Buenos Aires: Contexto, 1988).

6. Silvia Schenkolewski-Kroll, "Los movimientos juveniles: una faceta carente en la historiografía sionista de la Argentina," *Judaica Latinoamericana: Estudios Histórico-Sociales* 6 (2009): 209–19.

7. Beatrice Gurwitz, *Argentine Jews in the Age of Revolt: Between the New World and the Third World* (Leiden: Brill, 2016), 136.

8. Adrián Krupnik, "Cuando camino al kibbutz vieron pasar al Che. Radicalización política y juventud judía: Argentina 1966–1976," in *Marginados y consagrados: nuevos estudios sobre la vida judía en la Argentina*, eds. Emmanuel Kahan et al. (Buenos Aires: Lumiere, 2011), 311–27.

9. Silvina Schammah Gesser and Susana Brauner, "Militancia y prácticas culturales contestatarias: las segundas generaciones de judíos procedentes del mundo árabe en la

Argentina autoritaria," *Chasqui: Revista de Literatura Latinoamericana*, Special Issue, no. 5 (2013): 45–63.

10. Mary de Rabinovich, "Idealismo y juventud," *La Luz*, February 17, 1937, 33.

11. By "assimilation," Jewish Argentines meant loosening up religious practices, like abandoning *kashrut* laws, not keeping Sabbath, and not celebrating Jewish holidays. It also meant, for many, to join in political organizations.

12. "La juventud tiene que adoptar una posición de lucha para definirse," *Mundo Israelita*, April 19, 1941, 2.

13. Julieta Camji, "El judío argentino debe luchar por la libertad y los ideales sionistas," *Mundo Israelita*, June 28, 1941, 6.

14. Ibid.

15. Bahbout, "Realizaciones de la moshavá del Hejalutz," *Hanoar Hasefaradí*, March–April 1949, 2.

16. Bahbout, "La segunda moshavá del Hejalutz y los problemas de la juventud sefaradí," *Hanoar Hasefaradí*, January, February, March 1950, 13, 15.

17. Adriana Brodsky, *Sephardi, Jewish, Argentine: Community and National Identity, 1880–1960* (Bloomington: Indiana University Press, 2016), especially chap. 2.

18. Nissim Elnecavé, "Sionismo de colectas o colectas para el sionismo?" *La Luz*, May 1, 1942, 205–6.

19. CSS Minute books, May 5, 1940.

20. CSS Youth Department, Minute Books, January 4, 1945.

21. Adriana Brodsky, "'Miss Sefaradí,' and 'Queen Esther': Sephardim, Zionism, and Ethnic and National Identities in Argentina, 1933–1971," *Estudios Interdisciplinarios de América Latina y el Caribe* (2012): 35–60.

22. Comité Organizador de la Convención de la Juventud Sefaradí, Minute Books, June 12, 1945. Moisés Camji personal archive, Buenos Aires.

23. "Juventud Sionista Sefaradí," *La Luz*, August 30, 1940, 425.

24. "Acto cultural conmemorativo de la Declaración Balfour," *La Luz*, November 15, 1940, 567. These two Buenos Aires neighborhoods, Flores and Colegiales, housed two Sephardi congregations (and their various organizations) from two distinct geographical origins: Damascus and Rhodes respectively. The Balfour Declaration (1917) indicated British support for the "establishment of a Jewish nation" in Palestine.

25. Theodor Herzl (1860–1904) was the founder of (political) Zionism.

26. See invitations sent by the CSS Youth Department, October, November, December, 1941, Moisés Camji personal archive.

27. CSS, Minute Books, May 5, and May 19, 1940.

28. These blue tin boxes were everywhere; people would contribute coins to the fundraising effort of the KKL. See Michael Berkowitz, *Zionist Culture and West European Jewry Before the First World War* (Cambridge: Cambridge University Press, 1993), chap. 7.

29. Regina Menahem speech on November 25, 1945, at the 1st Sephardi Regional Convention of the KKL. Regina Menahem was the President of the Young Women's Committee. Moisés Camji personal archive.

30. See "Registro de Asistencias de la Comisión de Señoritas del KKL," June–December 1945. Moisés Camji personal archive.

31. Ibid.
32. Invitation to event, December 17, 1946. Moisés Camji personal archive.
33. See note 28.
34. "Discurso de la Srta. Regina Menahem," *Israel*, December 4, 1945, 19.
35. Ibid.
36. Nissim Elnecavé, "Sefaradim en la epopeya jalútzica," *La Luz*, April 1, 1942, 132–34.
37. "Una organización para la juventud sefaradí," *Israel*, March 12, 1948, 20.
38. Another institution was founded among Sephardim, the Organización Sionista Sefaradí (OSSA), which more openly supported ḥalutziut, but not exclusively Sephardi groups. "La Organización Sionista Sefaradí realizó una acción para los jalutsim," *Nueva Sión*, December 31, 1948, 6.
39. They joined Gordonia in 1952 after merging with another Sephardi Zionist Youth group from Montevideo (Uruguay) early in 1952. See Bar-Gil, *Juventud, visión y realidad*, 94.
40. Mapam, originally Marxist-Zionist, was founded in 1948, and it represented the Kibbutz Artzi movement; Mapai, was a center-left party originally founded in 1930, linked to the Kibbutz Hameuḥad movement.
41. "Excursión a la primera moshava sefaradí," *Hanoar Hasefaradí*, January–February 1949, 3, 7.
42. Macabi Sports Club had been founded in Buenos Aires in 1930. Hano'ar Hatzioni was a youth movement founded in Europe in 1926.
43. Interview with Iosef Duek, December 2011.
44. "Primera haflagah del Departamento de Juventud del Centro Sionista Sefardí. Una jornada feliz," *Hanoar Hasefaradí*, July 1948, 7.
45. Ibid. The "Hatikva" was the unofficial anthem of Israel until 2004.
46. "Excursión a la primera moshava sefaradí," *Hanoar Hasefaradí*, January–February 1949, 3, 7.
47. "Primera haflagah del Departamento de Juventud del Centro Sionista Sefardí," *Hanoar Hasefaradí*, July 1948.
48. Ibid.
49. Rebeca Memun, "Del diario de una javerá de la primera moshava Sefaradí: impresiones de mi primera mishmarut," *Hanoar Hasefaradí*, January–February 1949, 13–14.
50. Bahbout, "Realizaciones de la Moshavá del Hejalutz," *Hanoar Hasefaradí*, March–April 1949.
51. "Partieron para Israel los futuros madrijim," *Hanoar Hasefaradí*, June 1949, 8 and 15. This program was started in 1946 by the Jewish Agency, the organization created to promote and support Zionism and aliyah.
52. Nelson Pilosof, "La juventud sionista Tejezakna," *La Luz*, December 3, 1948.
53. Ibid.
54. Ibid.
55. Bar-Gil, *Juventud, visión y realidad*, 94.
56. New Zionist groups among Sephardim would form in late 1950s and early 1960s.
57. "Asamblea general ordinaria en Acción Sionista," *La Luz*, December 31, 1948.
58. "El sector sefaradí," *Nueva Sión*, April 9, 1948, 3.

59. Ibid.

60. Moisés Camji, "A 100 años de sionismo: importante activismo de la comunidad sefaradí de la Argentina." Unpublished manuscript, n.d. Moisés Camji personal archive.

61. The DAIA is the Delegación de Asociaciones Israelitas Argentina, the umbrella association that represents all Jewish institutions in the country. It was founded in the 1930s to confront the rise of antisemitism.

62. "Asamblea general ordinaria en 'Acción Sionista,'" *La Luz*, December 31, 1948.

63. "Un lúcido e interesante acto con la presencia de los madrijim Victoria Saal y Simon Dayan, se cumplió en Acción Sionista en su nueva sede," *La Luz*, September 29, 1950.

64. Interview with Raquel Saal, July 2013.

65. Lamerjav was created in 1949, and brought together four groups (which included Ashkenazim and Sephardim) to prepare for aliyah. They decided not to become affiliated with any political party.

66. The two groups which had split came together again in the mid-1960s.

67. I thank Rafael Arazi for composing a list of mixed marriages.

68. Cited in Diana Epstein, "Los judeo-marroquíes en Buenos Aires: pautas matrimoniales 1875–1910," *Estudios Interdisciplinarios de América Latina y el Caribe* 6, no. 1 (1995): 131n42. I thank Isaac Kaufman for this insight.

69. Judit recalls that there were single Ashkenazi young women during the training year, but no other Sephardi women. Interview with Judit Labatón, Or Haner, July 2013.

70. Speech delivered by Regina Menahem at the Primera Convención Regional del KKL, November 25, 1945.

71. Written testimony, Julieta Camji, July 1992, Moisés Camji personal archive. A Sephardi section within the WIZO-Argentina was founded in 1948; most members of WIZO were Ashkenazi. Yiddish was the language used by many during their meetings, especially during these decades.

72. Ibid.

73. Interview with Judit Labatón, July 2013.

74. Interview with Judit Labatón and interview with Raquel Saal, July 2013.

75. "Javer: Aprende tu idioma!" *Hanoar Hasefaradí*, January, February, March, 1950.

76. "Actividades del departamento de juventud del CSS," *Hanoar Hasefaradí*, July 1948, 8.

Bibliography

Primary Sources

Archives and Minute Books

Centro Sionista Sefaradí (CSS) Minute Books (Buenos Aires)
Isaac Kaufman personal archive (Buenos Aires)
Moisés Camji personal archive (Buenos Aires)

Interviews and Testimonies
Interview with Iosef Duek, December 2011
Interview with Judit Labatón, July 2013
Interview with Raquel Saal, July 2013
Written testimony, Julieta Camji, July 1992

Periodicals
Hanoar Hasefaradí, 1948–1950
Israel, 1945, 1948.
La Luz, 1937, 1940, 1942, 1948, 1950
Mundo Israelita, 1941
Nueva Sión, 1948

Secondary Sources

Bar-Gil, Shlomo. *Juventud, visión y realidad: movimientos jalutzianos en Argentina, de Dror y Gordonia a Ijud Habonim, 1934–1973*. [Translation of Ne'urim, hazon u-metsiút.] Colección Testimonios. Buenos Aires: Editorial Milá, 2008.

Berkowitz, Michael. *Zionist Culture and West European Jewry Before the First World War*. Cambridge: Cambridge University Press, 1993.

Brodsky, Adriana. "'Miss Sefaradí,' and 'Queen Esther': Sephardim, Zionism, and Ethnic and National Identities in Argentina, 1933–1971." *Estudios Interdisciplinarios de América Latina y el Caribe* (2012): 35–60.

——. *Sephardi, Jewish, Argentine: Community and National Identity, 1880–1960*. Bloomington: Indiana University Press, 2016.

Camji, Moisés. "A 100 años de sionismo: importante activismo de la comunidad sefaradí de la Argentina." Unpublished manuscript.

Epstein, Diana. "Los judeo-marroquíes en Buenos Aires: pautas matrimoniales 1875–1910." *Estudios Interdisciplinarios de América Latina y el Caribe* 6, no. 1 (1995): 113–33.

Goldberg, Florinda, and Iosef Rozen, eds. *Los Latinoamericanos en Israel: antología de una aliá*. Buenos Aires: Contexto, 1988.

Gurwitz, Beatrice. *Argentine Jews in the Age of Revolt: Between the New World and the Third World*. Leiden: Brill, 2016.

Krupnik, Adrián. "Cuando camino al kibbutz vieron pasar al Che. Radicalización política y juventud judía: Argentina 1966–1976." In *Marginados y consagrados: nuevos estudios sobre la vida judía en la Argentina*, edited by Emmanuel Kahan, Laura Schenquer, Damián Setton, Alejandro Dujovne, 311–27. Buenos Aires: Lumiere, 2011.

Patt, Avinoam. *Finding Home and Homeland: Jewish Youth and Zionism in the Aftermath of the Holocaust*. Detroit: Wayne State University Press, 2009.

Schammah Gesser, Silvina, and Susana Brauner. "Militancia y prácticas culturales contestarias: las segundas generaciones de judíos procedentes del mundo árabe en la Argentina autoritaria." *Chasqui: Revista de Literatura Latinoamericana*. Special Issue no. 5 (2013): 45–63.

Schenkolewski-Kroll, Silvia. "Los movimientos juveniles: una faceta carente en la historiografía sionista de la Argentina." *Judaica Latinoamericana: Estudios Histórico-Sociales* 6 (2009): 209–19.

11

Defying Traditional *Shtadlanut*

Jewish Self-Defense in Argentina

RAANAN REIN

On June 8, 1967, in the midst of the Six-Day War, several hundreds of people gathered in front of the Syrian Embassy in Buenos Aires. They began shouting, exclaiming against the "American-Jewish plot, Zionism and its collaborators in Argentina," and delivered rousing calls such as "Death to the Jews." The members of the Jewish Self-Defense Organization in Buenos Aires (known by its Hebrew name Irgún, which means organization) did not want to forfeit the field to the supporters of Arab countries and hurried to confront the protesters, several of whom were injured during the confrontation. "The war [in the Middle East] had arrived in Buenos Aires," the headline called out in the popular weekly *Así*.[1]

It was the first and last time in the 1960s that members of the semi-underground organization embarked on an open activity. The press coverage of the protest, including the publication of photographs of a few of the members, caused panic among the Jewish activists, who swiftly returned to patterns of activity developed in the early 1960s. Their targets now included not only antisemitic extreme right-wing organizations, but also groups supported by the Arab League delegation in Argentina.

The Israeli victory in the 1967 war evoked great enthusiasm among Jewish-Argentines and strengthened their self-confidence, as well as the Zionist identity of many of them.[2] Yet, as far as self-defense activity (instructed and motivated by Israeli officials) is concerned, the Six-Day War was not a turning point but only the beginning of a new stage in existing processes. In this regard, self-defense activities and their mutations were based, to a large extent, upon local needs and circumstances dictated on the one hand by the

Argentine national agenda, and on the other hand, by attitudes toward Jews manifested by different groups within Argentine society.

The rise of Juan Perón in the mid-forties, a few months after the end of World War II; his overthrow in September 1955 in a military coup, led prominently by Catholic nationalists; the kidnapping of Nazi war criminal Adolf Eichmann in May 1960 by agents of Israel's national intelligence agency, the Mossad; waves of antisemitism engendered by this abduction in the following years—all these should be considered as important milestones in the development and expansion of the Jewish Self-Defense Organization, much more than the Israeli military achievement in 1967.[3]

This chapter briefly traces the origins of Jewish self-defense in Argentina and the Jewish and Argentine ideological climate in which they developed, as well as the organization's structure, methods of recruitment of young men and women, and the preparation and training experienced by these young members, especially in the camp known as Macabilandia in the Province of Córdoba. My discussion accentuates the unique characteristics of the organization in Argentina, especially when compared with the Jewish Defense League, which operated at the time in the United States under the leadership of Rabbi Meir Kahane. Other Latin American cases, especially those of Venezuela, Brazil, Uruguay, and Mexico, highlight the fact that in Argentina the Jewish self-defense activities started earlier than in other countries of the Western Hemisphere, including the United States; that they were more extended in scope and expanded from the nation's capital to the periphery; and that their longevity was impressive.[4]

By focusing on the 1960s, I would like to emphasize the context of the "Youth Rebellion" that characterized the Americas at the time. In the 1960s, Argentina witnessed the youth's defiance against the adult world, its values and notions, that were perceived as mundane, dull, and normative.[5] It is in this context that the decision of Jewish youngsters to adopt a different approach to the struggle against antisemitism might be better understood. On the Argentine case, such expressions of youth rebellion became especially evident in the rising "Rock Nacional" of the same years and were reflected as well in increasing political involvement and violence.[6] The young generation in general, and the students among them in particular, became key actors in 1960s Argentine politics.

As active participants in the Self-Defense Organization, young Jews were able to construct their own separate identity, which was to a certain extent autonomous, personal, and creative. Their activities allowed them to highlight their Jewish masculinity, and also encouraged them to operate outside of accepted social norms, as well as to adopt an approach that challenged existing communal leadership demands. Many of the discussions as to the strategies to be adopted in the face of antisemitic violence are common to all Jewish communities in the Americas, north and south, past and present. These young Jewish men and women rejected *shtadlanut* (traditional lobbying of Jewish leaders) or the efforts to influence public opinion and turn it against antisemites. They opted for self-defense tactics.

"It's a Real Underground"

In late 1963, Abba Gefen, a diplomat at the Israeli embassy in Buenos Aires, was invited to dinner by Antonio M. Kristoffersen, the head of the Africa and Near East division of the Argentine foreign ministry. Kristoffersen wanted to discuss several matters "that might disturb relations between the two countries." Specifically, he referred to "military training" that Jewish youths were receiving in camps in the province of Buenos Aires under the supervision of Israeli instructors. He added that the camps changed location frequently and Hebrew was often spoken in them. "It's a real underground," said the Argentine official.[7] At the Foreign Ministry in Jerusalem, the report was received with much concern. The Israeli embassy was asked "to equip Kristoffersen with a detailed description of this new training in Argentina . . . above all to clear away his thought of the existence of an Israeli underground in Argentina."[8]

Argentine authorities' concern was aroused by the formation in Buenos Aires of Jewish self-defense groups that had resolved to confront the provocations of antisemitic, nationalist right-wing bullies. Allegations of a purported Jewish underground in Argentina were echoed in publications and speeches by both Arab and extreme right-wing groups. Thus, Hussein Triki, the representative of the Arab League in Buenos Aires, warned that "some twenty-six training camps for Israeli military personnel are operating on Argentine territory, and even the Spanish language is forbidden there."[9] The antisemitic campaign launched by the Peronist congressional deputy, Juan Carlos Cornejo Linares, included similar accusations.[10] The suspicion that young Jewish-Argentines were being trained by Zionist "agents" became an obsession for many Argentine military officers, and Jews kidnapped during the brutal military dictatorship of the 1970s were interrogated time and again about their alleged ties to "International Zionism."[11]

Such expressions of concern were the result of Jewish self-defense groups' activity in the 1960s and the beginning of the 1970s. The central questions to discuss are what their contribution and efficacy were, if any, at reducing violent expressions of antisemitism throughout the second half of the 1960s and the early 1970s. More specifically, what was the contribution, if any, of this struggle against antisemitism, racism, and xenophobia for the creation of a pluralistic, democratic Argentine society? What was Israel's role in these quasi-military groups? What sorts of actions did the members of these groups undertake?

Current historiography has hitherto steered clear of the subject, presumably fearing possible damage to Israeli-Argentine relations or to the image and status of Jews in Argentina.[12] Not only scholars, but community leaders and former members of Jewish self-defense groups have also preferred to avoid a discussion that might be exploited in some way by antisemites. Journalist Guga Kogan, a past member of the Self-Defense Organization, had considered writing a book on the subject but gave up on the project, following pressure from his fellow veterans in Argentina and Israel.[13] Mauricio (Tata) Furmanski, who had played a key role in Jewish self-defense in Latin America for over twenty years, left me a copy of his unpublished novelized memoir on condition that I would not use it as long as he was alive.[14] No wonder that most of the people I interviewed for this chapter preferred to be identified only by their first names or initials.

"We Want to be a Commando of Blood and Iron"

Only in fictional works do we find any clear reference to the Jewish self-defense groups and the role Israelis played in training young Jewish-Argentines. The following paragraph, for example, is taken from a short story by Hilel Resnitzky, published in Hebrew in 2006 under the title "Call Me Juan." The speakers are Yonatan—a Jewish-Argentine who studied Hebrew in Israel in 1960 and later returned there—and his cousin Akiva, who made *aliyah* (immigration to Israel) and has now come back to Buenos Aires as a *shaliaḥ* (emissary):

> Yonatan unfolded a strange story that hardly fitted his mild demeanor. He was in contact with a Jewish underground group, an Argentine version of the New York Jewish Defense League. While speaking, Yonatan demurred: "God forbid, not right-wingers. You know, here in Buenos Aires, we are all leftists, even Betar. Jewish young people are afraid of antisemites. They want to fight back. They want action."[15]

Later in the story one of the young people, Pablo, explains, "For now we are just a rag-tag commando, and in the future we want to be an iron commando." His friend Eduardo corrects him: "We want to be a commando of blood and iron."[16]

The Argentine government's concerns about Jewish underground activity were exaggerated, though not groundless. Likewise, concerns of the organized Jewish community about possible pogroms led by right-wing groups were excessive. In contrast to the opinion expressed by former members of these organizations, I believe that the Jewish self-defense organizations did not play an important role in deterring antisemitism during the 1960s and 1970s. It was the decision of various governments whether to confront (or not) the nationalist thugs. Self-defense organizations often shared the growing tendency to employ violence in order to promote political goals.

At times, these young Jewish organizations, to a certain extent, mirrored the antisemitic hooligans of Tacuara (Movimiento Nacionalista Tacuara), which first appeared in Argentina in 1957, or any other nationalist right-wing organizations in neighboring countries.[17] The lines separating different youth movements, marked with distinct ideologies in Latin America in general and Argentina of that time in particular, were not always clear; at times they were utterly vague. Accordingly, it is no surprise that several members of the Jewish self-defense groups found themselves, during the 1970s, operating under left-wing non-Jewish armed organizations. As mentioned by one of my interviewees, residing in Argentina: "a considerable number of members who had joined the self-defense groups later moved to the armed organizations."[18]

"Every Jew a 22"

The reference to Meir Kahane's Jewish Defense League in Resnitzky's story is interesting. In the late 1960s, Kahane established vigilante groups to protect New York's elderly Jews from local street gangs and hoodlums. Later on, he sponsored programs to teach Jews self-defense and the use of firearms. The Jewish Defense League (JDL) popularized the slogan, "Every Jew a 22" (referring to a 22-caliber gun for self-defense).[19] However, Jewish-Argentine self-defense groups were very different from Kahane's league. The demographic basis of what became known in Argentina as the Irgún, or sometimes Bitajón (security in Hebrew), was politically, ideologically, and perhaps also socially, more heterogeneous than the JDL.[20]

The Irgún's relations with the Jewish establishment were entirely different from the JDL set up. The organization also lacked Kahane-like charismatic leadership. Moreover, Israeli instructors played a crucial role in it. Apparently, Israel allowed itself to conduct certain operations in 1960s Argentina, through its embassy in Buenos Aires, that at the time would have been inconceivable in the United States. Judith Laikin Elkin has correctly noted Latin American Jews' reliance "on Israel for foreign policy leadership and defense."[21] This was especially true of Argentina's Jewish establishment from the 1950s onward. In this context, the Irgún can be viewed as a hybrid violent organization that mobilized an Argentine-born ethnic constituency seeking to improve its status in Argentina and strengthen its commitment to the real or imagined homeland of Israel.[22]

The organization of Jewish self-defense had first and foremost a psychological and moral significance. It was part of an effort to change the traditional stereotype of the Jew as a passive victim and send a clear message to the thugs of the extreme right that they could not injure Jews without paying a price for their acts, even under indulgent governments. It was also a function of contemporary identity politics in a transitional period in the history of Argentine immigrant society, a period that featured constant discussions of the ambiguous meanings of Jewishness and *Argentinidad*.[23]

Revisionist Zionism and the Fascination with Military Power

Self-defense activities were another way to strengthen Zionist attitudes among Jewish youth and encourage emigration to Israel. In this context, Holocaust themes and images (especially the Warsaw Ghetto uprising) were also used to inspire political engagement. Criticizing what they saw as the tragic passivity of Jews during the Holocaust, the young Jews in the Irgún were in fact saying, "never again." Participation in Jewish self-defense groups certainly strengthened Sephardic youngsters' consciousness of the magnitude and significance of the Shoah.[24]

Many Jewish young people—of all political and ideological hues—in both the United States and Argentina, were apparently much influenced by the Revisionist Zionist thinker Vladimir (Ze'ev) Jabotinsky, who, during the first decades of the twentieth century, warned of the dangers facing Jews in the diaspora and called for the establishment of a sovereign Jewish state in Palestine. He envisioned a new type of Jew: proud, generous, and fierce.[25] Born in Odessa in 1880, he founded the Jewish Self-Defense Organization there in 1903. As the prospects of additional pogroms increased, the Jewish Self-Defense Organization aimed to safeguard Jewish communities throughout Russia.

With Joseph Trumpeldor, Jabotinsky cofounded the Jewish Legion of the British army in World War I to fight against the Ottomans who then controlled Palestine. After he was discharged from the British Army in September 1919, he started training Jews in warfare and the use of small arms in Palestine. Jabotinsky died of a heart attack on August 3, 1940, while visiting a Jewish self-defense camp in Hunter, New York, that was run by Betar, the Revisionist Zionist youth movement founded in 1923 in Riga, Latvia.[26]

Menachem Begin, Jabotinsky's closest protégé, continued the latter's trajectory, through the Irgun Tzvai Leumi (aka Etzel), which struggled against British rule in Palestine in the mid-1940s. Begin's book, *The Revolt*, also had wide influence. The book was translated into Spanish and published in Buenos Aires in 1951 with a hand-written letter of Begin addressed to the Argentine readers.[27] Although Begin's political party Herut remained a minority in community institutions, the Israeli leader and his struggle against the British fascinated many Jewish youngsters in Argentina. Begin also visited Argentina more than any other senior Israeli politician. It is no coincidence that by 1962 Jewish defense groups in Argentina called themselves the "Irgún."[28]

Argentine Jews' personal sense of security had been undermined in the early 1960s as a result of a wave of antisemitism, following the kidnapping of Adolph Eichmann.[29] This wave of intimidation and violence against Jews, which continued well into the mid-1960s, took place under two democratically elected civilian governments: the Arturo Frondizi (1958–1962) and Arturo Illia (1964–1966) administrations, with a brief interlude under José María Guido, who was installed in the presidential palace by the generals of the armed forces. Both the Frondizi and Illia presidencies, despite their shortcomings, were a source of great hope for multitudes of liberal-minded Argentines who believed in democracy, including many Jewish-Argentines. The two presidents became symbols of a reformist era led by a representative government that enforced the rule of law, tolerance, civil liberties (including intellectual freedom), and a clear separation of church and state. The violent activities of the nationalists challenged these administrations and these values as much as they posed a threat to the Jewish community.

At the same time, the antisemitic incidents created a sense of solidarity among the beleaguered Jews and prompted, among other actions, two initiatives of particular significance to the Jewish community. First, Jewish parents joined forces to set up the first in a series of nationally accredited private Jewish day schools where pupils would not be vulnerable to antisemitic attacks. The result was the Tarbut School in Buenos Aires, founded in late July 1960. In these schools, the children were instructed in both the required Argentine curriculum and Jewish religion and culture. By opting for the name Tarbut (culture), the founders linked themselves to both Zionism and Jewish tradition. The Tarbut movement of Zionist, secular, Hebrew language schools flourished in interwar Poland and, on the eve of World War II, had tens of thousands of students in more than 250 institutions. The second initiative taken by Jewish-Argentines was the formation of Jewish self-defense organizations, initially in the capital, where approximately 80 percent of Argentine Jews made their home.

Never Again: Memories of the Shoah

Jewish self-defense groups began as the spontaneous initiatives of youngsters who decided to teach themselves judo, boxing, and other combat techniques in order to challenge the provocations of the nationalist hooligans. The 1930s had witnessed the growing influence and activity of right-wing nationalist, xenophobic, and antisemitic groups. On several occasions, at least, young Jews showed themselves unwilling to adopt passive behaviors.[30] During the election campaign of 1945–1946, many Jews feared attacks by nationalist groups who were among the supporters of presidential candidate Colonel Juan Perón. This, according to Daniel Finkelstein, led to the creation of self-defense groups, in which he participated. The news from Europe as to the magnitude of the Holocaust, says, Finkelstein, "certainly influenced us as well."[31] In La Plata, the capital city of the province of Buenos Aires, the local branch of Delegación de Asociaciones Israelitas Argentinas or DAIA, the umbrella organization of Argentina's organized community, gave a group of young Jews guns so that they could defend Jewish institutions from possible attacks by the Alianza Libertadora Nacionalista (ALN).[32]

After Perón had been in power for a few months, however, Jews lost most of their fears for their personal safety, as the president gradually adopted a clear policy against antisemitism and began to cultivate close ties with the newly established State of Israel. During the conflict between the Perón government and the Catholic Church in 1954–1955, anti-Peronist groups tended to identify Jews with the regime and used antisemitism in their propaganda. This trend was even more pronounced following the failed coup d'état of June 1955. As antisemitic manifestations grew, the Foreign Ministry in Jerusalem decided that the situation in Argentina called for aid to the local Jewish community. Prime Minister David Ben-Gurion sent the head of the Mossad, Isser Harel, to Buenos Aires to help the Jews there prepare to defend themselves if necessary.[33]

Carlos Perelman, who changed his name to Asher Porat following his immigration to Israel and later became a well-known physician, offered the following periodization for the development of Jewish self-defense in Argentina: spontaneous initiatives during the years 1939–1952; the "semi-organized" phase of 1952–1960, in the shadow of the growing polarization of Argentine society around Peronism; and the organized stage, which started with Eichmann's kidnapping and ended in 1976, with the military coup d'état of 24 March.[34] Porat himself first participated in self-defense training, together with a group of 50–70 Jewish youngsters, in a summer camp in the province of Buenos Aires in 1952. The youngsters saw themselves as the Jewish partisans who had fought against the Nazis. By the mid-1950s, these youngsters were already guarding Jewish institutions in the capital, as well as the building of the Israeli embassy. At this point, they were trained by Mossad agent, Alexander Eliraz, former Israeli champion in marksmanship.[35]

By the early 1960s, Jewish groups involving both Ashkenazi and Sephardi youth, were looking for ways to fight back against antisemitism. The new Irgún, quietly but heavily supported by Israel, was ready to meet this need. It was divided into separate intelligence and operational wings, each run independently. According to one of our interviewees, the operational wing included the youth movement battalion, with a unit for each separate youth movement; the club battalion; and the "unaffiliated youth" battalion, designed mostly to attract working-class Jewish youngsters with limited ties to Judaism or Zionism.[36]

Giora Divon's (formerly Jorge Dujovne) testimony is of particular importance. Divon, born in the Province of Entre Ríos, graduated from a high school in Rosario and was a member of the Zionist youth movement Dror Ḥalutz. He was eighteen years old when he arrived in Jerusalem, in 1953/54, where he attended the Makhon Lemadrikhei Ḥutz Laaretz (Institute of Jewish Diaspora Councilors), founded in 1946. The program included seminars in Jewish history, Zionist thought, the Bible, and Hebrew lessons, as well as physical training that took place in a camp based at the Negev area, involving self-defense training and the use of weapons.[37]

Upon his return to Buenos Aires, he maintained his ties with the Zionist movement, even after he was drafted into military service in the Argentine Navy. As a soldier in compulsory military service, he participated in the military uprising led by admiral Isaac Rojas aimed to overthrow President Perón in September 1955. In 1957 he emigrated to Israel. Divon joined Kibbutz Hukuk near the Sea of Galilee, completed a shortened military service, and was put in charge of the banana plantations. Following Eichmann's kidnapping and its subsequent wave of antisemitism, he returned to Argentina to assist the Jewish community due to the "great danger hovering over the Jews."[38]

At first, kibbutz members were reluctant to approve Divon's departure, but a special meeting held in Hukuk's dining hall, which Divon did not attend, took the opposite decision. Zivia Lubetkin, a leading figure in the Warsaw Ghetto uprising, was sent to the meeting by the Kibbutz Hameuḥad leadership. In a fiery speech, Lubetkin stressed that another Shoah was endangering Jews in Argentina; such concern was probably shared at the time by the leading figures of the kibbutz movement, such as Meir Yaari and Abba Kobner. Thus, Hukuk's members ultimately were convinced that no other choice remained but to enable Divon's departure to Argentina.

Divon arrived in Buenos Aires in March 1961 and shortly afterward was invited to meet with the Israeli ambassador Yosef Avidar, former head of the Haganah, the main Zionist paramilitary organization of the Yishuv in Mandatory Palestine. After the establishment of Israel in 1948, the Haganah became the core of Israel's Defense Forces (IDF) and Avidar served as one of the IDF's first major-generals. It was decided that due to the increasing number of reported antisemitic incidents, a team would be formed to coordinate the community's self-defense activity. The responsibility for all the intelligence work was assigned to Divon, along with Miguel Moguilevski and two others. Israeli *shliḥim* (emissaries) now worked alongside Jewish-Argentine activists, in coordination with Israeli diplomats, Mossad agents (one of them was Yehuda Harari, IDF colonel and one of the founders of the Paratrooper Division), and several leaders of the local community. At first, they used to meet in an office located in the Israeli embassy in Buenos Aires, or at the DAIA office in the building of the Asociación Mutual Israelita Argentina or AMIA. Later on, they began to gather in private houses in order not to overly emphasize the relations of the self-defense groups with official Israeli representatives in Argentina or the leadership of the organized community.

Divon's first responsibility was to develop and distribute a questionnaire to as many young Jews as possible. Within a short time, he created a database that included the details of 600 to 800 young Jewish-Argentines, who began gathering and communicating information to the organization. Such information could have arrived spontaneously or as part of a mission initiated by Divon, aimed to obtain a clearer picture of the various antisemitic activities within Argentine society. Several of these young Jews infiltrated the ranks of extreme right-wing organizations.

Recruitment

The Irgún's center of operations (which the activists called *el maté*, from the Hebrew word for headquarters) included a senior representative of the organized Jewish community (DAIA), the two people in charge of intelligence and operations, respectively, a representative of the provinces, an administrator, and sometimes a representative of the Israeli embassy, often known among the organization's activists as the *gallego*.[39]

Most militants in the Irgún came from the Zionist youth movements, with Hashomer Hatza'ir and its Mordechai Anielewicz Division playing the key role. However, Jewish self-defense groups were not limited to these bastions of middle-class, male Ashkenazi Jews. They also included Sephardi youngsters. E. S., for example, was a Bitajón militant in the community of Jewish immigrants from Aleppo, having been involved at the age of 16 or 17, following the antisemitic attack on Jewish Graciela Sirota by Tacuara thugs who tattooed a swastika on her chest. E. S. was the first Sephardi *madrikh* (instructor) in the organization. He was in charge of self-defense training and preparations for possible aliyah at the Club Oriente. He later trained and supervised several other Sephardi *madrikhim* (instructors), each of them in charge of 8–10 people. According to E. S., many young Sephardi people gathered information for the organization. Since many of them did not fit the Ashkenazi stereotype, they were able to infiltrate nationalist associations more easily. E. S. emphasizes that the Irgún and its activities helped unite diverse Sephardi communities in the interior provinces of Argentina, previously self-segregated by place of origin.[40]

The various cells of the Irgún included young women in their late teens. According to E. D., who was recruited in 1965 at the age of 18, almost one-third of the members in the unit in which he served were women.[41] Several members of the Irgún came from the lower socioeconomic classes. P. was from a home in which Jewish culture meant very little. He did not go to school, and after his father died, he helped support his family by selling ice cream in the street, near the Macabi clubhouse. In his words, "Someone took me to a course for instructors at the Jewish sports club. There, after three months, someone came before us and asked, 'which of you is capable of defending Jewish honour? If you are up for it, someone will contact you.'" Two weeks later, P. was assigned to a self-defense course.[42]

Training

> Some thirty young people, all from good Jewish homes, stood in two rows facing each other, waiting for a signal from the instructor. When they heard the command, each boy in turn would slap his partner in the face, and the recipient was supposed to take the blow without flinching. Then they switched places, so that the second boy hit the first. So went the first lesson in the Irgún's training course. The objective: to forge character and especially to eliminate the natural fear of being hit.
>
> The course would end after several weeks, when the trainees had been taught to defend themselves assertively, taking advantage of their opponents' weak points. The trainees were supposed to understand that these exercises were not James Bond games played for fun. The drills were intended to defend the Jewish community by instilling a powerful, violent, non-intellectual style.[43]

Thus began Guga Kogan's newspaper article, which was based on his personal experience and conversations with former members of the organization. Another ex-member, Esther, told me about drills after which she had to powder her face heavily to hide the bruises. [44]

Eli, for his part, emphasized the interrogation drills they underwent. The instructors would show up unexpectedly for different activities, take some of the trainees, and begin to interrogate them, to check whether their cover story held up. They were also given practice in inventing cover stories. The trainees were paired off and given five minutes to invent a believable cover story on which they would be interrogated. Some of the people I talked to describe the sense of operating in the underground that they experienced because of the way they were divided and kept in ignorance of the real names of the other young people in the group.

S. B.'s story is interesting in this respect. As a 16- or 17-year-old member of Hashomer Hatza'ir, he was recruited at the end of the 1950s by someone from the Jewish Agency. His first mission was to take a bus to the Paraguayan border and back and report on the trip to check whether there were police barricades or any special incidents on the way.[45] In retrospect he guessed that his trip had constituted part of the preparations for Eichmann's kidnapping, an investigation of possible escape routes.

He later took several courses in Argentina, including hand-to-hand combat, marksmanship, and the use of firebombs. In 1963, he went to Israel for further training in skills including physical fitness, marksmanship, breaking up demonstrations, and planning security operations. M. P., too—one of the few who received a salary from the Irgún—was sent in 1963 for advanced training in Israel.[46] A native of Bahía Blanca, he had been in charge of self-defense groups in the province of Buenos Aires before joining the Mordechai Anielewicz Division in the federal capital. From our interviews with former activists, it appears that dozens of young Argentines were sent to Israel for training throughout the 1960s. The instructor training program in Argentina took about a year. Candidates were then selected from among its graduates to go to Israel for an additional four-month course.

In the various camps held in Argentina—for example, the camp in the mountains in the province of Córdoba, operating since 1944 as a summer camp for Jewish youth and known as Macabilandia—trainees were often injured in the course of their maneuvers. Here and there I heard rumors of the brutality of these drills. For example, M. P. described how one of the trainers from Israel wanted the recruits to kill cats in a bag to acclimatize them to the experience of killing. "There were a lot of unhinged people, because the situation lent itself to that," M. P. explained.

Conclusion

The 2019 American Jewish Committee (AJC) survey of American Jews on antisemitism in America indicated the increase in antisemitism over the years 2014–2019 and that 88 percent of American Jews believe that antisemitism was a problem in the United States.[47] Far beyond the tragic attacks in Pittsburgh and Poway that have been in the limelight in late 2018 and the beginning of 2019, antisemitic incidents have become part of the social experiences of many Jews.

Echoing the concerns expressed by Jewish-Argentines in the 1960s, Bari Weiss asked in an op-ed in the *New York Times:* "What if the story of the Jews in America wasn't a straight line, but a pendulum, which had swung one-way and was now swinging back into the darkness of the Old World we were sure we'd left behind?"[48] After discussing various strategies to fight antisemitism, she concluded: "The long arc of Jewish history makes it clear that the only way to fight is by waging an affirmative battle for who we are. By entering the fray for our values, for our ideas, for our ancestors, for our families, and for the generations that will come after us." But the debate as to how to react to antisemitic violence continues in both Argentina as well as in the United States, where more than a few Jewish youngsters look with admiration at Israel's Jewish army and at Israeli characters in American cinema such as Zohan Dvir, the counterterrorist army commander played by Adam Sandler in the 2008 comedy *You Don't Mess with the Zohan*, or superwoman Gal Gadot, the Israeli actress and model, granddaughter of a Holocaust survivor who had served in the Israeli Defense Forces as combat fitness instructor. She first played a role in *Fast and Furious* (2009) and later became Wonder Woman (2017).

Concerns about how to react to antisemitic violence have arisen at times in Latin America as well, provoking discussions among Jews as to the proper ways to combat such violence. Of the possible repertoire of reactions to racism, xenophobia, and antisemitism, the young men and women of Argentina discussed here opted for an aggressive self-defense with its inherent dangers of mirroring violent antisemitism. Therefore, their struggle did not contribute to fostering a democratic and tolerant society.

The organization of Jewish self-defense in 1960s Argentina was a unique phenomenon; there was nothing comparable in the contemporary United States or Europe. During the 1950s and the 1960s there were attempts to train young Jews in Western and Arab countries, mainly to protect synagogues and community centers, yet none of these led to the establishment of such a systematized, hierarchical organization, which involved a large number of members and which existed for such a long time. Although an effort was made to "export" this model to other Latin American countries, it met with only limited success.

In Argentina itself, the Irgún contributed to a heightened Jewish and Zionist consciousness among young people, as well as a growing solidarity and cohesion within the framework of the organized community. The increase in immigration to Israel during the 1960s and 1970s was at least in part a result of these activities. Members who held "overly leftist views," believing that everyone should fight for a better society in Argentina, and not necessarily in Israel, were marginalized during the second half of the 1960s and eventually—toward the end of the decade—were either expelled or left to join one of the guerrilla groups.[49] The organization, like the various Zionist youth movements, clearly expressed the limits of political commitments outside of its own framework.

Nonetheless, the Irgún's violent activity did not contribute to building a democratic, pluralistic society in Argentina. There were other ways of fighting for an open, tolerant, inclusive, and just society. After all, non-Jews' unequivocal condemnation of the attack on Graciela Sirota, for example, was impressive in its magnitude. A very substantial number of non-Jews felt that expressing solidarity with Jewish-Argentines was part of defending freedom and democracy in Argentina.

It could even be argued that the Irgún mirrored Tacuara and its activities to a certain extent. The Jewish Self-Defense Organization was formed to counter the nationalists' antisemitic campaign, but in both organizations, most of the militants were in their late teens or early twenties, and in both groups, the use of violence for political purposes or to improve the status of a particular group was considered legitimate. In Argentina in the 1960s and 1970s, young people, both Jews and non-Jews, were challenging commonly held assumptions and well-established organizations and systems.

The proclivities of this new generation were manifested in various ways, including political radicalization as well as rock music. The ideological lines remained, in many cases, blurred. A few members of Tacuara found themselves, several years afterward, becoming guerrilleros in the Peronist Montoneros or in the People's Revolutionary Army that was affiliated with Trotskyism. Likewise, several members of the Jewish Self-Defense Organization also crossed the lines and worked alongside young Argentines who, only a few years before, had filled the ranks of the Catholic and antisemitic right. That was the case of A., who joined the Fuerzas Armadas Revolucionarias and passed to his new comrades information regarding the Jewish organization and its commander.

In this sense, the members of the Irgún were also boundary-crossers, although their struggle was an ethnic one rather than an antifascist campaign for a democratic Argentina. But did their activities effectively frighten antisemitic nationalist groups? Most of the people I interviewed tended to believe so, overemphasizing the importance of Tacuara and other nationalist organizations and the threat that they posed to the local Jewish community. In part, this had to do with typical Zionist attitudes. Adina Cimet wrote in her book on Mexican Jewry:

> [T]he interpretation of local Jewish issues was always presented with alarm. "Alarmism"—as it was called—as a mechanism Zionism used in viewing local problems, whose solutions were invariably found in

the ideals of Zionism. Zionist ideology posited that all "local" problems of Jews stemmed from their being in a geographical location that did not offer them their own polity. Eretz Israel was always portrayed as the single viable solution to this condition.[50]

Yehoshua Feigon, the emissary of Hashomer Hatza'ir to Buenos Aires in the early 1960s, estimated that the threat posed by Tacuara to the Jewish presence in Argentina was exaggerated by Jewish leaders "as a means to strengthen a Zionist Jewish identity and encourage aliyah to Israel."[51] At the same time, overemphasizing the importance of Tacuara also enabled the interviewees to exaggerate the success of their own actions against this and similar organizations:

> I certainly have my doubts as to whether the organization was indeed a major factor in the waning of antisemitism in 1960s Argentina. Most of the Irgún's activities were amateurish, and the decline in nationalist activity had to do mostly with the military dictatorship that took power in June 1966 and limited nationalist operations.[52]

Tacuara, the Guardia Restauradora Nacionalista, and similar organizations all enjoyed tacit support among sectors of the Catholic Church, the military, the police, and the traditional upper-class as long as they operated under civilian, democratic governments that showed "dangerous" liberal or popular tendencies. These antiliberal sectors hoped that extreme right-wing organizations would help undermine the Frondizi and Illia administrations. Once the military took power, however, in June 1966, there was no need to continue supporting the Tacuara-like organizations. Under the new military government, the Jewish defense organization also had to lower its profile and focus its attention on the Arab League and its propaganda activities in Argentina.

The Irgún, however, offered these youngsters a space where they could challenge the community leadership's discourse and form identities outside the traditional frameworks of Jewish Argentina. At the same time, it also contributed to the Jewish community's growing identification with the State of Israel and the Zionist enterprise. In this sense, the Irgún can be defined as a crossbreed violent organization that mobilized Jewish-Argentine youth to defend Jews and Jewish life in Argentina and strengthen its commitment to the Zionist cause.

Author's Note

For earlier versions of this chapter see my articles "Jewish Self Defense in 1960s and Early 1970s Argentina: A Mirror of Anti-Semitic Violence?" in *Israel (Studies in Zionism and the State of Israel)* [Hebrew], no. 25 (2018), 227–55, and (with Ilan Diner), "Unfounded Fears, Inflated Hopes, Passionate Memories: Jewish Self-Defense in 1960s Argentina," *Journal of Modern Jewish Studies* 11, no. 3 (2012): 357–76. I would like to thank the Fritz Thyssen Foundation for awarding me a research grant for my project "Fighting Anti-Semitism with a Club in Hand: Jewish Self-Defense in Latin America."

Notes

1. "La guerra llegó a Buenos Aires," *Así*, June 17, 1967, 3, 14–17, 32; "Frente a la embajada siria. Hubo refriegas: dos heridos," *Crónica*, June 9, 1967. *Así* started in the mid-1950s and within a few years sold a million and a half copies of three issues every week. The magazine devoted its pages to national politics, sports, and criminal affairs.

2. Haim Avni, "The Impact of the Six-Day War on a Zionist Community: The Case of Argentina," in *The Six-Day War and World Jewry*, ed. Eli Lederhendler (Bethesda: University Press of Maryland, 2000), 137–65.

3. Raanan Rein, *Populism and Ethnicity: Peronism and the Jews of Argentina* (Quebec: McGill-Queen's University Press, 2020); Raanan Rein, *Argentina, Israel, and the Jews: Perón, the Eichmann Capture and After* (Bethesda: University Press of Maryland, 2003).

4. On the Venezuelan case, see Isaac Cherem, *Judíos sin kipá: la autodefensa judía en la Venezuela de los 60* (N.p.: n.p., 2019). On the Uruguayan case, see Fernando Amado, *Mandato de sangre* (Montevideo: Sudamericana, 2012); Raanan Rein, "'We Had Our Own Problems and Therefore We Had Our Own Bitajón': Jewish Self-Defense in Uruguay, 1960–1978," in *Armed Jews in the Americas*, eds. Raanan Rein and David Sheinin (Boston: Brill, 2021), 143–72.

5. Valeria Manzano, *The Age of Youth in Argentina: Culture, Politics, and Sexuality, from Perón to Videla* (Chapel Hill: University of North Carolina Press, 2014).

6. Pablo Vila, "Rock nacional: crónicas de la resistencia juvenil," in *Los nuevos movimientos sociales*, ed. Elizabeth Jelin, vol. 1 (Buenos Aires: Centro Editor de América Latina, 1985), 83–148; Pablo Semán and Pablo Vila, "Rock Chabón: The Contemporary National Rock of Argentina," in *From Tejano to Tango: Latin American Popular Music*, ed. Walter Aaron Clark (New York: Routledge, 2002), 70–94.

7. A. Gefen to Israeli Foreign Ministry, November 26, 1963, 103/1, Israel State Archives (ISA), Ministry of Foreign Affairs (MFA), Jerusalem.

8. Ibid.

9. Quoted in Yehuda Adín, "Nationalism and Neo-Nazism in Argentina," [in Hebrew] *Betfutzot Hagola* 7, no. 33 (1965): 77. On Triki, his views and his activities, see Hussein Triki, *He aquí Palestina... El sionismo al desnudo* (Madrid: Afrodisio Aguado, 1977).

10. Juan Carlos Cornejo Linares, *El nuevo orden sionista en la Argentina* (Buenos Aires: Ediciones Tacuari, 1964), 93–95.

11. Graciela Ben-Dror, "Antisemitism in Argentina: From the Military Junta to the Democratic Era," *Antisemitism Worldwide 2002–3* (2004): 5–28.

12. For a brief mention, in passing, of Jewish self-defense in Argentina, see David Schers, "Antisemitism in Latin America," in *Violence and Defense in the Jewish Experience*, eds. Salo W. Baron and George S. Wise (Philadelphia: Jewish Publication Society of America, 1977), 239–53.

13. Author's telephone interview with Guga Kogan, September 7, 2009.

14. Furmanski passed away in 2019. See his unpublished manuscript *Historias de una época gloriosa* as well as author's interviews with Furmanski (Tel Aviv University, August 9, 2009, and his home in Moshav Aseret, September 2, 2009) and with his son Gusti (Skype conversation, June 12, 2019) and his daughter Nurit (Tel Aviv, June 16, 2019).

15. Hilel Resnitzky, *Artzot Moledet* (Fatherlands) in Hebrew (Tel Aviv: Chalonot, 2006), 69. For another novel describing clashes between Jewish-Argentine youngsters and extreme right-wing thugs, see Samuel Tarnopolsky, *La mitad de nada* (Buenos Aires: Macondo Ediciones, 1988).

16. Resnitsky, *Artzot Moledet*, 70.

17. Federico Finchelstein, *The Ideological Origins of the Dirty War: Fascism, Populism, and Dictatorship in Twentieth Century Argentina* (New York: Oxford University Press, 2014), chap. 5; Juan Manel Padrón, *"¡Ni yanquis, ni marxistas! Nacionalistas": nacionalismo, militancia y violencia política: el caso del Movimiento Nacionalista Tacuara en la Argentina, 1955–1966* (La Plata: Universidad Nacional de La Plata, 2017); Daniel Gutman, *Tacuara: historia de la primera guerrilla urbana argentina* (Buenos Aires: Sudamericana, 2003); Roberto Bardini, *Tacuara, la pólvora y la sangre* (Océano: México, 2002).

18. Author's interview with a group of six former members of the self-defense organization, Buenos Aires, July 2014. See also Adrián Krupnik, "Cuando camino al Kibbutz vieron pasar al Che. Radicalización política y juventud judía: Argentina 1966–1976," in *Marginados y consagrados. Nuevos estudios sobre la vida judía en la Argentina*, eds. Emmanuel Kahan et al. (Buenos Aires: Ediciones Lumiere 2011), 311–28; Ariel Nojjovich, "Movimientos juveniles sionistas socialistas bajo el terrorismo de Estado en Argentina," *Contra-relatos* 8 (2011): 133–60.

19. Meir Kahane, *The Jewish Defense League: Principles and Philosophies* (New York: n.p., 1971); Meir Kahane, *Never Again! A Program for Survival* (New York: Pyramid Books, 1971); Ehud Sprinzak, "Kach and Meir Kahane: The Emergence of Jewish Quasi-Fascism," *Patterns of Prejudice* 19, no. 3 (July 1985): 15–21; Judith Tydor Baumel, "Kahane in America: An Exercise in Right-Wing Urban Terror," *Studies in Conflict and Terrorism* 22 (October 1999): 311–29.

20. Curiously enough, Argentine military officers and policemen often used these Hebrew words while interrogating Jewish-Argentines suspected of "subversion." See Resnitzky to Anug, August 2, 1977, 24/6476, ISA, MFA, Jerusalem.

21. Judith Laikin Elkin, *The Jews of Latin America*, 3rd. ed. (Boulder: Lynne Rienner, 2014), 208.

22. Jeffrey Lesser and Raanan Rein, "Challenging Particularity: Jews as a Lens for Ethnicity in Latin America," *Latin American and Caribbean Ethnic Studies* 1, no. 2 (2006): 249–63.

23. Beatrice Gurwitz, "Zionism, Third Worldism, and Argentine Youth at the Crossroads," *Journal of Jewish Identities* 8, no. 2 (2015): 13–32.

24. Adriana Brodsky's interview with David Frastai, Modi'in, July 22, 2013, unpublished interview shared with author; Adriana Brodsky, "Argentine Sephardi Youth: Between Aliyah and Activism, 1960–1970," *Journal of Jewish Identities* 8, no. 2 (2015): 113–35; Gurwitz, "Zionism, Third Worldism, and Argentine Youth at the Crossroads."

25. Colin Shindler, *The Triumph of Military Zionism: Nationalism and the Origins of the Israeli Right* (London: IB Tauris, 2009), 116–32.

26. For a recent biography of Jabotinsky, see Hillel Halkin, *Jabotinsky: A Life* (New Haven: Yale University Press, 2014).

27. Menajem Begin, *La rebelión en Tierra Santa* (Buenos Aires: Santiago Rueda, 1951).

28. In Uruguay, the influence of revisionist Zionism on self-defense activities was more pronounced than in Argentina, in part due to the importance of the Ring family members on these activities. Author's interviews with Idan Ring, Tel Aviv, June–July 2019 and Miguel Ring, Givataim, July 7, 2019.

29. Raanan Rein, "The Eichmann Kidnapping: Its Effects on Argentine-Israeli Relations and the Local Jewish Community," *Jewish Social Studies* 7, no. 3 (2001): 101–30.

30. See, for example, Jacobo Timerman, *Prisoner Without a Name, Cell Without a Number*, trans. Toby Talbot (New York: Alfred A. Knopf, 1981), 114–15.

31. Author's interview with Finkelstein, Ramat Gan, June 2014.

32. Author's interview with David Hurovitz, Tel Aviv, May 2005. On antisemitic incidents in October 1945, see Daniel Lvovich, "Entre la historia, la memoria y el discurso de la identidad: Perón, la comunidad judía y la cuestión del antisemitismo," *Indice* 27, no. 24 (2007): 173–88.

33. Isser Harel, *Security and Democracy* (Tel Aviv: Idanim, 1989), 299–302.

34. Author's interview with Asher Porat, Tel Aviv, March 2014. See also Porat's memoir, *Ḥaluk lavan, kumtah sheḥorah : sipuro shel rofe tseva'i be-milḥamot Yiśra'el* [Hebrew] (Tel Aviv: Hakibbutz Hameuchad, 2011).

35. For Eliraz's autobiography, see *Sipur shel Yeled Ve-Hemshechim* [Hebrew] (Tel Aviv: n.p., 1998).

36. Telephone interview with S. B., August 11, 2009.

37. Author's interview with Divon, Tel Aviv, September 9, 2014.

38. Author's interview with Divon, Tel Aviv, September 9, 2014.

39. Author's interview with M. P., Ra'anana, September 16, 2009.

40. On the alleged separation between Sephardi communities, see Adriana Brodsky, "Re-configurando comunidades. Judíos sefaradíes/árabes en Argentina (1900–1930)," in *Árabes y judíos en Iberoamérica: similitudes, diferencias y tensiones*, ed. Raanan Rein (Sevilla: Fundación Tres Culturas del Mediterráneo, 2008), 117–34.

41. Author's interview with E. D., Tel Aviv, December 20, 2008.

42. Author's telephone interview with F. S., September 1, 2009.
43. Guga Kogan, "Ha-Irgun," [Hebrew] weekly supplement, *Al Hamishmar*, July 8, 1988, 11.
44. Author's interview with E. D., Tel Aviv, December 20, 2008.
45. Author's telephone interview with S. B., August 11, 2009.
46. Author's interview with M. P., Ra'anana, September 16, 2009.
47. See: "AJC Survey of American Jews on Antisemitism in America," AJC, accessed December 21, 2019, https://www.ajc.org/AntisemitismSurvey2019.
48. Bari Weiss, "To Fight Anti-Semitism, Be a Proud Jew," *New York Times*, September 6, 2019.
49. Krupnik, "Cuando camino al Kibbutz vieron pasar al Che," 311–27.
50. Adina Cimet, *Ashkenazi Jews in Mexico: Ideologies in the Structuring of a Community* (New York: State University of New York Press, 1997), 61.
51. Author's interview with Yehoshua Feigon, Jerusalem, March 30, 2003.
52. Ibid.

Bibliography

Primary Sources

Archives

Israel State Archives (Jerusalem)

Interviews

Adriana Brodsky's interview with David Frastai, July 22, 2013
Asher Porat, March 2014
Daniel Finkelstein, June 2014
David Hurovitz, May 2005
E. D., December 20, 2008
F. S., September 1, 2009
Giora Divon, September 9, 2014
Group of six former members of the self-defense organization, July 2014
Guga Kogan, September 7, 2009
Gusti Furmanski, June 12, 2019
Idan Ring, June–July 2019
M. P., September 16, 2009
Mauricio (Tata) Furmanski, August 9, 2009, and September 2, 2009
Miguel Ring, July 7, 2019
Nurit Furmanski, June 16, 2019
S. B., August 11, 2009
Yehoshua Feigon, March 30, 2003

Periodicals

Así (Buenos Aires, 1967)
Crónica (Buenos Aires, 1967)
Al Hamishmar (Palestine/Israel, 1943–1995)

Secondary Sources

Adín, Yehuda. "Nationalism and Neo-Nazism in Argentina." [In Hebrew]. *Betfutzot Hagola* 7, no. 33 (1965): 62–81.
Amado, Fernando. *Mandato de sangre*. Montevideo: Sudamericana, 2012.
Avni, Haim. "The Impact of the Six-Day War on a Zionist Community: The Case of Argentina." In *The Six-Day War and World Jewry*, edited by Eli Lederhendler, 137–65. Bethesda: University Press of Maryland, 2000.
Bardini, Roberto. *Tacuara, la pólvora y la sangre*. Océano: México, 2002.
Begin, Menajem. *La rebelión en Tierra Santa*. Buenos Aires: Santiago Rueda, 1951.
Ben-Dror, Graciela. "Antisemitism in Argentina: From the Military Junta to the Democratic Era." *Antisemitism Worldwide* 2002-3 (2004): 5–28.
Brodsky, Adriana. "Argentine Sephardi Youth: Between Aliyah and Activism, 1960–1970." *Journal of Jewish Identities* 8, no. 2 (2015): 113–35.
——. "Re-configurando comunidades. Judíos sefaradíes/árabes en Argentina (1900–1930)." In *Árabes y judíos en Iberoamérica: similitudes, diferencias y tensiones*, edited by Raanan Rein, 117–34. Sevilla: Fundación Tres Culturas del Mediterráneo, 2008.
Cherem, Isaac. *Judíos sin kipá: la autodefensa judía en la Venezuela de los 60*. N.p.: n.p., 2019.
Cimet, Adina. *Ashkenazi Jews in Mexico: Ideologies in the Structuring of a Community*. New York: State University of New York Press, 1997.
Cornejo Linares, Juan Carlos. *El nuevo orden sionista en la Argentina*. Buenos Aires: Ediciones Tacuari, 1964.
Elkin, Judith Laikin. *The Jews of Latin America*. Boulder: Lynne Rienner, 2014.
Eliraz, Alexander. *Sipur shel Yeled Ve-Hemshechim*. [Hebrew]. Tel Aviv: n.p., 1998.
Finchelstein, Federico. *The Ideological Origins of the Dirty War: Fascism, Populism, and Dictatorship in Twentieth Century Argentina*. New York: Oxford University Press, 2014.
Gurwitz, Beatrice. "Zionism, Third Worldism, and Argentine Youth at the Crossroads." *Journal of Jewish Identities* 8, no. 2 (2015): 13–32.
Gutman, Daniel. *Tacuara: historia de la primera guerrilla urbana argentina*. Buenos Aires: Sudamericana, 2003.
Halkin, Hillel. *Jabotinsky: A Life*. New Haven: Yale University Press, 2014.
Harel, Isser. *Security and Democracy*. Tel Aviv: Idanim, 1989.
Kahane, Meir. *Never Again! A Program for Survival*. New York: Pyramid Books, 1971.
——. *The Jewish Defense League: Principles and Philosophies*. New York: n.p., 1971.
Krupnik, Adrián. "Cuando camino al Kibbutz vieron pasar al Che. Radicalización política y juventud judía: Argentina 1966-1976." In *Marginados y consagrados. Nuevos estudios sobre la vida judía en la Argentina*, edited by Emmanuel Kahan, Laura

Schenquer, Damián Setton, and Alejandro Dujovne, 311–28. Buenos Aires: Ediciones Lumiere 2011.

Lesser, Jeffrey, and Raanan Rein. "Challenging Particularity: Jews as a Lens for Ethnicity in Latin America." *Latin American and Caribbean Ethnic Studies* 1, no. 2 (2006): 249–63.

Lvovich, Daniel. "Entre la historia, la memoria y el discurso de la identidad: Perón, la comunidad judía y la cuestíon del antisemitismo." *Indice* 27, no. 24 (2007): 173–88.

Manzano, Valeria. *The Age of Youth in Argentina: Culture, Politics, and Sexuality, from Perón to Videla*. Chapel Hill: University of North Carolina Press, 2014.

Nojjovich, Ariel. "Movimientos juveniles sionistas socialistas bajo el terrorismo de Estado en Argentina." *Contra-relatos* 8 (2011): 133–60.

Padrón, Juan Manuel. *"¡Ni yanquis, ni marxistas! Nacionalistas": nacionalismo, militancia y violencia política: el caso del Movimiento Nacionalista Tacuara en la Argentina, 1955–1966*. La Plata: Universidad Nacional de La Plata, 2017.

Porat, Asher. *Ḥaluḳ lavan, kumtah sheḥorah : sipuro shel rofe tseva'i be-milḥamot Yiśra'el* [Hebrew]. Tel Aviv: Hakibbutz Hameuchad, 2011.

Rein, Raanan. *Argentina, Israel, and the Jews: Perón, the Eichmann Capture and After*. Bethesda: University Press of Maryland, 2003.

———. "Jewish Self Defense in 1960s and Early 1970s Argentina: A Mirror of Anti-Semitic Violence?" *Israel (Studies in Zionism and the State of Israel)* [Hebrew], no. 25 (2018): 227–55.

———. *Populism and Ethnicity: Peronism and the Jews of Argentina*. Quebec: McGill-Queen's University Press, 2020.

———. "The Eichmann Kidnapping: Its Effects on Argentine-Israeli Relations and the Local Jewish Community." *Jewish Social Studies* 7, no. 3 (2001): 101–30.

———. "'We Had Our Own Problems and Therefore We Had Our Own Bitajón': Jewish Self-Defense in Uruguay, 1960–1978." In *Armed Jews in the Americas*, edited by Raanan Rein and David Sheinin. Brill: Boston, 2021.

Rein, Raanan, and Ilan Diner. "Unfounded Fears, Inflated Hopes, Passionate Memories: Jewish Self-Defense in 1960s Argentina." *Journal of Modern Jewish Studies* 11, no. 3 (2012): 357–76.

Resnitzky, Hilel. *Artzot Moledet* (Fatherlands). [In Hebrew]. Tel Aviv: Chalonot, 2006.

Schers, David. "Antisemitism in Latin America." In *Violence and Defense in the Jewish Experience*, edited by Salo W. Baron and George S. Wise, 239–53. Philadelphia: Jewish Publication Society of America, 1977.

Semán, Pablo, and Pablo Vila. "Rock Chabón: The Contemporary National Rock of Argentina." In *From Tejano to Tango: Latin American Popular Music*, edited by Walter Aaron Clark, 70–94. New York: Routledge, 2002.

Shindler, Colin. *The Triumph of Military Zionism: Nationalism and the Origins of the Israeli Right*. London: IB Tauris, 2009.

Sprinzak, Ehud. "Kach and Meir Kahane: The Emergence of Jewish Quasi-Fascism." *Patterns of Prejudice* 19, no. 3 (July 1985): 15–21.

Tarnopolsky, Samuel. *La mitad de nada*. Buenos Aires: Macondo Ediciones, 1988.

Timerman, Jacobo. *Prisoner Without a Name, Cell Without a Number*. Translated by Toby Talbot. New York: Alfred A. Knopf, 1981.

Triki, Hussein. *He aquí Palestina . . . El sionismo al desnudo.* Madrid: Afrodisio Aguado 1977.
Tydor Baumel, Judith. "Kahane in America: An Exercise in Right-Wing Urban Terror." *Studies in Conflict and Terrorism* 22 (October 1999): 311–29.
Vila, Pablo. "Rock nacional: crónicas de la resistencia juvenile." In *Los nuevos movimientos sociales,* edited by Elizabeth Jelin, 83–148. Vol. 1. Buenos Aires: Centro Editor de América Latina, 1985.
Weiss, Bari. "To Fight Anti-Semitism, Be a Proud Jew." *New York Times,* September 6, 2019.

Contributors

Zachary M. Baker is the Reinhard Family Curator Emeritus of Judaica and Hebraica Collections in the Stanford University Libraries, where he also served as Assistant University Librarian for Collection Development. Previously, he was Head Librarian of the YIVO Institute for Jewish Research (New York City). He has published extensively in the fields of Yiddish Studies and Judaica bibliography and is a member of the core team of the Digital Yiddish Theatre Project.

Adriana M. Brodsky is professor of Latin American and Jewish History at St. Mary's College of Maryland. Her book *Sephardi, Jewish, Argentine: Creating Community and National Identity, 1880–1960* appeared in 2016. She has published on Sephardi food, schools, beauty contests, and Latin American Jewish history in general. She is now finishing a manuscript on Argentine youth in Zionist movements (1940s–1970s). Since 2014, she has been copresident of the Latin American Jewish Studies Association.

Sandra McGee Deutsch is professor of history at the University of Texas at El Paso. She is the author of *Counterrevolution in Argentina, 1900–1932: The Argentine Patriotic League*; *Las derechas: The Extreme Right in Argentina, Brazil, and Chile, 1890–1939*; and *Crossing Borders, Claiming a Nation: A History of Argentine Jewish Women, 1880–1955*. *Crossing Borders* received the Latin American Jewish Studies Association 2011 Book Award for best book on Latin American Jewish Studies published between 2008 and 2010. Currently she is working on a book manuscript entitled *Gendering Antifascism: Women's Activism in Argentina and the World, 1918–1947*. Deutsch also coedited (with Kathleen M. Blee) *Women of the Right: Comparisons and Interplay across Borders* and (with Ronald H. Dolkart) *The Argentine Right: Its History and Intellectual Origins, 1910 to the Present*. In addition, she has written numerous articles and chapters on fascist and antifascist movements, women, and Jews in Latin America. The University of Texas at El Paso gave her the Outstanding Faculty Award in the Humanities in 2016.

Lucas de Mattos Moura Fernandes is a doctoral student in Social History at the Federal University of Rio de Janeiro (UFRJ). He is a researcher at the Interdisciplinary Nucleus of Arab and Jewish Studies. He has been working with the documentation of Brazil-Morocco diplomacy since 2013, conducting historical research in the Archives of the Itamaraty Palace. In addition, he teaches philosophy and human sciences for young people in public schools on the outskirts of Rio de Janeiro, Brazil. His master's thesis, "Negociando com naturalidade: questões de identidade e cidadania na comunidade brasileira no Marrocos (1860–1906)," was "approved with praise" in August 2018.

Isabel Rosa Gritti is associate professor at the Federal University of Fronteira Sul (UFFS)-Erechim in Rio Grande do Sul. She received her M.A. and Ph.D. in Brazilian History at the Pontifical Catholic University of Rio Grande do Sul (PUC-RS). Gritti is the author of *Imigração judaica no Rio Grande do Sul: a Jewish Colonization Association e a colonização de Quatro Irmãos* and *Imigração e colonização polonesa no Rio Grande do Sul: a emergência do preconceito.*

Tamar Herzog (https://therzog.fas.harvard.edu/), who is the Monroe Gutman Professor of Latin American Affairs at Harvard and an affiliated faculty member at the Harvard Law School, received her Ph.D. at the EHESS in Paris in 1994. She is the author of *A Short History of European Law: The Last Two and a Half Millennia* (available also in Spanish and Mandarin, and forthcoming in Portuguese, Italian, and Korean), *Frontiers of Possession: Spain and Portugal in Europe and the Americas* (available also in Spanish, Portuguese, and Brazilian Portuguese), *Upholding Justice: State, Law and the Penal System in Quito* (available also in French and Spanish), *Defining Nations: Immigrants and Citizens in Early Modern Spain and Spanish America* (available also in Spanish and French), *Ritos de control, prácticas de negociación* (available also in French) and *Mediación, archivos y ejercicio*. She is the author of over 100 articles and book chapters published in the United States, Canada, the United Kingdom, Italy, France, Spain, Portugal, Germany, Brazil, Mexico, Colombia, Argentina, Peru, Ecuador, and Israel.

Elisa Kriza is a scholar of cultural history and comparative literature. She holds a Ph.D. from Aarhus University, Denmark, and is currently teaching and conducting research at the University of Bamberg, Germany. Her research focuses on the cultural and political interconnections between Eastern Europe and other regions, such as Latin America, Western Europe, and the United States. Her second book, *Understanding Yiddish Movies: Religious Symbols and Cultural Context,* was published in German. She has written about Latin American

Jewish culture for the weekly *Jüdische Allgemeine* and she has analyzed antisemitism in literature in *Jahrbuch für Antisemitismusforschung* and *German Life and Letters*. Her first book was entitled *Alexander Solzhenitsyn: Cold War Icon, Gulag Author, Russian Nationalist? A Study of His Western Reception*. Among her many articles, "Blood Carnival and its Variations in Mexican and Soviet Subversive Satires by René Avilés and Fazil Iskander" appeared in *Comparative Literature Studies*.

José C. Moya is professor of history at Barnard College and director of the Greater Caribbean Studies Center at Columbia University. He has authored more than fifty publications, including *Cousins and Strangers: Spanish Immigrants in Buenos Aires*, a book that received five awards for its contributions to migration and Latin American studies. He is the editor of a number of volumes, among them *Atlantic Crossroads: Webs of Migration, Culture and Politics between Europe, Africa, and the Americas, 1800–2020*.

Dana Rabin is professor and chair of the Department of History at the University of Illinois, Urbana-Champaign. A historian of eighteenth-century Britain, her scholarship examines the cultural and legal relationships between British subjects, the law, nation, and empire. She teaches global history, British history, and the history of crime.

Katalin Franciska Rac is a historian and archivist, currently the Jewish studies librarian at Emory University. She specializes in the modern history of Central European Jewry and their transnational connections. Her publications probe the dynamic relationship between nationalism, imperialism, academia, and Jewish integration in Hungary. She is interested in exploring other aspects of the Central European cultural experience as well. In the essay "How Shabbat Cholent Became a Secular Hungarian Favorite" published in *Feasting and Fasting: The History and Ethics of Jewish Food*, she connects food studies with the research on Central European nationalism and Jewish integration.

Raanan Rein is the Elias Sourasky Professor of Latin American and Spanish History and former vice president of Tel Aviv University. He is also head of the S. Daniel Abraham Center for International and Regional Studies. Rein is the author and editor of more than forty books and numerous articles and book chapters. He is a member of Argentina's National Academy of History and former president of the Latin American Jewish Studies Association (LAJSA). The Argentine government awarded him the title of Commander in the Order of the Liberator San Martín for his contributions to Argentine culture.

Hilit Surowitz-Israel is assistant professor in the Religion Department at Rutgers University. She is coauthor, with Laura Leibman and Michel Hoberman, of *Jews in the Americas, 1776–1826*. She is currently completing her manuscript: *American Diasporas: The Creolization of Religion in the Colonial Atlantic World*.

Lenny A. Ureña Valerio is associate director for program development in the Latin American and Iberian Institute at the University of New Mexico. She received her B.A. in history from the University of Puerto Rico and her M.A. and Ph.D. in Central/East European history from the University of Michigan, Ann Arbor. Her primary research and teaching interests include imperial/colonial studies, European migration to Latin America, Polish diaspora in Brazil, history of medicine and public health, and historical methods and theories. She is the author of *Colonial Fantasies, Imperial Realities: Race Science and the Making of Polishness on the Fringes of the German Empire, 1840–1920*, winner of the 2020 Kulczycki Book Prize in Polish Studies awarded by the Association for Slavic, East European, and Eurasian Studies. The book also received honorable mention for the 2020 Heldt Prize for best book by a woman in Slavic/East European/Eurasian Studies awarded by the Association for Women in Slavic Studies. She is currently president of the Consortium for Latin American Programs (CLASP).

Neil Weijer is curator of the University of Florida's Harold and Mary Jean Hanson Rare Book Collection. His research and teaching focuses on the history of early books and manuscripts both in their physical and digital forms. He holds a Ph.D. in Medieval History from Johns Hopkins University as well as an M.Phil. in Medieval History from Cambridge University. He is the author of the article "Gathering Places: William Lambarde's Reading" that appeared in the *Journal of the Warburg and Cortauld Institutes* 81 and of "Re-Imagining Digital Things: Sustainable Data in Medieval Manuscript Studies," coauthored with Michelle Warren, in *Digital Philology*.

Index

Page numbers in *italics* refer to illustrations.

Abi Yetomin ve Dayan Almanoth society. *See* Yeshiva(s): Abi Yetomin ve Dayan Almanoth society
Acapulco: node of New Christian trade and financial network, 132
Acción Feminina por la Victoria (AF). *See* Feminine Action for Victory
Activism: Jewish, 15, 249, 278; Jewish women's, 21; Jewish women's antifascist, 255; left-wing, 278; of marginalized groups, 15; political, 253; of Sephardic youth, 278, 296; of Sephardic young women, 279; Zionist, 16, 258
Activist(s), 15; former, 314; human rights, 256; Jewish, 302; Jewish-Argentine, 311; Jewish women, 15, 255, 19; Jewish in Russia, 28n39; left-wing, 27n36, 278; Sephardic, young, 17; Sephardic, young, of the Irgún, 312; in Victory Board, 251; Zionist, 281
Adela, Buenos Aires province, 292
AF. *See* Feminine Action for Victory
Africa, 44; Africa and Near East division of the Argentine foreign ministry, 304; Brazil's imperial ambitions, 11, 150; European imperialism, 9, 11; Jewish and New Christian migration to, 119; link between Brazil and North Africa, 161; Lusitanian/Portuguese colonies in, 109, 133; North Africa, 9, 11, 131, 134, 135, 161; Portuguese, 126; Portuguese trading posts, 119; South Africa, 20, 24, 133; in Yiddish travelogues, 179
African(s), 70, 117; African American film actors, 226n54; Afro-descendants, 117; Euroafrican, 127; slaves/enslavement (*see* Slave[s])
Agadir, 112
Agricultural: in Brazil, 234–35 (*see also* Fazenda Quatro Irmãos); Jewish, 15, 20; movement, 20; pre-agriculturalist groups, 128; settlements/colonies in Americas, 10; settlements/colonies in Argentina, 179, 189–90, 254–55 (*see also* Basavilbaso; Moisés Ville; Rivera); training, 292–93
Aleichem, Sholem: short stories, 13, 179, 211–12, 217; voice, 193; Yiddish, 185
Aleppo, 312
Algeciras, 167
Alhambra Decree, 4, 24n10, 108
Alianza Libertadora Nacionalista (ALN), 309
Aliyah. See Migration: to Palestine and Israel
Alliance Israélite Universelle, 150
Allies (World War II), 249–51
American Jewish Historical Society, 22n3
Americas: European discovery of, 4; groups prohibited to migrate to, 39, *41*, 47n5; home of Ashkenazic and Sephardic communities in early modern period, 101n12; Ibero-America, 118; Latin American countries, 17; migration to (*see under* Migration); multicultural, 1–3; opportunities in, 110; permission to migrate to, 39; Portuguese communities, 94; resources (*see* Commodity); Sephardic Jewish religiosity in, 94; shelter and refuge, 56, 110; Spanish Indies, 125; South America, 13; Southern Cone, 13

Amézaga, Juan José de, 253
Amsterdam, 8, 89; Caribbean's subservience to, 94; connection to non-Iberian Jewish congregations, 91; Judaism legal, 128; Ma'amad, 94; as mother-congregation, 84, 94; node of New Christian trade and financial network, 132; Portuguese Jewish Community, 91, 123; as a quasi-imperial center, 8; as a religious center, 89–90, 98; Talmud Torah of, 83, 85, 89–90
Anatolia, 131
Ancestry. *See* Descent
Anglican(s), 58, 72n14; male, 59, 67
Anglican oath, 58–59; abolition in Scottish universities, 72n15
Angola, 109, 119, 122, 128
Antifascism: advancing Jewish integration, 16; in the Americas, 250; continuing experiences in countries of origin, 255; as global connections, 264; Jewish, 261, 264; subject of academic study, 250; as a vehicle of local integration in Argentina and Uruguay, 251, 265; of women, 250–51, 266n2
Antigua, 56
Anti-Nazi Action for Aid to the Soviet Union and Other Peoples in the Struggle (ANA), 252; Ladies' Commission (Uruguay), 252, 257
Antisemitic movement and riots. *See* Antisemitism
Antisemitism, 117, 186, 211, 223, 279; ACJ survey on, 314; in Argentina, 255; in Berlin, 209; DAIA's role in fighting, 300n61; defense against, 257; European, 296; fear of, 186, 286; fight against, 17, 280, 303, 305, 310; following the capture of Adolf Eichmann, 303, 305, 308, 311; in Hollywood films, 216; in Latin America, 315; in Lisbon in 1506, 114; modern racial, 115; response to, 281; self-defense mirroring, 315; in Ukraine, 217; in the United States, 315; in Uruguay, 260
Antwerp, 122; node of New Christian trade and financial network, 132
Arab(s), 169; Arabic countries, 17; Arabic language, 41, 43, 110, 125; Arabic-speaking Jews, 255, 297n1; communities in Latin America, 20; groups in Argentina, 304; Jews in Arab countries, 315; supporters of Arabic countries, 302; world, 117–18
Arabian Peninsula, 120
Arab League, 302, 318; representative of, 304
Aragon, 124; laws of 1414 similar to Ayllon laws, 111; New Christian office holders, 114
Arendt, Hannah, 115
Argentina: barriers between Israel and, 294; connection with Israel, 17, 305; democracy in, 316–17; Dirty War, 17; emigration from, 296; failed coup d'état of June 1955, 309; identification of Jews, 16; ideological climate, 303; inhospitable to Jews, 264; in the 1960s, 303, 307, 315–16; JCA in, 191; Jewish activism, 15; Jewish agricultural settlements and settlers, 10, 15, 20, 190–91, 255; Jewish establishment, 307; Jewish politics, 16–17; Jewish underground in, 304; migration to, 250; as a node of international Yiddish theater network, 176, 190; Nomberg's visit in, 195n12; non-democratic, 255; prostitution and white slavery in, 133, 180, 186; restricting immigration, 184; Schwartz's impressions of, 13, 178; solidarity work in, 264; Tevye considering to emigrate to, 214–15; use of Zionist vocabulary, 19; women in, 251; Zionism in, 16, 278, 318. *See also* Asociación Mutual Israelita Argentina; Delegación de Asociaciones Israelitas Argentina; Israel: relation with Argentina; Jew(s): in/of Argentina; Self-defense organizations
Argentinidad, 307
Armada Revolts, 153
Ascamot, 101n9, 101n12. *See also* Jewish community(ies): bylaws
Ashkenazi. *See* Ashkenazic
Ashkenazic: in Argentina, 16, 255, 257, 259, 312; Argentine definition of, 268n33; Ashkenazic/Sephardic dichotomy, 131; Ashkenazic-Sephardic divide, 16; barriers between Ashkenazic and Sephardic Jews, 279, 282, 292; culture, 2; diaspora, 5; disputes with Sephardic Jews in St. Eustatius, 8; institutions in, 259; involvement in labor organizations, 259; in Israel, 135; in Jewish-Argentine self-defense groups, 312; Jews, 9, 100n4; in and from Latin America, 135; members of Mikvé Israel, 88;

members of Shearith Israel, 87; outnumbering Sephardic Jews in the Americas and Europe, 103n25, 134–35; population growth in Europe, 9; in Suriname, 23; tension between Sephardic and Ashkenazic Jews in the Caribbean, 101; traffickers, 133–34; western expansion, 12, 134
Ashkenazim. *See* Ashkenazic: Jews
Así, 302
Asociación Mutual Israelita Argentina (AMIA), 311
Assimilation, 110, 125, 298n11; of New Christians, 129; silent, 42; threat of, 203; in Yiddish film, 222–23
Atlantic, 108, 132; colonization of, 112; crossing, 39–40, 47n6, 93; early modern Atlantic world, 6; economy, 57, 109, 119, 133; islands (Spanish and Portuguese), 133; North African Atlantic coast, 112; Portuguese Jewish early modern, 84–85, 96–98, 124; two sides of, 9, 55. *See also* Trade: Atlantic
Attias, Jacob, 160–61, 164
Auto(s)-da-fé, 116, 126
Ayudismo, 252, 254, 260. *See also* Activism
Ayudista(s), 259. *See also* Activist(s)
Azamor, 112
Azores, 112, 122

Bahia: early population of, 122; New Christian enclave, 129, 133
Bahía Blanca (in Argentina): Victory Board chapter, 255–56
Bahrain: Portuguese trading post, 119
Baldomir, Alfredo, 253
Balfour Declaration, 298n24
Barbados, 60; Jewish population, 56; Jewish slave-owning households, 123; Jews of white population, 124; Kingston, 63; New Christian enclave, 133
Barcelona: node of New Christian trade and finance network, 132
Basavilbaso (in Argentina): Victory Board chapter, 255
Begin, Menahem, 308
Belmonte (in Portugal): Crypto-Jews, 118
Benin: Portuguese trading post, 119
Bermuda: 1674 Act, 70
Beser, 177, 192

Bevis Marks (in London): mother-congregation of British Caribbean, 86
Birobidzhan, 179
Bitajón. *See* Jewish Self-Defense Organization (Argentina)
Blackstone, William, 57
Bnei Anusim, 118
Bohemia: origin of Jews in Salonica, 131
Brazil, 121, 182; chancellery, 154; coffee industry in, 232; community in Morocco, 164–67, 168–69; Consul General in Morocco, 160; consular representation in Morocco and North Africa, 149, 153–54, 170; Consulate in Morocco, 170; Consulate in Tangier, 167–68 (*see also* Tangier); declaration of independence, 149; desirable for Jewish migration, 149; diplomatic and consular papers, 151, 168; "discovery" by Portuguese, 121; Federal Decree 998B, 160; immigration and colonization policy, 232–33; immigration authorities in, 168; imperial ambitions in Africa, 11, 150; Jewish agricultural settlements, 10; Jewish colony in Morocco, 151, 154, 158; Land Law of 1850, 232; Ministry of Foreign Affairs, 154, 167–68; Ministry of Justice and Internal Affairs, 169; Moshe Sharett's visit, 20; naturalization process and citizenship, 11, 168–69, 171n10; republican government of, 167; Schwartz's impressions of, 13, 178, 182; self-defense, 303; state, 170. *See also* Jewish Colonization Association: in Brazil
Brest, Leon, 178, 193n3
Britain. *See* England
British: culture, 69; expansion, 59; goods, 57; government, 62; imperial project and endeavors, 69; men, 69; nation, 68; national identity, 7, 69–70. *See also* Empire: British
Bruges: Portuguese trading house, 121
Buenos Aires: Ashkenazic burial society in, 259; children of colonists in, 190–91; commercial hub in Spanish Indies, 125; Jewish self-defense groups in, 304; New Christian enclave, 133; Sephardic communities in, 282; as "sin city," 186; slave traffic, 133; Syrian Embassy in, 302; theater world of, 177; training farm and summer camp in the province of, 290–93, 304, 310. *See also* Yiddish: theater in Argentina

—neighborhoods: Boca and Barracas, Once, San Fernando, Villa Crespo, Tigre, 288; Colegiales, 284, 298n24; Flores, 287, 291, 296, 298n24
—and Schwartz: stay in, 178–79; articles about, 184–87; return to, 196n34
Bukovina, 176
Bulgaria: Jews expelled from, 131; region, 135

Caboclos, 233, 242
Calimerio, Adoniram Maurity de, 164, 165, 167, 168
Canary Islands, 123
Cape Verde: Portuguese occupation, 112; Columbus's stop, 119
Caracas, 87; Judaism illegal in, 130
Caribbean: Atlantic Portuguese Diaspora, 8; biased scholarship on Jewish communities, 95; British Empire, 56; Jewish belief/religiosity in, 94; as part of the Americas, 2; Tacky's Revolt, 74n34
Carta ejecutoria de hidalguía, 7, 25n18, 53, 54–55
Cartagena: Inquisition, 40, 111; New Christian enclave, 133; principal port of slave trade, 123
Cartagena, Bishop Alfonso de, 137n27
Castile: Habsburg, 124; Jewish assimilation in, 110
Catholic Church, 114, 309, 317
CCFI. *See* Feminine Central Israelite Committee
CCIU. *See* Central Israelite Committee of Uruguay
Center: British metropolitan elites, 66; cosmopolitan British, 58; imperial, 5; of international Yiddish theater world, 13, 26n31; London as trade, 56; as mother-congregation (*see* Jewish community[ies]: mother-congregation); -periphery binary or relations, 9, 19, 26n28, 71; of Portuguese Jewish Diaspora in the Americas, 85, 98 (*see also* Amsterdam; Curaçao); of religious authority, 100; of Yiddish culture, 12, 19
Central Israelite Anti-Nazi Committee of Aid to the Soviet Union (CICA), 257
Central Israelite Committee of Uruguay (CCIU), 257

Charles II (of England), 60
Charleston: relation with Curaçao, 87, 124
Children of Jews and African slave women, 63, 127
Chraa. See Muslim(s): law in Morocco
Christian(s):
—Catholic(s): authorities, 115; education in Argentine public schools, 252; efforts in US film industry, 205; in England, 58, 71; Jewish converts, 6, 100n4, 112; majority in Iberia, 6; nationalists in Argentina, 303
—Protestant(s): communion, 61; English in Jamaica, 61; Protestantism as British identity, 69, 71; sects in London; women members of Feminine Action, 252, 261, 271n74; women members of the Victory Board, 251
—Quaker(s), 61–62
Citizenship. *See* Naturalization
Class: Brazilian consular services, 160; as in education, 294–95; middle class, 195n19, 216, 251, 277; neighborhoods of mixed, 254; as a social category, 3, 59, 109, 129; travel, 181, 189; working class, 182, 251, 254
Colaço, José Daniel, 11, 149, 151–52, 160–61
Colegio Mayor de San Bartolomé of the University of Salamanca, 38
Colonies: in Americas, 124; Caribbean, 56; England's or British, 56–58; exploitation, 15; France's in North Africa, 28n40; Jewish agricultural, 10, 189–91, 237, 256; Lusitanian, 133; "national" in Buenos Aires, 184; Portugal's in Africa, 109, 118, 133. *See also* Naturalization: in Britain or British colonies
Columbus, Christopher, 24n10, 108, 119; second, 26n32
Commentaries on the Laws of England, 57
Commodity: brazilwood, 121–22; coffee, 182; forest products, 238–39, 241; land, 149, 232–34; sugar, 57, 121–24, 133, 182
Compagnie Auxiliaire de Chemins du Fer au Brésil, 235–26
Congregation(s). *See* Jewish community(ies)
Conqueror, William the, 64
Consularization: 164, 169. *See also* Naturalization: mobilization of Brazilian citizenship

Index · 333

Convención de la Juventud Sefaradí (Sephardi Youth Convention), 284
Converso, 39, 94, 100n4, 109, 136n3; in Aragon, 114; in Castile, 111, 113–14; as Crypto-Jews, 112; in Iberian World, 8, 117; identity and culture, 8, 118; of Jewish origin, 39–40, 44–45, 47n5; Muslims or Muslim origin, 37–40, 42, 44–45; physicians, 111; Portuguese, 116; as "potential Jews," 128; prohibited to migrate to the Americas, 47n5; recently baptized, 109; socioeconomic success, 117; Spanish, 110, 124; in Spanish America, 111; suspicion of, 115; synonym for, 131
Converts. See Converso
Córdoba (city in Argentina): Schwartz's performance, 189–90; Victory Board, 255–56
Córdoba (province in Argentina): Macabilandia, 303, 314; Zionist summer camps, 288
Coronavirus, 223
Correia, Rivadávia, 169
Cristão(s)-novo(s). See New Christian
Cromwell, Oliver, 60
Crypto-Jew(s), 110, 112, 118–19, 126; in Brazil, 124; identity, 8; effect on multireligious character of Latin America, 130; Portuguese, 125–26; presumed, 114. See also New Christian
Crypto-Judaism, 40; suspicion of, 111, 123
Culture(s): of belonging, 18; British, 69; converso, 118; high, 176; Iberian, 45; as identifying feature, 42; Jewish, 2, 293, 309; material, 8, 93, 96; Muslim, 45; popular, 176; Schwartz's culture shock, 187; subculture, 203; Yiddish, 12, 14, 201–2, 223
Curaçao: New Christian enclave, 133; trade hub, 84
—Jewish community, 8; cemetery, 125; demand of retention of Sephardic rite, 88; following Amsterdam's example, 84–85, 88–90; ma'amad, 85, 94; mimetic expressions of Amsterdam's Jewish communal life, 94; as mother-congregation in, 84–85, 95, 98–99; as "new Amsterdam," 105n56; poor Jews, 103n29; quasi-imperial networks of, 13; religious life, 96; as religious hub, 84; rise to economic success, 84; synagogue, 92

Delegación de Asociaciones Israelitas Argentina (DAIA), 257, 300n61, 309, 311–12
Dar-al-Islam. See Muslim(s): societies
Denization, 58
Derechinsky, Jaime, 291
Der Shpigl, 178, 194n7
Descent: Christian, 116; conflation of Jewish and Portuguese, 39–40, 130; of conversos, 116; European, 116; hyper-, 116; hypo-, 109, 116, 121; Iberian, 101; in Iberian world, 53; Jewish, 45; Jewish and Muslim, 37–38, 44, 115; mixed, 63, 71, 74n37, 116 (see also Mulatto[es]); mixed religious, 114; noble, 7, 53–55; Ortega family, 53; Portuguese, 126; practice of recording, 7; pretense of Arab, 43; Spanish and Portuguese, 63, 100n4
Despechados. See under Jew(s): in Curaçao
Dhimmi (protected persons), 120
Diario Popular (DP), 256, 267n6
Dias, Branca, 122
Diaspora: Atlantic Portuguese, 8; Bialystoker, 26n28; Caribbean Jewish, 8; consciousness of Portuguese Jews, 93, 98–99; diasporas, 22n8, 24n13, 129–30; East European Jewish, 181; Iberian Jewish, 8; Jewish, 4, 5, 9, 226n67; New Christian, 122, 128, 131–32; New Christians' mercantile (commercial and trade), 109, 133–34; North African Jewish, 12; Sephardic commercial, 129; of Spaniards of Jewish origin, Western Sephardic, 8–9, 100n4, 104n49, 45; of Yiddish speakers, 176, 180, 204
Difference: categories of, 70; between conversos of Jewish and Muslim descent, 39–40, 44–45; denization and naturalization in England, 58; between the experiences of Africans and Iberian Jews in the Americas, 117; intra-Iberian, 113; Jewish, 3, 19; Jewish difference from Catholics and Dissenters, 69; physical difference of Jews, 115, 117, 138n28; between Sephardic and Ashkenazic women in Argentina, 16; in whiteness, 59
Di Presse, 178, 192, 194n7
Diversity: Americas, 3 (see also Americas: multicultural); in Brazil, 169; in Britain, 58; ethnic, 22n4; Feminine Action, 253; Jewish, 1, 131–32; linguistic, 19; in Salonica, 131

Edelman, Fanny, 256
Edict(s) of Tolerance, 10
Edict of Expulsion (from Spain). *See* Alhambra Decree
Edward I (of England), 56
Eichmann, Adolph, 308
Elnecavé, Nissim, 286, 291
Emancipation: Dutch Jews, 127; in Great Britain, 60; in France, the Netherlands, and UK, 134
Emissary, 90, 305, 311, 317
Empire: as agent of globalization, 24n13; Austria-Hungary, 10; Aztec, 110; of Brazil, 11; British, 70; early modern, 4; German, 10; imperial framework(s), 9; Inca, 110; Ottoman, 10; Portugal's, 128; Russian, 10, 20, 176; Russian, Tsarist, 210
England, 69, 121; Bank of England, 56; Christian, 67; Crown of, 57; diversity of, 58; House of Lords, 67; immigrants, 58; inclusion and belonging, 7; Parliament, 61, 66–67; White Paper, 205. *See also* Colonies: England's or British
Equatorial Guinea: Portuguese trading post, 119
Erechim region (in Brazil), 233
Eretz Israel, 214
Essaouira, 90, 112; Brazilian consular office, 165
Europe, 5, 10; as dangerous home to Jews, 215; Eastern Europe, 13–14
Exile, 37–39, 214, 226n67; from Iberia, 112, 131–32
Expulsion: as an attempt to assimilate, 42; from England in 1290, 56, 60; of former Muslims from Spain, 38, 41; of Jews from Iberia, 100n4, 112–13; of Jews from Portugal, 100n4, 113; of Jews from Spain, 108, 190; of Jews from Zaydi Imamate of Yemen in 1679, 127

Fascist(s) and fascism: in Argentina, 251, 255; European, 205, 216; in Uruguay, 252, 255, 260
Fazenda Quatro Irmãos, 14, 233, 236; forest products, 239 (*see also* Commodity); reforestation, 241
Feminine Action for Victory (AF), 249, 253–54; inclusion in Jewish Studies, 250; Jewish participation, 254, 256–57; Jews in board, 258; predecessor—Ladies' Commission, 257; relationship with CCFI, 260–61; relationship with Victory Board, 254
Feminine Central Israelite Committee (CCFI), 257, 259–64
Fernandes, Diogo, 122
Ferrara Bible of 1553, 83, 100n3
Flanders: cloth dyers, 121; Habsburg domain, 124
Fonseca, Isaac Aboab da, 123–24
Forverts, 178, 190, 194n7
1492 (year of), 4, 9, 24n10, 38, 100n4, 108, 112, 190
1497 (year of), 39, 100n4, 108, 113
1499 (year of), 113
Frondizi, Arturo, 308; administration, 317
Fuerzas Armadas Revolucionarias, 316

Galicia: Austrian, 176
Galut. *See* Exile
Gambia: Portuguese trading post, 119
Gefen, Abba, 304
Germany, 20; Nazi Germany, 204–5; roots of Ashkenazic Jews, 100n4; twentieth-century, 117. *See also* Empire: German
Gift: to assert religious authority, 84–85, 98; bags for children in Allied countries, 258, 261; building of Snoa, 92; *The Gift* (Mauss), 93 (*see also* Mauss, Marcel); marker of the community, 99; as opposed to commodity, 98; religious objects as, 8, 85; representation of power and religious identity, 93–96; wedding, 210
Goes: AF section, 257
Goldene medina, 216
Great Britain. *See* England
Guardia Restauradora Nacionalista (Argentina), 317
Guido, José María, 308
Guinea: *lançados*, 119–20; Portuguese trading post, 119–20
Guinea Bissau: Portuguese trading post, 119
Gunboat diplomacy, 152

Haganah, 311
Ḥakham(im), 89, 102n16, 103n20
Ḥalutz(im/ot) (pioneers), 279, 286, 295
Ḥalutziut, 283, 286–88, 295–96

Index · 335

Hamburg: node of New Christian trade network, 132
Hanoar Hasefaradí, 284, 294–95
Hasokhnut Hayehudit Leeretz Yisrael. See The Jewish Agency for Israel
Havdalah ceremony, 212
Ḥazan, 103n19; of Philadelphia, 87; of Shearith Israel, 86–87
Hebrew, 28n39, 136; Argentine Zionist youth learning, 289–90, 294–95, 310; Bibles, 83; in Hanoar Hasefaradí, 295; language schools in Poland, 309; tomb inscriptions in Curaçao's old Sephardic cemetery, 125
Hebron, 90, 91, 100n5; impoverished Jewish community, 84; relationship with Curaçao, 104n37; Talmudic academy, 91. See also Yeshiva(s): Abi Yetomin ve Dayan Almanoth society; Honen Dalim society Hermandades. See Yeshiva(s)
Herzl, Theodor, 298n25
Ḥevrah (voluntary, mutual-aid society), 186
Hidalgos, 53
Hidalguía, 53
Hirsch, Baron Maurice, 10, 189, 191, 233–34
Hirschbein, Peretz, 179–81, 186, 206
Hispanicity, 19, 109
Hollywood, 216
Holocaust: helping victims, 255; images of, 307; in Nueva Sión, 290; Uruguayan public opinion, 271n77; youth aliyah after, 277
Holy Land. See Land of Israel
Honen Dalim society. See Yeshiva(s): Honen Dalim society
Hope of Israel, 60
Humboldt, Alexandre von, 26n32
Hungary: origin of Jews in Salonica from, 131; Yiddish speakers, 176

Iberia, 37, 44–45, 118; colonization, 150; culture, 45; heritage, 101n7; identification with Iberian past (see Spain: emotional ties and loyalty to); late medieval, 117; maritime expansion, 9; medieval, 28n38; mini-, 131; origins, 135; policy against, 309; Spain and Portugal, 4; territories, 43, 45; union of Spain and Portugal, 40, 109, 111, 124, 128, 132; world, 8, 53, 108–9, 126–27, 129, 132

Iberian(s), 115; exiles, 135. See also Jew(s): Iberian Jews/Diaspora
Iberian Peninsula. See Iberia
Identity: British, 7, 69–70; collective, 23n9, 44, 134; descent as, 56, 116; discourse, 6; ethnic, 115, 281; individual, 6; Jewish, 3, 211, 220, 222, 260, 278, 281, 285; loss, 216, 218; New Christian, 134; politics, 307; religious, 7–8, 55, 93, 96, 98; young Jews', 303; Zionist, 302
Illia, Arturo, 308; administration, 317
Imperialism: colonization companies, 232–33; of Europe in Africa and Asia, 9; of Europe in the Americas, 4; nineteenth-century, 115; Portuguese in Morocco, 152; Royal African Company, 57; South Sea Company, 57; West India Company, 85
India: outside imperial control, Kerala, 128; Portuguese colonial outposts, 120; Yiddish travel narratives, 179
Indigenous people: assumptions about, 180; denied political rights in British Empire, 61; elite, 63; land occupation in Brazil, 233 (see also Caboclos); Schwartz's discussion of, 182, 195n22; targeted by Inquisition, 111
Indonesia: Portuguese colonial outpost, 120
Inquisition: concern about Portuguese New Christian, 128; in Lisbon, 118; in New Castile, 110; records of Portuguese conversos, 116; in Spain, 47n6; in the Spanish colonies, 40, 111, 126; Schwartz reminded of, 190
Inter-American Commission of Women (IACW), 250
Intermarriage: between Ashkenazic and Sephardic Jews, 292; between European descendants and people of color, 129, 182; between Old and New Christians, 48n14, 114
—between Jews and non-Jews in Eastern Europe, 203, 212, 215; fear of, 223; representation in non-Yiddish-language movies, 216; in US today, 217; in USSR, 226n73
Iran: Portuguese trading post, 119
Iraq: Portuguese trading post, 119
Irgún. See Jewish Self-Defense Organization (Argentina)

Irgun Tzvai Leumi (aka Etzel), 308
Islam: force of globalization, 24n13; in Spain after Reconquista, 43
Islamic. *See* Muslim(s)
Israel, 286; agricultural settlements, 20; embassy in Buenos Aires, 307, 310–11; as the Jewish collective, 212; land of, 285; magazine, 287; migration to, 17, 307; migration to agricultural settlements in, 20; as a modern nation, 282; as a place for displaced Jews, 286; relation with Argentina, 17, 305; as religious center, 296
Israel's Defense Forces (IDF), 311
Istanbul: destination of Iberian Jews after expulsion, 135; node of New Christian trade and finance network, 132

Jabotinsky, Vladimir (Ze'ev), 307–8
Jacob Franco, Moseh de, 86
Jalutzi(m). See Ḥalutz(im/ot)
Jalutziut. See Ḥalutziut
Jamaica, 7, 56, 60, 132; Assembly, 62, 64, 66; Curaçao's generosity, 87; Jewish community, 60, 62; Jews in the white population, 124; kosher meat trade, 89; New Christian enclave, 133; racial balance, 65; racial hierarchies, 64; slave owner Jews, 123
JCA. *See* Jewish Colonization Association
Jerusalem, 92
Jeshuat Israel (Touro) congregation in Newport, 86–88, 97
Jeshurun, Ḥakham (of Curaçao), 86–88, 102n16
Jew(s): acceptance of, 261; admission to the body politic, 69; Arabic-speaking, 255; Lusitanian, 130; banned to move to the Americas, 47n5; barred from holding office, 63–64; in Barbados, 123; in Brazil, 123, 150; in British colonies, 59–60; conversos, 6, 44; "cultural Jews," 129; in England/Britain/British Empire, 7, 56, 64, 67–68; denied the vote, 64; engagement with antifascism, 264; Ethiopian, 100n4; in Europe, 4, 13, 223, 279, 296; exemplary, 218; former, 40, 43; as generic term for non-blacks, 119; gentile discussions of, 75; German, 133; history of, 280–81; Iberian Jews/Diaspora, 4, 8–10, 46, 117–18, 120, 135; inclusion of, 262; intellectuals, 217; invisible, 128; involved in maritime activities, 110; in Jamaica, 60, 62, 71, 123; Ladino-speaking, 255; Latin American, 135; in London, 71; Maghrebi (from Morocco and Algeria), 131; marrying non-Jews in the United States today, 217; Mizrahi, 130, 135; and modern colonialism, 29n40; in Morocco, 12, 20, 131, 149–51, 154, 167–69; *Musta'arabim* (from Arab lands), 131; as a nation, 64, 224n25; naturalized Brazilian-Moroccan Jews, 149–50, 158, 169–70; nomenclature in sixteenth-century Italy, 131; of non-Iberian descent, 45; non-Portuguese, 127; as nonwhites, 7; North America, 195n19; Oriental, 132; among other groups, 3, 47n5; participation in Europe's overseas expansion, 57, 111; as part of white population, 123; in Poland, 216; in Portugal, 40, 112–13; position in Muslim societies, 120; "potential," 129, 134; practicing, 44; as race, 23n9; release of captive Jews, 91; in Rio de Janeiro, 182; in Safi, 119; in Serbia, 135; in South Africa, 24n12; in (late medieval) Spain (also as Castile and Aragon), 38, 112, 120; Spanish, 39, 46; symbolic, 211, 213; *Toshavim* (in Morocco before 1492), 131; in Tucacas, 88, 127; *Twansa* and *L'grana* in Tunisia, 131; in the United States, 23n9, 24n12, 223; visible, 127; in Western Europe, 108; "without synagogues," 128, 129, 130, 134; Yemenite, 100n4; young Jews in Western and Arab countries, 315. See also Ashkenazic: Jews; Crypto-Jew(s); Israel; Sephardic: Jews; Zionist[s])
—in/of Argentina, 16, 185, 189, 265, 268n29, 280, 305; Jewish women, 264; kidnapped, 304; violence against, 308; young in Argentina, 17, 279, 281, 303, 307
—in Curaçao, 84–86, 90: poor Jews, 88, 103n29
—in Uruguay, 183, 254, 259–60, 263–65, 268n29, 309, 311: Central European, 259; in Montevideo, 259
—Eastern European, 133, 176, 179–80, 203; Galician and Bessarabian, 130; Moldavian and Ukrainian speakers, 130; Yiddish speakers, 130, 176, 217
Jew Bill. *See* Jewish Naturalization Act of 1753

Jewish Agency for Israel. *See* The Jewish Agency for Israel
Jewish-Argentines. *See* Jew(s): in/of Argentina
Jewish Colonization Association, 10, 189, 191, 233; in Brazil, 10, 234–35, 239; as colonization company, 233, 242; council, 234; Lamerjav, 291; timber industry, 14, 236–39, 241–42; Victory Board chapters, 255
Jewish community(ies), 8, 57; in the Amazon region, 150; in the Americas, 304; in Argentina, 178, 187, 308, 312; in the Atlantic world, 94; Bialystok, 12; in Buenos Aires, 298n24; bylaws, 99 (see also *ascamot*); Charleston, 124; colonial settlements, 20; in Curaçao, 8, 83–84, 90, 96 (*see also* Mikvé Israel); day schools, 308; diversity in the Americas, 19; experience, 127; German, 95; global Portuguese, 90–91; of Hebron, 100n5; in Jamaica, 60; Levantine, 130; in London, 68, 86; in Madras, 57; Mikvé Israel in Philadelphia, 87; Moroccan, 159–61; mother-congregation, 84, 86, 88–90, 94, 98–99; non-Iberian, 91; parents, 308; Portuguese, 39, 85, 100; satellite congregations, 97; Sephardic, 101, 130; Shearith Israel in New York, 86–87; Sicilian, 130; sister congregation, 87; Spanish and Portuguese in London, 68; Venezuelan, 88; women in, 15; Yeshuat Israel, later Touro, in Newport, Rhode Island, 86–87. *See also* Amsterdam
Jewish Daily Forward. *See* Forverts
Jewish Defense League (JDL), 303, 306
Jewish Legion of the British Army in World War I, 308
Jewish Naturalization Act of 1753, 7, 59, 67–70; repeal, 67
Jewishness: ambiguous meaning in Argentina, 307; Christian protection of in England, 75n50; of Columbus, 108; heterogeneity, 2; and identification with the State of Israel, 28; as immutable trait, 116; mutuality with trade as a marker of, 129–31
Jewish Self-Defense Organization (Argentina), 306–8, 317; in Argentine society, 316; center of operation, 312; class and gender of members, 312; connection to Zionism, 312, 315, 317; members in Buenos Aires, 302; supported by Israel, 310
Jewish Self-Defense Organization (Odessa), 307
Jewish societies. *See* Yeshiva(s)
Jizya (tax), 120. *See also* Muslim(s): societies
João II, King, 112
Johnson-Reed Act of 1924, 179
Joseph II, Habsburg Emperor, 10. *See also* Edict(s) of Tolerance
Journals of the Assembly of Jamaica, 61
Judaism, 203; allegiance/ties to, 44, 310; in the Americas, 111; in Castile, 110; future of, 280; in the Iberian world, 126; Inquisition cases related to, 126; institutional, 129; as opposed to Marrano religion, 129; in the New World, 123; private practice, 60; revival of/return to, 125, 127; secret practice (*see* Crypto-Judaism); in Spanish America, 109
Junta de la Victoria (JV). *See* Victory Board
Juventud Sionista Sefaradí (JSS), 283–84. *See also* Departamento de Juventud del Centro Sionista Sefaradí (CSS Youth Department)
JV. *See* Victory Board

Kahane, Meir, 303, 306. *See also* Jewish Defense League
Kenya: Portuguese trading post, 119
Keren Hayesod, 283
Keren Kayemet Leisrael (KKL), 234, 283; Young Women's Committee, 280, 293, 296
Khmelnytsky Uprising in 1648–1657, 127
Khromada (Ukrainian administration), 213
Kibbutz(im): Alumot, 291; Artzi movement, 299n40; example of communal idea, 286; Giv'ot Zaid, 290; Hameuhad, 311; Hukuk, 311; make the desert flourish, 20; move to, 283; Neot Mordekhai, 291; Or Haner, 290; work on, 277
Kosher meat and slaughtering: in Curaçao, 89; slaughterer, 186
Kristoffersen, Antonio N., 304

Labatón, Judit, 292–94, 300n69
La Luz, 280, 282
Lançados. *See* New Christian

Land of Israel, 14; for Argentine Sephardim, 285; support sent from Amsterdam and Curaçao, 90–91, 103n36. *See also* Hebron; Jerusalem; Safed

Language(s): of biological superiority, 115; of colonialism, 152, 171n12; communal, 28n39, 101; difference among Argentine Jewish women, 258; as marker of ethnicity, 129; mix, 125; racial, 115; of Sephardic intellectual and literary expression, 125; use multiple, 19; of Zionism, 295

La Plata: Victory Board section, 256; DAIA branch, 309

Law: Ayllon laws of 1412, 111; of blood purity, 24n17; Brazil's Land Law of 1850, 232–33; element of British culture, 69; English, 57–59, 73n27, 73n30; Jamaican, 71; Jewish community bylaws, 23n9, 99, 101n9, 101n12; Jewish dietary, 89; Nuremberg Laws, 204; rule of law in Argentina, 308; rule of law in England, 71; Spanish ban to enter the Americas, 46n4; of Spanish and Portuguese citizenship of 2015, 135; use of, 70. *See also* Jewish Naturalization Act of 1753; Plantation Act of 1740

Leeward Antilles, 83

Letters of patent, 58

Levy, Bucas, 292

Libre Israel, 285

Liebgold, Leon, 222

Liege subject, 57–58, 63–64

Lima: auto-da-fé in 1639, 126; Inquisition, 40, 111; node of New Christian trade and financial network, 132; Portuguese in, 123, 125

Limpeza de sangre. See Purity of blood

Limpieza de sangre. See Purity of blood

Lineage. *See* Descent

Lisbon: anti-Jewish riots, 114, 118; node of New Christian trade and finance network, 132

Livorno, node of New Christian trade and finance network, 132

Livro de Registro de Súditos Brasileiros Residentes no Marrocos em 1900–1901 (Book of Registration of Brazilian Subjects in Morocco in 1900–1901), 164–65, 173n46

London: center of foreign trade, 56; imperial government in, 62; as if opposite Jamaica, 66; Spanish and Portuguese community in, 68, 86–87

Lopez, Ḥakham, 86

Lopez da Fonseca, Mosseh, 86

Loronha, Fernão de, 121–22

Lynn, Henry, 201, 217–18

Ma'amad, 101n9; Amsterdam, 94; Curaçao, 85, 94

Macabilandia, 303, 314

Macabi Sports Club (in Buenos Aires), 28n38, 287, 291, 299n42; clubhouse, 312

Macau: node of New Christian trade and finance network, 132

Madagascar: Portuguese trading post, 119

Madeira, Portuguese settlement, 112; named after commodity, 122; sugar production, 123

Madrid: node of New Christian trade and finance network, 132

Makhon Lemadrikhei Ḥutz Laaretz (Institute of Jewish Diaspora Councilors), 289, 310

Malacca: node of New Christian trade and finance network, 132

Malawi: Portuguese trading post, 119

Mallorca (Spain): Crypto-Jews, 118

Mandatory Palestine. *See* Palestine: Mandatory

Manila: node of New Christian trade and finance network, 132

Manuel I, King, 113–14, 119

Mapai, 287, 299n40

Mapam, 287, 299n40

Maraha/Maraghe (Persia): Jewish communities, 90

Mauritania: Portuguese trading post, 119

Mauss, Marcel: *The Gift*, 93, 96–97

Medicine: in Spain, 111

Medina del Campo: node of New Christian trade and finance network, 132

Mediterranean: Jewish migration from, 9, 19; Jewish migration to, 9; trade, 57. *See also* Middle East

Menasseh ben Israel, 60

Merchants, 113; naturalized Brazilian in Morocco, 172n32; non-Anglican, 62; peddlers, 24n12; Portuguese, 40, 121, 123; Sephardic, 8

Index · 339

—Jewish: in England, 57–58; in Morocco, 163, 166
—New Christian, 114, 121–22, 129, 132; core of world-dominant Atlantic economy, 133–34; dominate slave traffic, 133; veneration of Saint Moses among, 130
Metropole. *See* Center
Middle East: emigration from, 19, 130; migration, 9
Middle Passage, 130, 133
Migration, 203; and agriculturalism, 15; ban on migration to Americas, 39; from Arabic-speaking countries to Latin America, 20; cross-Atlantic, 18; cross-continental, 18; and ecology, 21; to the Erechim region, 233; global structures erected by, 5; of Iberian Jewry, 9; intra-Caribbean, 56; Jewish and New Christian to Africa, 119; to Palestine and Israel, 20, 277–78, 283, 287, 289–90, 293, 305, 312, 317; of New Christians, 126; of people, 100; perceptions of, 11; Portuguese to Spain and Spanish America, 40, 125; representation, 12, 201; as a result of antisemitism, 216; as source of the Americas' multicultural societies, 3; southern or south of, 232, 235; from Spain to the Indies, 109; from Spain to Portugal, 108; and travelogues, 13; to Uruguay, 183, 250; in Yiddish cinema studies, 202
—to Brazil: JCA's support, 233, 239 (*see also* Jewish Colonization Association: in Brazil); levels seen by Schwartz, 182; of Moroccan Jews, 149–51; of Old Christians, 126; policy (*see* Brazil: immigration and colonization policy)
—emigration, 10, 12; of Eastern European Jews, 176, 233; routes from Morocco to Brazil, 155; from Spain, 110–11
—global, 9; of Portuguese New Christian, 109
—Jewish, 10, 20, 150–51; immigration to Brazil, 11, 21, 182, 233; migration to Portugal, 112
—Moroccan Jews: to Amazon, 11, 150; from Brazil to Morocco, 11; from interior of Morocco, 155
Mikvé Israel: Curaçao, 83–86, 89, 94, 98; Philadelphia, 87
Minhag, 87, 103n25

Moços judeus, 118
Mogador. *See* Essaouira
Moisés Ville, 190–91, 254–55; Moisesville, 291; Victory Board chapter, 263
Montevideo: Feminine Action chapters, 253; Schwartz's visit, 182–83
—neighborhoods: Barrio Sur, 257; Cerro, 257; Ceudad Vieja, 256; Goes (Ruis), 257; Palermo, 257; Pocitos, 257; Villa Muñoz, 257
Montoneros, 316
Moors, 47n5, 119
Morocco, 11
Moskovskii Kamernyi Teatr', 188
Mossad, 303
Mother-congregation. *See* Jewish community(ies): mother-congregation
Movimiento Nacionalista Tacuara, 306, 312, 316–17
Mozambique: Portuguese trading post, 119
Mulatto(es), 46n4, 63, 70, 74n35, 116. *See also* Nonwhite
Muniz, Jacob E., 158–59
Muslim(s): culture, 45; law in Morocco, 163; Morocco, 150; societies, 37, 43, 120
—Iberian Muslims, 46; integration in Castile, 43

Nação. See Nation: Portuguese
Nagasaki, 132
Namibia, 119
Nation, 129; British, 67–68; building, 295–96, 297, 298n24; Jews as or Jewish, 203, 224, 285–86, 296; Portuguese, 100, 101n7; Portuguese of the Hebrew Nation, 130; power through consular protection, 157; Yiddish diasporic, 176
Nationalism: in Brazil, 160; Jewish, 280; Yiddish cultural, 176
Nationalists: Argentine, 251–52 (*see also* Fascist(s) and fascism: in Argentina), 308; Catholic Argentine, 303
Naturalization, 2; in Brazil, 11, 150–51, 169, 171n9; Brazilian Protected Person, 168; in Britain or British colonies, 61, 62; of Jews in England, 7, 56, 58, 68; Feminine Action, 253; mobilization of Brazilian citizenship, 155–64; providing mobility, 11–12; secular, 134; Spanish and Portuguese in 2015, 135; Victory Board, 251

Networks: British imperial trade, 66; ethnoreligious network and trade, 114; as global structure, 5; Jewish colonial and metropolitan, 69; Jewish commercial, 57, 85; Jewish communal, 9; Jewish quasi-imperial, 13; Jewish religious, 98; New Christian, 85, 88, 122, 129, 132; women's activist, 255

Neve Sedek society. *See* Yeshiva(s): Neve Sedek society

New Christian, 7–8, 113, 132, 134; assimilation, 114, 118, 129; bankers, 128; in Brazil, 27n33, 109, 119, 127; in Cape Verde, 128; in Castile and Aragon, 114; community, 129; as conversos, 136n3; distinction between Old and, 118; enclaves on the Atlantic, 133; as an ethnic group, 132; ethnogenesis of, 109, 113; investors, 27n33, 119, 121–22; of Jewish descent, 39, 134; of Jewish and Muslim descent, 39; as "Jews without synagogues," 119; *lançados*, 119–20; migrants from Portugal to Spain, 126; migration to Africa, 119; migration to Asia, 120; migration to Lusitanian colonies, 109; of Muslim descent, 42, 44; partial (half-, quarter-, and one-eight-), 116; in Portugal, 113, 118, 121; Portuguese, 124–26, 128; religiosity, 128–29; as secret or Crypto-Jews, 125–26, 128; *Tem parte de cristão-novo*, 121. *See also* Diaspora: New Christian; Merchants: New Christian; Networks: New Christian

New World. *See* Americas

New York, 87, 88, 89, 90, 105n56; Jewish Defense League, 306; Jewish labor movement, 28n39; kosher meat trade, 89; Shearith Israel, 86–87, 102n18; *The Yiddishe Mama* set in, 217–18; Yiddish theater, 13, 177–78, 190

Nigeria: Portuguese trading post, 119

Nomberg, H. D., 179–82, 195n12

Non-Anglicans, 58, 67; traders, 62

Non-Jewish: colonial companies, 10; ideological movements, 6; left-wing organizations in Argentina, 306; neighbors and regimes, 1–2

Non-Jews, 9; antifascist activists, 15; in Argentina, 316; cooperation between Jews and, 250, 260; JCA land sale to, 238; in *Tevye the Milkman*, 211–13

Nonwhite, 7, 116

Nueva Sión, 290

Nuñes, David, 61

Octoroons, 116. *See also* Nonwhite

Old Christian(s), 38, 111, 119, 129; distinction between New and, 118; from Portugal in Brazil, 126. *See also* Intermarriage: between Old and New Christians

Olinda: New Christian enclave, 133

Oman: Portuguese trading post, 119

"One-drop rule," 116. *See also* Racism

Ordenanzas reales para la Casa de la Contratacion de Sevilla, 41, 47n5

Organización Sionista Sefaradí (OSSA), 299n38

Or Haner (kibbutz), 290

Origin(s). *See* Descent

Ortega y Vilches family, 53

Ovando, Nicolás de, 47n5

Pacific: nodes of the New Christian trade and finance network, 132; Portugal outposts, 128

Palestine: British immigration policy, 205; emigration to, 20; home of different Jewish communities, 19; Jewish agricultural movement and settlement, 10, 190; Mandatory, 17, 311; support for, 90–91; in Yiddish books, 179

Palos (Spain), 108

Pampas: agricultural colonies, 179 (*see also* Agricultural: settlements/colonies in Argentina); Jewish life, 190–91

Paradesi, 121. *See also* Portuguese Jews: in India

Pardo, Ḥakham Josiau, 86

Pardo, Saul, 86

Partido Socialista Independiente (PSI) (in Argentina), 185

Paso Del Rey: summer camp, 291

Pau-brasil. *See* Commodity: brazilwood

Paver, Chaver (Gershon Einbinder), 206

Paysandú department (in Uruguay), 256

People of color, 61, 70, 74n37

People's Revolutionary Army (Argentina), 316

Perez, Leon, 291

Pernambuco: Dutch, 123; New Christian

enclave, 122, 133; Portuguese reconquest, 60, 123
Perón, Juan, 303, 309
Peronism: Peronist Montoneros, 316; polarization of Argentine society, 310
Persian Gulf: Portuguese trading posts, 119
Petite Côte: New Christians, 120
Phenotype, 116–17. *See also* Racism: modern; Whiteness
Philadelphia, 87
Plague wedding, 223
Plantation: coffee in Brazil, 232; Jewish owned sugar, 123–24; New Christian-owned, 122; Portuguese king's, 122
Plantation Act of 1740, 7, 59, 61–62, 70, 73n30
Poland: Nazi invasion, 202; Schwartz's theater tour in, 211; Tarbut movement, 309; Yiddish speaking Jews, 176, 201
Pombal, Marquis de, 118
Porto: node of the New Christian trade and finance network, 132
Portugal: after 1497, 113; colonial outposts in Asia, 120, 128; Judaism, 113; Portuguese-English alliance of 1385, 121; trading posts in Africa, 119; treaty with Morocco in 1880, 152. *See also* Empire: Portugal's; Iberia; Migration: Jewish; New Christian: in Portugal
Portuguese Jews, 8, 39, 85, 88, 101n7, 123 (*see also* Nation: Portuguese); associated with trade, 129–30; associated with trade in London, 68; associated with trade in Western Europe, 125; in India, 121; in Italy, 125
—in the Americas/Caribbean/Atlantic World, 84–85, 88–90, 93–94, 97, 126; lack of textual production, 99
—in Curaçao, 84–85; religious life, 96
Portuguese nation. *See* Nation: Portuguese
Prejudice: against merchants, 158; racial, 117; religious, 115; against Spain, 63
Proops, Joseph, Iacob, & Abraham de Salomon, 83
Prostitution. *See* White slavery
Protestantism: element of British culture, 69, 71
Provence: origin of Jews in Salonica, 131
Purity of blood, 6, 38, 43, 47n5, 53, 109, 115–16; abolition of distinction between Old and New Christians, 118; racial elements in, 24n17, 137n28

Quadroons, 116. *See also* Nonwhite

Race, 137n28; absence of racial segregation in Argentina, 182; mixed-race, 63, 71; New Christians as ethnoracial group, 113; Othering, 71; racial construct(s), 3; racial diversity in England, 58; racial hierarchy in Jamaica, 64–65, 71; racial taxonomies, 109, 115–16
Racism: Jewish acceptance of racial theory, 23n9; modern, 116; religiously coded, 6. *See also* Antisemitism
Recife: first synagogue in Americas, 123; New Christian enclave, 133
Recopilación de Indias, 39, 46n4, 47n5
Refugees: Jewish in Uruguay, 183, 257; in Portugal, 111–12
Rendeiros, 119
Resistencia (in Argentina), 255–56
Resnitzky, Nehemias, 291
Resources. *See* Commodity
Rhineland: origin of Jews in Salonica, 131; origin of Jews in sixteenth-century Italy, 131
Rio de Janeiro: Schwartz's visit, 178, 181
Rio Grande do Sul, 232, 234–35
Rio Hacha, 87
Rivera, Primo de, 45
Rivera (in Argentina), 255
Rojas, Isaac, 311
Rollansky, Samuel, 189
Romania: agricultural settlements, 20; modern Yiddish theater, 176; Yiddish-speaking Jews, 176
Romaniots, 131
Rosario (in Argentina): JSS members, 288; Schwartz's performance in, 189–90; Victory Board chapter, 256

Safed: Holy Land community receiving support from Curaçao, 90, 104n38
Safi (in Morocco), 112; Portuguese trading post, 119
Saida Jewish community (in Morocco) receiving support from Curaçao, 90

Salonica: "Jerusalem of the Balkans," 131; Jewish community receiving support from Curaçao, 90; Judaism legal, 128; node of the New Christian trade and finance network, 132
Salvador, Joseph, 68
Sanches, Abraham, 62–63, 66
Santa Cruz. *See* Brazil
Santa Fe (in Argentina): Schwartz's performance in, 189; Victory Board chapter, 256
São Tomé, 119; "model," 122
Saslavsky, Dalila, 256
Saudi Arabia: Portuguese trading post, 119
Saul, Ḥakham Yahacob (of Smyrna), 90
Schwartz, Maurice, 12–14, 26n31, 177, 210; emigration from Pale of Settlement, 195n16; travelogues, 181. *See also* Buenos Aires; *Tevye the Milkman*
Segregation: of Jews from non-Jews, 213, 215, 220
Seixas, Gershom Mendes, 87
Self-defense organizations, 27n36, 306; Jewish self-defense groups, 17, 260, 307
Senegal: Portuguese trading post, 119
Senegambia: New Christian settlement, 120, 127–28
Sepharadí. *See* Sephardic
Sephardi. *See* Sephardic
Sephardic: Caribbean, 95; empowerment, 88; ethnic, 131, 135; religiosity, 94; rite, 88, 103n25; Western, 134. *See also* Diaspora
—Communities: in the Americas, 101n12; in Argentina, 277, 282; in Brazil, 150; in Ciudad Vieja, 256; in Curaçao, 83 (*see also* Curaçao; Mikvé Israel); in Holy Land/Palestine, 90–91; inclusion of non-Iberian members, 45, 88; in New (Amsterdam) York from Recife, 86; in Tucacas from Livorno, 127
—Jews, 100n4, 297n11; in Amsterdam, 123; in CCIU; women in Argentina, 16, 293–94; young Sephardic Jews from Greece, Yugoslavia, Bulgaria, 286; youngsters, 307, 310, 312
—Youth organizations: in Argentina, 286; in Montevideo, 289–90; Zionist youth movement in Argentina, 277, 279, 281
Sephardim. *See* Sephardic: Jews
Sephardization, 131

Servi camerae regis (serfs of the royal chamber), 64
Seville, 53, 110; node of New Christian trade and finance network, 132
Sforim, Mendele Moicher (Sholem-Yankev Abramovich), 179, 206
Shaliaḥ. *See* Emissary
Sharett, Moshe, 20
Shearith Israel (New York), 86–87, 89
Shoah. *See* Holocaust
Shoḥet (ritual slaughterer). *See* Kosher meat and slaughtering: slaughterer
Shtadlanut, 304
Shtetl, 130, 207
Shund, 177, 189, 206, 217; filmmakers, 217
Sicily: origin of Jews in Salonica, 131
Sierra Leone: Portuguese trading post, 119–20
Sirota, Graciela: attack on, 312, 316
Six-Day War, 302
Slave(s): abolition of slavery, 73n30; African, 57, 119, 121, 123, 130; barred from passage to Americas, 46n4; Jewish slave owners, 123; Jewish status described as of, 65; laws, 62; Jews, 117; from the Sahel and East Africa, 117; slave labor replacement, 232; slavery, 117, 133; Sub-Saharan Africans, 117; trade, 70, 109, 121–23, 133; from West Africa, 117. *See also* Tacky's Revolt; White slavery
Smyrna (Izmir) Jewish community, 90
Snoa, 92
Sociedad Zwi Migdal, 186. *See also* White slavery
Sola, Mendes da (of Curaçao), 89
Somalia: Portuguese trading post, 119
Sousa, Washington Luís Pereira de, President, 182
South America. *See* Americas: South America
Southern Cone. *See* Americas: South America
South-north axes of exchange, 9
Soviet Union (USSR): agricultural settlements, 190; aid to, 16, 250, 254; Jews in, 224n25; in the 1930s, 204
Spain, 4; cultural prestige, 135; early modern, 7, 44; emotional ties and loyalty to, 6, 19, 28n38; emotional ties and loyalty to Iberian Peninsula, 44–45, 125, 132; expulsion

of Jews, 24n10, 108; Hispanic traditions, 45; interference in Morocco, 152–53; medieval, 38; multicultural kingdom and empire, 7, 44; prejudice against, 63; readmission to, 46; Republican, 267n8; return to democracy, 45; Spanish America, 40; 1391 pogroms, 111
Spanish Civil War, 260
St. Eustatius, 62, 85
St. Thomas: receiving support from Curaçao, 87
Study of Jews in Americas, 19, 22n3, 94, 150, 250
Sugar. *See* Commodity
Sugar mill, 122; mechanics, 122; owners, 119, 129
Suriname: intra-communal relations, 23n9; Jewish households owning slaves, 123; Jodensavanne, 124; receiving support from Curaçao, 87
Svirsky, Raquel P. de, 258, 261
Synagogue: in the Americas, 101n6; first in the New World, 123; Mill Street, 86; Newport, 86; Paradesi (Portuguese) in Cochin, 121; Snoa, 92, 104n41

Tacky's Revolt, 74n34
Tacuara. *See* Movimiento Nacionalista Tacuara
Tangier: Brazilian Consul, 155, 156–57, 160, 161, 164, 165; office of Consul General of Brazil, 151
Tanzania: Portuguese trading post, 119
Tarbut School and movement, 309
Teatro Argentino, 178
Teatro Colón, 188
Teatro Excelsior, 189
Teatro IFT or Idisher Folks-Teater, 192
Teatro Nuevo, 178
Teatro Odeón, 188
Terra, Gabriel, 252
Teubal, Nissim, 28n38
Tevye the Milkman, 13, 201, 210–17; DVD version, 204
The Jewish Agency for Israel, 291, 299n51, 313
The Light Ahead, 201, 206–10, 216
The Yiddishe Mama, 201, 217–22
Thrace, 131

Threat(s): associative links to migration, 14, 68; existential, Jews faced, 210; fascist threat in Argentina, 264; foreigners perceived as, 69; on Jewish community in Argentina, 308, 316–17; Jewish suffrage in Jamaica perceived as, 71; New Christians' economic clout as, 128; Yiddish culture facing, 201–2
Tiberias, 90
Tish'a B'av, 24n10, 108
Tme'im, 187
Toledo: *sentencia decreto* of 1449, 38
Touro Synagogue. *See* Jeshuat Israel
Trade: Atlantic, 133, 134; British colonial, 58; Dutch entrepôt, 83; illicit, 85; in luxury goods, 57; opportunities in Sub-Saharan Africa, 111; plume, 24n12. *See also* Kosher meat and slaughtering; Networks; Slave(s): White slavery
Traders. *See* Merchants
Transnational/ism: conversation among scholars, 21; East European Jewish Diaspora, 180; historical phenomena connecting global and local forces, 4; Jews as transnational people, 21n11; about transnational history, 265n2; Yiddish film industry, 201; Yiddish speaking community, 26n28; Yiddish theater, 176, 193n2, 197n42; Zionist politics, 16
Travel: tourism, 181; in Yiddish film industry, 201; writing (*see* Travelogue)
Travelogue: advocacy for migration, 13, 32n26; as (auto)ethnography, 180; Schwartz's, 13, 178–79, 188–89, 194n7; Yiddish, 179
Treaty of Madrid (1880), 156, 159, 164–65
Treifene medina, 216
Triki, Hussein, 304
Tucacas (in Venezuela): only Sephardic community in Spanish America, 127; poor Jews settle in, 88
Tucumán (in Argentina): Victory Board chapter, 255–56

Ukraine: famine, 204; Jewish agricultural settlements, 20; setting Jewish film plots in, 216–17
Ulmer, Edgar, 206, 209
Union Juvenil Israelita de Flores, 284

United Arab Emirates: Portuguese trading post, 119
United States, 9; American Jewish Committee (AJC) survey, 314; Hayes Code, 205; Israeli characters in American cinema, 315; Jewish agricultural settlements, 10; Jewish Defense League, 303; Johnson-Reed Act, 179; oldest congregation in, 86; Yiddish films, 201. *See also* New York
Uruguay: immigration to, 250; Jewish agricultural settlements, 10; Jewish population in 1917, 259; Jewish population in 1930, 183; Schwartz's impressions of, 178

Vainberg, Rosa, 263
Veracruz: Spanish American port of slave trade, 133
Verónica (Buenos Aires province): training farm, 292
Viceroyalty of New Spain, 111
Victory Board (JV), 249–50, 263
—chapters: in Buenos Aires, 251, 256; outside Buenos Aires, 255; in Jewish agricultural colonies, 255, 263
Voyage. *See* Travel

West India Company (Dutch), 85
Whitehall Conference of December 1655, 60
Whiteness: definition of, 59, 70; in Jamaica, 65; as a legal category, 70; legal whitening, 63; as norm, 117; privileges of, 71
White slavery, 133; sex trade, 186; Sociedad Zwi Migdal, 186
Windsor Proclamation of December 1661, 60
Wolof Kingdom, 120
Women: African slaves of Jewish owners, 63, 127; aid activism, 252; antifascist, 250–51, 255; Argentine Jewish, 254; local integration, 16; political activism, 253; Schwartz's observation in Buenos Aires, 186; suffrage in Uruguay and Argentina, 265; young Zionist Sephardic, 279, 292–94
Women's International Zionist Organization (WIZO), 293, 300n71
World War I, 29
World War II, 205, 285

Yemen: Portuguese trading post, 119. *See also* Zaydi Imamate of Yemen
Yeshiva(s), 90; Abi Yetomin ve Dayan Almanoth society, 91; Honen Dalim society, 90; Neve Sedek society, 91
Yiddish: Argentine dailies, 178; author(s), 13; films and film industry, 13–14, 201–3; global language, 12; international Yiddish theater world, 177; language spoken in WIZO Argentina, 300n71; literary language, 12; New York's Yiddish Art Theater, 12, 177–78, 187–88; speaking communities, 176; speaking immigrants, 181–82; speaking world, 14; spoken in Moisés Ville, 191; studies, 193; theater in Argentina, 190, 196nn30–31; travel in Yiddish literature, 179
Yiddishism, 176
Yiddishland. *See* Diaspora: of Yiddish speakers
Yishuv, 179, 311
Yom Kippur, 88, 183, 221
Young Women's Committee. *See* Keren Kayemet Leisrael: Young Women's Committee
Youth Rebellion, 17, 303–4
Yugoslavia: AF affiliates from, 253, 257; former, 135; Sephardic youth from, 286; Uruguayan Jews from, 253

Zaydi Imamate of Yemen, 127
Zhitlovsky Cultural House (Montevideo), 257, 260
Zionism, 10; in Argentina, 16, 278; conservative, 258; Hebrew, 19, 295; Revisionism, 307–8, 320n28; transnational, 16, 27n34; Yiddish, 176; Yishuv, 179
Zionist(s): education, 282, 285, 310; identity, 302; pioneer movement (*see* Ḥalutziut); radical, 17; Sephardic, 16–17, 281–82, 283–85; young Argentine Sephardic, 279; young women, 294; youth movement, 279, 282, 287
—organizations: Acción Sionista, 287, 290–91; Centro Sionista Sefaradí, 282–85, 296; Comité Juvenil Sionista Sefaradí (Sephardi Zionist Youth Committee); Departamento de Juventud del Centro Sionista Sefaradí (CSS Youth Department), 283–84, 293–94;

Gordonia, 290, 299n39; Hano'ar Hatzioni, 287, 299n44; Hashomer Hatza'ir, 283; Hejalutz, 287, 289–90, 291–92, 296; Hejalutz-Tejezkana collective, 290; Ijud/Iḥud Habonim, 290; Lamerjav, 287, 300n65; Mordechai Anielewicz Division, 312, 314; Peulah, 296; split within, 291; Tejezakna, 289–90; Zionist Socialist Youth, 290